From 1964 to 1985 Brazil was governed by a military dictatorship unlike its predecessors but soon to become the model for other authoritarian regimes in South America. It attracted civilian technocrats and foreign investors to engineer an "economic miracle," and to consolidate its economic model it initiated sweeping political change that was intended to rid Brazilian society of radical social movements and the state and political system of traditional politics and elites. This study demonstrates that military aims notwithstanding, a traditional political elite has persisted in Brazil through two regime changes——one to and one from authoritarian rule. During the dictatorship, traditional politicians retained considerable power in the state governments, which were their traditional redoubts. In particular, they continued to occupy high-level appointed offices that permitted them to retain control of patronage, their most important political resource. Since the transition to democracy, as prominent Brazilian intellectuals have charged, genuine political debate has fallen victim to a restoration of oligarchical power and clientelistic practices typical of traditional Brazilian politics.

Continued on back flap

From 1964 to 1985 Brazil was governed by a military dictatorship unlike its predecessors but soon to become the model for other authoritarian regimes in South America. It attracted civilian technocrats and foreign investors to engineer an "economic miracle," and to consolidate its economic model it initiated sweeping political change that was intended to rid Brazilian society of radical social movements and the state and political system of traditional politics and elites. This study demonstrates that military aims notwithstanding, a traditional political elite has persisted in Brazil through two regime changes – one to and one from authoritarian rule. During the dictatorship, traditional politicians retained considerable power in the state governments, which were their traditional redoubts. In particular, they continued to occupy high-level appointed offices that permitted them to retain control of patronage, their most important political resource. Since the transition to democracy, as prominent Brazilian intellectuals have charged, genuine political debate has fallen victim to a restoration of the oligarchical power and clientelistic practices typical of traditional Brazilian politics.

This study argues that the military project was severely constrained by the pattern of mediation between state and society that it inherited, the expansion of the state's productive, regulatory, and distributive roles that underlay its model for economic stabilization and development, and the need to marshal political support for the largely symbolic elections that it permitted as part of its strategy for governing. State-led capitalist development led to an expansion of clientelism in that it enhanced both the state's resource base and the number of clients dependent on state programs, at the same time that more competitive elections made the resort to clientelism, and the traditional politicians who could marshal votes on this basis, more compelling. By leading a negotiated transition away from authoritarian rule, traditional political elites secured prominent positions in the postauthoritarian state and political system.

TRADITIONAL POLITICS AND REGIME
CHANGE IN BRAZIL

TRADITIONAL POLITICS AND REGIME CHANGE IN BRAZIL

FRANCES HAGOPIAN

Tufts University

CAMBRIDGE
UNIVERSITY PRESS

Published by the Press Syndicate of the University of Cambridge
The Pitt Building, Trumpington Street, Cambridge CB2 1RP
40 West 20th Street, New York, NY 10011-4211, USA
10 Stamford Road, Oakleigh, Melbourne 3166, Australia

First published 1996

Printed in the United States of America

Library of Congress Cataloging-in-Publication Data
Hagopian, Frances.
Traditional politics and regime change in Brazil / Frances
Hagopian.
p.   cm. – (Cambridge studies in comparative politics)
Includes bibliographical references and index.
ISBN 0-521-41429-6 (hc)
1. Brazil – Politics and government – 1964–1985.   2. Brazil –
Politics and government – 1985–   3. Elite (Social sciences) – Brazil.
4. Patron and client – Brazil.   5. Authoritarianism – Brazil.
I. Title.   II. Series.
JL2481.H34   1996
320.981′09′045 – dc20   95-20453
CIP

A catalog record for this book is available from the British Library.

ISBN   0-521-41429-6 Hardback

For my parents

Contents

Tables and figures

FIGURES

Preface

Fifteen years after it had been established in 1964, most observers believed that the Brazilian "bureaucratic-authoritarian" regime had marginalized economic and political elites. Indeed, in a survey of the literature as of 1979 on post-1964 Brazil, I detected not one mention of the survival of the country's "traditional elites." Accordingly, when I embarked on this study, I had no reason to doubt that they had fallen; I wondered only if and how they might have protested their fate, and if their presumed opposition, perhaps in alliance with other subaltern forces, to military-technocratic rule may have been consequential for regime instability. I was naturally disconcerted, then, in an interview for a Social Science Research Council dissertation fellowship, when one of the members of the screening committee, a historian familiar with the Brazilian hinterlands, badgered me to defend the usefulness of a study that was bound to uncover what everyone already knew – that traditional elites persisted throughout Brazil.

In struggling to reconcile these two pictures – one of a major, if temporary, revolution at the highest echelons of the national Brazilian state, and one of remarkable continuity at lower levels of the political system – this study became a book about regime change as well as a book about Brazilian politics. More accurately, this book is about two regime changes – one to and one from authoritarian rule. It does not seek to cover old ground on the causes of the breakdown of democracy and transition from authoritarian rule, but rather to explain what regime change ultimately meant for broader political change. It focuses on how the economic models and political ambitions of new authoritarian regimes revised or were constrained by the political systems they set out to conquer and the nature of their own exit from power. In attempting to fulfill two agendas – to contribute to a body of general theory on regime change and political continuity, and to explain the role of "traditional politics" in the Brazilian political system – the book treads a fine line between comparative politics and Brazilian politics. Such a strategy risks disappointing "Brazilianists" with the presentation of old facts to a new audience and comparative political scientists uninterested in the debates that preoccupy country specialists. Nonetheless, I hope that both will find something of value in the attempt, and that the book will not only sharpen our interpretations about Brazilian politics but also that its theoretical contributions will be richer for drawing from my own research than they otherwise might have been had I relied on the standard interpretations, or the "stylized facts," of Brazilian politics.

In researching and writing this book, I became convinced that the past, present, and at least immediate future of Brazilian politics could not be understood without reference to clientelism, regionalism, and other elements of traditional politics. I focus on the resources and strategies of the agents of political continuity, the group I have (some would say stubbornly) called the traditional political elite. After examining economic and institutional influences on political change and continuity, I concluded, contrary to my education and previous intellectual leanings, that structural incentives of either an economic or political variety were inadequate for explaining the powerful currents of political continuity, and that a set of powerful individuals had indeed made a giant contribution to preserving archaic state structures and channels of mediation between state and society. Having arrived at this new (for me) intellectual terrain, I found myself in search of a framework for understanding the preservation of traditional power structures. To the extent that social scientists think about elites, most are either closet Marxists, who attribute elite power to their economic resources, or Weberians, who locate sources of traditional power and authority in social position, religious beliefs, and ascription. Yet, what I discovered was that clientelistic mediation held the key to the survival of traditional elites in the crannies of an expansive Brazilian state. Accordingly, I came to appreciate the importance of the bridges that the "state" and "society" build to one another. In the case of traditional Brazilian politics, those channels spanned territory, and since political representation has often been organized along territorial rather than class or ethnic lines as in other societies, the book approaches the problem of political change through the lens of territorial politics.

In a time when most political scientists cannot agree on an epistemology of comparative politics, there is a general prejudice against studying "only" one country (unless that country is the United States), and this prejudice, as might be expected, is even stronger against a regional study. I should therefore explain why a book that finds itself as part of a comparative politics series should concentrate on the politics of one state in one country. I would contend that a single-country study is just as capable of comparing itself at various points to other countries' experiences as a two-country comparison that is parsimoniously designed to illuminate the explanatory significance of a single dimension of difference. When social phenomena are reducible to univariate causality, such a research design can be elegant; when they are not, a single-country study permits the discovery of multivariate causation by switching comparisons to highlight a particular variable and the flexibility of witnessing complex social phenomena in their entirety.

A regional focus additionally offers the advantage, especially in a federal but even in centralized systems, of understanding various levels of state behavior and state–society interaction. In a political system soaked with clientelism, such as the Brazilian, it opens a window on the modification, persistence, or interruption of political patterns. Despite a tradition of Brazilian scholarship that calls attention to the mosaic of regional patterns (Lima, 1983; Soares, 1973; Schwartzman, 1975), and a number of excellent comparative regional histories (Wirth, 1978; Levine, 1978; Love, 1971, 1980; Lewin, 1987), most recent political science research about Brazil has clung to a national focus. Many studies that identify themselves as national in scope are in fact analyses of the most advanced regions – Rio de Janeiro and especially São Paulo. As such, they have a collective blind spot and, if the analysis in this book is correct, have paid a price for their myopia.

If the highest price of neglecting the study of subnational politics in Brazil is that the persistence of traditional politics has been at best overlooked and at worst denied, it is also the case that informed observers dance around the reality that squarely faces even the sojourner to Brazil because social scientists, and many Latin Americanists in particular, tend to study the forces they champion. But if it is true that any demonstration of the persistence of traditional elites in power breeds a profound pessimism for the prospects of an expansion of the political market for previously excluded groups and the consolidation of a full democracy, it is equally true that without an accurate assessment of the structures of power, it is impossible to chart a realistic course for political change. Ignoring traditional politics will not make traditional political elites and practices "go away."

Earlier versions of portions of Chapter 7 appeared previously as " 'Democracy by Undemocratic Means?': Elites, Political Pacts, and Regime Transition in Brazil," in *Comparative Political Studies* 23, 2, (July 1990): 147–70, and "The Compromised Consolidation: The Political Class in the Brazilian Transition," in Scott Mainwaring, Guillermo O'Donnell, and J. Samuel Valenzuela, eds., *Issues in Democratic Consolidation: The New South American Democracies in Comparative Perspective* (Notre Dame, Ind.: University of Notre Dame Press, 1992), pp. 243–93; part of Chapter 8 as "After Regime Change: Authoritarian Legacies, Political Representation, and the Democratic Future of South America," in *World Politics* 45, 3 (April 1993): 464–500; and a general overview of the book as "Traditional Politics against State Transformation," in Joel S. Migdal, Atul Kohli, and Vivienne Shue, eds., *State Power and Social Forces: Domination and Transformation* (Cambridge: Cambridge University Press, 1994), pp. 37–64.

No one writes a book without help, but I had more than some law of the academic enterprise should permit. The research for this study was conducted in successive field trips in 1980–82, 1985, and 1989 funded by dissertation grants from the Joint Committee of the Social Science Research

Council and the American Council of Learned Societies and the Fulbright
Commission, a seed-money grant from the Helen Kellogg Institute of the
University of Notre Dame, and a travel grant from the Monadnock Fund of
Harvard University. A residential fellowship from the Kellogg Institute and
a junior faculty presidential leave from Harvard University allowed me to
write first a dissertation and then a book. I also benefited enormously,
practically unscrupulously, from people whom I barely know, and cannot
possibly name. Some are low-level public employees in Minas Gerais, Brazil, who took a special interest in an American who would write a book
"just about Minas Gerais." Others are professors and former graduate
students at various political science departments who formed the vocal and
skeptical audiences for the early presentations of this work in the most
challenging of all scholarly formats – job talks.

But for these and other colleagues, acquaintances, and adversaries who
are too numerous to name, there are those whose criticisms and praise,
intellectual inspiration, and faith in me and this project were so crucial to
its completion that the mere token mention of their names seems ruefully
inadequate. For their special roles, I must single out Guillermo O'Donnell,
who inspired my research agenda for nearly two decades; my teacher Suzanne Berger, who not only showed the way to studying traditional classes
and supervised the dissertation on which this book is based but also
equipped me in every meaningful way to become a scholar; and my friend
Elisa Pereira Reis, who convinced a young graduate student that Portuguese was really an easy language to conquer, if not master. Norma de
Goés Monteiro opened to me the biographical archives of the Centro de
Estudos Mineiros, which made possible the elite study upon which this
work is based. To Miriam and Luiz Santiago, and their sons Leonardo,
Marcelo, and Henrique, I owe a debt that only those who have labored
through the logistical nightmare and personal loneliness of the travails of
fieldwork in a foreign country can possibly understand.

Among my many generous colleagues over the years, Scott Mainwaring
read the entire manuscript in two distinct incarnations, prodding me to
back down from exaggerated claims and saving me from various and as-
sorted confusions and errors, large and small. Several years ago, in a stage
play over which he has expressed embarrassment but I hope not regret,
Jorge Domínguez sliced the principal arguments of this work to shreds. The
three years of effort required to reconstruct them on a more solid foundation were no sooner completed than he read and commented extensively
upon the entire manuscript, raising new dilemmas. For those which I was
able to resolve the book is better. The intellectual imprint of Joel Migdal
and the participants in the workshop on state–society relations that he
organized is very much in evidence in this work. Susan Eckstein, James
Glaser, Stephan Haggard, Silvia Raw, Thomas Skidmore, Peter Smith,
Myron Weiner, Alexander Wilde, and Enrique Zuleta all commented on

parts of earlier versions of the manuscript, and Brian MacDonald helped to make it intelligible. I am also grateful for the crucial and timely support of my former department chair, Robert O. Keohane, who not only allowed an overwhelmed mother the time to write this book by sheltering her from many of the most onerous responsibilities of being a junior faculty member at Harvard University, but also kept her afloat in this profession.

Finally, few female academics have a husband like mine who, as one friend and astute observer of our profession once observed, "support their careers 200 percent." My husband Tony Messina has lived with this work as long as I have. Without his intellectual and personal support and companionship, his babysitting services at home and in the field, and his not so gentle prodding, this work would today be lost in the junkyard of unfinished doctoral dissertations. To my son, Michael Messina, I feebly offer this book as partial if inadequate compensation for those long hours during early childhood when he was remanded to the video cassette recorder to view every inane and violent cartoon and action hero on offer. I can only hope that when he is old enough to read it, he will find some cause to be proud of me. My father, Leo F. Hagopian, will not have that chance; he did not live to see the book that he always hoped I would write. It is to his cherished memory, and to my mother, Elizabeth Hagopian, who stood at his side and behind me for a lifetime, that I dedicate *Traditional Politics and Regime Change in Brazil.*

Glossary of abbreviations and Portuguese terms

Açominas	Aço Minas Gerais S.A., federally owned state steel company.
ARENA	Aliança Renovadora Nacional (National Renovating Alliance). Progovernment political party, 1965–79.
bancada	A state's delegation of representatives to the Chamber of Deputies.
BDMG	Banco de Desenvolvimento de Minas Gerais (Minas Gerais Development Bank).
BEMGE	Banco de Estado de Minas Gerais (Bank of the state of Minas Gerais).
BNDES	Banco Nacional de Desenvolvimento Econômico e Social (National Economic and Social Development Bank, formerly the National Economic Development Bank, BNDE).
BNH	Banco Nacional de Habitação (National Housing Bank).
boiá-fria	Temporary agricultural laborer who resides in an urban area and commutes to the fields.
cabo eleitoral	Political ward boss.
café com leite	Political alliance between states of Minas Gerais and São Paulo during Old Republic.
câmara municipal	Local council.
Carioca	Resident of the city of Rio de Janeiro.
cassados	Citizens stripped of political rights and elected mandates by the military regime.
CDI(MG)	Companhia de Distritos Industriais (Industrial Districts Company), not to be confused with the CDI/MIC.
CDI/MIC	Conselho de Desenvolvimento Industrial (Industrial Development Council), a national government agency of the Ministry of Industry and Commerce.

CEMIG	Centrais Elétricas de Minas Gerais, state of Minas electric company.
COHAB	Companhia de Habitação, state of Minas housing agency.
coronel, coroneis	Local political bosses.
coronelismo	Rule by local bosses.
cruzado	Brazilian unit of currency introduced in 1986.
cruzeiro	Brazilian unit of currency until 1986, and again in 1990.
CUT	Central Unica dos Trabalhadores. Central labor union formed in 1983.
CVRD	Companhia Vale do Rio Doce (Rio Doce Valley Company). A federal state enterprise primarily involved in iron mining.
DER	Departamento de Estradas e Rodagem (Highway and Road Department).
DIAP	Departamento Intersindical de Assessoria Parlamentar. A labor lobby group.
diretório	The directorate of a political party from which members of the executive commission are elected, found at national, state, and local levels.
ESG	Escola Superior de Guerra (Superior War College).
Estado Nôvo	New State. Vargas dictatorship, 1937–45.
fazenda	A large farm.
fazendeiro	A large-land owner, but not synonymous with *latifundário*.
FIEMG	Federação de Industrias do Estado de Minas Gerais (Minas Gerais Federation of Industries).
FL	Frente Liberal (Liberal Front). A dissident group within the PDS that emerged in 1984 to support direct elections and Tancredo Neves's presidential candidacy in the electoral college.
FJP	Fundação João Pinheiro, research institute of state of Minas Planning Department.
FPE	Fundo de Participação de Estados. Federal revenue-sharing fund for states.
FPM	Fundo de Participação de Municípios. Federal revenue-sharing fund for municipalities.
FRIMISA	Frigoríficos Minas Gerais S.A., state of Minas meat-processing plants.
FUNRURAL	Fundo de Assistência ao Trabalhador Rural (Rural Workers' Assistance Fund). Rural social security fund.

Guanabara	Greater Rio de Janeiro city, formerly a separate state, incorporated into the state of Rio de Janeiro in 1974.
Gaúcho	Resident of the state of Rio Grande do Sul.
IBAM	Instituto Brasileiro de Administração Municipal (Brazilian Institute for Municipal Administration). An independent agency that assists municipal governments.
IBGE	Fundação Instituto Brasileiro de Geografia e Estatística. The official census and statistical institute.
ICM	Imposto sobre a circulação de mercadorias ("tax on the circulation of merchandise"). A value-added tax, which is the main source of revenue for the states.
INDI	Instituto de Desenvolvimento Industrial (Industrial Development Institute).
legenda	A party slate.
MDB	Movimento Democrático Brasileiro (Brazilian Democratic Movement). Opposition party, 1965–79.
METAMIG	Metais de Minas Gerais S.A., state of Minas mining and metals corporation.
Mineiro	Resident of the state of Minas Gerais.
MTR	Movimento Trabalhista Renovador (Movement for Labor Renewal). A progressive splinter of the PTB before 1964.
município	The Brazilian municipality. An administrative unit broader than a city or town. The closest equivalent in the United States is the county.
Paulista	Resident of the state of São Paulo.
PDC	Partido Democrata Cristão (Christian Democratic Party).
PDS	Partido Democrático Social (Democratic Social Party). Progovernment party formed in 1979.
PDT	Partido Democrático Trabalhista (Democratic Labor Party). Formed in 1979 under leadership of Leonel Brizola.
PFL	Partido da Frente Liberal (Party of the Liberal Front).
PL	Partido Libertador. A Gaúcho-dominated party, 1945–65.
PMDB	Partido do Movimento Democrático Bra-

	sileiro (Party of the Brazilian Democratic Movement). Formed in 1979.
PP	Partido Popular (Popular Party). Formed in 1980, dissolved in 1982.
PR	Partido Republicano (Republican Party). Near monopoly party during the Old Republic, resurrected in 1945 by Artur Bernardes.
PRM	Partido Republicano Mineiro (Minas Republican Party).
PRN	Partido de Reconstrução Nacional (Party of National Reconstruction). Formed by Fernando Collor de Mello in 1989 to support his presidential candidacy.
PRODECOM	Programa de Desenvolvimento de Comunidades (Community Development Program).
PRP	Partido Republicano Paulista (São Paulo Republican Party).
PSB	Partido Socialista Brasileiro (Brazilian Socialist Party).
PSD	Partido Social Democrático (Social Democratic Party). Pro-Vargas party, 1945–65.
PSDB	Partido da Social Democracia Brasileira (Party of Brazilian Social Democracy). Formed in 1988 as splinter of PMDB.
PSP	Partido Social Progressista (Social Progressive Party), 1945–65. Populist, São Paulo–based party dominated by Adhemar de Barros.
PT	Partido dos Trabalhadores (Workers' Party). Formed after 1979 party reform.
PTB	Partido Trabalhista Brasileira (Brazilian Labor Party). Pro-Vargas party, 1945–64. Reorganized after 1979 by Ivete Vargas, Vargas's grandniece.
SEPLAN	Secretaria de Planejamento e Coordenação Geral. Minas Gerais state Planning Department.
situação	The "ins," or the party or group in power.
SNI	Serviço Nacional de Informações (National Information Service). The national military-run intelligence agency.
sublegenda	A party "subticket," introduced by the military regime. Up to three candidates of the same party were permitted to contest the same office awarded under the plurality system.

SUDENE	Superintendência do Desenvolvimento do Nordeste (Superintendency for the Development of the Northeast). Development agency for Brazilian Northeast.
tenente	Army lieutenant.
Tenentismo movement	*Tenente* protest movement of the 1920s against the Old Republic.
TRE-MG	Tribunal Regional Eleitoral de Minas Gerais. The Minas regional electoral court.
UDN	União Democrática Nacional (National Democratic Union). Anti-Vargas party, 1945–65.
Usiminas	Usinas Siderúrgicas de Minas Gerais S.A., federally owned state steel company.

Up to a certain point, trading posts and favors is a normal fact of any political system. What has become abnormal in our current political situation is that favor is traded for favor, post for post. In other words, there is no more politics, no more political debate. . . . The result is that we are witnessing a restoration of oligarchical power, the same type of power that was utilized in 1964 to contain popular pressure.

– Fernando Henrique Cardoso,
Interview with *Veja,* June 29, 1988

The political tradition molded by the oligarchs and the dictatorships is still with us.

– Francisco Weffort,
Democratizing Brazil, 1989, p. 334

1

Introduction: Traditional politics, new authoritarianism

From 1964 to 1985 Brazil, Latin America's largest and most industrialized country, was governed by a military dictatorship, which on the surface was unlike its predecessors and was soon to become the model for other authoritarian regimes on the continent. Like other military governments before it, it deposed an elected president, repressed labor unions in order to carry out an austerity program, and imposed a moratorium on politics. Within a few brief years of coming to power, however, it shunned former allies and enlisted the support of new ones in the international arena to impose its own vision of radical economic and institutional change on the nation. If the military copied parts of its design for a new institutional configuration from the tapestry of earlier Brazilian history, its blueprint unambiguously looked to the future, not the past.[1] In order to accomplish a sophisticated set of economic and security objectives, the new governors set out to demobilize and depoliticize society. In the name of national security, they did not hesitate to torture their enemies, real and imagined, who did or merely appeared to harbor "Communist" sympathies or oppose military rule. This military dictatorship was South America's first "bureaucratic-authoritarian" regime.[2]

The Brazilian "Revolution" of 1964, as the military called its coup d'etat, had two broad goals: to foster economic development and to recast politics. In the economic realm, Brazil's new military governors initially sought to control inflation and attract foreign investment. In the longer term, predominant factions within the military that envisaged Brazil as a future great

1 Whether the post-1964 Brazilian military regime represented a rupture from democratizing trends of the late 1950s and early 1960s or a return to Brazil's authoritarian political past was a subject of considerable debate. The theme dominated the agenda of the justifiably celebrated *Authoritarian Brazil* (Stepan, 1973a), and much of the debate about Brazil in the 1970s in general.
2 The term was, of course, coined by O'Donnell (1973) to describe the military regimes of Brazil and especially Argentina. If Argentina provided O'Donnell with his model for the contribution of economic crisis to social conflict and political instability, the Brazilian military regime became the archetype of the bureaucratic-authoritarian regime. He later applied the label to authoritarian regimes in Uruguay and Chile (O'Donnell, 1978).

power wished to harness the resources of the state to sustain a massive development project. In order to accomplish these immediate and long-term economic objectives, the military believed that sweeping political change was necessary. The pressing goal of economic stabilization required that the "popular sectors," or the lower and middle classes, be politically demobilized in order to moderate wage demands. Reining in inflation and labor militancy would, in turn, improve the climate for foreign investment.

The broader development aims mandated a more profound reform of the way politics had traditionally practiced in Brazil. The military viewed the pervasive political clientelism, occasional corruption, and inefficient allocation of public resources to boost personal political careers that had traditionally characterized Brazilian politics as systemic obstacles to economic growth and ultimately political stability that needed to be rooted out of the state. Brazil's new governors thus planned to reorganize the state in such a way as to increase its administrative efficiency and capacity for autonomous action. In particular, they set out to concentrate power in the federal executive, then in military hands; centralize the state's fiscal resources; and depoliticize the policy-making process by transferring major policy decisions to a technobureaucracy. Initial differences within military ranks over how "hard" authoritarian rule should be and the extent to which the military state should sever its bonds with civilian elites were submerged over time in favor of a project to purge the state of all vestiges of patronage politics – the antithesis of technocratic rationality – and liberate it from the grip of politicians who put personal ambition ahead of the national interest and insulate it from their whims. By forcing regionally based political elites to surrender their dominance over the political system, military governors hoped to fulfill a century-old military dream: to create a national politics out of the mosaic of states' politics, to discard regional identities and loyalties, and to make Brazil a "great power" (*grande potência*).[3]

Military ambitions were realized to a great extent in the economic realm. During the late 1960s and the 1970s, growth rates soared, and extensive physical infrastructure was laid, and intermediate, consumer durables, and capital goods industries became sufficiently well established that they now not only serve the domestic market adequately, but they are also important earners of foreign exchange, easily eclipsing traditional exports. At the close of the period of military rule in 1985, Brazil's economy was the eighth largest in the Western, capitalist world. Most observers agree that policies of the military, and not merely fortuitous circumstances, contributed to this

---

3 McDonough's interviews with representatives of various Brazilian elite groups revealed that "the men who took power in 1964 were probably more concerned with those among their peers whom they considered as incompetents and demagogues than with a convulsion emanating spontaneously from the mass of the population, whom they tend to view as malleable and largely indifferent to politics" (1981b: 233).

pronounced economic success.[4] Recently even its opponents and detractors have grudgingly credited the regime with developing Brazil economically (Barros de Castro and Pires de Souza, 1985; Hirschman, 1987: 19–22), even though most would agree that the price tag – a $120 billion foreign debt – may have been too high.[5]

In contrast to the success of its economic program, military efforts to reform the political system produced mixed results. On the one hand, the bureaucratic-authoritarian regime scored several quick political strokes. It increased the military presence in the state and usurped control of the state police forces away from politician-governors. It also by and large succeeded in its primary short-term goal: containing the popular mobilization of the late 1950s and early 1960s. It limited popular influence over state policy and effectively excluded popular classes from politics, removed the administration of social security from the hands of labor leaders, set back peasant organization two decades, and preserved the distribution of income as one of the most skewed in the world. Although these changes will not likely be permanent, they have not been entirely reversed with democratization. Even after its exit, the military was able to flex its muscle over certain consequential political decisions; the presidential system enshrined in the 1988 constitution is a case in point. Since being legalized, Brazil's Communist parties attract only a small fraction of the electorate. Today, moreover, economic policy is still formulated and carried out by high levels of the cabinet ministries and state banks with formal responsibility for the economy, with little input from elected representatives. Even with the power to review the budget acquired through the 1988 democratic constitution, Congress has yet to become a full partner in government with the executive.

On the other hand, this military revolution was incomplete. Most obviously, its efforts to eradicate populism and "radicalism" ultimately failed. The formerly exiled populist leader and bête noire of the military, Leonel Brizola, triumphantly returned to national politics as soon as the military declared a national amnesty in 1979. More gradually but clearly more significantly, the Worker's Party has achieved steady electoral success on a platform of unreconstructed socialism. What is even more intriguing is that military rule proved to be no more capable of waging a war against traditional politicians than it was at rendering extinct populists and socialists. In Brazil today, three decades after the implantation of the bureaucratic-authoritarian regime and ten years since the military returned to the bar-

4 This has been questioned, however, by two highly respected economists. Bacha (1977) and Fishlow (1973, 1989) argue that the growth rates of the miracle were bound to occur, given excess capacity.
5 Also, Fernando Henrique Cardoso, in an interview with *Veja* (6/29/88: 6), compared the Sarney administration with its predecessors, stating that it was "undeniable that under the authoritarian regime there was a surge of modernization stimulated by the state."

racks, traditional politics and politicians have persisted despite military plans for their demise, military-sponsored economic modernization, and the important political mobilizations from below accompanying the transition to democracy. Clientelistic bargains, corruption, and other remnants of traditional politics are more than vestigial and, in some cases, have been changed in ways that have served to strengthen, not weaken them. Regional elites still broker major political questions and there is a great deal of continuity in elite ranks from the military to the current democratic regime. As Cardoso and Weffort lament in the quotations that begin this book, genuine political debate in Brazil has fallen victim to a restoration of oligarchical power and clientelistic practice.

In retrospect, the failure of the Brazilian military regime to bring about lasting momentous change may not appear quite so startling. Even with the monopolistic control over state force and state institutions that led to a widespread loss of life, violations against those persons accused of believing the wrong things, and economic immiseration for the majority, not one of the bureaucratic-authoritarian regimes fulfilled their bold projects of excising populism, socialism, and clientelism from the body politic, creating controlled democracies, and transforming the economic and political organization of their states and societies (cf. Garretón, 1989: 108; Gillespie, 1991: 50–51; A. Valenzuela and J. S. Valenzuela, 1986: 184–85). Their ambitions were obviously constrained by the lack of clarity of their transformative projects. What Garretón (1989: 108) calls their "defensive" or "reactive" projects – to repress and demobilize labor – were from the outset more clearly delineated than their "offensive" or "foundational" designs for new patterns of state–society interaction. In cases where their objectives were clear, South American militaries were also timid, unwilling (mercifully) to resort to the lengths of genocide or totalitarian control perhaps necessary to destroy the existing foundations of social and political life (cf. Garretón, 1989: 169). Nonetheless, even if the commitment of the Brazilian and other South American militaries to their political projects wavered, their reluctance to dance their own waltzes must in itself be explained.

The failure of the Brazilian military regime in particular to insulate the state from populist and clientelistic pressures and to eradicate traditional politics, moreover, cannot simply be dismissed as quixotic from the start. Most students of Brazil writing at the height of the dictatorship did not doubt that the military, willing to use force, enjoying international backing, and facing a subdued and disorganized opposition, could readily achieve its economic and political goals.[6] The Brazilian state was long regarded as a bureaucratic leviathan rising above a weak civil society, and scholars who

---

6 Although Celso Furtado (1968), Hélio Jaguaribe (1968), and much of the Brazilian left characterized the coup soon after it had occurred as a conservative regression doomed to fail, most observers overestimated its potential for stability once its repressive and economically modernizing face had been revealed.

otherwise disagreed about the origins, purpose, and future prospects of the regime concurred that the military had acquired vast power by virtue of seizing its reins. With the longest reign of all the bureaucratic-authoritarian regimes – twenty-one years–the Brazilian military also had more opportunity than the other South American dictatorships to rewrite the political map. Two decades of state-sponsored industrialization and agricultural modernization rapidly transformed the least urban, least literate, and least participatory of the countries that fell under bureaucratic-authoritarian rule into an urban society with a preponderance of urban industrial and service-sector workers. By the close of military rule, the most important participant group in the political market was no longer poorly informed peasants dependent upon landlord patrons but millions of young voters with no attachments to the parties that had officially ceased to exist in 1965 and no experience in precoup politics.[7]

Certain that military efforts to change Brazilian society would bear fruit, scholars did not stop to confirm whether the regime's policies had in fact produced a lasting break, intended or unintended, from previous political patterns, nor did they consider whether such change, if it took place, was subject to reversal. Once military rule weakened, however, scholars heralded the contribution of a stronger labor movement and civil society to the collapse of the dictatorship and the task of democratic consolidation. They even believed that the authoritarian disruption and devaluation of traditional politics provoked fundamental change in virtually every facet of political life.[8] They also assumed that because Brazil achieved the highest growth rates of any military regime, because its weak parties were replaced by new ones, and because its period of authoritarian rule was the longest, Brazilian politics would change more than politics in neighboring Chile, Uruguay, and Argentina. In fact, politics in Brazil may have changed less than in any other case of bureaucratic-authoritarianism as a result of the two regime changes of the past thirty years. This enduring strength of traditional politicians, along with the frustration of political and social change, has now been observed but still not explained.[9]

Taking the consequences of regime change for granted is not unique to scholarship on Brazil but is symptomatic of comparative research about

7 According to Remmer (1985: 271), as of 1980, nearly half of the adult population was less than thirty-five years old, and hence had not participated in the pre-1964 electoral system.

8 The emergence of new parties, voters, and forms of association and representation led at least one observer to predict that "contrasts between the pre-1964 Brazilian democratic regime and any future one are likely to be unusually marked by comparative standards. . . . [A]uthoritarian rule has altered fundamentally the political cleavages, party organizations, patronage networks, and electoral loyalties that shaped the outcome of political conflict before 1964" (Remmer, 1985: 270). In her entry on Brazil in the 1985 *Handbook of Latin American Studies*, Sarles (1985: 554) commented "the literature on Brazilian politics suggests that the country will never return to the pre-1964 form of democracy."

9 See, for example, Campello de Souza (1989).

politics in the former "bureaucratic-authoritarian," other recently authoritarian, and even former Communist countries. Because scholarly attention has been fixed sequentially on the albeit intellectually intriguing and practically important tasks of identifying factors provoking transitions from authoritarian rule, sustaining the processes of political liberalization, and consolidating constitutional democracies – the questions of why, how, and for how long regime change takes place that have been the focus of Huntington (1991) and others (e.g., O'Donnell and Schmitter, 1986) – a series of theoretical problems relating to the limits and consequences of regime change has been neglected. The literature on Latin America and other regions has paid little systematic attention to examining the capacity of authoritarian regimes to achieve their political projects and the issue of whether politics was transformed in intended or unintended directions by military rule. Most seriously, it has generally failed to provide a convincing causal explanation for why particular forms of political organization persist and others fade away after transitions from authoritarian rule.

This book attempts to answer why, despite controlling the state and resorting to force, the military could not control the directions of change in the Brazilian state and society, and considers as well the broader theoretical issue of the effects of regime change on patterns of political recruitment, competition, and representation. It addresses the understudied empirical question of what the lasting impact of authoritarian rule, its attendant development success, and its demise has been on traditional politics in Brazil, and also examines the fate of the traditional political elite, whose recent role in Brazilian politics has been systematically neglected. This research strategy is premised on the assumption that political behavior is not determined by the incentives offered by economic relations or political institutions to such an extent that political agents are not free to pursue strategies to revise those relations and institutions and that they cannot be effective in doing so. Indeed, in Brazil the traditional political elite blocked the transformation of political institutions and arrangements in ways that perpetuated a less than democratic traditional politics. Given the power of this class in Brazilian politics today, the role it played during the authoritarian regime and the transition from authoritarian rule, moreover, illuminates not only the Brazilian experience with authoritarianism per se, but also the prospects for the consolidation of a truly competitive democracy.

THE PROBLEM ELABORATED: REGIME CHANGE AND POLITICAL CHANGE IN BRAZIL

For scholars, the regime change of 1964 in Brazil was a watershed in the country's political development. Although virtually all observers recognized immediately that the practices of the new military regimes represented a sharp departure from the politics of the semicompetitive democracy that had preceded it, they did differ initially over the issue of how "new" this brand of authoritarianism was. A minority believed that the military regime of 1964–85 was something familiar to and consistent with Brazilian history. For the "patrimonialists" (such as Faoro, 1958; Malloy, 1979; Roett, 1984; Schwartzman, 1975, 1982), centralized rule was Brazil's "normal" political condition, interrupted only by two periods of loose federalism: the Old Republic (1889–1930) and the semicompetitive democratic era (1945–64).[10] The roots of Brazilian authoritarianism, according to Schwartzman (1970, 1975, 1982), lay in the co-optation by the too strong patrimonial state of any attempt at genuine representation on the part of civil society.[11] In the twentieth century, the interests of civil society were kept segmented, weak, and subject to state control by corporatist labor laws and institutions that prohibited plural representation and competition among organizations for membership – structures best described by Schmitter (1971).

Others, most notably the "structuralists," rejected the notion that authoritarianism was rooted in Brazil's political past and believed that the military regime was like nondemocratic governments of the past only in the most superficial respects. If patrimonialists viewed Brazil as destined to authoritarianism by birth, "structuralists" believed that the authoritarian regime had come about as a result of the country's marriage to the international economy. Cardoso (1973, 1979) in particular characterized the "new authoritarianism" as a political response to a new structural situation of external dependency. For a late-developing, capitalist country to industrialize in a time of the "internationalization of the market," he contended, it would have to dismantle its populist coalition that had supported import-substituting industrialization and turn outward to foreign investors. The structuralist perspective implied that other countries pursuing similar economic policies under comparable constraints would also fall victim to the new authoritarianism. This argument subsequently won the day when democratic regimes met their demise in the faltering economies of Argentina, Uruguay, and Chile and were replaced with military regimes that changed national economic course in each country by force.

Once authoritarian regimes were established in Brazil's neighboring states, it did not take long for scholars to highlight the common political patterns that distinguished them from "old" authoritarian regimes. They were most easily differentiated from their predecessors in their origins, purpose, and tenure. Guillermo O'Donnell (1973), who baptized these re-

---

10 Although not a "patrimonialist," Skidmore (1973) likened the military regime of 1964 to the "semifascist" dictatorship of Getúlio Vargas known as the Estado Nôvo (New State) (1937–45).

11 His analysis diverges sharply from the more common view that authoritarianism springs from an excess of demands from society placed on a too-weak state with insufficient institutional development, the view best expressed by Huntington (1968) as political decay.

gimes "bureaucratic-authoritarian," persuaded virtually all students of Latin American, if not comparative, politics that they had come into being as a response to the economic and political strains engendered by the "exhaustion" of the easy phase of import-substituting industrialization. At precisely the moment when these economies bumped up against the limits of the expansion of the domestic market for existing industries, inflationary pressures inherent in this development model, which were caused by trade imbalances and the wage increases that the working class was able to extract as a partner in the populist coalitions, surfaced. Stagnation and inflation, in turn, set off distributional conflicts that led to what Huntington (1968) has called "mass praetorianism."[12] The straightforward if sometimes grisly purpose of bureaucratic-authoritarian regimes was to rekindle growth and alleviate inflationary pressures by demobilizing and depoliticizing their conflict-ridden societies.

In taking the unprecedented decision to remain in power, the military fundamentally revised its relations with civilian elites. Whether directly serving the oligarchy, or assuming temporary total control in the hands of a single military strongman, a *caudillo*, old-style military intervention in Latin America had not attempted to restructure politics, only perhaps, as classically described by Anderson (1967: 96–97), to "brutally restrict entrance of other new power contenders into the political arena." Military governments in Latin America, Anderson claimed, assured "holders of important power capabilities in the society" that their position in the society would not be endangered and permitted them "some participation in the political process." Even in Brazil where the military intervened in politics in the years leading up to the 1964 coup not to empower strongmen or to prop up the oligarchy but to heed calls from civilians to oust a particular executive or prevent him from assuming power in the first place – a pattern described by Stepan (1971: 62–66) as the "moderator model" – the military did not retain power for itself, its ambition was limited, and its role in reshaping the state nonexistent.

In bureaucratic-authoritarian regimes, by contrast, militaries retained power in order to implement their own political agendas.[13] Schooled in a

12 "Mass praetorianism" is a condition of hypermobilization in modern society where levels of political participation markedly exceed the level of political institutionalization and where "social forces confront each other nakedly: no political institutions, no corps of professional political leaders are recognized or accepted as the legitimate intermediaries to moderate group conflict." In the absence of accepted procedures, each group employs means of direct action on the political scene that reflect its peculiar nature and capabilities: "The wealthy bribe; students riot; workers strike; mobs demonstrate; and the military coup" (Huntington, 1968: 80, 88, 196).

13 Cardoso (1979: 35–36, 41) argued that the military in bureaucratic authoritarianism departed from old *caudillo* politics, in which a single general or a colonel imposed personal orders by decree, in that it acted as an institution as such when assuming power, and did so in order to restructure society and the state. In Cardoso's view, such a military posture had

"new professionalism" at the Superior War College in Brazil and similar military institutions in other countries, they acted foremost to defend their institutional interests (Stepan, 1973b). In Brazil, governing according to the precepts of "national security doctrine" – the military's home-grown analysis of the ills of the Brazilian political economy that threatened national security (Alves, 1985) – the military not only "deactivated" the lower and lower-middle classes, but also, disgusted with economic disorder and the lack of material progress under the rule of politicians (Skidmore, 1973), it accumulated power in a way that "endangered" the position of older power elites. Turning to economists and engineers for technical solutions to thorny economic and social problems, the military both depoliticized key areas of economic and social policy and created a new, technocratic elite. This view of a centralizing state determined to squash societal mobilization and invest heavily in intermediate and capital goods industries described by O'Donnell was entirely consistent with the presumption of the "patrimonialists" that the Brazilian state intruded into most spheres of economic, administrative, and social life. Despite their real differences, "patrimonialist-corporatists" and "structuralists" shared a common view of the centralized Brazilian state that became only more economically and politically powerful during the period of military rule.

Leading scholars alleged, moreover, that accompanying this transformation of the Brazilian state was the exclusion of the traditional political elite from the new ruling coalition. Cardoso (1973: 146–47) contended that traditional sectors and politicians, the "older ruling sectors," "lost their relative power position in the total structure" in the wake of radical economic change, and that "the position of the career politicians, generally identified with the dominant classes in the previous arrangement," was "extensively undermined" by the military's attack on federalism and its structural changes in the political realm that involved a shift of power and the arenas of interest representation from parliament and the political parties to the executive branch of the state. For similar reasons, McDonough (1981b: xxviii, 99) asserted that many formerly well entrenched elite groups, including politicians as a class and most notably those who had been associated with the so-called Revolution of 1930, were marginalized from power. "The concentration of power by the military and the civilian technocracy began to deprive these elites of their constituencies. They were made increasingly irrelevant." Roett (1984: 39–40) had no doubt that a new elite of military and technocrats, concerned with efficiency, performance, and stability, had captured the state apparatus and become the dominant group of the Brazilian patrimonial state. Schwartzman interpreted the "Revolution" of 1964 as the "triumph of the center" and a bureaucratic, patrimonial state over the regional

become possible only recently, because previously the professional structure of the armed forces was less fully developed, and because the civilian oligarchies were far more powerful: they "needed only occasional military intervention in order to exercise their dominance."

oligarchies that had previously held power. With no notable exception, all accepted the view of a ruling coalition that comprised at its core a modern military and a civilian technocratic elite,[14] and a state whose top echelons, in Cardoso's (1975: 178–79) words, had become the "*chasse gardée* of the military and bureaucrats."

The dominant analyses of Brazilian politics reflected reasonably accurately the heady days of the authoritarian regime in the early 1970s. The military effectively pursued first a stabilization program and then a new development model that favored large-scale, advanced, largely foreign and state industry over small domestic manufacturers that produced for the internal market. Within a few years of assuming power, military rulers had expanded the powers of an executive branch effectively insulated from popular, electoral pressure and immune from constitutional checks on its authority. They struck a new partnership with technocrats, whom they named to top national cabinet posts to oversee major policy decisions, and distanced themselves somewhat from their former allies, the traditional economic and political elites who had coconspired to overthrow the populist regime.

The possibility that the account of post-1964 Brazilian politics that these compelling analyses collectively suggested was less than entirely accurate was suggested initially not by scholarship but by the turn of events. Both those scholars who attributed Brazilian authoritarianism to its patrimonial past and those who placed its origins in its dependent capitalist present were at a loss to explain why the regime first began to open and subsequently lost control over the transition process. As Cardoso (1989: 299) confessed "In 1971 when I wrote my essay for *Authoritarian Brazil,* 'Associated-Dependent Development: Theoretical and Practical Implications,' I did not see any possibility of the Brazilian regime's metamorphosis." The regime's persistence appeared to be inevitable to him and to others, he wrote, either because they believed dependent development *required* a centralization of power, or because they believed the "authoritarian vocation" to be "inherent in the historical formulation of Brazilian society." Because of these analytical errors, it was even more difficult than it would otherwise have been before 1974 to detect the cracks in the leviathan that was the Brazilian state, and so scholars overstated the magnitude of the changes they observed and underestimated the chances for the reversibility of these new patterns.

Once liberation was underway, scholarship on Brazil came to recognize the limits of the new authoritarianism and the collective predictive failure of the dominant interpretations of Brazilian politics in the 1970s. Following O'Donnell's (1979) identification of tensions within the bureaucratic-

---

14 Illustrative of the confidence in this belief, McDonough (1981a: 79) began his study of Brazilian elites during the Médici government by flatly asserting: "The objective [of this study] is not to discover the power structure, as if there were serious doubt about its existence or even much mystery about its composition."

authoritarian regimes,[15] scholars viewed the military regime in Brazil as less monolithic than presumed during the period of hegemony of the hard-liners, and attributed the political opening primarily to the divisions within (1) the state elite (the military institution) (Stepan, 1988) or (2) the ruling coalition (the military and the bourgeoisie) (Bresser Pereira, 1978; Faucher, 1981; Martins, 1986).[16] Subsequently, others, obviously impressed by the opposition mounted by a civil society that was stronger and more resilient than earlier analyses had appreciated,[17] contended that the state was considerably weaker and less able to implement its political agenda than previously believed by the "patrimonialists" and the "structuralists."[18]

A third school of revisionist scholarship looked to the political beliefs of the regime's societal opposition to understand why the regime had to abandon its ambitious political project (Lamounier, 1984, 1989a, 1989b; McDonough, 1981b). Bolivar Lamounier (1989a: 47) charged that analysts of Brazil who contributed to *Authoritarian Brazil*, with the notable exception of Juan Linz, failed to predict the inability of the authoritarian

15 O'Donnell (1979) identified at least two "tensions" capable of fracturing these regimes: (1) the erosion of the military's claim to govern on behalf of the nation, and the exposure of its rule as based on fear; and (2) the antagonism within the bureaucratic-authoritarian alliance between the military, which was nationalistic, on the one hand, and the technocracy and leading segments of national capital, which were "internationalized."

16 Stepan (1988), perhaps the most articulate spokesperson of the view that liberalization began within the military, argued that the soft-liners in the military-as-government, in order to defend the integrity of the military-as-institution, initiated a policy of "decompression" to reign in the military-as-security community. Bresser Pereira (1978), Faucher (1981), and Martins (1986) all underscored the importance of the withdrawal of bourgeois support from the authoritarian, governing alliance in triggering the transition from authoritarian rule; the "antistatism" campaign waged on the part of the São Paulo business community posed great difficulty for a military regime that prided itself on its good relations with domestic entrepreneurs. Faucher (1981) attributed the disillusion of the bourgeoisie to discontent with the second National Development Plan, and Martins (1986) to the highly centralized style of policy making characteristic of the Geisel administration.

17 Objecting to economic recession, political repression, or both, various segments of civil society resisted the dictatorship. The "Progressive Church" began this resistance (Alves, 1985; Della Cava, 1989), which was subsequently joined by women's movements (Alvarez, 1990), urban popular movements (Mainwaring, 1987, 1989b), a "new union" movement (Keck, 1989; Moisés, 1979; Tavares de Almeida, 1981), and a Worker's Party (Keck, 1992). Economic recession in particular damaged a regime whose only legitimacy formula was economic growth and national aggrandizement (Mainwaring, 1986b).

18 Stepan (1985) rejected this simple dichotomy, arguing that the state set the conditions for the growth and strength of civil society, which in turn became a dynamic opposition to the regime's controlled political opening. In a later analysis (1989: xi–xii), he combined these contending perspectives in arguing that intraelite divisions caused the regime to crack, and civil society's opposition prevented it from reneging on its promise to continue the process of liberalization: the momentum of transition was sustained by what he coined the "dialectic of regime concession and societal conquest." Diniz (1986) has similarly claimed that although the political opening began well before civil society was heard from, it took directions that its sponsors did not intend, and these can only be explained by popular pressure.

regime to institutionalize itself in the 1980s because they "underestimated the importance of liberal-representative traditions, of the electoral process and the party formations, of the symbols associated with them and the resistance which they still potentially represented.[19] In Lamounier's view, these traditions and symbols amounted to no less than an underappreciated tradition of political pluralism. Although he qualified Brazil's polyarchy as a "perverse" one that lacked a strong tradition of political organization independent of the state, Lamounier (1989a: 72) nonetheless argued that adherence to pluralist values within and outside military circles softened military rule. The ambivalence of Brazil's elites and masses about authoritarianism, in turn, forced the military to retain the trappings of democracy – the Congress and especially elections – even if these institutions and procedures were robbed of their full meaning by the dictatorship. Eventually, after 1974, these elections assumed the nature of plebiscites on the regime, precipitated a realignment of the electorate along the axis of the two parties created by the military, strengthened the opposition first in the industrialized cities of the Southeast (especially São Paulo) and eventually in the towns of the hinterlands, and ultimately forced the military to open the political system more than originally planned. Brazil's liberalization was, in his words, an "opening through elections" (1984).

Lamounier was quite correct to point out that political scientists consistently erred in underestimating the importance of elections in authoritarian Brazil. His focus on the rise of an electoral opposition enabled him to offer a credible explanation for why the political project of the military eventually failed. However, this same focus also failed to explain three central problems: (1) the considerable degree of electoral *success* that the military enjoyed in much of the country up to 1982 not attributable to its manipulations of electoral law (known as *casuismos*);[20] (2) whose discomfort with authoritarian rule was decisive in the breakup of the authoritarian regime (although his emphasis on elections seems to weigh on the side of mass opinion);[21] and, most seriously, (3) how the military was able to exert such

19 Linz (1973: 241–44) argued that the Brazilian regime would encounter severe difficulties in attempting to legitimize authoritarian rule. It lacked both traditional bases of legitimation of authoritarian rule: a charismatic leader and corporatism. Its military organization was bureaucratic, not headed by such a figure as Nasser, and the bases of corporatist rule would be difficult to achieve because its fascist variant was internationally discredited; the Catholic Church would not likely play along; and it would be difficult to harmonize a corporatist solution with the federal structure of the country and the traditional rule of state governors.

20 *Casuismos* refer to a wide variety of arbitrary laws and institutional practices designed by the authoritarian regime to serve its interests and undermine the electoral chances of the opposition (Lamounier, 1989a: 59, Weffort, 1989: 334).

21 McDonough (1981b), who also attributes the origins of political liberalization to the failure of the military-technocratic elite to establish ideological hegemony among political, reli-

control over the transition from authoritarian rule,[22] and what followed the authoritarian regime. The "mere" rise of an electoral opposition could no better predict the shape of the post-1985 competitive regime in Brazil than the other prevalent explanations for the slowly developing transition from authoritarian rule in Brazil. If Lamounier had been correct that an electoral realignment of regime-shaking significance forced the transition to Brazilian democracy, then the new electoral forces that undermined the authoritarian regime should have been successful in directing the transition and imposing a modern, plural democratic politics during the first decade of civilian rule. Yet, they were not.

There is perhaps no better illustration of the loss of control by the democratic opposition over the transition from authoritarian rule than the presidential succession of 1984–85. At the same time that tens of millions of Brazilians took to the streets to campaign for direct elections for president, sporting buttons that proclaimed, "Eu quero votar para presidente" (I want to vote for president), the governors of the states of Minas Gerais (Tancredo Neves) and São Paulo (André Franco Montoro) met in the resort city of Poços de Caldas, Minas Gerais, to "select" the opposition candidate for president in a procedure reminiscent of the manner in which Brazilian presidents were chosen at the turn of the century in the Old Republic (by a system known as "governor's politics," because the governors of the same two states made the selection).[23] Since then, in the first decade of civilian rule, traditional politicians have retained control of several major political parties and the state houses of many of Brazil's most important states, run up a staggering debt during a spree of wild clientelism in the late 1980s and early 1900s (cf. Ames, 1991; Mainwaring, 1991a), and projected their power in the national political arena through influencing cabinet appointments and presidential successions.

Of course, Lamounier was not alone in failing to predict the dramatic role that would be played by the traditional elite in the construction of a democratic regime. No serious observer of Brazil held out the possibility in the mid-1970s that traditional elites would have assumed the leadership of the regime change of the 1980s or that traditional politics would persist well after regime change. Persuaded of the military's earnestness by its rhetoric and early actions, and reasoning that entrusting fiscal authority and economic decision making to technical elites posed a threat to the operation of the oligarchical patronage system, prominent observers agreed that tradi-

gious, and labor leaders, unambiguously credits the defection of these elites from the authoritarian regime for its inherent instability and ultimately its downfall.

22 To my knowledge, there has been only one recent attempt to answer this question. Ames (1987) has argued that the military, to ensure the survival of its *influence*, if not its incumbency, embarked on a spending spree targeted to specific classes and regions, in order to maximize its political support.

23 Governor's politics is explained in Chapter 2.

tional, regional political elites and the clientelistic politics that they practiced began an irreversible decline after 1964. They were also influenced by the enduring dominant belief in social science that economic development that creates new industries sets in motions such processes as urbanization, unionization, and pluralization that eventually undermine traditional elites and traditional politics. Finally, most agreed with Lamounier's compelling argument that the military regime that created new political parties inadvertently also introduced new cleavages and forged new political identities, leaving Brazilian politics considerably more complex than standard and stale views about power and influence of the traditional political elite and traditional Brazilian politics would suggest.

Despite capturing slices of reality, these views were incomplete as descriptions of politics under the military and inaccurate as predictors of the future. The bureaucratic-authoritarian regime was a military-technocratic edifice only when the state was defined narrowly as the national executive and the power structure as governing only economic policy. During the dictatorship traditional elites dominated subnational governments and occupied a crucial role in the governing coalition as mediators at lower levels of the political system. When the military was challenged to shore up its sagging support, it revitalized its alliance with the traditional political elites who, in Cardoso's words (1973: 147), "expressed at the overt political level the class alliance in terms of which power had been organized since the old Republic," and abetted this elite in its wholesale practice of state clientelism. When the political winds shifted in favor of democracy, regional, traditional political elites figured prominently in the transition to a more democratic regime. Just as surely as their support helps to explain the persistence for two decades of bureaucratic-authoritarianism, their "defection" finally made possible the transition from authoritarian rule. Indeed, the derailing of the military's political project to transform the state and recast politics and the eclipse of the authoritarian regime is just as likely attributable to the enduring strength of *traditional* politics and *traditional* political elites as to the force of *modern* politics.

Despite urbanization, industrialization, the rise of a new union movement, an awakening consciousness of women, and the electoral breakthroughs of a genuine labor party, elite politics continues to be deeply embedded in Brazilian political life. Before offering an explanation for why this is so, we must examine the nature of traditional politics in Brazil.

TRADITIONAL POLITICS AND THE TRADITIONAL POLITICAL ELITE

When, more than twenty-five years ago, David Maybury-Lewis (1968: 161) wrote, "Politics everywhere entails patronage but in the Brazilian interior it involves little else," he spoke for virtually all observers of Brazil who assumed the practice of clientelism by regional oligarchies and local bosses to be pervasive. With the development of the past quarter century, scholars have backed away from the maximalist nature of this claim. Most now take as given that clientelism is of diminishing importance in the modern, partisan electoral politics of the more developed Brazilian Southeast but still rampant in the interior of the politically "backward," less developed Northeast.[24] Recently, Lamounier (1989a: 47) has challenged the common wisdom even more forcefully, charging past perceptions to be exaggerations, and expressing frustration that scholars have long overestimated the pervasiveness of the clientelism, corruption, and personalism of traditional Brazilian politics: "Our party and electoral history was then (in the early 1970s) and perhaps still is buried in stereotyped, often anecdotal descriptions, in which the practices of fraud, personalism, and clientelism are given an obviously unacceptable interpretive weight."

Lamounier's challenge is not to be taken lightly, because it calls to our attention that old and new stereotypes have for too long substituted for careful empirical research. Paradoxically, despite widespread *mention* of traditional politics in our literature on Brazil, we have few serious studies of clientelism, personalism, and corruption in contemporary Brazilian politics. In comparison with historians who have documented the stories of particular regional oligarchies during the Old Republic (Levine, 1978; Lewin, 1987; Love, 1971, 1980; Wirth, 1977) and anthropologists who have chronicled the control exercised by local political bosses and their families in small rural towns (see references in Murilo de Carvalho, 1968–69), political scientists in the past two decades have neglected the "oligarchy," the "politics of patronage," and *coronelismo* from the research agenda and their more general analyses of Brazilian politics.[25] As a result, there is little consensus on what traditional politics entails, and we lack a common understanding of the mechanisms underlying traditional politics and of the contemporary role of traditional politics and politicians in the larger political system.

24 Although this may be changing in the state of Ceará, where successive state administrations have challenged traditional political machines and improved the delivery of social services, most scholars would nonetheless probably still consider it to be a fair characterization of the politics of the region as a whole.

25 Early works by political scientists that made significant contributions to our understanding of the role and mechanisms of traditional politics were Murilo de Carvalho (1966, 1968–69) and Soares (1973). Since then, among the very few works that have successfully illuminated the evolution of the practice of clientelism in Brazil are Cammack (1982), Diniz (1982), Ames (1987, 1994), and Mainwaring (1991a). These more recent works have highlighted the importance of clientelism during military government (Cammack), the machine-like nature of modern clientelism in the state of Rio de Janeiro during the military regime under the opposition governor Chagas Freitas (Diniz), and the broader implications for Brazilian political institutions of the persistent strength of politicians that make use of clientelism (Ames and Mainwaring), but by and large have not placed the exercise of clientelism within a framework of traditional politics.

In this work, "traditional politics" implies a system of political organization that is authoritarian in the sense that political power is narrowly concentrated, access to decision making is restricted, channels of political representation are arranged hierarchically, and political competition is strictly regulated. Similar to politics in the various authoritarian regimes described by Linz (1975), traditional politics is demobilizing and essentially nonideological. What distinguishes traditional from other authoritarian politics are its peculiar patterns of political representation, competition, and recruitment. In "modernizing" authoritarian regimes, political parties might be submerged altogether or used as instruments of resocialization by a strategic state elite, and state leaders may either attempt to mediate interests through functional groups or deny such representation where it predates authoritarianism. In traditional politics, by contrast, political parties are more likely to be vehicles of oligarchical control, and interests to be mediated by patron-client relationships, which feed into a broader pattern of political representation that is organized along territorial, not functional, lines. The basis of the limited political competition that characterizes traditional politics also differs from that typical of modern authoritarian politics. Whereas in the latter politicians and parties define themselves along ideological lines or by association with a particular set of "conservative" issues – such as liberal economic policies, a proclerical stance, or promotion of a conservative social agenda – the primary cleavages of traditional politics are based on particularistic concerns, and factions are defined by and identified with personal cliques. Finally, political recruitment in traditional politics, although relatively closed, is not monopolized by a single, central state elite. More typically, it is dominated by an "oligarchy" of families that cross the blurred boundaries between state and society, and membership in or alliance with these families is key to political advancement.[26]

Traditional politics in Brazil is based on the three pillars of clientelism, regionalism, and personalism. Because it evolved under different circumstances in different parts of Brazil, a variety of forms can be identified, ranging from an extremely personalistic variant of clientelism in the Northeast hinterlands to a machine-based form of clientelism practiced by the opposition Brazilian Democratic Movement (MDB) in Rio de Janeiro during the dictatorship (Diniz, 1982). This work assumes that "traditional clientelistic" and "modern" forms of political mediation do not exist in pure form in separate, territorially demarcated zones, but that they coexist in Brazil's regions and in the Brazilian state. This coexistence, moreover, is not temporary, corresponding to a transitional phase of Brazilian development when the state is not yet capable of entirely penetrating national territory, as Nunes Leal (1977: 1) argued. Nor is one side likely to triumph

---

26 In this sense, traditional oligarchies more closely resemble the familiastic and personalistic oligarchies described by Lewin (1987) than the bureaucratically or collegially organized ones.

over the other, as implied by Soares (1973) in interpreting the events of 1964 as the simple victory of the traditional, conservative half of Brazil over the modern half, and by those who assume an inexorable march toward a "modern" politics. The battle between these forces is protracted, and it creates a dualism within the state, in systems of interest representation, in the electorate, and in various realms of public policy. When traditional and modern forces clash, neither side retains its purity. The bumping up of traditional against modern politics and each with economic constraints and opportunities "contaminates" both. Their interaction produces hybrid political forms, and practices that are normally thought of as "traditional" become "modernized," and the practices of the state and modern political parties are somewhat perverted by the presence and actions of traditional political elites. Thus, clientelism is not confined to personal relationships in rural areas as it was in the nineteenth and early twentieth centuries, but exists in the modern state and is exercised in the public, political sphere. Similarly, the same modern political parties that court the votes of union members and the university professors in some parts of Brazil are in others racked by personal and family feuds.

Underlying traditional politics in Brazil today is a system of domination founded primarily not on "status" in the Weberian sense but on control of material resources in a society marked by extreme economic inequality, particularly where the market has not yet penetrated, where it has been distorted, or where it has malfunctioned. In thousands of municipalities across Brazil, local bosses exploit the economic dependence of their clients on resources they own or control to boost their power and position. Although land clearly constituted the power base of traditional elites for most of the twentieth century, and still does in many parts of Brazil, traditional politics is no longer sustained on the basis of landholding alone. Even where land still serves as the basis for local dominance, it does so only within a political system that backs up local control with state resources. With economic development and territorial integration, the dependence of the client population has shifted from land to the state. At the state level, the most important material resource in establishing dominance is the manipulation of public resources that comes from controlling the state apparatus.

In this work the "traditional political elite" refers to a dominant class that does not occupy a single position in the productive structure, whose members' economic resources may be quite heterogeneous, and whose power derives from the exercise of politics itself. Both politicians of national prominence and their local allies, the local political bosses of the cities and towns of the interior, are included under the rubric of "traditional political elite." The group that dominates state politics is referred to as the "oligarchy" because its numbers are relatively small, its ranks relatively closed, and its power concentrated in few hands. Although once fitting the label of an economically based "export-oriented oligarchy," this elite today is a politi-

cal oligarchy. Local elites base their power on their roles as political mediators who deliver the political support of their subjects and state benefits
from their masters to one another. The dominance of local political bosses is
sustained by the productivity of their alliance with state-level elites.

Traditional political elites are distinguished from "professional politicians" and bureaucratic and other "nontraditional" or "modern" political
elites by their family background and the manner in which they exercise
domination – through highly personalized clientelistic networks, which are
themselves most often family-based.[27] The *traditional* political elite is to a
large extent interrelated through kinship, although nonfamily members can
through political friendship and connections gain entry to this elite. Lewin
(1987: 11) corrects the possible misperception that oligarchical politics was
synonymous with family politics when she explains that even by the late
nineteenth century in Paraíba, a "backward" state of the Northeast, "family ties alone could not provide an adequate nexus for local political organization and mobilization," that they "had ceased to be relied upon as narrowly as they had for securing an elite parentela's vital interests, and indeed, that they never had been the exclusive connecting bonds in politics
that the term "family system of politics" connotes in the anthropological
literature."

The concept of "traditional political elite" and the political success of its
members do not require that elite members have a shared political vision,
common ideology, or world view. During the military regime, members of
the traditional political elite infiltrated the ranks of both the opposition and
the government. Most old elites in the opposition were as apt to behave in
"traditional" ways, mobilizing a personal vote through family-based clientelistic networks, as did their counterparts who formally supported the
regime. Although there have been cases in which politicians of traditional
elite descent stake out positions genuinely distinct from the rest of the
oligarchy and at times are even actively committed to defeating the traditional order, this latter group is sufficiently small that no qualifications
need be placed on this definition.

The traditional political elite has shown itself on occasion, as in 1964, to
be capable of unity and common purpose in defending traditional politics
and privilege, but common purpose does not preclude competition within
its ranks. In fact, since the period of extraordinary noncompetitiveness
during the Old Republic (1889–1930), this class has been as divided and
politically competitive as most others. In 1945, the fundamental division
was between backers and opponents of Getúlio Vargas; in 1985, between
those who followed Aureliano Chaves and Tancredo Neves into the opposition, and those who remained loyal to the military regime. What is signifi-

27 The classic work of Oliveira Vianna (1974, I: 242–57) traces the extension of family clans
   into electoral clans, and the process by which great families became "major segments" of
   national political parties at the local level.

cant is that its divisions, often personally motivated, have defined the principal divisions in Brazilian politics. Intraelite rivalries have determined the number of political parties and how broadly based their membership will be, and who may participate in government and who will be relegated to the opposition.

The blurry lines of the "traditional political elite" have doubtless led many scholars, anxious for a neater categorization, to redraw the boundaries of this group. The temptation is to redefine divisions within the elite according to their positions in the productive structure, not to differentiate traditional and "modern" political elites, or to base an understanding of traditional elites exclusively on family lineage or social origin. These approaches hold substantial appeal in that in each of these formulations group identity is clear and membership can be unambiguously ascertained. Moreover, these classifications in and of themselves suggest hypotheses for group behavior: an economic elite has defined, material interests; and a political elite whose only glue is shared positions in a legislative body, for instance, can be viewed either as representatives of some other dominant group or power elite, or as self-interested power maximizers.[28] In contrast, problematic for understanding the political cohesiveness and behavior of a regional oligarchy is its lack of apparent motivation for political domination and clear sense of whom its members represent, with how much autonomy they act, and by whom they have been co-opted.[29]

The advantage gained by establishing distinct group boundaries is outweighed by the disadvantage of losing sight of what is common to the traditional political elite per se. Economically defined terms such as "agrarian elites" or "bankers" cannot capture the sources of cohesion and political behavior of this group, and the significance of its survival for political change. "Agrarian elite" may accurately, if ambiguously, describe both landed aristocrats and an agrarian bourgeoisie that controls large tracts of land, employs wage laborers, has at its disposal at least moderately sophisticated technology, and produces for large domestic and foreign markets, but cannot satisfactorily include a lawyer, whose family lands lie fallow, with investments in little more than urban property or short-term, savings bank deposits. If this lawyer is a prominent member of the political elite and is descended from a great line of landowner-governors, to view him as a middle-class, liberal professional would be to overlook the full scope of his power resources, his probable path to local, state, or national prominence, and the ends of his public activity. In Brazil, the rise of lawyers and other

28 The latter is the view of Ames (1987) and Geddes (1994).
29 One possible motivation, suggested by Schwartzman (1982: 23–24), is that public administration is a good in itself. Chilcote (1990: 154–55) reports that the ties of the ruling classes of Juazeiro and Petrolina to public officials and agencies outside their areas enabled them to channel state and federal funds for the construction of roads, reservoirs, dams, and irrigation systems to their ranches.

professionals to government does not necessarily imply the replacement of one class (agrarian elite) by another (liberal professional). Nor would the power of a banker derive from his wealth and the support of the financial community alone if he is served by a ward boss who served his father. Conversely, a sociologically based definition of traditional elite that excludes members with the "wrong" family lineage may miss the connection between the traditional political elite and the practice of traditional politics.

If social scientists have difficulty in identifying "traditional elites," conceiving of them as a distinct political class, and understanding the rationale for their behavior, Brazilian society does not. The "traditional families" (*famílias tradicionais*), "old leaderships" (*velhas lideranças*), and "conservative classes" (*classes conservadoras*) are known to all, and remain part of the Brazilian daily lexicon. The task of social science is to explain systematically who they are, why they survive and continue to monopolize power, and the effects of their dominance on political organization and practice.

REGIME CHANGE AND POLITICAL CONTINUITY: THE ROLE OF STATE – SOCIETY RELATIONS

What can account for the broad failure of the military regime to transform the Brazilian state and society and for traditional politics to survive two regime changes? Political science offers surprisingly few possible explanations for political continuity, which it most often relegates to a residual category – the absence of change.[30] A structuralistic perspective that seeks the impetus to political change in socioeconomic change interprets continuity as a result of economic stagnation and anticipates that, where economic development takes place, political change will soon follow. Decades of robust economic growth and political stasis in Brazil strongly suggest that such a line of argumentation is wholly inadequate to explain political change as well as its absence.

A second familiar view attributes political continuity to the influence of "culture," a set of attitudes and beliefs about politics and political relationships that are understood to be so stable that they work to defy any ambitions to create a new political order, The problem with such a view is that culture is quite often *not* stable but quite remarkably pliant. Values and beliefs have the capacity to shift sharply and rapidly in times of regime change, as occurred in Germany in the first decade after military defeat of Nazism (Verba, 1965), as well as gradually and across generations, as appar-

---

30 One intriguing exception is Berger and Piore (1980). The authors have argued convincingly that the economic and political needs of the "modern" sector – to distribute uncertainty, and to control labor and remain competitive – have kept alive "traditional" classes (small shopkeepers, independent property owners, and small peasant farmers) and production units. But this framework does not account for why change might not take place should the "modern" sector attempt to bring it about.

ently has taken place in Western Europe in the postwar period as a result of sustained economic prosperity (Inglehart, 1977, 1990). When crudely applied, as they all too often are, culturally based explanations for stalled political development are unsatisfactory precisely because they dodge the fact that continuity in cultural patterns too needs to be explained.

Students of regime change in Latin America have largely been as optimistic about political change as social scientists more generally (Hagopian, 1993: 469–70). A few notable exceptions, however, that do attempt to explain political continuity in the context of regime change have done so with considerable promise by focusing on the contribution of politics. One potential source of continuity is alleged to be the "freezing" effect of authoritarian rule. Inspired by the Lipset and Rokkan (1967) metaphor, some observers (Rial, 1989; A. Valenzuela and J. S. Valenzuela, 1986) expected bureaucratic-authoritarian regimes to have a limited political impact on party systems, party–constituent relations, and political leaders for at least five reasons: (1) the tenacity of symbolically rooted partisan loyalties; (2) the name recognition enjoyed by party leaders during the times when political activities are banned; (3) the ideological hardening of parties not forced to compromise or to moderate their appeals in the electoral arena but which are instead struggling to stay alive in the hearts and minds of their militants, ever faithful to the party line; (4) the assumption of leadership by party activists of the new social movements and civil associations that supplant parties as the natural sphere of political activity; and (5) the diversion of partisan energies into clandestine work that reinforces existing party organizations by hindering the creation of new structures and networks (Garretón, 1989: 169–70).

The "freezing" metaphor aptly captures to a large extent the various dimensions along which preauthoritarian political parties and leaders survived the authoritarian episode in some countries. Chilean parties targeted for elimination by the military regime reappeared on the political scene as soon as some political space was opened in 1983 (Garretón, 1989: 169). The reemergence of Uruguay's "traditional" parties, and the similarity of their vote totals in the 1984 elections to those registered in the 1971 election (Rial, 1986), lend credence to Gillespie's (1986) claim that they survived in "suspended animation." But the formation of an entirely new party system in Brazil and electoral realignment elsewhere suggest, as Remmer (1989: 49–51) has persuasively argued, that the "freezing" hypothesis is unable to account for variation in the effects of authoritarian rule on party systems – to predict when it impedes electoral realignment and when it may actually provoke it.[31]

31 Remmer (1989: 70) proposes as an alternative that "the degree of party-system continuity linked with redemocratization in Latin America over the past four decades is positively associated with party system age and preauthoritarian party system continuity and negatively associated with electoral growth, political repression, and the organization of sup-

Continuity in political systems has also been attributed to political institutions and electoral laws that create incentives for political actors to reproduce familiar patterns of political behavior.[32] Students of Uruguay have credited the double simultaneous vote (DSV) with retaining the two-party system (Gillespie, 1986; and especially González, 1985),[33] and a growing consensus argues that the persistence of Brazil's comparatively underdeveloped parties, weak party discipline, and persistent clientelism can be traced to its open-list, multimember district version of proportional representation (Ames 1991, 1994; Lamounier, 1989b; Mainwaring, 1991b, 1992–93). These analyses have considerable merit, although the rapid rise of a third electoral force in Uruguay – the leftist Frente Amplio and Nuevo Espacio coalitions – without reform of the DSV does challenge their validity. As explanations for why the Brazilian military project to transform the state and society failed, and why the traditional political elite emerged from bureaucratic-authoritarian rule with its dominance intact, moreover, they must be considered at best incomplete. The fact that candidates for the programmatic Workers' Party (PT) campaign very differently (i.e., without promising to be the best brokers of particularistic benefits) in the same electoral system suggests that political competition is not driven exclusively by institutional arrangements.

Finally, a third potential source of political continuity is claimed to be the compromise that provides the basis for the construction of democratic regimes. Karl (1990) has argued that features of past regimes may be written into the constitutional and other founding arrangements of the new during two types of "elite-ascendant" regime transitions that she calls "imposition" and "pact" and which Linz (1978: 35) calls *"reforma,"* Mainwaring and Share (1986: 177–79), "transition through transaction," and Huntington (1991: 113–14), "transformation." Either by imposing or securing through negotiation their requirements for adhering to a democratic order, elites can "freeze" democracies, effectively impeding their ability to evolve and extend themselves.

Comparative evidence supports the contention that democratization is

port in noncompetitive elections." Moreover, the longer authoritarian regimes remained in power, the greater the change from the political status quo ante. The merits of this framework, and its applicability to Brazil, are discussed in Chapter 6.

32 This tradition is of course not new but dates back to Sartori's (1966) analysis of the contribution of the proportional representation electoral systems of France and especially Italy to the survival of ideological parties in party systems that were characterized by what he called "polarized pluralism."

33 The double simultaneous vote permits parties to present more than one list in each election, and the number of seats for each party is determined using a modified d'Hondt form of proportional representation, first for the party as a whole and then by the same method among rival factions of each party. Presidential elections, held at the same time, are also subject to the DSV; the victor is the candidate who polls best on the ticket of the party whose combined vote total is highest (Gillespie and González, 1989: 212–13).

often slowed or stopped in regimes spawned by political pacts negotiated with traditional and authoritarian elites. In Italy after Agostino De Pretis persuaded opposition deputies from the Destra Party newly marginalized from power and state spoils in 1876 to shift their votes to the government majority in exchange for personal benefits, access to state patronage, and the right to rule locally – to "transform" themselves from the opposition into a stable part of the governing majority – all effective opposition was eliminated from the Italian parliament; for decades, southern deputies voted with any government, regardless of program or ideology, that supported their practice of clientelism. The organization of politics "around personality and patronage rather than ideas and practical programs . . . ultimately emptied the very concept of 'party' of any meaning beyond that of a loose congeries of personal clienteles" (Chubb, 1982: 21). In Colombia, during nearly three decades of formal and effective consociational, coalition rule, traditional and conservative political elites limited popular mobilization, access to higher education, and agrarian reform, and slowed the process of extending democracy to a glacial pace (Berry and Solaún, 1980; Hartlyn, 1988; Wilde, 1978).[34] Such a framework, indeed, goes far in explaining why several features of Brazilian politics survived the transition to democracy (Hagopian, 1990, 1992).

What is less clear is how and why countries embark on particular transition paths. Responding to Przeworski (1986, 1989), who viewed regime change as the outcome of largely subjective strategic choices made by political actors,[35] Karl (1990: 6) saw a country's choice of path as the product of "structured contingency," or, the structural constraints placed upon political actors by the political institutions and especially the socioeconomic structures already present. The strength of various actors at the moment of regime transition is explained, if at all, in relation to factors that change more slowly than the life of most authoritarian regimes, such as a country's natural resource base, social structure, or position in the international economy.

In attempting to explain the considerable degree of political continuity in Brazil during and after the regime of a modernizing military dictatorship, this book also assigns considerable importance to the nature of regime change. But it departs from this literature in viewing the choices that actors make in times of transition, and their prospects for success, as constrained more by politics than by socioeconomic structures. My concep-

---

34 To end civil war and military dictatorship, Colombia's two traditional, warring parties, the Liberals and the Conservatives, formed a National Front government, agreeing to share equally until 1974 (regardless of vote totals) all legislative and administrative posts while alternating the presidency. Parity between the two parties in all legislative bodies, the cabinet, the Supreme Court, governorships and mayoralties, and the bureaucracy was constitutionally guaranteed.

35 His ideas are further developed in Przeworski (1991, 1992).

tion of "politics," moreover, is broader than mere electoral arrangements, administrative structures, and even the institutions of the state.[36] It also includes the competition of aspiring political representatives, their relationship to the political institutions that they operate, and the pattern of their interactions with their constituents – the representative relations between the state and society. Such a focus assumes not only that "state–society relations" influence the nature of regime change, but also that the way in which previous regime change affects those relations helps to explain the capacity of a national executive to effect changes in the broader pattern of political organization.

State–society relations in this work encompass the ways in which the state and society are independently organized as well as the networks through which societal interests are mediated and the state marshals consent in a political system.[37] The state, for example, can be either federal or unitary, with power more or less concentrated and administration more or less decentralized. Societal associations can be organized vertically or horizontally, more or less independently of the initiatives of the state or political parties, on a class, group, or other basis, and along ideological or nonideological lines. Societal interests can be mediated through ideological political parties that make collective appeals to functionally defined groups, by clientelistic political parties that appeal to individuals and territorially defined groups, or outside party structures by corporate groups. Consent is organized through these same channels by the state, which can be either "stronger" or "weaker" than society. More than one type of state–society relation can be present within the same country and even represent the same group or individual – one may be a member of a corporatist rural union and also be part of a patronage network headed by a deputy. State–society relations shape social organization, structure incentives for individual and collective political behavior, and set the parameters within which the state can design a strategy to mobilize support. They are

36 Although studies of state institutions can be quite valuable for explaining economic policy making (Hall, 1986; Geddes, 1990), they are less useful for studying how political systems accept and resist change.

37 Unfortunately, the view of state–society relations embedded in most political analyses of Brazil and comparative politics generally tends to focus separately on *either* the state or society, and to privilege one as acting upon the other (cf. Migdal, 1994). The "first-generation" state–society scholars by and large worked within liberal and "instrumentalist" Marxist frameworks; behavioralists, modernization theorists, and students of class analysis were "society-centered" in that they privileged the centrality of class conflict and the actions of social forces in explaining political change. To these analysts, the state was a reflection of societal conflict, and the instrument of the class victorious in that conflict – the "dominant" class. The "second generation" institutionalists and "structural" Marxists (e.g., Nordlinger, 1987; Skocpol, 1979; Stepan, 1977) were "state-centered" in that they identified institutions as key to the capacity of the state to pattern social and political life. For a useful review of these frameworks, see Kohli and Shue (1994).

the essence of a political regime as defined by Cardoso (1979) and Collier (1982).[38]

I begin this work with the premise that how state–society relations are configured makes a difference for the degree of change regimes are able to effect, not by provoking or precluding change altogether, but by establishing constraints and opportunities within which regimes and other political actors must work. Whether and what kind of change takes place follows from the way in which particular regime strategies and policies interact with these networks. The book argues that in authoritarian regimes, the success a state elite may have in attempting to transform the state, reorganize society, and redraw the relations of the state with society is progressively enabled or constrained by (1) the legacy of the way in which society is organized politically and attached to the state; (2) the manner in which authoritarianism is formatted onto preexisting links between society and the state – that is, whether these networks are altered, preserved, or destroyed by regime policies; and (3) the nature of regime transition. More specifically, in those bureaucratic-authoritarian regimes in which the preexisting networks of mediation between state and society could be repaired, the military was constrained from rebuilding them on a different foundation; where they had malfunctioned more dramatically, the transformative projects of military regimes were more active and sweeping (though not necessarily more effective). In both cases, their "defects" shaped military strategies for authoritarian rule. They determined, for instance, whether corporatist networks were created, exploited, or targeted for destruction. Once the restrictions on political activity were defined, political alliances between regime and segments of society forged or severed, and economic policies and plans formulated, whether authoritarian regimes contributed to or blocked political change depended rather on whether they left intact or attempted to reorganize the basis on which political interests had been organized previously, and whether the economic policies and political strategies that they pursued privileged or dismantled preauthoritarian networks of mediation between states and societies. The vitality of these channels was in turn important for their impact on the strength and weakness of various social and political forces, their negotiating positions, and their own aspirations and priorities at the moment of regime transition. The process of negotiation and regime transition itself benefited certain political actors and disadvantaged others; it allowed dominant actors to write into founding political arrangements and institutions rules and procedures that would benefit them in the longer term.

38 According to Cardoso (1979: 38), a political regime encompasses the "formal rules that link the main political institutions (legislature to the executive, executive to the judiciary, and party system to them all), as well as the issue of the political nature of the ties between citizens and rulers (democratic, oligarchic, totalitarian, or whatever)." For Collier (1982: 60), a regime is the structure of formal, legitimate power of the state.

The Brazilian military inherited a political system whose primary form of state–society relations was regionally based, highly personalized, networks of political clientism that traversed public–private boundaries. The pattern of economic development it pursued ahead enhanced the opportunities and political returns for those who distributed state patronage. The authoritarian regime's political strategy to hold elections in a context of circumscribed political competition that limited opportunities for factional realignment and elite turnover paradoxically preserved traditional politics and politicians. When, then, regime change took place, traditional regional political elites in Brazil were in a strong position to forge a new governing coalition, to dictate policy, and to command considerable electoral force.

Such a framework requires a focus not only on the process of transition, which has been examined extensively, especially for the Brazilian case, but also on the period of military rule, which by contrast has been surprisingly understudied. Perhaps because, as Karen Remmer (1989: 24) has observed, "Scholars moved from the study of democratic breakdown to the study of democratic transitions without pausing to analyze the authoritarian phase that came in between," they failed to recognize the potential that studying the period of authoritarian rule holds for explaining how particular transition paths were shaped, why some patterns of political organization should emerge or reemerge and others fail to, why some actors were left stronger than others after authoritarian episodes, and why representative relations take certain directions and not others – in short, why change or continuity takes the form that it does.[39] Demonstrating such an argument also requires attention to the mechanisms of traditional politics – where they are located.

THE INQUIRY

Most studies that attempt to judge change and to ascertain who is powerful typically focus on the national executive and bureaucracy, national political parties, and national corporate bodies. A focus on national politics, however, is inappropriate for observing the indicators of change or sources of continuity in traditional, oligarchical political systems. In such political systems, the "state" comprises not merely the institutions and appointed positions of the national bureaucracy and executive branch, but also its legislative branch as well as its subnational components, including the elective positions of state and local governments and the local outposts of state and federal agencies. Such a focus is particularly inappropriate for Brazil, where an extensive state presence in the economy generated multiple points where "society" and the "state" intersected, and where a "national

---

39 J. S. Valenzuela and A. Valenzuela (1986), McClintock and Lowenthal (1983), and Cavarozzi and Garretón (1989) are fine exceptions.

politics" probably does not exist as one entity but only as a cluster of regional politics.[40] Most parties do not have national scope – until very recently, the Democratic Labor Party (PDT) was a party of primarily two states, Rio de Janeiro and Rio Grande do Sul,[41] and the PT, of São Paulo. Not to disaggregate research on the Brazilian state, territorially *as well as* institutionally, is to presume erroneously, or at least without any means of confirmation, that the hypothesized shift in power from decentralized points of the system to a single national center has already taken place, and that interests are no longer organized and represented on a territorial basis, but, as in modern political economies, on a functional basis.[42]

Studying traditional politics: The territorial dimension

In Brazil, political machines are organized regionally and the epicenter of oligarchical politics is found on the periphery. Traditional political elites ruled Brazil from the states; their power has historically been regional in scope and based in the state political machines. A work that purports to study the fate of traditional political elites and traditional forms of political organization must therefore bring to its investigation a focus on state-level politics. But if this study should focus primarily on the state level, it cannot do so exclusively. In particular, it cannot ignore local politics. As Soares (1973: 98), one of the few political scientists to investigate the relationship between traditional and modern politics, explains:

even though states do not depend on any one municipality in the same way that the municipalities depend on them . . . traditional politics, characteristic of many Brazilian states, resides in oligarchical municipal politics . . . and cannot be understood without reference to it. It was precisely the existence of oligarchical politics in tens or hundreds of *municípios* that made possible the supremacy of traditional politics on the state level, in detriment to a modern politics, based on class interest. The politics of many Brazilian states would be fundamentally different if municipal politics were characterized by a full electoral-political participation of less favored

40 Lima (1981) has argued convincingly that in the 1945–64 period, there was no single pattern of national politics, merely an amalgamation of many state patterns, Also highlighting Brazil's regional political diversity, Soares (1973) has demonstrated that parties behave differently in different parts of Brazil.

41 On this basis, Soares (1984: 65–73) projected that the party's leader, Leonel Brizola, could not win a direct presidential election. Indeed, not only did Brizola fail to make it past the first round in the 1989 election, but his vote was highly concentrated in those two states. He received 50 percent and 61 percent of the vote respectively in Rio de Janeiro and Rio Grande do Sul, but only 1.5 percent of the vote in São Paulo (Ames, 1994: 98). In 1990 the PDT did elect the governor of Espírito Santo and in 1994, the governors of Mato Grosso and Paraná.

42 Writing of advanced industrial societies, Tarrow (1978: 6–7) suggests that as social and economic problems gravitate to the level of greatest centralization – the national state – territorial units (cities, provinces, and regions) find their representative function in decline. He notes, moreover, that this trend is especially pronounced where technocrats are privileged decision makers.

social sectors, if there were not domination by traditional families, and if the political parties represented the interests of different social classes and not the different oligarchical and traditional families.

Given the critical importance of local politics to the power base of traditional elites, even a small change in local politics might rock the foundation of the oligarchical system. Transformation or its absence at the local level is particularly significant. Because the expected effect of socioeconomic change is to undermine traditional dominance first at the local level, as was the case historically, it is important to look to the local level for early indications of *change*. If a transformation of the elite is likely to take place as the result of industrialization, even if it takes decades for this change to filter up through the various levels of the political system to the national cabinet, the independent effects of socioeconomic change should be visible at the local level. Various elite studies concur that it is at the local level of the political system that the preliminary evidence of elite transformation can and should be sought.[43] A focus on local politics also affords us an opportunity to seek possible sources of *persistence*. If the political changes attempted by an authoritarian regime that originate at the *national* level are to take hold, they should filter down to the lower levels of the political system. If they do not, the absence of change locally, in turn, enhances the ability of a regionally based oligarchical elite to contest efforts at political centralization.

One objection to this research plan might be that it obscures how meaningful regional power is in a centralizing regime. If "real power" were centralized within the federal state apparatus and concentrated in a few ministries, then the enduring dominance of traditional elites in the states would be largely symbolic and irrelevant for the major decisions governing Brazilian society. With the centralization of power and finance complete, regional elites might be mere pawns of a more powerful bourgeoisie or military, and permitted to rule in their states in exchange for supporting the national regime. To compensate for this problem, I insert the analysis in a national context, and study state–national linkages, the extent and limits of fiscal centralization, and the interplay of state and national politics. But even if it were true that traditional politics persisted only in the states and the scope of power of the traditional political elite was thus limited, this in

43 Frey (1965: 262) describes the pattern of bottom-up changes in the Turkish elite in the twentieth century as "capillary action": "the lowest levels of formal power are affected first. If pressure continues, middle leaders are then altered, and only after a noticeable time lag is there a seepage into the highest levels of leadership and the cabinet." This pattern is consistent with that discovered by Putnam's (1976) and Matthews's (1954) historical studies of elite transformation in Britain. Matthews's study showed a lag of almost a century between the time the middle-class bourgeoisie became dominant in the electorate and the time it became dominant in the British cabinet, some thirty to forty years after middle-class members of Parliament became common (1954: 42–43).

itself would constitute a significant finding about the organization of politics and possibilities for change in a federal system,[44] especially if such a failure to change local and state politics had led to the demise of the national regime.

To understand the socioeconomic origins of clientelistic politics, to trace the impact of industrialization on the structure of power, and to reconstruct the network of alliances and transactions that uphold the oligarchical political system require an analysis that bridges the levels of territorial politics. Given the complexity of traditional, territorial Brazilian politics, too many important connections would be lost were this study to focus on a single level of government. Yet, in Brazil, the sheer size of the physical territory, the proliferation of administrative units, and the nation's economic, political, and cultural diversity pose considerable difficulties for designing research. A state-level comparison of traditional political forces, however attractive, would test variation in the effects of only one independent variable and presumes the existence of at least two comparable regional oligarchies for research. This work pursues an alternative approach to test the effects of industrialization *and* political centralization on traditional political elites: to focus on one regional oligarchy and to make use of controlled comparisons of local politics, state–local linkages, and state–national fiscal and political relations. The regional political elite and state politics of choice are those of Minas Gerais.

The case of Minas Gerais

Minas Gerais has long been one of Brazil's most important states, and its political elite, often called Brazil's "political class," especially powerful and resilient. Deposers of elected presidents and nonelected dictators, its members are Brazil's keepers of political tradition. Throughout the twentieth century, a powerful local oligarchy dominated state politics in Minas and exerted great influence in national politics, more than its economic resources would suggest it "should have." During the Old Republic (1889–1930), it negotiated a power-sharing agreement with its São Paulo counterpart that allowed it in alternate election years to handpick the president of the republic. As Brazil modernized, the Minas political elite was not forced to cede national power in order to preserve local power.[45] The four major regime changes in this century – the collapse of the Old Republic in 1930, the restoration of democracy in 1945, the military "Revolution" of 1964, and the transition to civilian government in 1985 – were all provoked by

44 Key's (1984) classic work about politics in the South of the United States of course demonstrated precisely the ways in which the power of traditional elites in the Southern states spilled over into the American Congress.

45 Such an argument, first advanced by Gramsci (1971), has been frequently made about the terms under which southern Italian elites accepted unification with northern Italy.

the Mineiro political elite, who respectively led the Liberal Alliance against the hegemony of São Paulo, authored the *Manifesto dos Mineiros* which condemned the Vargas dictatorship, led the civilian–military conspiracy against the elected president João Goulart, and forged the alliance of old-regime elites and their opponents to launch the presidential candidacy of Tancredo Neves and oust the military regime that it had conspired to implant. The Minas elite ultimately outlasted even the military itself.

Because of its historical political influence, the Minas elite represents in a sense the "most likely" oligarchy to survive the centralizing efforts of the military regime and as such raises possible problems for generalization. Yet weaker regional oligarchies in authoritarian Brazil were not exposed to nearly the same degree to the effects of the economic development model of the military regime that was alleged to threaten the foundations of traditional power and politics. Following the regime change in 1964, a state technocracy came to power in Minas in the late 1960s and engineered a superlative economic recovery from decades of stagnation. The local miracle produced average annual industrial growth rates of 16 percent, the highest in Brazil during the 1970s, and made Minas the country's third most industrialized state. The industrialization of Minas Gerais serves as a quintessential example of dependent development as defined by Cardoso (1972, 1973), Evans (1979), and others. State and foreign capital played a prominent role, the intermediate and capital goods sectors received most industrial investment, and a local technocracy managed economic policy. In contrast to the industrialization of São Paulo, which might be and has been described as "spontaneous" (Cardoso, 1965) in that it was effected largely by private sector capitalists, that of Minas was neatly contrived, stimulated by select state interventions and, from the late 1960s, state-directed; Minas Gerais in 1980 had more state enterprises than any other Brazilian state (IBGE, 1980c: xxxvi). It represents the purest case of "state-led capitalist development" in Brazil.

The similarity of its pattern of development to the national model led many observers to make similar claims about state politics that scholarly consensus held to be true of national politics. One observer, noting the prominent roles of the state government, state and foreign capital, and technocracy in the upper echelons of the state apparatus, represented the industrialization of Minas, in both its economic and political dimension, as a "replica" of the larger Brazilian model of industrialization (Grossi, 1977). The same observer (Grossi, 1977: 262–63) was joined by others (L. Andrade, 1980; Cintra, 1979) in claiming categorically that the regime had eliminated "traditional" politicians in Minas from power because (1) they were no longer found in the key posts for decision making (which had gravitated more and more toward the executive branch), and, most important, (2) their source of power and the system itself in which they held a prominent place was in the process of disappearing. With the importance of elections diminished in a regime in which "real power" was exercised in bureaucratic circles, Cintra (1979: 151) contended, "Elites from such states as Minas Gerais, whose sizeable electorate accounted for the power they wielded in the center, have fallen into ostracism."

It is also reasonable to choose Minas Gerais for a case study of the effects of regime change and economic development on traditional politics because of its broad diversity. Minas borders, and serves as a bridge between, the underdeveloped Northeast and the industrialized and Europeanized South. Its politics reflects this tension: in 1982, it elected an opposition governor, as did the states of São Paulo and Rio de Janeiro, but with the support of both metallurgical workers from the metropolitan region of the state capital and the "steel valley" and landed elites from the northern part of the state – an area included by convention and by statute in Brazil's Northeast region. The Jequitinhonha Valley, to the northeast, is as poor and backward as any region of Brazil. The residents of the southern and southwestern parts of the state, both prosperous agricultural zones, on the other hand, are integrated in the São Paulo orbit. They read São Paulo newspapers and root for Paulista *futebol* teams. If one can generalize from the experience of a single Brazilian state, Minas Gerais affords greater warrant to do so than the more frequently studied southeastern states.

ORGANIZATION OF THE STUDY

This book is organized to illuminate the interactive effects of regime change on the networks of mediation between state and society in Brazil. Its inquiry can be conceptually divided into three parts: (1) elaborating the configuration of state–society relations prevailing on the eve of the 1964 coup d'etat; (2) examining how the economic and political strategies pursued by the military regime altered, preserved, or destroyed those relations; and (3) identifying the degree to which these patterns were reinforced or disturbed in the transition from authoritarian rule to democracy.

Turning first to the pattern of state–society relations inherited by the Brazilian military, Chapter 2 examines the foundations and adaptation of traditional politics in Minas Gerais. Regional oligarchies that dominated national politics from the overthrow of the emperor in 1889 to the Great Depression profited from the establishment of a republic in Brazil that conceded substantial political and fiscal autonomy to the states. The Minas elite stifled political competition in the state and within its own ranks by centralizing control over political recruitment, the electoral system, and the state judiciary and police forces in the state and single-party executives. The collapse of export markets and the quasi-Bonapartist Vargas dictatorship (1937–45) disrupted the state political machines and divided this oligarchy. Nonetheless, with the reimposition of democratic procedures after World War II, the traditional political elite of Minas Gerais reestablished its domi-

nance despite a reasonably wide franchise and relatively open political competition. It did so largely by modernizing clientelism and by creating a party
system to accommodate its own internal competition and organize the consent of its political clients. Traditional politicians were abetted in shifting the
practice of clientelism from the private sphere to the state by two waves of
bureaucratic expansion coupled with the continued fiscal dependence of
municipalities on the state government. These state patronage networks that
were less coercive than the private patron–client relations of agrarian society
became the dominant form of political mediation prior to the onset of authoritarian rule.

Next, the book turns to the regime's economic strategy. Chapter 3 out-
lines the expansion of the state's role in the economy and the regional and
national pattern of industrialization that reinforced the state–society relations of traditional politics. In the first decade of bureaucratic-authoritarian
rule, the resources of the Brazilian state sector proliferated, levels of state
investment and employment rose, and the state's regulatory capacity expanded even above and beyond levels reached as a result of state economic
intervention in the 1930s, 1940s, and 1950s. In Minas Gerais, direct investments by state enterprises in infrastructure, industry, and agricultural modernization, and state financial and institutional support for foreign and
domestic private investors, generated a local economic miracle. Contrary
to expectations that the military's economic program would shake the foundations of the traditional political system by strengthening industrial classes
and the modern economy, the regime's policies invigorated networks of
political clientelism and the power of local political elites. The state-led and
state- and foreign-financed industrialization did not produce a regional
bourgeoisie to challenge the traditional political elite at any level of the
political system. Peasants displaced by agricultural modernization were
only partially incorporated into industrial employment; some formed an
underemployed and undercompensated, seasonally employed, agrarian
wage labor force; they and others that resided in mushrooming urban areas
became "state clients," dependent in whole or in part on state employment,
credit, direct and indirect transfers, and other benefits. The growth of the
public economy (1) increased the volume of resources available for state
patronage, (2) drew in ever larger numbers of clients participating in existing clientelistic networks, and (3) created "state patrons" among the state's
political representatives. The political role and importance of this elite
were only enhanced as the stakes in controlling state power in Brazil rose.

In the next three chapters, the book examines the design, revisions, and
results of the nebulous political project of the Brazilian military. Chapter 4
focuses on the impact of bureaucratic authoritarianism on political recruitment and state power in Minas Gerais, with particular attention devoted to
the questions of the extent to which politicians were supplanted in the
executive branch of the state by technocrats after the coup, and the politi-

cal fate of those elites who occupied powerful public office before the 1964 coup d'etat, including the "oligarchy." An examination of the career paths of the cabinet secretaries and other top state executives from 1956 to 1982 shows that if the military intended to evict traditional politicians from the state – as its emasculation of the legislature and early promotion of techno-crats suggested it might – it did not. Traditional political elites returned to the state cabinet in the early to mid-1970s, and retained important sources of state patronage throughout the dictatorship. A "technocracy" did not materialize, and traditional politicians survived in top state posts to an even greater extent than did politicians without roots in traditional families.

Chapter 5 examines the role played by state–society relations in modifying the military project, and of state-sponsored political clientelism in strength-ening traditional elites and the bases of traditional politics. The economic and political strategies pursued by the military in the regime's first decade had not fundamentally altered preexisting state–society relations. At-tempted fiscal centralization fell short of undermining a central feature of traditional Brazilian politics – the dependence of local politicians on state-level regional elites. After 1974, electoral competition intensified and the regime struggled to retain legislative majorities. When even despite re-peated manipulations of electoral law the regime's need for political and electoral support became more acute in the second decade of bureaucratic authoritarianism, the military accepted as necessary to the regime's survival a wholesale revision of its strategy for contesting elections and political mediation. Constrained by the state–society relations it inherited as well as the traditional and emerging bases of partisan identification, it redirected the expanding state resource base and state programs in Minas Gerais and elsewhere in the 1970s through highly politicized networks operated by the traditional political elite. The massive distribution of state patronage not only shored up electoral support for military rule for several years (until the most serious economic recession in Brazil in fifty years rapidly eroded mass tolerance for military rule) but it also strengthened clientelistic networks of state–society mediation and traditional politics.

Despite the fact that the military ultimately controlled state resources and should have been able to direct patronage funds through any office-holders, it was unable even to replace traditional political elites with new political elites in the state. Chapter 6 addresses this puzzle by examining the consequences of the Brazilian military's decision to stage restricted electoral competition. From the beginning of the authoritarian period, the high-level participation of the traditional political elite in the regime was virtually locked into place because incumbent traditional politicians, firmly entrenched in key state positions for controlling state patronage before the onset of rapid industrialization, were well placed to use the resources of their offices, which were enriched by the state's extensive penetration of the economy, for political gain. Their advantage was reinforced by the military's decision in 1965 to appoint governors and create a two-party system in which a progovernment party, organized and controlled by members of the traditional political elite at all territorial levels of the political system, would be virtually guaranteed electoral hegemony. The political networks that served as bridges between the state and society through which clientelism was disbursed, moreover, were their personal patrimony and not available to the military simply by virtue of seizing the upper ranks of the central state. Ultimately, the military's political program restricted elite political recruitment. Elite turnover was reduced especially at the municipal level, where recruitment paths were virtually closed, but at the state level, too, turnover rates were down sharply from the precoup period.

Chapter 7 examines the role played by traditional politicians in the transition to a democratic regime and the broader impact of the process of regime change on state–society relations. An outcome that preserved traditional politics and the hegemony of regional political elites was not predetermined, but neither was it completely a chance development. When military rule tottered, the traditional political elite that had been favored by the military and shielded from political competition during the dictatorship was well placed to take the lead in the transition to democracy and the birth of the "New Republic."[46] Striking a series of political bargains to regain their control over state clientelism that had eroded with the restoration of state-level political competition, members of the Minas elite underwent a metamorphosis in their political identities and partisanship. By "transforming" itself, the elite emerged from the transition in the inner circles of power in the state and the three major political parties, and it used its position of leadership to shape the political institutions of the New Republic and preserve the political advantage it had gained during authoritarianism over its civilian and military competitors. The study concludes its investigation with the influence exerted by traditional politicians on the democratic constitution of 1988, subsequent elections, and democratic governance in the 1990s.

Chapter 8 reexamines and extends the theoretical framework advanced in this book and the tentative conclusions reached about political continuity and the regime change in Brazil by subjecting it to comparative analysis. The experience of other bureaucratic-authoritarian countries shows that different regime strategies, superimposed on different state–society relations, and ended by different kinds of regime transitions, produced more political change. Clientelistic networks, the politicians that organized them, and the parties that distributed patronage suffered a decline in Uruguay where the regime failed to expand the state's role in the economy and suspended the political parties and closed Congress. Corporatism in Argen-

---

46 The "New Republic" (A Nova República), a phrase coined by Tancredo Neves in his presidential campaign, has been widely used to describe the post-1985 civilian regime.

tina was severely weakened by a regime that preferred to kill labor leaders than co-opt them, and ideological parties in Chile survived a ruthless attack by the military but in an altered state.

In the perspective suggested by this research, there is reason for profound pessimism for the future of the Brazilian political system and the welfare of the 80 percent of the population for whom the economic growth of the 1970s bore no fruit and the galloping inflation accompanied by recession of the late 1980s and early 1990s hit hardest. As Brazil inches toward democracy and delivering long-overdue social justice to its population, the survival of the traditional political elite may compromise the ability of the political system to transcend its authoritarian heritage, something it must do if it is to represent national and particularly popular interests. To date, the political strength of this class has acted as a brake on a genuine opening of the political system in Brazil, and there is little reason to believe that socioeconomic development alone, which helped to reproduce traditional politics during the dictatorship, will now be a catalyst for democratic development.[47] If old elites can continue to dominate the political system, then even if formal democracy can survive rumored coups each time the military is displeased with civilians, the vast majority of the population will reap neither its political nor material fruits. Indeed, there is mounting evidence that – even as a genuine labor party has established an enduring presence on the political landscape, the populace stands ready to organize itself to stop military autocrats and corrupt civilian leaders alike, and a social democratic president takes the reins of government with a competent economic team – exaggerated state clientelism is ruining the economy and eroding popular faith in political institutions. Yet, although democracy's early years have not been promising, the conclusions of this study may be revised by political events. Sustained, open political competition may still undermine the patterns of politics that state-led economic development, bureaucratic authoritarianism, and the transition from authoritarian rule alone could not.

47 A new variant of modernization theory, which gained considerable adherence after the regime transition of 1985, believed that the socioeconomic development made possible by the military had paved the way for democracy in Brazil. In his perceptive review of this and other explanations for democratization in Brazil, Cardoso (1989: 311) observed that this belief rested on the view that a "democratic subproduct," which was "the consequence of social differentiation provoked by economic development, by the growing specificity of social roles required by growing secularization of and rationalization of society, and by the need for standardization of norms appropriate for a modern industrial society," unexpectedly grew up in civil society.

2

Oligarchical power and traditional politics in Minas Gerais

The first republic of Brazil was an archetypal oligarchical republic fashioned by regional elites to preserve their dominance within their respective states. The Old Republic (1889–1930), as it was known, restricted real political participation to a bare fraction of the population. Among participant groups, elites of smaller states were as helpless as the urban middle classes of the larger ones to challenge successfully the hegemony of the oligarchies of the strong states. These elites who were "coffee barons" or represented coffee interests used their political success to make coffee the nation's leading source of foreign exchange and wealth and thus to enrich themselves. The pattern of traditional, authoritarian politics practiced by these noncompetitive, regional oligarchies was underwritten by electoral fraud and the dependence of local governments on the state and, at the local level, by a grossly unequal distribution of land and the use of public and private force.

After four decades, the "oligarchical republic" ruptured from within amid discontent in military circles and a crisis in the coffee economy. The "Revolution" that deposed the Paulista president and delivered power to Getúlio Vargas of Rio Grande do Sul strengthened the central state and expanded the scope of its activities; set in motion the processes of economic moderation and the incorporation of new, especially urban, classes and sectors into the political system; and effectively ended the oligarchy's monopoly over the state and politics. Though agrarian elites remained in control of the rural areas and were able to deny rural workers the full rights of citizenship up until the military coup of 1964, it is taken for granted in the conventional wisdom about Brazil that the political centralization carried out by Vargas caused the state and national power of regional oligarchies to decline steadily after 1930; the expansion of political participation that followed the restoration of competitive elections in 1945 accelerated their demise; and politicians campaigning on populist platforms in the postwar period gained in strength, especially in rapidly growing urban areas, at the expense of traditional political elites who practiced clientelism.[1]

1 Weffort (1970: 390), for example, claims that the Revolution of 1930 ended oligarchical hegemony when it did away with "the system of access to power through the traditional

Whatever the merits of these familiar arguments for some parts of Brazil, they do not hold true for Minas Gerais; they probably understate elsewhere as well as the resilience and adaptability of traditional politics to modern circumstances; and they do not present a complete or entirely accurate picture of the political inheritance of the military regime. During the Estado Nôvo regional oligarchical machines were undermined and regional oligarchies reconfigured, but state appointments continued to be made according to political criteria and resources for state patronage were still available to traditional political elites. In the postwar period, despite relatively open and competitive politics, modern political parties, burgeoning cities and industry, and populist politicians who courted and were committed to platforms championing the causes of working-class voters, the traditional oligarchy of Minas Gerais maintained its grip on the state political system; however, now divided by Vargas into rival camps, it no longer, with its Paulista counterpart, could overtly control the national presidency and the Congress.

This chapter examines the underlying structures of oligarchical hegemony laid during the Old Republic, their survival and adaptation during the postwar "experiment in democracy,"[2] and the clientelistic strategies adopted by the elite-dominated parties of the postwar era. From a closed oligarchy that in the Old Republic ruled by centralizing state politics, by eliminating competition, and by pressing into alliances with it the local elites (known as *coroneis*) whose power resided in private, economic sources of domination, this elite shifted its power base and strategies for political domination as necessary to keep pace with economic and political change. With the declining value of controlling land and police forces, it took refuge in the state and political advantage of state expansion without bureaucratic insulation under Vargas. With the intensification of electoral competition in the postwar period, it learned to compete politically under conditions of a gradually expanding electorate, principally by adapting traditional clientelism to a more urbanized environment. When the military regime took power in 1964, it inherited, then, an elite-dominated political system permeated by traditional politics in which clientelism pervaded the state and electoral systems.

TRADITIONAL POLITICS IN THE OLD REPUBLIC

For most of the life of the Old Republic, power was held by the regional oligarchies of the strongest states. The rule of these elites was sustained by a pattern of authoritarian political organization superimposed over a highly

families and economic groups, which would have enabled the oligarchy to renew itself within its own group." Also see Weffort (1978), Cardoso and Faletto (1979), and Laclau (1979).
2 The expression is Skidmore's (1967).

unequal distribution of economic resources that suppressed the two most basic levers of democratization: political competition and participation. The Minas oligarchy in particular consolidated its power in the public sphere and based its longevity on its command of the state apparatus and a single party. In the state the traditional political elite found the material resources and military protection to perpetuate its rule; in the party, it found an uncontested vehicle for achieving and retaining state power.

Oligarchy and federal republic

On gaining independence from Portugal in 1822, Brazil's form of government continued to be an empire, and even the royal family remained the same: the Portuguese emperor was succeeded by his young son.[3] After nearly seven decades of remarkable stability in which the Crown held a slight advantage in the balance of power between itself and the imperial elite, the empire fell swiftly and suddenly when military and agrarian elites, the two imperial political actors of consequence, separately withdrew their support for the emperor. São Paulo coffee planters turned against the emperor for his handling of the abolition of slavery,[4] and the military did so to advance its own corporate interests and because it believed, erroneously, that overthrowing the emperor would weaken the planters (Reis, 1980: 102).[5] With the forced abdication of the emperor in 1889, a republic was established.

The persistence of traditional political organization in Brazilian politics has its origins in the way in which the institutions and alliances that founded the Brazilian republic were constituted. While the military had as

3 In 1808, when Napoleon invaded the Iberian peninsula, the Portuguese royal family fled to Brazil, its colony, and there established its court. After the defeat of Napoleon and the monarchy's return to Portugal, Dom Pedro I remained behind, and declared Brazil's independence in 1822.

4 Many planters hastened to join the São Paulo Republican Party (PRP) after the passage of the Golden Law in 1888, the fourth in a series of abolition laws that over the course of nearly four decades gradually ended slavery in Brazil. The aims of the Paulista coffee planters in opposing the emperor and the imperial parties and converting to the Republican cause were not so much to save or to reinstitute the institution of slavery, but to carry out abolition on terms more favorable to themselves (J. Martins, 1977; Reis, 1980: 58–77). The planters of the Paraíba Valley hoped for indemnification for freed slaves (Love, 1980: 108; Reis, 1980: 105). Those in the frontier zones expected that a republic would override the emperor's objections to subsidize imported labor (Reis, 1980: 111–12). Their efforts helped to win federal government subsidies for immigration that covered the transportation costs of 63 percent of the 158,420 immigrants who entered São Paulo between 1888 and 1890, and 80 percent of the 719,595 who came between 1891 and 1900, mostly from Italy (Villela and Suzigan, as cited in Reis, 1980: 45).

5 The sources of military discontent sprang from internal disciplinary questions and civilian–military disputes. After the war with Paraguay, military budgets were cut and civilians appointed to the war ministry. For an overview, see Reis (1980: 97–99), and for an account of how these issues became salient in Rio Grande do Sul, see Love (1971: 30–31).

its ambition so replace the empire with a strong central government committed to the positivist ideal of "order and progress," civilians who favored a federal system in order to maximize regional autonomy won the day (Cardoso Silva, 1982: 147; Cintra, 1979: 131). By 1891, the elites of the economically strongest states had wrested control of the new republic from the military and framed a constitution that guaranteed a decentralized, federal republican structure that accorded the states even wider latitude than did the United States federalism from which it drew its inspiration: each state was entitled to draft its own constitution; negotiate commercial treaties with foreign governments and borrow money from abroad; and levy taxes on exports, rural and urban lands, property transfers, industrial activities, and professional activities (Reis, 1980: 132). The union, in contrast, was entitled only to import and stamp taxes. The constitution also delegated to the states the authority to regulate municipal rights.

Brazilian federalism strengthened the strongest states and their oligarchies vis-à-vis the union, and progressively weakened the already weak. The two leading state elites to emerge were those of São Paulo and Minas Gerais. Economically ascendant and with the best organized of the provincial Republican Parties in the last two decades of the empire (Love, 1980: 102), it was natural that São Paulo would have assumed a leading role in national politics and that a Paulista planter would become Brazil's first elected civilian president in 1894. Why, on the other hand, the elite of Minas Gerais, a state lacking economic wealth and antecedent political organization, rose in national politics is far less obvious.

The Minas political elite was descended from the *bandeirantes*, or fortune seekers that settled in the state during the gold rush of the seventeenth and eighteenth centuries, who were enriched by the award of titles of nobility and large tracts by the Crown.[6] After the once gold-rich mines of Minas Gerais became exhausted in the mid-eighteenth century and the bases of the regional economy changed and diversified, they ventured into agricultural and commercial activities. At the time of the constitution of the republic, this now semimodern, increasingly heterogeneous economic elite included coffee barons, old mining-based wealth, cattle and dairy ranchers, and even small, local industrialists based in different topographical, economic, and political territories in the state (Wirth, 1977: 69–72). Even despite the moderate recovery of the regional economy with the introduction of coffee to southern Brazil in the second half of the nineteenth century – in 1880, Minas Gerais became the second most important Brazilian producer of coffee (Lage de Resende, 1982: 25, 29) – the state's economy was not sufficiently dynamic to catapult its elite to national political prominence and to take a leading role in the Brazilian union.

6 The rich mines that provided gold and other precious metals to Portugal named the province; "Minas Gerais," in Portuguese, means "General Mines."

Nor was the Minas elite in a strong position politically. It was less well represented in the ranks of the imperial elite than its counterparts from Rio de Janeiro, Bahia, and São Paulo.[7] Moreover, its Republican movement was weak. As the "mainstay of the Bragança monarchy" (Wirth, 1977: 98) it was a latecomer to the Republican movement: in Minas, Republican clubs were organized only in 1888, were few in number, and did not attract large coffee-growers as they had in São Paulo (Cardoso Silva, 1982: 147).[8]

Why the Minas elite initially shared in national power can be attributed to its political utility to the hegemonic Paulista coffee elite. The São Paulo oligarchy had originally reasoned that a federal system that granted the states a considerable degree of autonomy would best suit the coffee economy. It was soon forced to rethink this localist strategy, however, when it became apparent that its economic interests depended in large part on *national* financial and exchange policies, as well as the fulfillment of foreign commitments (Carone, 1978: 99–100). To assure the profitability of coffee, the coffee barons would need central government backing. This, in turn, was possible only with the organized, political support of other states in the Congress. As the most populous state in the union, and hence the one with the largest delegation to the Chamber of Deputies – thirty-seven representatives – Minas Gerais was a natural target for Paulista affections. (The Paulista *bancada* had only twenty-two delegates). In 1898, the newly elected Paulista president, Campos Salles, offered to his Minas counterpart shared control of the national executive in exchange for the support of the Minas congressional delegation for his monetary policy. The arrangement concentrating power in the hands of governors of the two most powerful states of the Old Republic, São Paulo and Minas Gerais, was known as the *política dos governadores*, or, the "politics of the governors." Bahia, a northeastern state and the third largest with twenty-two representatives in Congress, assumed the role of a junior partner in this coalition. Weaker states with small militias were made fiscally dependent upon the central government and subject to federal military intervention.

The *café com leite (café au lait)* alliance between the coffee-producing São Paulo and the dairy-producing Minas Gerais proved to be lucrative

---

7 Political hegemony during the second reign (1840–89) belonged to Rio de Janeiro, the country's administrative and financial center and its principal port (Cardoso Silva, 1982: 146), and Bahia (Murilo de Carvalho, 1980: 104–7). In 1885, Minas had 22 percent of the population but only 16 percent of the deputies in the imperial legislature (São Paulo had nearly 20 percent). Rio de Janeiro, Bahia, and Pernambuco all had more ministers.

8 Not only was the Minas Republican movement considerably less developed than those of São Paulo and Rio de Janeiro, where the first Republican clubs were organized as early as 1870, but it also lagged behind even that of Rio Grande do Sul, organized in 1882. In Rio Grande, the Republican movement enjoyed strong support, and acquired a coherent programmatic outlook: it opposed slavery (Rio Grande had few slaves and antislavery was gaining in popularity) and endorsed Comtian positivism (Love, 1971: 26–27).

indeed for its participants. Paulistas and Mineiros rotated the federal executive for twenty-eight of the thirty-six years that civilians controlled the Old Republic, and of the two occasions in 1910 and 1919 when natives of these two states did not occupy the presidency, in only the first did the winning candidate (Marechal Hermes da Fonseca) not receive the official endorsement of the "governors." The Minas oligarchy in particular reaped several self-perpetuating sources of power after the "governors' politics" alliance was sealed in 1898: broad access to federal patronage (Wirth, 1977: 106); the top leadership posts in Congress of president and majority leader of the Chamber of Deputies (except from 1904 to 1914 when the post of majority leader was occupied by the powerful Pinheiro Machado of Rio Grande do Sul) (Wirth, 1977: 175); a significant presence on parliamentary commissions (in 1903, Minas congressmen occupied three of the nine seats on the important budget committee alone [Lage de Resende, 1982: 213]); and considerably more frequent and longer stints as titleholders in the key Ministries of Finance, Justice, and Public Works than the elite of any other state. Mineiros held these cabinet posts for 28 percent of the period from 1898 to 1930, Gaúchos for 16 percent, and Baianos for only 9 percent (Wirth, 1977: 106, 174).

Minas was even more successful politically than its partner, São Paulo, whose political influence, Schwartzman (1975: 120–23) has pointed out "never corresponded to that which its growing economic weight would suggest." Despite representing Brazil's most powerful planters and nascent bourgeoisie, Paulista politicians occupied the posts of ministers of finance, justice, and public works for only 8 percent of the period from 1898 to 1930. To be sure, as Schwartzman (1975: 120–21) has conceded, it was possible for the Paulistas to secure from the central government much of what they needed, especially in the line of coffee support, without occupying presidential and ministerial posts.[9] Yet, São Paulo was visibly discontent with the levels of support it received from the union. Paulista officials and representatives complained bitterly in published works and in the Constituent Assembly of 1933–34 of the state's tax burden, which had increased from 13 percent of federal receipts in the 1890s to 30 percent in the decade from 1928 to 1937 (Schwartzman, 1975: 123). They argued that São Paulo paid more taxes into union coffers than the federal government spent in São Paulo, in effect "subsidizing" other states – in particular Minas

---

9 Paulista coffee growers at one time received almost 70 percent of the resources of the Bank of Brazil (Pena, as cited in Schwartzman, 1975: 121); the Paulistas controlled the administrative machinery governing coffee interests; and they were able, on three separate occasions during the Old Republic, to induce the central government to contravene the market through "valorization schemes" in order to boost the international price of coffee. When the world market price for coffee was low, the federal government purchased stocks from the planters (financed by borrowing abroad), then sold the stocks in the international market when world prices became more favorable, which they were bound to given Brazil's dominant position in the international coffee market.

Table 2.1. *The Minas elite in the Old Republic (in %)*

	Wirth (177)	Martins (542)	Fleischer		
			P (19)	VP (12)	FD (241)
Family ties	41.0	51.7	73.7	50.0	32.8
"High elite"		77.8			
Local politics experience		42.3			
Principal occupation					
Industry	17.8	10.9			
Commerce	5.6	6.2	5.3	8.3	8.6
Agriculture	16.7	21.9	5.3	0.0	3.3
Lawyer	67.9	52.7			
Judges	17.3	28.1	47.3	25.0	38.8
Professors	32.2	29.6	15.8	41.7	9.1
Other professions[a]	48.6	51.8	26.3	25.0	33.3
Other public employees	n.d.	22.2	0.0	0.0	4.3
Finance and banking	15.0	5.4	0.0	0.0	2.9
Region (political base)					
Center (Metalúrgica)	53.5	19.0	22.2	10.0	31.0
Mata	19.2	14.4	22.2	30.0	25.0
South	11.1	21.4	38.9	20.0	19.8
North	6.1		0.0	10.0	7.8
Jequitinhonha			0.0	10.0	3.9
Rio Doce (East)	2.5	34.3	5.6	10.0	3.0
West	6.1		11.1	10.0	6.9
Triângulo	1.5		0.0	0.0	2.1
Outside state		10.9			

Note: The three author's sample sizes (in parentheses), time periods, and universe of posts vary slightly. Martins's study covers the years from 1889–1930; Wirth's from 1889–1937; and Fleischer's from 1890–1937. Wirth includes governors, lieutenant governors, state cabinet secretaries, presidents of state banks, members of the executive commission of the Republican Party, government leaders in the Legislative Assembly, and the equivalent posts on the federal level. To Wirth's posts, Martins adds deputies and senators. Fleischer's data are subdivided into state presidents (P), vice-presidents (VP), and federal deputies (FD).
[b]Encompasses engineers, journalists, and physicians in Wirth's and Martins's studies. This category is unspecified in Fleischer's data set.
Sources: Wirth, 1977: 142, 147, 245; Martins, 1983; Fleischer, 1982: 48.

Gerais. Their claims were based in fact. São Paulo contributed five times as much to the federal treasury as Minas in 1925–30, and between seven and eight times as much in 1931–37 (Love, 1980: 261–62), but Minas Gerais obtained the greater benefits in areas such as rail construction; 40 percent of all federal rail construction in the 1920s was in Minas (Wirth, 1977: 179).

The disparity in rail construction was so pronounced that by 1928, 28 percent of the federal railway network was located in Minas (70 percent of the state's rail network), but only 4 percent in the state of São Paulo (12 percent of the São Paulo rail system) (Schwartzman, 1975: 123).

The Minas elite that was to gain political dominance was from the beginning a traditional elite organized into clan networks that formed zonal power groups (Rebelo Horta, 1956: 59; Oliveira Vianna, 1974,1: 218–19, 224–33). Throughout the Old Republic, family ties were a crucial feature of the Minas political elite. Forty-one percent of 177 top executive, legislative, party, and administrative elites from 1889 to 1937 studied by Wirth (1977: 142) were related to at least one other member of the elite through first cousin, directly, or by marriage,[10] as were 51.7 percent of the broader elite of 542 elites (including deputies and senators) studied by Martins (1983: 4–6) (Table 2.1). Intraelite linkages were even more pronounced in "high-level office": 77.8 percent of those who reached federal executive and cabinet-rank office had ties to the elite, and only one governor (of fifteen) during the Old Republic did not have identifiable clan ties within the state. Not only were family connections an important asset in climbing the political ladder, but they were also used as a criterion for appointment to the state bureaucracy. In 1900, 38 percent (226 of 584) of public functionaries in Belo Horizonte belonged to 87 clans (Siqueira, 1970: 178–79).

In contrast to the Paulista political elite, which was primarily an agrarian and industrial elite – over 40 percent had a stake in the export economy (mainly coffee) and 28 percent were industrialists – the Minas elite was concentrated in professional and bureaucratic occupations. Only 17.1 percent of the Mineiro elite were linked to the coffee trade and 17.8 were industrialists. Lawyers in both states were well represented in the political elite (67.9 percent in Minas and 69.3 percent in São Paulo), but in Minas the most common professions after lawyer were educator (at the secondary or university level) (32.2 percent) and journalist (23.8 percent) (Table 2.2). Known landowners represented a small portion of the state's political elite during the Old Republic.[11] Wirth (1977: 145) positively identified only 35 members (16.7 percent) of his sample of the Minas elite as *fazendeiros*.[12]

10 This figure may be an underestimate, since the data are not complete.

11 They may have represented a small proportion of the imperial elite as well. According to Murilo de Carvalho (1980: 78–87), the percentage of ministers who by occupation were landowners and merchants for the entire period (1822–89) was less than 5 percent; senators, less than 15 percent; and deputies, less than 10 percent, although over 40 percent of ministers did have landholdings and another 11 percent engaged in commerce and/or finance.

12 Wirth (1977: 145) concedes that there are considerable methodological difficulties in stating such figures with confidence: data on rural property ownership are poor – newspaper biographies and obituaries, the richest data sources for elite studies, usually focus on a person's educational and professional achievements rather than his assets, including rural properties; and most members of the elite had multiple careers – two-thirds of the *fazendeiros* had two or more careers (Martins also found an average of 2.6 occupations for

Table 2.2. *Old Republic oligarchies: Minas Gerais versus São Paulo*

	Minas Gerais		São Paulo	
	%	N	%	N
Member of agricultural export complex[a]	17.1	210	40.3	233
Fazendeiro	16.7	210	37.7	239
Industrialist	17.8	214	27.8	241
Merchant	5.6	213	16.6	241
Lawyer	67.9	212	69.3	241
Educator	32.2	213	21.2	241
Journalist	23.8	214	26.6	241
Member of, or related to, imperial elite,[b] through first cousin, cosanguinal or affinitive, or direct descendant through grandson	16.2	185	19.7	239
Related to at least one other member of same state elite, through first cousin, cosanguinal or affinitive	46.3	177	42.5	240
Break with state establishment's position over presidential succession in				
1909-10	10.7	149	7.9	164
1921-22	4.6	151	.6	178
1929-30	5.9	136	3.2	125

[a]Included in the agricultural export complex are: (a) agricultural society officers; (b) exporter, manager or director of, or investor in, exporting firm; (c) *fazendeiro*, and (d) *comissário* (a short-term lender to *fazendeiros*).
[b]Imperial elite includes senators, or titleholders of barão (baron) and above.
Sources: Love, 1980: 283, 286; Wirth, 1977: 242, 245, 246, 247.

The coffee elite was even smaller. Of 108 *fazendeiros* classified by Martins (1983: 3–4) (21.9 percent of his sample), only 35 were born in the coffee-producing regions of the state, and but 13 (2.5 percent) could be categorically identified as coffee planters. On the other hand, landowners and coffee growers in particular were better represented in the upper echelons of this elite (Fleischer, 1982: 48; Wirth, 1977: 143, 147).

each politician). Given these difficulties, Wirth is probably correct to assume, as he does, that many, perhaps the majority of the Minas elite, owned *fazendas*.

From its origins as a coherent political class, the Minas oligarchy became increasingly professionalized after 1900. Officeholders elected in that year brought with them and continued to accumulate more political experience than their predecessors. The new deputies had held twice as many political posts, and their careers were more than twice as long, as the cohort they replaced (Fleischer, 1982: 21). Schwartzman (1975) has claimed that from this time the Minas political class – more actively involved in politics than other regional Brazilian elites – became Brazil's political class. Weaker economically than São Paulo and militarily than Rio Grande do Sul, Minas was more dependent on the union and "had no choice but to play a central role in national affairs" (Wirth, 1977: 181).

Oligarchy and state politics

With the state of Minas Gerais lacking economic and military power, the national political influence and success of the Minas oligarchy was predicated, as John Wirth (1977) has persuasively argued, on its internal unity. Because the state's strength followed from the size of its delegation in the federal Congress, it was crucial that the thirty-seven members of the Minas delegation, or *bancada*, not divide along ideological or issue-oriented lines. In the republic's second decade, leaders of the Minas oligarchy achieved a high degree of internal unity by eliminating competition within the single dominant political party and then, with the force of state institutions, by suppressing dissent and subordinating municipal to state government. With these measures, this noncompetitive oligarchy consolidated its hegemony throughout the state's territory.

The ruling clique that would form the core of the Minas oligarchy seized control of the Minas Republican Party (PRM) at the turn of the century with a successful coup against its executive commission. The governor, Silviano Brandão (1898–1902) (at the time referred to as the state president), and the party secretary asked loyal, local political bosses to organize party branches in their municipalities and secured their proxies for all important commission votes, which effectively left their state opposition isolated and without a base of support in the interior (Lage de Resende, 1982: 177–78). Once in charge, this group proceeded to interpret and refashion party rules at every opportunity in such a way to increase its power and advantage over its internal opposition, as well as to perpetrate electoral fraud, conduct party purges, and engage in other irregular practices (Lage de Resende, 1982: 182–84). After 1901, the executive commission grew more powerful. It drew up party tickets, party conventions rubber-stamped its decisions, and its members named their own replacements. Over this body presided the governor. A prominent Mineiro politician and executive commission member, Levindo Coelho (1957: 117–18), recalled that the governor typically handpicked his successor and analyzed one by one a slate of party candidates for president of the state, vice-president, senators, and federal and state deputies vetted by the party hierarchy, "taking into consideration not merely their political worth, but their fitness, level of education, moral qualities, services lent and activities they developed of genuine public benefit." The final list submitted to the executive commission by the governor was almost always approved unanimously.[13]

Having asserted firm control over the only party in the political system, the ruling clique introduced a battery of legislation to bring under executive control other branches of the state that could be employed against any political rivals, concentrate power in the governor, and deprive municipalities of some powers and resources that they had enjoyed in Minas in the early years of the republic. Governor Silviano Brandão made two previously independent branches of the state, the police force and the judiciary, subordinate to the executive. The state police (Brigada Policial) was placed under the supervision of the secretary of the interior and used more frequently to intimidate opposition strongholds in the state and even to remove the local group in power (Lage de Resende, 1982: 193–94, 196–97). The judiciary lost its independence under Brandão's successor, Francisco Sales (1902–6). Formal competitions to fill district judgeships were eliminated in 1903, and the governor thereafter freely appointed whomever he wished to these posts. He was also able to remove them through his direct representative, the *procurador geral* (the equivalent to the state's attorney general), and the president of the Senate (a member of the executive commission of the PRM) (Lage de Resende, 1982: 198). With the politicization of the judiciary, electoral legislation could be rewritten and fraudulent practices concealed to guarantee victory for the ruling state oligarchy.[14] Aspiring voters known to be in opposition were denied registration and those already registered were purged from the rolls (Lage de Resende, 1982: 201). At the same time, the courts looked the other way when local political bosses arranged for the registration en masse of illiterates and then instructed them in how to vote.[15]

13 The relative strength of the governor and executive commission may have varied, According to Wirth (1977: 108–10), Artur Bernardes, who became governor in 1918, strengthened the position of the governor, but after his successor Raul Soares died in 1924, the control of the PRM reverted to a "collegium of regional satraps."

14 Fraud was commonplace in the Old Republic. One could even say it was institutionalized, The most widely used tactics were the registration of the dead or otherwise absent (known as *fosforos*) and the wholesale writing in of voters (*eleições a bico da pena*) (Cammack, 1982: 57). Since the declared results were subject to review at all levels from the local electoral board to the floor of the Chamber of Deputies itself, fraud invariably benefited official candidates. One indication of the extent of fraud was that the new registration for the election of a Constituent Assembly in 1933, which included women for the first time, still produced scarcely more than two-thirds as many registrations as there had been votes cast in 1930.

15 Tightening up the restrictions on the voting of illiterates as a means of curtailing the power of the landed oligarchy would come to be a demand of urban, liberal constitutionalist groups later in the Old Republic. The urban bourgeoisie stood to benefit from an enforce-

Finally, the state oligarchy presided over an erosion of municipal autonomy. The state legislature, with the active support of local landowners, merchants, and industrialists wishing to reduce their tax burden, formally withdrew from local legislative bodies their right to levy taxes on rural property and half their revenues from the tax on property transfer (the state appropriated the other half) (Lage de Resende, 1982: 199–200). It also removed from the municipalities the right to demarcate municipal limits and create districts. The frequent manipulation of municipal borders by state authorities was motivated overwhelmingly by political considerations. "Dismembering *municípios* and creating new ones, [the governor] destroyed opposition strongholds and answered the calls of local bosses to be freed from the *município* to which they belonged in exchange for unconditional loyalty. . . . [The law's] purpose was merely to satisfy local bosses for blatant electoral purposes" (Lage de Resende, 1982: 196).

Local politics and traditional clientelism

Emasculating municipal government and intimidating and eliminating all potential local opposition had the effect of fostering fiscal and political municipal dependence on state government. Municipal dependence, in turn, shaped state–local linkages, local politics, and the system of traditional clientelism known as *coronelismo* that underpinned the exercise of political dominance by the state oligarchies in the Old Republic.

More than a sum of dyadic patron–client relationships, *coronelismo* was a system of local bossism that bridged levels of government and organized intergovernmental relations. The local patrons known as *coroneis* (colonels) for the titles they and their forebears once held as the local commanders in the National Guard,[16] were all-powerful within their domains: they had their own militias and they controlled local judicial officials. In the larger political system, local political bosses served as the henchmen of the state oligarchy. Although the local rule of political bosses predated the Old Republic, *coronelismo* as a system that subordinated local bosses to the state oligarchies came into full force during the oligarchical republic. In his classic work, Nunes Leal (1977: 1) understood *coronelismo* in this time frame as a pact between public authority, which although becoming stronger was still unable to establish its supremacy throughout its territory, and local private power holders, whose power was in decline. According to the terms of this pact, central, public authorities designated local chiefs as their representatives in the hinterlands.

ment of the literacy requirement because the illiterate vote was manipulated by the agrarian elites.

16 They retained their titles long after the National Guard was disbanded in 1831. On the origins, structure, and functions of the National Guard, see Uricoechea (1980: 64–75), and on the relationship of the *coroneis* to the Guard, see Pang (1973: 67–69).

Coronelismo has been called without exaggeration the foundation of the traditional political order in the Old Republic (Reis, 1980). In São Paulo, the richest state in the Brazilian union, no less than Minas Gerais, the Republican Party relied on local bosses to support its rule (cf. Love, 1980: 130–31). In the Center-South where state oligarchies were strong, *coroneis* who hoped to retain power in their communities or to rise in state politics courted the favor of the state elite and conformed to its will. Governing resource-starved municipalities that were vulnerable to armed intervention by state militias, local chieftains were easily persuaded to ally themselves with the winning side in state politics. An opposition *coronel* had no resources with which to implement local programs and distribute the kinds of benefits that he needed to solidify his local support and he ran the real risk of being overthrown. Not all state oligarchies were equally adept at disciplining local bosses and controlling state territory. *Coroneis* in the geographically isolated hinterlands of the Northeast enjoyed more independence from relatively weak state oligarchies; they could sustain themselves in power with or without the support of the ruling state parties and they could even threaten regional oligarchies with overthrow when they allied their armies with the enemies of the state oligarchy in the federal government (Cintra, 1979: 136; Pang, 1973: 72–73, 74–76, Reis, 1980: 143).

Coronelismo flourished under the same local economic conditions of a traditional agrarian society that generally sustain traditional political clientelism – the grossly unequal distribution of land and other material resources. Direct economic dependence and status differentials allowed local, private elites to establish political clienteles. The *coroneis* were usually the largest landowners in the area under their "jurisdiction" but they could also be pharmacists or other professionals in urban centers.[17] These local chiefs dominated public employment and civil life. As described classically by Carone (1978: 253–54), the *coronel's* followers "lived on his prestige, his strength, and his money."

For his dependents he provided land to cultivate, release from jail, and aid in illness; in return for these favors, he demanded loyalty, services, indefinite residence on his lands, and participation in his armed groups. To relatives and friends he distributed public employment, lent money, guaranteed credit; he protected them from the police and judicial authorities, and helped them to evade taxes. He was the "judge," who heard complaints about land disputes and even cases of runaway single girls. He was merchant as well as farmer. Not only was he a producer, but he also acted as

17 All *coroneis* were not landowners. Pang (1973: 77–79) identifies at least seven types of *coroneis*: the *coronel*-landowner; the *coronel*-merchant; the *coronel*-industrialist; the *coronel*-priest; the *coronel*-warlord; the *coronel*-"bandit"; and the *coronel*-party cadre (a category that subsumes both the party bureaucrat and the city ward boss). The *coronel*-"bandit" and the *coronel*-priest were more typical of the hinterlands of the Northeast, while merchants, industrialists, and, above all, the party cadres were preponderant in the Center-South.

intermediary between the small producer and the market. With the greatest financial resources, he represented the fundamental economic power of the *município*. He was a "man of faith," for he was the one who promoted and gave an official character to religious ceremonies.

The *coronel* was an exclusive mediator in a vertically organized, hierarchical system of domination (Cintra, 1979: 128). He shepherded his followers to the polls on the backs of farm trucks and instructed them for whom to vote (thus the *"voto de cabresto,"* or, the "herd vote"); voters rarely knew for whom they had cast their ballots.[18] In exchange for delivering these votes to the state oligarchy, the *coronel* secured for his municipality roads, employment, and other resources (Pang, 1973: 75), and for himself, he won the exclusive right to fill through appointment all powerful posts in his jurisdiction, a prerogative that reinforced his power to an even greater degree. The ability of the *coroneis* to deliver the vote of their clients to the state oligarchies became more important when voting rates rose during the Old Republic and select elections became subject to contestation. Not motivated by ideological considerations, state oligarchies pragmatically supported whoever could deliver the most votes. If a local challenger could demonstrate that he was more "worthy" than the incumbent of state support, the state party machine would often shift allegiance to the newcomer, and the old *coronel* would lose his followers to the new local boss.

Rigid *coronelismo* of the variety practiced in the Center-South restricted political competition at all levels of the political system. In Minas Gerais, the state oligarchy severely limited competition among *coroneis* in order to maintain unity among its supporters so as to preserve its national position. Minas Gerais was perhaps exceptionally driven to maintain unity, but Wirth (1977: 227–28) has observed that in São Paulo as well there was a trend toward growing gubernatorial power, that little room existed for new types of political organizations to develop or compete, and that, despite the greater economic growth and social diversity in São Paulo, Paulista politics were not more open and participatory and less traditional than Mineiro politics, at least up until 1930, and "ambiguously so after that." The state establishment in São Paulo that headed a Republican Party at least as professional and organized as the PRM (Love, 1980: 130–31) was even better able than the Mineiro to impose discipline within elite ranks in each of the three contested presidential successions – 1910, 1919, and 1922 (Table 2.2). Wirth asserts that co-optation, clientelism, and violence were just as important to consolidating the hegemony of the Paulista as the Mineiro elite.

18 In a classic dialogue retold by Rouquié (1978: 19), a voter in the state of Pernambuco asks his *coronel*, "Chief, I have done everything as you asked me to. Now I would like very much to know who I have voted for," to which the *coronel* responds, "My son, never ask me that kind of question and above all do not forget that the vote is secret."

In firm control of state politics, with no real challenge from any social sector, and benefiting amply from the status quo, the Minas oligarchy had every reason to be content with its arrangement with the union during the Old Republic. Yet the republic fell, and change was thrust upon it.

THE REVOLUTION OF 1930 AND POLITICAL CENTRALIZATION

The year 1930 was a watershed in Brazilian history. That October amid a "crisis of oligarchical hegemony," the Old Republic came to an end with the broad-based "Revolution" that placed Getúlio Vargas in the presidency. During the 1920s, the Old Republic had been racked by revolts of *tenentes*, young army officers – predominantly lieutenants – with reforming ambitions,[19] and worker's strikes. Against this backdrop, the formal collapse of the oligarchical system was precipitated by an economic depression and a crisis in the coffee economy. Perhaps the most crucial reason for the demise of the Old Republic, however, was the eruption of intraoligarchical, regional rivalries that led to the breakdown of "governors' politics." The decision of the Paulista president Washington Luís to renege on the fundamental agreement on which the *café com leite* alliance had rested – alternation of the presidency – by attempting to impose as his successor Julio Prestes, a Paulista, strained the governing partnership beyond repair.[20] The Mineiros retaliated against their former ally by backing the candidate of the "Liberal Alliance," the Gaúcho Getúlio Vargas, who headed a loosely knit coalition of *tenentes*, their civilian allies, and the political establishments of the smaller states eager to exploit the fissure between São Paulo and Minas. When Prestes was declared victor, those in the opposition claimed fraud and un-

19 Resenting the oligarchical grip on the national political scene, the *tenentes* staged armed revolts in 1922 in Rio de Janeiro and again in 1924, both of which were repressed. They are best known for marching more than 15,000 miles through the Brazilian hinterland in the "Prestes Column" to carry their message to the interior of this country. After three years of eluding federal troops, the column disbanded in 1927 and several of its members went into exile. Great importance has been attached to the role played by this march and the Tenentista movement more generally in eroding the legitimacy of the Old Republic (Carone, 1975: 123–47, as cited in Reis, 1980: 246–47; Forjaz, 1977). The *tenentes* enjoyed a considerable degree of power in the early years of the provisional government (1930–33), but lost influence after 1932, in part because their presence in government angered other coalition members (Skidmore, 1967: 10). Campos Coelho (1976: 89–91) claims that by 1932, the *tenentes* had been thoroughly co-opted by the civilians with whom they were associated.

20 Allegedly, his motivation was to ensure the continuation of his economic policies in depression-stricken Brazil. Pang (1973: 85) cites as reasons for his breach of the governor's agreement a personality conflict with the governor of Minas to whom the nomination would have fallen, Antonio Carlos Ribeiro de Andrada; serious differences in economic beliefs; and domestic pressure from São Paulo.

leashed their state militias on the federal government.[21] With troops advancing on Rio de Janeiro (then the nation's capital) from Rio Grande to the south, Paraíba to the north, and Minas Gerais to the west, senior officers deposed President Luís in October 1930 in order to avert what they saw as an impending civil war (Skidmore. 1967: 5–6). Ten days later, they delivered power to Getúlio Vargas who became president of Brazil.

The Vargas presidency brought great change to Brazil, embodied in state expansion, political centralization, and a sharp shift in economic priorities and development strategies. One interpretation of the 1930 "Revolution" credits the bourgeoisie, supported by emerging urban middle and working classes, with the overthrow of the oligarchical republic. Another sees the demise of the Old Republic as brought about by a "revolution from above," which ultimately strengthened the central state apparatus, loosened it from the grip of the coffee-exporting oligarchy, and used its enhanced autonomy to enact policies that favored industrial interests.[22] Both views suggest that, in effecting structural changes and realigning the state to accommodate those changes, the Vargas regime was a "modernizing dictatorship" that ultimately represented a victory of the "bourgeoisie" and the central government over the powerful state oligarchies. From this common view follows the customary interpretation among students of Brazilian

21 What catalyzed the "Liberal Alliance" to act was the assassination of Governor João Pessoa of Paraíba, its vice-presidential candidate, by a Washington Luís–backed local political enemy (Coelho, 1957: 127).

22 Fausto (1981) has methodically demolished both theses. He demonstrates (pp. 29–43) that the building industrial bourgeoisie did not instigate, propel, or even endorse the "Revolution of 1930," in either their areas of greatest concentration (São Paulo and Rio de Janeiro) or in the states that championed the Vargas revolt (Rio Grande do Sul and Minas Gerais). The bourgeoisie never presented an industrial program as an alternative to the system based on coffee interests, nor did it align politically with the "revolutionary" forces. During the presidential campaign of 1929, the principal industrial associations of São Paulo publicly endorsed the candidacy of Julio Prestes and shunned the Partido Democrático, which opposed Washington Luís and joined the Liberal Alliance. Even after Vargas had come to power, these industrialists supported the state political elite against Vargas in the 1932 constitutionalist revolt. Outside São Paulo, there is no evidence of any connections between the Frente Unica in Rio Grande do Sul, which launched the Vargas candidacy, and any industrial interests of that state (or any other). In Minas Gerais, what few industrialists there were in this period (largely concentrated in Juiz de Fora) were allied with Antonio Carlos. Finally, nowhere in the election manifestos of the Liberal Alliance was there any indication of a pro-industrial program.

Fausto (1981: 47–50) also demonstrates that the Vargas regime did not represent a "revolution from above," which promoted industrialization and development on behalf of the industrial bourgeoisie. Some representatives of industry were appointed to high posts in the Bank of Brazil and the Ministry of Labor, and state incentives helped to establish cement factories in the country. Yet, Vargas's tariff and exchange policies from 1930 to 1937, which were designed to benefit coffee, were harshly criticized by industrial representatives in the Chamber of Deputies, and there is no evidence that any coherent set of policies was adopted to favor industry.

politics that during the Estado Nôvo – Vargas's authoritarian government in place from 1937 to 1945[23] – the regional oligarchies, especially those of Minas and São Paulo which had benefited most from political decentralization, found themselves marginalized from power and helpless before a barrage of legislation that favored industry at the expense of agriculture, the union at the expense of the states, and the new elites at the expense of the old.[24]

Vargas did in fact change fundamentally the nature of the relationship between the regional oligarchies and the central government by disrupting the state political machines, strengthening the national administrative apparatus, and enhancing bureaucratic autonomy from the regional elites (cf. Campello de Souza, 1976: 85; Miceli, 1979: 132; Skidmore, 1967: 33). In order to subordinate these oligarchies to the union and to strengthen the federal executive, he dismissed federal and state legislatures and named "interventors" as the new chief executives in the states. These interventors, who were by and large natives of the states of which they were appointed but on the fringes of their states' political machines, were more apt to act as loyal agents of Vargas in the states than the governors whom they replaced. In the early years of his regime, Vargas imposed military officers as interventors in recalcitrant states and, in the larger of these, he frequently rotated the interventors in order that they might not develop local interests and a local identity. Many state political machines received their new chief executives bitterly; Vargas's appointment of a *tenente*, João Alberto, as state interventor in São Paulo caused strained relations for two years between São Paulo and the central government (Fausto, 1981: 31), culminating in the Paulista's 1932 failed armed revolt against Vargas and the union known as the "constitutionalist revolution." To maximize the power and autonomy of the federal government (and to check the interventors), Vargas also created a new layer of federal bureaucracy in 1938. The "Administrative Department of Public Service" (DASP) was given the responsibility for preparing the budget and other duties normally performed by the legislature. This emerging parallel power was presided over by bureaucrats and staffed by engineers, agrono-

---

23 Patterned after Italian fascism, the Estado Nôvo enacted corporatist labor and social welfare legislation, and bore the stamp of economic nationalism. Unlike European fascist regimes, Vargas's "semifascist" state had no party to mobilize support for the dictator; rather, Vargas banned parties altogether, disingenuously calling for a democracy that did not place parties as intermediaries between citizens and the state.

24 Exceptions to this view are rare but they do exist. Recently, Chilcote (1990: 71) wrote of the effects of the Vargas regime on politics in Juazeiro, Bahia: "Theoretically, the Vargas revolution consolidated Brazilian politics at the national level and undermined the strength of the patriarchy in local affairs. The real impact of the Vargas period upon Juazeiro politics is difficult to assess for the traditional families continued to prevail."

mists, and statisticians – persons considered immune from clientelistic pressures.[25]

If in the short term the Vargas reforms threatened the practice of traditional politics, their effects on the long-term position of the regional oligarchies was actually quite limited. The administrative reform of 1938 neither shielded the bureaucracy from politicians nor professionalized its higher ranks. Lower-ranking functionaries were admitted to the bureaucracy by the competitive civil service examination known as the *concurso*, but at least 1,173 new "independent" positions created at the higher ranks of the state ministries (the *cargos isolados*) by the reform's "Lei do Reajustamento" were filled by the executive according to "ad hoc" criteria, which in practice meant on a clientelistic basis (Miceli, 1979: 137–38). Thus, what Miceli (1979: 133) has called the "colossal expansion" of the bureaucratic machinery of the state into new areas of regulation and distribution, and the growth of the federal state's powers for new purposes, strengthened public power vis-à-vis the private sector and the union vis-à-vis the states, but did not deny politicians per se access to state patronage. The circumvention of the *concurso* distinguishes the Brazilian reform in its design and effects from a similarly intentioned reform in Germany. The German reform, which treasured the civil service examination, gave the civil service control over its own recruitment, mobilized a constituency for bureaucratic autonomy, and effectively insulated the bureaucracy from politics (Shefter, 1977: 423–25). Ultimately, the Brazilian federal bureaucracy was not only not professionalized by the Vargas reform, but its loyalties were turned immediately toward the figure of Vargas and, in the long run, toward whichever party or group controlled the presidency. This politicization of the higher echelons of the state bureaucracy made it at the time "one of the decisive support bases for the regime" (Miceli, 1979: 134). In the future, the prerogative to fill the second- and third-tier positions in the state would become one of the largest prizes in negotiations among aspiring governing parties and party factions.

During this transitional period in Brazilian history, the bureaucratic ranks of the state became an even greater redoubt of the traditional elite. As Sérgio Miceli (1979) has demonstrated for the case of São Paulo, intellectuals were recruited from traditional families in decline, and sons of traditional families seeking an escape from agriculture were the principal beneficiaries of the sharp increase in opportunities for employment at higher levels of the state bureaucracy. Intellectuals from traditional Minas families such as Francisco Campos, Abgar Renault, and Rodrigo de Mello

25 Graham (1968: 27–28) argues that the DASP became a "superministry" and that in the states, the regional presidents of the "DASPinhos" (little DASPS) were even more powerful than the interventors. State laws and decrees declared by the interventors were valid only when approved by the *daspinho;* the *daspinho,* moreover, reported to the president of the republic on all appeals against the interventor.

Franco Andrade were appointed to fill top posts (*cargos de cupula*); second-tier, advisory positions such as private secretaries and cabinet chiefs (*cargos de confiança*); positions governing culture (museum and library directorships); offices in traditional domains of the bureaucracy whose powers were expanded with the intervention of the state into such areas as arbitrating labor disputes (the diplomatic service, courts); and even new technical posts (Miceli, 1979: 145–58).

The first representatives of the traditional elite to benefit from the Vargas revolution were not among the leaders of the incumbent state political machines, nor, according to Miceli (1979: 132), were they loyal to them: "The intellectuals of the Vargas era were tied much more closely to the eminent personalities of the bureaucratic elite than to party leaders of the political factions of their respective states." The monopoly of the executive commission of the Republican Party over state politics was broken by Vargas's use of political appointments, and especially the appointment of mayors by his designated interventors. Yet, despite these challenges to the state political machines, the Vargas revolution did not seriously damage the long-term interests and power of the Minas oligarchy. Unlike its São Paulo counterpart whose opposition to Vargas earned it only political and military defeat, the Minas oligarchy that had joined the Liberal Alliance pursued a strategy of cooperation with the provisional government similar to that which had won it a place of prominence in the Old Republic. In exchange for backing Vargas in his bid for the presidency and offering the Minas state militia to help crush the Paulista revolt, the elected governor, Olegário Maciel, was permitted to remain in his post of chief executive until his death in 1933. Vargas had a particularly close relationship with the Minas politician whom he named to be Maciel's successor as state interventor, Benedito Valadares.

The Minas elite that profited from supporting Vargas was not identical to that which had controlled the machinery of the PRM on the eve of the "Revolution of 1930," but it was also not the case that an entirely new regional elite was created by the center or that the incumbent pre-1930 oligarchy merely became the "outs" of the 1930s and 1940s (Table 2.3). Rather, the once unified PRM split into different camps. More than half of its executive commission led by former governor and President Artur Bernardes remained with the PRM in opposition to Vargas. Others, most notably Antônio Carlos de Andrada and Wenceslau Bras, joined with Olegário Maciel to form the Partido Progressista, which supported Vargas. Belying the notion that Vargas supporters were challengers to the state elite, twelve of the nineteen members of the executive commission of the new party had held legislative or high executive posts during the Old Republic, and only three were newcomers to the political elite (Wirth, 1977: 114). After 1945, approximately an equal number of the members of the executive commissions of both parties (including their political heirs) emerged as Vargas

Table 2.3. *The Minas oligarchy and the Vargas interregnum*

	1930-36 party		Post-1945 party	
	Pro-Vargas	Anti-Vargas	Anti-Vargas	Pro-Vargas
Executive commission, PRM 1926-30				
Julio Bueno Brandão				D
Francisco Alvaro Bueno de Paiva[a]				
João Pio de Souza Reis[a]				
Teodomiro Carneiro Santiago[a]				
Artur da Silva Bernardes		X	X	
Alaôr Prata Soares		X		
Afonso Pena Junior		X	X	
Eduardo Carlos Vilhena do Amaral		X		
Afrânio de Melo Franco		X	D	
Augusto Mário Caldeira Brant		X	X	
Levindo Duarte Coelho		X		X
Wenceslau Bras Pereira Gomes	X			H
Antônio Carlos de Andrada	X		X	
José Monteiro Ribeiro Junqueira	X			
Alfredo Sá[a]				
Fernando de Melo Viana				X
José Bonifácio de Andrada e Silva	X		X	
Post-1930 elites[b]				
Benedito Valadares Ribeiro	X			X
Gustavo Capanema	X			X
Cristiano Monteiro Machado		X		X
Virgílio de Melo Franco		X	X	
Noraldino Lima	X			X
Washington Ferreira Pires	X			X
Pedro Aleixo	X		X	
Otacílio Negrão de Lima	X			X
Odilon Duarte Braga	X		X	
José Francisco Bias Fortes[c]	X	X		X
Olavo Gomes Pinto		X	D	
Djalma Pinheiro Chagas		X	X	

Note: D = descendants; H = political "heir."
[a]No data were available on post-1930 partisan affiliation.
[b]Includes four members of the executive commission of the PRM and eight members of the executive commission of the Partido Progressista (1932–36) who had not served on the executive commission of the PRM in the pre-1930 period, and for whom post-1945 data were available.
[c]Bias Fortes switched loyalty from the PRM in opposition to the Partido Progressista in 1932.
Sources: Wirth, 1977: 97–98, 110–16, 248–53, 255–60; Carone, 1976: 305; Benevides, 1981: 27–30, 35; Oliveira, 1981: 109; Hippolito, 1985: 129; Rebelo Horta, 1956: 66, 67–68, 71–72, 74–75, 76–77, 79, 86, 87–88; and author's bibliographical data file.

supporters and opponents.[26] Former governors Wenceslau Bras (and his protégé Noraldino Lima), Bias Fortes (and his son), Raul Soares (and his political heir, Levindo Coelho), and Melo Viana were among the most prominent representatives of the state oligarchy to ally with Vargas. They, along with Benedito Valadares – the "outsider" appointed by Vargas to govern Minas – were descended from Minas' most traditional families (Rebelo Horta, 1956: 76–77). For a member of the oligarchy, being in the opposition was no longer the political dead end that it was in the Old Republic. Political alignments drawn in 1930 were far more fluid and politicians who made the "wrong" choices could reenter the inner circles of power far more easily than in the Old Republic. Cristiano Machado, a "Bernardista," and Bias Fortes, son of a Minas governor who would one day become governor himself, spent brief periods in the opposition before returning permanently to the Vargas fold. Even permanent opponents of Vargas were hardly marginalized from power. Two prominent opponents of Vargas – Milton Campos and José de Magalhães Pinto – became state governors in the postwar period.

The apparent permanent effects of the Vargas interregnum on the Minas oligarchy were to provide it with a new basis of power in a state whose role in regulating the economy increased for over half a century, and to split it into two warring camps polarized along a pro- and anti-Vargas axis of conflict, which in the postwar period defined the political parties. After 1945, the Minas elite would never again be as unified as in the Old Republic. Expanded political competition forced the oligarchy to discover new ways to survive, divided, in a formally democratic regime.

OLIGARCHY AND "POPULIST" DEMOCRACY

With the defeat of the Axis powers and fascism in 1945, the Estado Nôvo was dissolved. The military, which had sent an expeditionary force to Italy to fight on the side of the Allies, pressured Getúlio Vargas to fulfill his promise to restore democracy in Brazil. After the growth of new social classes, the reform of the state apparatus, and the realignment of elite political and economic interests, restoration could not entail a simple return to pre-1930 politics. The one-party politics of the Old Republic was no longer feasible, nor could two states exclusively continue to dominate national politics. Elite divisions served as a catalyst to open the political system to greater competition, but multipartism expanded opportunities for political contestation at different levels of the political system for all

26 Wirth (1977: 247) reports that 22 percent of the larger sample of the Minas political elite of the Old Republic broke with the Olegário Maciel administration (1930–33); 15 percent when Valadares was appointed as interventor in December 1933; and 14.5 percent when the PRM and the Partido Progressista were fused by Valadares in 1936.

classes. Political participation also increased markedly in the postwar Brazilian republic: five million new voters were added to the electoral rolls between the last election for the Chamber of Deputies in 1934 and the 1945 election. The percentage of the population participating in the 1945 presidential election rose from 5.7 in 1930, the year of the previous presidential election, to 13.4, and it continued to climb to 18.1 in 1960 (Love, 1970: 9). Many of these new participants, especially from the urban areas of the South, were incorporated into the political system through loose associations with leaders, parties, and institutions, which together have been called "populist."

Multipartism and the political incorporation of new groups under the populist rubric notwithstanding, the transition from Estado Nôvo to postwar democracy that permitted the full participation of the traditional elite did not result in a truly open political system. Populist governing coalitions headed by charismatic politicians such as Getúlio Vargas, Adhemar de Barros, and Jânio Quadros nominally united the interests of the urban middle, lower-middle, and working classes with those of the industrial bourgeoisie as they did across Latin America in the postwar period. But, in practice, mass political participation was hierarchically organized by elites and access to the state was channeled principally through corporatist and clientelistic networks. The elaborate corporatist structure mounted by Vargas during the Estado Nôvo – crowned by the Consolidated Labor Code (CLT) of 1943 – strictly mediated the interests of organized labor for decades to come (Erikson, 1977). Citizens in most rural areas and even in many urban areas not fully integrated into corporatist institutions continued to rely on clientelistic networks for their link to the formal political system – to the extent that they were incorporated at all into the body politic. Even after the broadening of political contestation and participation, patronage networks controlled by the traditional political elite that operated in thousands of communities across Brazil, especially in the Northeast and Minas Gerais, worked to maintain the traditional order and generally to deform political representation. If these networks were stable, however, the nature of clientelism did not remain static in the face of political and economic change. Rather, clientelism was adapted to a political landscape transformed by the growth of the parties and voters, and state expansion, urbanization, and economic development caused its role in the political system to become more pervasive.[27]

27 Cammack (1982: 57) goes so far as to suggest that Nunes Leal's 1949 claim that *coronelismo* reached its apex in the Old Republic was too influenced by contemporary events (see Nunes Leal, 1977). He points out that prior to 1930, less than 4 percent of the population was eligible to vote, and argues that the prevalence of fraud probably made dependent votes attached to an *individual* a less valuable asset than control of the electoral machinery.

The modernization of clientelism

In 1966, José Murilo de Carvalho puzzled over how it was possible that in the Minas *município* of Barbacena – which then had a total population of over 55,000 persons, of whom over three-quarters resided in the urban portion of the district – two of the most important traditional families in state politics, the Bias Fortes and the Andradas, dominated local and state politics within the municipality. Obviously, he reasoned, with such elevated levels of urbanization, land ownership could no longer be the base of local economic power and political domination, especially given that the rural areas had become a zone of subsistence farming (1966: 169). What he discovered was that in a city in which two textile factories employed about 1,300 persons, commercial establishments about 1,500, and the combined branches of federal, state, and local government, 5,000 (of an urban electorate of about 14,000), these families ruled through the control of public appointments and the use of urban-based political machines (1966: 177–79).

The shift in the basis of clientelism Murilo de Carvalho observed in Barbacena took place in scores of municipalities across Minas Gerais over the course of the two decades after the fall of the Estado Nôvo. A steady growth of the public sector in the postwar period allowed politicians who had moved into the state during the Vargas interregnum to build a base for mounting large-scale patronage operations. New ministries and departments of the direct administration were created and new spaces of negotiation between the executive branch and various economic sectors were opened (Miceli, 1979: 133). From 1947 to 1960, government spending rose from 17.7 to 29 percent of gross domestic product (Schmitter, 1971: 246). The increase in state resources available for patronage kept pace with the expansion of the political market, and changes in the 1934 constitution rendered these resources at least as valuable a political club to wield over local politicians as they had been in the Old Republic. Municipal shares of public revenues dropped from 11.8 percent in 1930 to 8.2 percent in 1945 (FJP, n.d., I: I-13). After a slight rise in the 1950s, the municipal government's share of public sector expenditures dropped precipitously in the early 1960s to 5.9 percent (Table 2.4).

Postwar clientelism combined elements of traditional and modern politics. It was still "traditional" in the sense that (1) political power was based on the rule of powerful *traditional* families descended from the days of the empire, even if it was not a closed dictatorship of families; and (2) voters more often demonstrated loyalty to individuals than to parties. In highly personalistic campaigns, politicians from governor to local councillor competed for their positions on the basis of their ability to deliver the maximum number of votes to higher levels or state resources to lower levels – an ability enhanced by family connections – and not on the basis of their party's programs, policy proposals, or records of administrative compe-

Table 2.4. *Public sector expenditures, 1939–64 (in %)*

Year	Federal govts.	Federal parastatals	Union total	State govts.[a]	Municipal govts.
1939	56.6	2.4	59.0	31.3	9.7
1947	42.6	11.7	54.3	39.4	6.4
1950	41.7	14.6	56.3	36.2	7.6
1952	35.0	14.7	49.7	42.2	8.1
1955	35.7	18.2	53.9	38.6	7.5
1957	35.4	19.5	54.9	37.1	8.1
1960	34.3	20.2	54.5	39.2	6.2
1962	37.0	21.6	58.6	35.4	5.9
1964	36.9	21.5	58.4	34.1	7.5

[a]Includes parastatals.
Source: FJP, n.d., I: I-21.

tence in office. Clientelism also still segmented citizens on a territorial basis. But it was also "modernized." As Minas became more urban (Table 2.5) and its work force entered the secondary and tertiary sectors, voters could no longer be herded onto the back of a truck and instructed for whom to vote by the *coronel*. Overtly traditional forms of domination, though still important in the hinterlands, were inadequate to keep the state's population in submission and coercion gave way to more subtle mechanisms of control. Aspiring local political chiefs had to make a different sort of electoral appeal to increasingly independent voters. Greenfield's (1977: 151) account of the power base of a doctor who assisted friends and neighbors in a town in the Minas Mata stands in marked contrast to that of the *coronel* described by Carone:

The cashing in of . . . debts is the basis of his political strength. In contrast with the *coroneis* of the Old Republic, whose position was based on force, power, and the ability to frighten and intimidate . . . , the position of Dr. Santos and the politicians of 1946 to 1968 was based on generosity, constant giving, and the inability, or so it appeared to the outsider, to say no to the continuous requests of those who considered their patronage network and voting bloc.

No longer exercising virtually total power in their domains, the role of local bosses as political mediators between local communities and state government became an ever more important basis for the consolidation of their local power. Unlike elected representatives elsewhere whose mediating role features the negotiation of "collective" transactions for their constituents in the legislative arena, Brazilian deputies and mayors in the postwar period engaged in a form of local brokerage politics akin to that described by Valenzuela (1977: 159–61) for the case of Chile. They processed the claims of their constituents for both "particular" (judicial par-

Table 2.5. *Brazil and selected states: Urban population, 1940–60 (in %)*

State	1940	1950	1960
Minas Gerais	25.0	29.9	39.6
Northeast[a]	23.4	26.4	33.9
Rio Grande do Sul	31.2	34.1	44.4
Guanabara[b]	86.1	96.9	97.5
São Paulo	44.1	52.6	61.8
Brazil	31.2	36.2	44.7

[a]Includes the states of Maranhão, Piauí, Rio Grande do Norte, Paraíba, Pernambuco, Alagoas, Sergipe, and Bahia, as well as the island territory of Fernando de Noronha.
[b]Before 1974, the greater metropolitan area of Rio de Janeiro.
Source: IBGE, 1979a: 74.

dons and schoolteaching jobs) and "categoric" (bridges and paved roads) goods through "individualistic" transactions conducted in the executive branch of the state.

As the nature of the relationship between local boss and voter changed, so too did the relationship change among politicians in the political hierarchy. Even in more rural municipalities, the expansion of the political market, territorial integration, and party competition forced traditional politicians to stake their local power ever more on the state clientelistic chain. Local rivals competed by entering into alliances with state and federal authorities in which they accepted federal or state aid and protection in exchange for delivering votes. Local rivalries and political competition were increasingly defined by denser clientelistic networks. In a vertically integrated system defined by competition for clientelistic resources, winning office and delivering state patronage depended to a large extent upon the ability to build political-electoral coalitions that bridged territorial units. Candidates to local office in even remote towns could not insulate themselves and their campaigns from state and national political contests.

State clientelism was also crucial to state elections. State patronage furnished by state and federal executives to the candidates of their parties (or allies) defined the campaigns for the Senate, the Chamber of Deputies, and the state Legislative Assemblies. As Ribeiro (1964: 96) vividly describes the 1962 elections in Ceará,

The federal government lavishly favored PTB [Brazilian Labor Party] candidates. . . . Federal meddling took the form of eliminating jobs, substituting heads of the principal federal agencies, distributing about 100 ambulances, using official vehicles, and making electoral donations of medical and surgical instruments and a substantial quantity of medicine. . . . Beyond this, the federal government, by various means, displayed malicious hostility toward government authorities in Ceará, denying them the collaboration of federal authorities. For its part, the state government mobilized its apparatus to support the candidates for the "Union for Ceará," principally the candidates of the Partido Trabalhista Nacional, the party organized by the state governor when he split away from the PTB. . . . As a form of electoral influence, the government gave away jobs, used its own vehicles, and bestowed highway contracts in an attempt to offset federal government interference. On the municipal level, most mayors used municipal funds for electoral ends – to sponsor their own successors, or to get themselves elected to the state Legislative Assembly.

In the competitive postwar Brazilian electoral system, clientelism served more than simply to organize local support for national parties and politicians who competed on some other basis. Because the practice of clientelism by the traditional political elite deeply penetrated mass political parties, it became a defining feature of those parties, structuring the manner in which they represented their constituents and competed or allied with each other at the state and local levels.

Parties of the oligarchy

When the Brazilian political system was reopened in 1945, the leading regional oligarchies organized national elite parties to mobilize mass support in a competitive electoral system. Though they were unable to recreate regional parties, they did gain considerable autonomy and power for the regional directorates.[28] Even more significant than their direct control over parties that enjoyed an impressive measure of electoral success, traditional political elites were able to restrict the representativeness of the entire party system that prevailed during the postwar Brazilian republic. Their intense personal rivalries defined partisan lines at precisely the moment when new parties were being formed, their extension of clientelism into the state induced parties they did not control to resort to patronage-based electoral appeals, and they diluted the programs, policies, and capacity to change national politics of parties that purported to represent primarily nonelites by pulling them into national, regional, and especially local electoral alliances.

The postwar party system was organized by and in response to Getúlio Vargas and his henchmen as the former dictator ignominiously left office, and it remained divided along pro- and anti-Vargas lines for its entire life (cf. Alexander, 1973). The political officials and elites of the Estado Nôvo won top posts on two of the three major parties – the elite-dominated

28 Hoping to recreate Old Republic politics, and especially the *café-au-lait* alliance, representatives from São Paulo and Minas Gerais argued that the political parties should be regional entities (Hippolito, 1985: 120–21). Getúlio Vargas, however, created *national* parties over their objections with the support of such states as Pernambuco and Rio de Janeiro. Nonetheless, parties, and the PSD in particular, were in practice managed regionally. State-level directorates (*diretórios*) named the municipal *diretórios* and elected representatives to the national *diretório* and convention.

Social Democratic Party (PSD) and the mass-based Brazilian Labor Party (Campello de Souza, 1976: 109). The PSD fit to a tee the description offered by Shefter (1977: 415) of an "internally mobilized" party, or, one "founded by elites who occupy positions within a prevailing regime and who undertake to mobilize a popular following behind themselves in an effort either to gain control of the government or to secure their hold over it." In the states, the PSD was organized by the interventor, and incorporated the appointed mayors (named by the interventors), members of the state administration, many of the Old Republic's local political bosses (Roett, 1984: 56), and other government supporters. Whoever opposed the state interventor, even if he wished to support Vargas, was relegated to the opposition. The first national president of the PSD was the Minas interventor and Vargas confidant, Benedito Valadares. One of two elite parties that dominated the national political scene in the first decade after the war, the party was managed in a familiar oligarchical fashion – Hippolito (1985) coins the PSD the "Michelian party par excellence – by an elite whose primary goal was to retain control of the state party machine at all costs, an aim that it accomplished reasonably well.[29]

The National Democratic Union, or UDN, was the principal rival to the PSD formed by Getúlio Vargas's enemies. Members of "dethroned" oligarchies, people who had once supported Vargas or had served in his government but for one reason or another had broken with the former dictator, traditional liberals, and various leftist currents who stood to profit from a return to democratic competition and rights came together under the UDN umbrella in order to hasten the departure of Vargas (Benevides, 1981: 29–31). Some of these actors were traditional enemies, divided by intense personal and ideological rivalries since the days of the empire. Some were true to liberal principles, others to socialist appeals, and still others represented the old state oligarchies. But despite their differences they all favored a return to constitutional, if restricted, democracy. The UDN had its origins in the celebrated 1943 document, the *Manifesto dos Mineiros*, a call for an end to Vargas's Estado Nôvo and a return to democratic liberties signed by ninety-two Mineiros (Benevides, 1981: 34–35).[30] Among the signatories of the document were some of the most prominent Mineiro politicians of the postwar years – Pedro Aleixo, Milton Campos, and Vir-

29 The nomination of Juscelino Kubitschek for governor of Minas in 1951 to some extent represents an exception to the iron control they maintained over the party; Kubitschek's candidacy was not the first choice of the party machine, but rather was won in a grass-roots campaign. Yet, Kubitschek was neither an "outsider" to oligarchical circles nor did he make any attempts to reform the PSD. Rather, in his bid for the governship, he demonstrated the ability to secure votes, to win the adherence of local elites to the PSD, and the other prerequisites for membership in the higher echelons of the oligarchy.

30 Benevides (1981: 35) suggests they did so to outflank Vargas, who was himself moving in this direction – undoubtedly due to the impending Allied victory in the war and the presumed demise of fascism in Europe.

gílio de Melo Franco. This motley UDN united in 1945 around the presidential candidacy of Brigadier General Eduardo Gomes,[31] but the party was subsequently unable to retain its disparate elements. Among its most significant defections were former president and governor of Minas Gerais, Artur Bernardes, who resurrected the Republican Party (PR); Adhemar de Barros of São Paulo, who founded the Partido Social Progressista (PSP), and the Gaúcho wing of the party which broke away to form the Partido Libertador (PL). Barros's PSP, which became the major electoral force in São Paulo, rarely allied with the UDN after the 1945 election (Benevides, 1981: 47 – 49).

Stereotyped views about the differences between the PSD and UDN, if ever true nationally, quite inaccurately represent the parties' characters at the state and local levels of the political system. Although the PSD was perceived as a rural-based party of agrarian elites, and the UDN as a liberal-democratic champion of urban middle-class interests, their local leaders were in fact drawn from the same classes. Surveying over 27,000 members of both parties' municipal directorates in Minas Gerais, Carvalho (1960: 283) found that 43.5 percent of the members of the PSD were farmers and cattlemen, compared with 42.1 percent for the UDN. They also both represented rural constituencies, with the UDN enjoying only little more urban electoral support than the PSD. On the national level, the product–moment correlations between vote for the UDN and degree of urbanization were $-.26$ in the 1950 federal deputy elections and $-.10$ in 1962, and for the PSD, $-.34$ and $-.55$, respectively (Soares, 1973: 219).

If, moreover, the PSD and the UDN espoused different ideologies in national campaigns – the UDN projected itself on the national scene as a principled, liberal-democratic opposition to a former dictator – these ideologies rarely filtered down to the local level and were not easily recognized in the campaigns of local parties. Reflecting on their lack of program and ideology, Murilo de Carvalho (1966: 172–73) has called the political parties of Barbacena "merely artificial frames required by electoral legislation." He observed that "party positions could be inverted without any transformation, as the party chiefs themselves recognize." What defined parties and party competition were personal rivalries, and postwar politics in Barbacena was "entirely conditioned by the struggle of the families." Political elites there and elsewhere were separated by factional, rather than ideological or programmatic differences; which party local elites chose to

---

31 Of all "illustrious old politicians," the support of Artur Bernardes for the Brigadier (as he was called in Brazil) was the most difficult to secure. On being invited to join the UDN, Bernardes recalled that Gomes had flown a revolutionary mission against his government in 1924 (Bernardes was president of Brazil from 1922 to 1926), but left open the possibility that "if he has all the qualities that people attribute to him, there is no reason that he shouldn't be my candidate to lead this country" (Benevides, 1981: 48).

join in the Brazilian interior was most often determined in response to the partisan affiliation of their enemies.

The third major party of the postwar period, the PTB, was the second party of Vargas's creation in 1945 – and Vargas was even elected president of Brazil in 1951 as the party's standardbearer. It was neither a multiclass, "catchall" party nor a vehicle for the political aggrandizement of regional oligarchies. Its local leaders were distinguished from those of the oligarchical parties in their origins – only 17.8 percent of the members of its municipal directorates belonged to the agrarian sector – and the party drew most of its support from the urban areas: the correlation between percent urban and the vote for the PTB was .68 in 1945, .66 in 1950, and .34 in 1962 (Soares, 1973: 219, 222, 228). After the outlawing of the Communist Party in 1947, the PTB was the only electorally viable mass party in this system espousing support for labor and economic nationalism. Yet, the PTB joined in national electoral coalitions for most of the postwar period with the PSD. Moreover, like the PSD and the UDN, the PTB did not bring its ideological message to local election campaigns.

In this elite-dominated system, every major legal party practiced clientelism at some level. The PSD was the quintessential clientelistic party and the supreme party of the "ins." In the entire period from 1945 to 1965, the PSD's access to national state resources was interrupted only briefly after Vargas's suicide in 1954, and for the seven months of the Quadros presidency in 1961. Among the attributes deemed most essential for a politician to rise in the party and enter the elite group that controlled state-level politics were to (1) be a top vote-getter; (2) have public resources to distribute; and (3) be able to liaise with local leaders (Hippolito, 1985: 124–27). Although in the opposition for the most of the postwar period, the UDN, too, behaved as an "internally mobilized" party.[32] Despite its poor prospects for winning presidential elections, its strategy for gaining and retaining state and municipal offices was, like that of the PSD, predicated on dispensing patronage. Even the populist parties of the era competed and governed by resorting to clientelism. The São Paulo–based PSP, reputed to be personalistic as well as populist, in fact behaved as a clientelistic party with ties to the state (Cardoso, 1978: 50; Lamounier, 1980: 33), and the leaders of the PTB, though less addicted to clientelistic campaigning, did nonetheless rally the support of labor by distributing social security benefits through the Ministry of Labor.

Clientelism shaped the nature of party competition, intensifying patterns of coalescent behavior fostered by electoral laws and multipartism. If mi-

---

32 Lamounier (1980: 33) has categorized the vote for the UDN as based on ideological, not clientelistic expectations. If this characterization is an accurate representation of the way in which the party presented itself nationally, in the interior of Minas Gerais and other states, clientelistic expectations and voter attachments to "personalities," or individual politicians, were more evident.

nor parties with only geographically limited bases of support had incentives to enter into electoral coalitions for sheer survival, in a system which the winning parties gained a monopoly over the distribution of patronage, leaders of major parties too, reduced their risk of electoral defeat by forming alliances to contest state and local elections. In the Northeast coalescent behavior was so prevalent that in the 1954 elections, 62 percent of all congressional representatives were elected by party alliances and coalitions (Soares, 1967: 480). In 1962, such multiparty electoral alliances were formed to contest local elections in twelve of a sample of twenty-four municipalities.[33]

With party programs lacking content and well-defined positions on salient issues, these local electoral coalitions were forged among unlikely allies based on purely local personal and tactical considerations. In Minas Gerais, the Republican Party that Artur Bernardes resurrected joined electoral coalitions with both the UDN and the PSD in various local and state elections in Minas Gerais from 1945 to 1964. Even the PTB, locally, formed electoral alliances on the sheer basis of political expediency with those same parties that it castigated in the national arena. Like the PSD and the UDN, its ideology was sufficiently vague to allow it flexibility in local coalition building. The PSD and UDN at times cast aside their bitter rivalry to ally when confronted by a serious electoral threat. In small towns alliances shifted from election to election as a response to the fluctuations in party fortunes that followed from the favors granted by a particular state administration to the local party in power. For example, in the small predominantly rural municipality of Dores do Indaiá, which was still dominated politically in the 1950s by *fazendeiros*, from one election to the next the UDN and PSD allied to combat a local PR administration, then split. After parting, the UDN entered into a coalition with the PR and, in doing so, drove the PSD to join forces with the PTB (Eloy de Carvalho Guimarães, 1956: 177–78). These alliances further diluted the potential that nonoligarchical parties might have carried for breaking the oligarchical grip on state power.

The limits of populism

In Brazil, the smooth functioning of corporatism and clientelism – the twin pillars of postwar state and elite domination – buttressed by the elite-serving character of the political parties placed populism on a more stable footing than in any other country in Latin America with the possible exception of Mexico. The effectiveness of these mechanisms of control avoided for Brazil the collapse suffered by most multiclass, predominantly urban-based popu-

33 My criteria for choosing a sample of twenty-five *municípios* for electoral analysis are discussed in note 2, Chapter 6. (Here, the sample size is reduced to twenty-four because data for the 1962 election in the *município* of Curvelo were missing.)

list coalitions that could not contain popular mobilizations, economic disorder, and their own internal divisions. Nonetheless, even the Brazilian oligarchy eventually bumped up against the limits of clientelistically controlled populism. Added to the most frequently cited causes for the breakdown of Brazilian democracy in 1964 – the strains caused by the structural limitations of import-substituting industrialization (O'Donnell, 1973) and the recurrent inflation that this development strategy generated but could not control (Wallerstein, 1980); the elite conspiracy to change the regime and the economic development model (Dreifuss, 1981); the failure of political leadership to navigate the national crisis (Stepan, 1978); and the condition of polarized pluralism that cost Congress its effectiveness and the president a stable base of support (Santos, 1986) – change in the regional party systems upset the delicate balance of power that had preserved oligarchical hegemony for two decades. Although clientelism was able to contain populist electoral pressure in Minas Gerais, in select other regions populist parties grew in strength to an extent that they eroded the dominant position of the parties of the oligarchy within the governing coalition and threatened their national majorities. Ultimately, regionally based traditional political elites that faced the danger of losing control of national political institutions plotted with the military against the populist democracy.

In Minas Gerais support for the three parties of the traditional political elite remained firm. From 1945 to 1962, the share of the state's delegation to the Chamber of Deputies elected by the PSD dipped from 57.1 to 43.8 percent, but that of the UDN – buoyed by the election of the state executive in 1947 and 1961 – rose from 20 to 33.3 percent (Table 2.6). Combined, these two parties of the oligarchy retained virtually the identical share of seats in the federal Chamber – 77 percent – that they had captured in 1945. The state Republican Party suffered a decline but nonetheless elected a delegation of four to the Chamber of Deputies in 1962, which represented the only Republican deputies left in the Congress. In the state-level elections, too, the PSD, UDN, and PR polled well, together garnering nearly two-thirds of the seats (65.9 percent) in the Minas Legislative Assembly. The PTB doubled its share of the vote in this period but elected only 12.5 percent of the state's congressional delegation and 14.6 percent of the state legislature in 1962. Small parties, moreover, did not gain a single state representative to the federal Chamber.

In sharp contrast, national electoral support for the PSD, UDN, and PR eroded during the course of the postwar era to the advantage of the PTB and small parties. Of the two major parties, the PSD by far suffered the steeper decline in popular support; the percentage of its representatives in the Chamber of Deputies plummeted from a dominating 52.8 in 1945 to 28.9 in 1962. Outside Minas Gerais the PR did not elect a single representative to the Chamber in 1962. The PSD and UDN combined won 43.3 percent of the seats in all state legislatures in 1962 – to 53.7 percent in

Table 2.6. *Brazil and Minas Gerais: Party strength, federal and state legislatures, 1945–62 (in % of seats)*

Party[a]	Chamber of Deputies		Minas delegation		All state Assemblies[b]		Minas Legislative Assembly	
	1945	1962	1945	1962	1947	1962	1947	1962
PSD	52.8	28.9	57.1	43.8	41.4	23.8	40.3	22.0
UDN	29.0[c]	22.2	20.0	33.3	26.3	19.5	22.2	31.7
PR	2.4	1.0	17.1	8.3			19.4	12.2
PTB	7.7	28.4	5.7	12.5	9.9	17.4[d]	8.3	14.6
PSP	.7	5.1		2.1				11.0
PL	.3	1.2						3.7[e]
PDC	.7	4.9					1.4	2.4
PRP		1.2					1.4	2.4
PST		1.7						
PTN		2.7					5.5	
PRT		.7						
PSB		1.2						
MTR		.7						
PCB[f]	4.9						1.4	
PPS	1.4							

[a]PSD-Social Democratic Party; UDN = National Democratic Union; PR = Republican Party; PTB = Brazilian Labor Party; PSP = Social Progressive Party; PL = Liberator Party; PDC = Christian Democratic Party; PRP = Party of Popular Representation; PST = Social Labor Party; PTN = National Labor Party; PRT = Rural Labor Party; PSB = Brazilian Socialist Party; MTR = Movement of Labor Renewal; PCB = Brazilian Communist Party; PPS = Popular Sindicalist Party.
[b]Data available only for the three major parties for Legislative Assembly races outside of Minas Gerais.
[c]The UDN vote in the Chamber of Deputies race in 1945 includes 2.1 percent of the vote obtained by the UDN-PR coalition.
[d]The vote for the PTB in the 1962 state Assembly races represents the total vote obtained by the PTB-PSP-PL coalition.
[e]The vote for the PL in the Legislative Assembly race in Minas Gerais in 1962 represents the total vote obtained by the PL-MTR coalition.
[f]The PCB was outlawed after 1947.
Sources: Bastos, 1964: 321, 325; Hippolito, 1985: 199, 276, 285; Tribunal Superior Eleitoral, 1973: 102–7.

Minas. Nationally, the PTB surpassed the UDN and nearly supplanted the PSD as the largest party; the labor party's share of seats in the Chamber of Deputies rose from a mere 7.7 percent in 1945 to 28.4 percent in 1962, a rate more than twice as great as that registered in Minas Gerais. Across Brazil, moreover, small parties elected 20 percent of the Chamber in 1962, leading to what Santos (1979) has called the "accelerated fragmentation" of the party system. According to Sartori's (1976) index of party system fragmentation, on the eve of the coup Brazil's was the eighth most fragmented party system that existed in the world at any point in the period from 1945 to 1973 (Santos, 1986: 70).

Voting in Minas Gerais deviated from a national average but not a national pattern. Brazilian electoral politics in the period from 1945 to 1964 consisted of distinctive regional party systems, prompting one observer to characterize national voting as little more than an aggregation of various regional trends (Lima, 1981: 30). Brazilian populism was essentially a regional, not an urban phenomenon. The PTB and other populist parties did not increase their vote evenly in Brazil's urban areas, as is widely believed, but where regional political elites used them as vehicles for advancement. Populist parties generally were strongest in Rio Grande do Sul and in São Paulo (where their appeal was enhanced by the personages of Adhemar de Barros and Jânio Quadros), and most of the national representatives of the PTB in particular were from Rio Grande (Vargas's home state).[34] If the advance of the PTB and small populist parties had regional origins, however, it had national consequences. In many parts of Brazil, it appeared that the system was becoming truly competitive, and oligarchic victories could no longer be assured.

If the electoral decline of parties of the oligarchy was alarming, the growing strength of the labor party and a host of minor parties mattered all the more because the nature of the PTB itself began to change. In the first decade of the postwar republic, the PTB contributed to the stability of the oligarchically controlled party system. Its potential effectiveness as a labor party was undermined by its alliance with the elite-dominated PSD in national elections, with parties representing any class or program in local elections, and with state corporatist institutions. The populist politicians of the PTB played an important role in mediating the state's relationship with labor unions, which by law were subordinated to the Ministry of Labor and bound by the decisions of the labor courts on a range of issues from wage levels to the legality of strikes. The fact that labor, an excluded constituency, came to be represented by what was also an "internally mobilized" party successfully co-opted many Brazilian voters. With the Communist Party outlawed, anti-Vargas forces at the mass level had virtually nowhere else to go, except to such populist leaders as Jânio Quadros.

In the decade leading up to the coup, however, populist pressures that began outside the party system pushed their way into the PTB. The self-organizing efforts of peasants who had been excluded from the populist coalition in Brazil challenged the labor party to take up the banner of the rights of rural laborers. Emboldened by a series of successful strikes in the

---

34 Trindade (1978) suggests the populist–antipopulist divide was the most important axis of political conflict in the state of Rio Grande do Sul.

1950s and the inauguaration of a populist president in 1961, moreover, labor unions themselves became less quiescent. As its representation in the Congress grew, the PTB became more responsive to its constituencies that pressed for the creation of a social welfare state.

The strained PSD-PTB coalition that had joined the oligarchy and state-sponsored labor movement finally broke apart when Jânio Quadros unexpectedly resigned the presidency in 1961. Above the vociferous objections of most representatives of the oligarchy but according to the constitution, the office passed to the vice-president, João Goulart, a PTB politician and Vargas's ex-minister of labor. The loss of influence over the national executive of the real power holders in the system – the regionally based traditional elites – provoked a national political crisis. Supporters and opponents of change drew new lines of cleavage in the political system that cross-cut party boundaries. The "Ala Moça" of the PSD (the group that Hippolito [1985] calls "reformers") and the "Bossa-Nova" wing of the UDN (similarly committed to reform) united with the PTB in favor of agrarian reform, economic nationalism, liberal social policies, and an independent foreign policy. In response, the oligarchy united across party lines, not hesitating to seek extraconstitutional means to defend oligarchical privilege and power.

The traditional elite of Minas Gerais, joined by its counterparts in other states, plotted and launched the military coup of 1964 (Motta, 1971; Schneider, 1971: 97–99; Starling, 1986: Stepan, 1971: 199–201, 207). Two decades after the fact, the state secretary of public security, José Monteiro de Castro, admitted that Minas, which was very resistant to the structural changes proposed by Goulart, conspired against the president ("On many nights we flew to secret meetings with military officers"), that a "cabinet of unity" was formed by then governor Magalhães Pinto, and that the landowners ("the most ardent revolutionaries") offered arms and money to him in his capacity as secretary of public security (as cited in *Istoé*, 7/25/84: 92–94). The coup was led by Minas Governor Magalhães Pinto, General Guedes, commander of the 4th Infantry Division located in Minas, and General Mourão Filho (Stepan, 1971: 207). Military conspirators considered the cooperation of the governor of a major state who had the backing of his own state militia to be a prerequisite for initiating any attempt to overthrow the elected president; the militia would be necessary to resist any attempt, however unlikely, on the part of the Goulart government to launch a preemptive coup, and Guedes had a long-standing agreement with Magalhães Pinto to close the state borders in order to resist Goulart (Stepan, 1971: 199–200).

Once the military moved, support from elite political parties was immediately forthcoming. Predictably, the UDN, which had taken the lead in spurring the military to seize power, was first to praise the coup.[35] In an official

---

35 Carlos Lacerda, the anti-Communist Carioca journalist and former governor of Guanabara, and UDN president Mineiro Bilac Pinto, often publicly denounced the government of João Goulart in the early months of 1964 (Benevides, 1981: 124).

statement issued on April 3, the party commended "the patriotism, bravery and lack of personal ambition on the part of the Armed Forces," and placed itself "entirely at its side in every way, for whatever measure is necessary, in order to save democracy" (as cited in Benevides, 1981: 125). To attract the support of the wavering PSD, ex-president Juscelino Kubitschek, the party's titular head, was promised that a member of the PSD, the Mineiro José Maria Alkmim, would be named vice-president in the revolutionary government (Skidmore, 1988: 22). Once the coup was an accomplished fact, much of the PSD did back the military in the Congress. Its hesitation was understandable given that the rival UDN was the prime instigator of the military movement. Its adherence to the "Revolution" is testament to the ability of the traditional political elite to close ranks.

CONCLUSIONS

From the outset of the Brazilian republic, agrarian-based regional oligarchies established their hegemony through noncompetitive political parties in a political system noticeably marked by municipal dependence on state authorities. The oligarchy governing Minas Gerais was among the most noncompetitive and successful to dominate state and even national politics. The mere presence of a political oligarchy in a traditional agrarian society is in itself quite unremarkable and the uncontested hegemony of the oligarchies of two states over a territory as vast as Brazil for three decades is perhaps only slightly less so. What is striking is that a system of closed politics based on economic and state coercion headed by an oligarchy should have survived nearly two decades of state centralization, economic modernization, and expanded political competition and participation.

The regime changes of 1930 and 1945 represent lost opportunities for attacking oligarchical hegemony. The economic and political strategies pursued by Vargas and his most powerful supporters served to reinforce, rather than dismantle, the supporting structures of traditional politics. Municipal dependence on state government was exaggerated, a politically controlled bureaucracy expanded, and internally mobilized political parties controlled by the regional oligarchies virtually monopolized political competition and representation. The oligarchy, in fact, was better able to adapt traditional politics to economic and political change than any other group was able to take advantage of these political openings to reorient the bases of political association, competition, and, above all, representation. Temporarily replacing the leadership of the state political machines was no substitute for structural political change.

The Minas oligarchy in particular reemerged from the centralizing Estado Nôvo bruised and divided but still dominant in the state and political party system. With society already organized politically to support the practice of territorially based clientelism, its members captured and channeled the growing resources of an increasingly interventionist state to integrate the newly participant and nonparticipant classes created by economic development into patronage networks. Traditional politicians grafted the practice of clientelism onto the new party system, although under the conditions of competitive mass politics of the postwar era oligarchically controlled parties relied on less coercive forms of clientelistic political representation than had prevailed during the Old Republic. The multipartite political system established after World War II served the interests of the regional political oligarchies well for two decades. It brought urban labor into the system and attenuated its potential influence, but it nonetheless could not prevent urban and rural labor from escalating their demands for political and economic participation and, eventually, the system from breaking down.

Even more impressive than its own survival, the Minas political class was able to shape the organization of state and even national politics along traditional lines for decades to come. Its first legacy was that of regionalism as an enduring cleavage in Brazilian politics. During the Old Republic, power resided in the states, politics was organized along regional lines, and separate state Republican Parties had little in common. Because of the regional fragmentation of the oligarchy and the parties that represented it, "class divisions didn't occur along national lines, and internal divisions within the dominant classes took a regional character" (Fausto, 1981: 91). Even as the federal state was strengthened over time and the balance in the state–federal relationship tilted toward the union, national class and even more narrow socioeconomic interests did not develop and became translated into national political programs and parties.[36]

Second, clientelism became ingrained in Brazilian political culture as the dominant means of competing electorally and the primary mode of political representation more broadly. Clientelism generally is not a form of domination limited to agrarian societies or used to incorporate migrants and other political "marginals" during some "transition time" that will soon disappear with economic change. Rather, as Shefter (1977: 405–8) has persuasively argued, parties adopt electoral strategies for reasons that have little to do with their social bases; they choose to employ or resist patronage and other strategies based on the costs associated with mobilizing their support-

36 Most historians would agree that very different subregional economies (sugar vs. coffee) generated dissimilar and even competing interests among the agrarian elites of the different states of Brazil at the same time that, in the largest urban centers, there was an overlapping of interests between agrarian and industrial bourgeoisies. Temporary cross-regional alliances to promote the interests of coffee growers were the exception that proved the rule. Cammack (1982: 56) dissents from this consensus. He argues that throughout the Old Republic, policy considerations and economic interests were decisive in shaping alliances and divisions within the state and between the state and federal government. He bases this claim on the differential impact of certain policies on different regional landed interests in Minas Gerais.

ers. In Brazil, even parties that "should have" developed different electoral strategies and governing styles in a mass democracy dared not incur the costs of challenging clientelism. Indeed, there was no competitive political party that did not resort to patronage-based electoral strategies, and virtually no rival politicians competed for votes in any other manner. No matter how "modern" it became, moreover, clientelism remained highly personalized. Patronage was funneled primarily through the political parties, but clientelistic relations were always mediated by politicians and distributed through their personal networks.

Because regionalism, clientelism, and personalism permeated the political parties and framed the way in which society was organized and represented to the state more broadly, society was deprived of opportunities for developing horizontal, national solidarities through parties or other organizations or institutions. Brazilian-style federalism, which centralized fiscal and political power in the executive branch of state government, diminished the competitiveness of local politics. Partisan divisions that overlapped with elite political alliances corresponded rather poorly to class or more narrowly defined economic interests, and parties that were used as vehicles to dispense patronage for the particularistic ends of traditional politicians were robbed of distinctive identities and did not evolve into genuine conduits for nonelite representation. Traditional politicians and their personal rivalries were destined to outlast any particular political party to which they temporarily belonged. The regionalism, clientelism, and personalism of traditional politics, in short, were deeply embedded in state–society relations on the eve of the 1964 coup d'etat.

3

The modern political economy
of traditional politics

The military regime that came to power in 1964 set a new economic course
for Brazil. Originally, the military had hoped to follow up economic stabilization with an ambitious program to rationalize production and encourage
large-scale capitalist development by attracting private domestic and foreign investors to advanced consumer durable and capital goods industries.
The problem with what was initially a liberal economic plan was that the
domestic private sector was too weak and capital-poor to take the initiative
to lead this development, and foreign capital needed to be prodded to
assist in developing Brazil. For the military to fulfill its economic project, it
needed to find some means to compensate for the deficiencies of the private sector. The solution it settled on was a more expansive role for the
state.

The Brazilian state, like other states of late developing countries in Latin
America and the Third World, had intervened extensively in the economy
at least since the Great Depression in order to stimulate industrial development.[1] After the regime change in 1964, however, the state's interventionist role grew more active and pervasive and its nature changed from that
typical of a state in a late developing capitalist society to one that has been
called "state capitalist" (Baer, Newfarmer, and Trebat, 1976). The state
organized and controlled investment, launched major new lines of industries, and steadily increased its domination over the private sector of the
economy. It also provided capital for joint ventures with foreign enterprises

1 The state has taken a leading role in economic development in late-industrializing countries
  at least since Bismarck used the state to support the German iron industry. Industrialization
  in the late-developing countries of Germany, Austria, Italy, and Russia hinged on the state's
  organization of channels of capital investment (Gerschenkron, 1962). In the "late-late"–
  developing economies of Latin America, industrialization also required the state to become
  a producer (Hirschman, 1971). Baer et al. (1976) suggest that states in Latin America were
  forced into entering certain sectors deemed to be in the national interest in which investment requirements were high and maturation periods were long, such as energy and steel in
  the case of Brazil, because the alternatives – to make industrialization exclusively dependent on foreign capital and technology or forgo it altogether if foreign investors were
  uninterested – were unacceptable.

and negotiated foreign investment on reasonably favorable terms for Brazil.[2] Its success in attracting multinational capital to invest in dynamic manufacturing sectors (in a departure from the old multinational pattern of investing exclusively in primary-sector activities – mining and agriculture) led Cardoso (1972) and Evans (1979) to label Brazil's phenomenal growth "dependent development." The state played a less celebrated but equally central role in an agricultural modernization nearly as impressive as the industrial transformation.

Many of the political analyses of Brazil in the 1970s anticipated that such a fundamental economic transformation would be accompanied by profound political change inherently threatening to traditional elites for two reasons. First, the rapid evolution of a predominantly agricultural economy into an industrially based one was expected to reproduce the shift of political power from rural to urban elites evidenced in other, earlier industrializing countries.[3] Second, because this industrialization took place under the aegis of state and foreign capital, it was believed that government technocrats, state enterprise managers, and the military itself would become the new dominant class. Both political effects were expected within the state of Minas Gerais because of the broad similarities between the regional pattern of development and the national model. Much of the Brazilian "economic miracle" of the early 1970s was located in Minas Gerais – the Brazilian state established major steel and metalworking plants in Minas in the 1970s and foreign investors responded en masse to fiscal incentives offered by the state.

2 According to Evans's account (1979), the Brazilian state pressured foreign corporations to participate in local capital accumulation. With their status (and investments) vulnerable to nationalistic attack, foreign firms acquiesced, and took local partners for political protection. In exchange, both public and private local capital won from their new foreign associates the technology they sorely needed to become competitive.

3 Of course, such an expectation has not been borne out in other late-developing countries (cf. Kurth, 1979), and is itself based on a stereotyped view of European and American history that is only half true. In the first developers, the onset of industrialization did not suddenly transform either the economy or politics. Traditional elites held up "bourgeois democracy" for decades, indeed centuries, after industrialization was well underway, and accounts of "conquering bourgeoisies" have little foundation in fact. In the *Communist Manifesto* of 1848, Marx and Engels (1972: 339) described a "one hundred year rule" of a bourgeoisie, which, in England, the country in which it was the most advanced, had been enfranchised for only sixteen years, and had won its first important political battle – the abolition of the Corn Laws – a mere two years earlier. In the South of the United States after the Civil War, traditional aristocrats retained both their land and a strong political base in their state governments, which enabled them to wield disproportionate influence in the Senate (Moore, 1966; Key, 1984). Mayer (1981) compellingly argues that the old regime remained in place and in power *throughout* Europe until World War I. Most remarkably, even today, the aristocracy in Britain enjoys an important representation in the British cabinet and Parliament. Despite this ample historical evidence to the contrary, however, a belief in the inevitability of political change following an industrial revolution still holds considerable appeal.

This chapter examines the economic model adopted by the military regime, and its application in Minas Gerais. Its analysis of industrial investments, agricultural modernization, and the urban labor market suggests that, in fact, state-led capitalist development did have significant political repercussions, but not in the predicted direction. In Minas Gerais, the movement of national resources from agriculture into industry did not transfer power to industrial elites because the local bourgeoisie played only a secondary role in the state's industrialization. Government technocrats and state enterprise managers who administered regional industrialization, moreover, did not become a force in local or regional politics. The modernization of agriculture evicted peasants from the rural areas, but outside of the metropolitan region of Belo Horizonte, they did not become a political army of industrial workers. Rather, given the preponderant role played by the state in the provision of employment, transfer payments, and other resources, they were integrated into the public sector of the economy. By increasing state resources available for production and distribution both absolutely and in relation to the private sector, and by driving upward the number of potential clients, state intervention enhanced the political value of state positions, which offered unanticipated opportunities to extend dominance for a political elite already rooted in the state. Not only did state-propelled economic modernization not undermine the power base of the traditional political elite and erode traditional politics, as "free-market" capitalism might have, but it laid a structural foundation on which traditional politics could be revitalized.

State-led capitalist development does not always engender traditional, patronage politics. The resources of an interventionist state are available to whoever or whatever political party or coalition controls the access to the branches of the state that distribute them. If the resources of such a state are distributed collectively through automatic transfers, their recipients often view them as a right of citizenship, and parties are more likely to make gains by committing themselves to defending them than are politicians who pledge to distribute them on a particularistic basis. If, on the other hand, such universal entitlements do not exist, politicians who are perceived as best equipped to deliver pork will be rewarded. The congruence between this economic model and traditional politics in Brazil followed from the fact that expanded state intervention and foreign investment were superimposed over a political system already organized along clientelistic lines. When the economic programs and policies of the military regime multiplied the points of intersection of the state and society, state sanctions and resources could be and easily were applied according to particularistic criteria. The economic strategy for stimulating growth pursued by the authoritarian regime nourished a form of political representation that was pervasive on the eve of the military coup, clientelism, reinforcing the bases of dominance of those who occupied state office – in this case, a traditional elite.

STATE INTERVENTION IN BRAZIL

Before the advent of the Chicago boys, Thatcherism, and the wave of neoliberalism that has swept the Third World, the economies of few countries in the late twentieth century conformed to classic notions of "liberal" capitalism. Both the postwar welfare states of advanced industrial societies and interventionist states of the contemporary Third World regulated public utilities, finance, and industry, provided physical infrastructure and other subsidies for the private sector, and, above all, delivered public goods – education, health care, and a wide array of welfare programs – to their citizens. State intervention in the economy enhanced private profit by socializing the cost of overhead and by absorbing losses in key service industries, and state provision of employment and distribution of social services and benefits assuaged the harshest features of laissez-faire capitalism for the laboring classes. In Latin America in the postwar period, countries from Mexico to Chile abetted industrialization and economic growth through public financing for the private sector, the regulation of trade and investment, and the ownership of public utilities and basic productive enterprises. In Brazil in particular, the state under Vargas made forays into steel, mining, electricity, and petroleum in the 1940s and early 1950s (Evans, 1979: 87–93). But after 1964, Brazilian development became "state-led" in that the state additionally was the motor of economic development: it set basic prices; contributed substantially to the domestic product through its capital and current expenditures; was the leading financier, controlling savings and investment; and established a broad array of productive enterprises in the commanding heights of the economy. The Brazilian military government developed an aggressive economic strategy that heightened state intervention in the economy, sharpened the tools of regulation and distribution, and through its own investments even manipulated foreign and domestic private investors. This model of state-led capitalist development contrasts sharply with the neoliberal economic programs adopted roughly contemporaneously by neighboring military governments in Chile, Uruguay, and Argentina, which reversed historical patterns of state intervention. Only the Peruvian military pursued a strategy of state capitalism comparable with the Brazilian, but it did so with less success.[4]

After the change of regime, the Brazilian state significantly expanded its network of productive sector enterprises, One hundred eight federal state enterprises were added to the state sector from 1967 to 1973 (Araujo, 1977: 238), and new ones continued to be created even after the "miracle" had been exhausted and acrimonious antistatism complaints had been voiced

4 FitzGerald (1979) argues along similar lines that the growth in the state sector in Peru after 1968 was a direct response to the failure of domestic capital to sustain industrialization or negotiate effectively with foreign enterprise.

Table 3.1. *Brazil: The state's productive sector, 1974–83*

Sector	State firms: % of net assets			
	1983(1)	1980(2)	1975(3)	1974(4)
Mining	62.0	61.5	61.0	62.0
Metallurgy (metal products)	60.5	37.8	40.0	34.0
(iron and steel)	(81.6)	(62.5)		
Chemicals and petroleum	50.8	58.0	55.0	
(chemicals and petrochemicals)	(25.0)	(22.4)	32.0[a]	
(petroleum)	(82.7)	(85.0)	98.0	
Transportation and storage	88.9	89.6	89.0	78.0
(railroads)	(100.0)	(100.0)		
(storage)	(75.1)	(78.8)		
Public utilities (services)	98.3	98.5	90.0	88.0

[a]Martins does not make plain which subsectors this figure comprises, and thus we should not necessarily conclude that the state's share of this sector has declined. *Sources:* (1) *Visão*, 1984; (2) *Visão*, 1981; (3) Martins, 1985: 251, 252; (4) Baer et al., 1976; Faucher, 1980.

loudly by the business community. Toward the close of military rule in 1983, there were 683 public sector companies (195 federal, 372 state, and 116 municipal), 110 of which were added in the six-year period from 1977 to 1983 (*Visão*, 1983: 431). These enterprises dominated the commanding heights of the economy. In the 1970s and early 1980s, they consistently topped the "Who's Who" list of leading corporations compiled by the business magazine *Visão*: in 1982 79 state enterprises controlled three-quarters of the net assets and accounted for half of the sales, profits, and employment of the 200 largest nonfinancial corporations (*Visão*, 1983: 23). From 1974 to 1983, the share commanded by public enterprises of the net assets of the largest nonfinancial firms in Brazil rose from 39 percent (of 5,113 companies) (Baer et al., 1976) to 50.5 percent (of 8,480).[5] In some areas state economic activity even eclipsed that of the private sector. State enterprises dominated the petroleum, transportation and storage, mining, metallurgical (especially steel), and public utilities sectors for at least a decade (Table 3.1). Only in the case of the petroleum industry did the state's participation decline: exploration by foreign corporations was permitted after the oil shocks of the 1970s in order to alleviate Brazil's acute energy crisis. The state's presence was insignificant in only six, mostly

5 The *Visão* list includes only corporations, which has the effect of understating the role of private national capital.

traditional, sectors of the economy (footwear, textiles and clothing, leather and rubber, beverages and tobacco, electronics, and nonmetallic minerals).

Unlike in many advanced industrial societies where governments subsidize lame ducks to maintain vital services and service industries, in Brazil state enterprise in both the productive and financial spheres generated surplus for most of the period of military rule.[6] Prior to 1964, Brazil's state enterprises behaved pretty much as state enterprises do in "liberal" capitalistic economies. Public sector pricing, especially in the railway services, electrical energy sector, and steel industry, essentially subsidized the cost of industrial inputs to the private sector (Faucher, 1980: 16; Mendonça de Barros and Graham, 1978: 8). This practice fueled inflation and drained the national treasury. Following the coup, a priority and accomplishment of the stabilization plan was for these enterprises to operate in the black in order to finance investment spending. Assigned high-quality managers and permitted autonomy in their operations and price setting, Brazilian state enterprises became profitable in absolute terms, by international standards, and relative to the private sector (Trebat, 1983: 175–80).[7] In the 1970s, they were "a more secure and remunerative portfolio investment for prospective stock-holders than private firms" (Mendonça de Barros and Graham, 1978: 14). Only in the 1980s when a severe recession had a more damaging impact on public than private sector firms did their performance seriously falter (*Visão*, 1983: 23).

The state also dominated financial markets. In 1983 112 state financial institutions accounted for over half (51.2 percent) of the net assets of Brazil's financial sector. State financial institutions were by far the most important source of investment capital for the private sector: in 1974, the

6 Trebat (1981: 49) found rates of profitability (current surplus as a percent of net worth) in public enterprises in the mining sector to have averaged over 20 percent from 1966 to 1975; in petrochemicals, 18.7 percent; and in electricity, 7.4 percent. Even steel, which suffered losses in the years from 1966 to 1969, rebounded after 1970 to achieve rates of profitability of 4.3 percent from 1970 to 1975. In 1980, during an economic downturn, the rate of return of state enterprises in the primary (mining) sector was 11.3 percent, in manufacturing industry, 6.9, in the financial sector, 13 percent, and in public utilities, 3.8 percent (*Visão*, 1981: 414–32). The only declining public service taken over by the Brazilian state, and the only significant component of the state sector that was unprofitable, was the railroads (Abranches, 1977: 9).

7 According to a 1972 survey of 318 of the largest nonfinancial firms in the country (Doellinger and Cavalcanti, as reported in Baer et al., 1976: 79), the profitability (here defined as the unweighted average of before-tax profits divided by equity) of state enterprises was higher (17.6) than that of both private Brazilian (16.4) and multinational (15.8) firms. The results of a 1974 survey of 731 firms in 48 different sectors conducted by Wilson Suzigan (as reported in Cipolla, 1977: 99) do not show quite as favorable comparative rates of state enterprise profitability, but they are still quite good: profits in the state sector were the highest of the three sectors (state, foreign, national private) in capital goods; the lowest in intermediate goods; and more profitable than national private, less than multinational, in durable consumer goods.

state supplied 72 percent of all investment loans to private borrowers, and 44 percent of working capital loans (Cipolla, 1977: 100); in 1983, 72 percent of all loans conceded by Brazil's development and investment banks were made by the official federal and state government development banks (and one public investment bank) (calculated from *Visão*, 1984: 386). The actual percentage of investment originating from within the state is even higher, for these figures do not include the investments of the National Housing Bank (BNH) targeted to urban development and housing.[8]

Along with the extensive reach of the state into production and finance, the state's leverage over private economic activity was enhanced. As buyers of capital goods, public enterprises were an important market for domestic heavy industry (Mendonça de Barros and Graham, 1978: 8), and the large capital investments of these firms also had a multiplier effect on the entire economy. In 1974, state-owned enterprises alone accounted for more than 26 percent of all investment in the Brazilian economy, and the combined contribution of the public sector (state enterprises plus government investment) to investment exceeded 60 percent (Coutinho and Reichstul, 1977: 63). The state's revenue base was also sharply increased: between 1965 and 1969, the number of federal income taxpayers rose from 400,000 to 1.5 million (FJP, n.d., I: II-2). Revenue was also enhanced by indexing tax payments in arrears. During military rule, the gross tax burden (27 percent in 1973 and 28 percent in 1981) was the highest in Latin America, as was the public sector's gross capital formation until it was surpassed by Mexico's after 1975 (Baer et al., 1976: 73; FitzGerald, 1979: 214; Banco Interamericano de Desarrollo, 1984: 231, 262, 273, 289, 357, 391).

During the 1960s and 1970s, state expenditure rose in real terms, on a per capita basis, and in relation to the gross product. General government expenditures (including state and municipal governments, but excluding state enterprises) as a percent of GDP climbed from less than 20 percent in 1949 (Baer et al., 1976: 73) to approximately 24 percent in the 1970s (IBGE, 1983: 948, 956). In comparative terms, this rate was higher over a period of these two decades than that of the other major economies in Latin America. While the central government was the principal beneficiary of increased state revenues, this visible increase in spending extended to other branches of government: the states of Brazil, taken as a whole, saw their shares of gross product rise on average nearly 10 percent per year from 1970 to 1976 (FJP, n.d., I: IV-14).

At least two theoretical implications for politics follow from these data. First, this model of development conferred enormous power on state elites. The state's own contribution to investment, its control over crucial variables that determine private investment decisions, the concentration of

---

8 In 1980, nearly half of housing loans originated in the BNH; some were authorized directly, the rest through other financial institutions, All private commercial housing bank loans were from credit lines made available by the BNH (IBGE, 1983: 902).

economic decision-making power in its higher echelons, and its network of productive enterprises in key economic sectors gave it a considerable degree of power over the private sector and made the occupants of state office important formal and informal power holders in the political system. So extensive was their power that state elites have been referred to by Brazilian observers as a "state bourgeoisie" (Cardoso and Faletto, 1979: 210; Martins, 1985: 237, Singer, 1975, as cited in Malloy, 1979: 184). Such claims build on one that maintains that in state capitalism the state's participation in the economy does not necessarily complement private economic activity (Freeman, 1982), but rather that public sector accumulation implies a confrontation with, and perhaps even the partial or total elimination of, the private sector (Sorj, 1983: 73). State enterprises attempt to maximize profit in order to accomplish state, not private objectives; state elites are not accountable to the bourgeoisie (though this does not preclude an alliance between these classes), and state elites use the state's control over investment and production to achieve state-defined economic goals.[9] Such a reality is quite distinct from that of liberal capitalist society as conceptualized by traditional liberal and Marxist views. Despite their wide differences, both schools of thought agree that "real power" in capitalist society resides outside the state, which is one, but not the only or the most important, locus of power in society; the state in both views is in fact dominated by civil society.[10] The considerable powers of the Brazilian state also exceeded those attributed to modern states by recent theories that have persuasively argued that the capitalist state may structure social and political relations as well as take command of the economy and economic decision making (Evans, Rueschemeyer, and Skocpol, 1985; Hamilton, 1982; Nordlinger, 1987; Stepan, 1977).

Second, the economic reach of the Brazilian state shaped several important patterns of representation of mass and even elite interests. The growth of state resources and regulatory powers in the Vargas era laid the basis for contemporary clientelism and gave rise to state corporatism (Erickson, 1985; Schmitter, 1971). The intensification of state economic activity under

---

9 What state elites choose to do with their levers of control over the economy forms the basis of Guimarães's (1977: 197) distinction between two types of capitalism with a prominent role for state elites: "politically oriented" and "state-directed" capitalism. A politically oriented regime is one in which political groups (bureaucracies, parties, militaries) define political objectives for the state that imply an expansion of governmental activities that deliberately create new lucrative opportunities for private groups. In "state-directed" capitalism, political groups mobilize the state apparatus to impose direct controls over the economy, restructure markets, and control resources for the realization of priority policies.

10 Liberal theorists have argued that there exist plural centers of decision making (Truman, 1951; Dahl, 1961); elite theorists, that private elites influence policy in their favor because of the resources they command in the private sector of the economy (Mills, 1956; Domhoff, 1967). The state is thus viewed alternately as a useful ally or pawn of some other, more powerful, societal group or groups.

the military regime, in particular in providing employment and distributing social services, heightened the political importance of state clientelism. The overlapping of public and private activity and the intrusion of the public sector into private activity (through its command of regulatory decisions), moreover, structured a new pattern of interest representation primarily for elites that Cardoso (1975: 206) called "bureaucratic rings." Bureaucratic rings metaphorically described alliances that cut horizontally across the public and private bureaucracies and united parts of an economic sector controlled by private enterprise with segments of the state bureaucracy. Only through "bureaucratic rings" of influence could the private sector in Brazil establish the contacts with relevant ministers of state, agency and council heads, and their undersecretaries necessary to conduct business in a highly regulated environment in which the major financier, supplier of inputs, and purchaser of goods was often the state.[11]

THE INDUSTRIALIZATION OF MINAS GERAIS: STATE AND BOURGEOISIE

Under military rule, the interests of the federal and state governments, local elites, and foreign and national businessmen converged around developing the sluggish regional economy of Minas Gerais, particularly industry in intermediate and dynamic sectors. The state in Minas expanded its role in the regional economy and economic development in a manner strikingly similar to that of the national state. From 1947 to 1969, public expenditure grew annually by 6.5 percent (FJP, n.d., I: IV-13), and from 1971 to 1977, by nearly 17 percent (FJP, n.d., I: IV-13). In real terms. state expenditure per capita nearly tripled between 1960 and 1977 (FJP, n.d., III: 141, 145). Public sector spending in Minas Gerais also increased as a share of the gross domestic product: state spending alone (state direct administration, parapublic agencies, foundations, and enterprises) reached 19.0 percent in 1977 (SEPLAN, 1978, 6, 2: 253, 252). When to this is added the spending of the federal and municipal governments within the state, as well as that of the social security institutes (the National Institute of Social Insurance, INPS, and the Rural Worker's Assistance Fund, FUNRURAL) and educational foundations, that figure rises to 28.9 percent (SEPLAN, 1978, 6, 2: 255).

To administer a richer and increasingly complex state government, a number of new federal and state enterprises and parapublic agencies and foundations were created. Between 1960 and 1977, the number of state agencies, foundations, and enterprises rose from 45 to 124 (SEPLAN, 1978, 6, 1: 112). Taken together, these parapublic agencies and foundations represented approximately one-fifth of all nonentrepreneurial public spend-

---

11 This theoretical point has received empirical support from McDonough's (1981a) study of the frequency of contacts between entrepreneurs and state ministries regulating affairs of interest to them during the administration of Emílio Garrastazú Médici (1969–73).

ing in the 1970s. Through these institutions, the state provided vital services. The most important (those with the largest budgets) delivered roads, water, and energy, administered social security, sold agricultural inputs, constructed elementary schools, and even ran the lottery (FJP, n.d., III: 103, 113–14).

Beginning in the mid-1960s, the state coordinated a pro-industrial economic policy, creating several agencies to accelerate development and promoting technocrats within them to responsible positions (L. Andrade, 1980), enacting fiscal and other incentives for private investors, and providing directly a majority of investment and financing capital. Among the more prominent of the new state agencies were the Industrial Development Institute (INDI), created in 1969 to accelerate the state's economic growth, and the Industrial Districts Company (CDI), created in 1971 to provide basic infrastructure necessary for industrial plants. INDI aggressively courted investors throughout the developed world (Grossi, 1977; Suzzi, 1980). The CDI cleared land and supplied water and sewerage facilities at state expense in order to reduce the cost of new industrial investment and enhance the attractiveness of various sites throughout the state for potential investors.

Substantial fiscal incentives guaranteed Minas's success in inducing private capital to invest in the state. From 1969 to 1975, 278 firms investing in new plants or plant expansion in the state received a tax rebate of 25.6 percent of the federally levied but state-collected value-added tax (ICM). When the federal government outlawed such manipulation of the ICM in 1975, Minas replaced this incentive with yet another attractive one, a Fund for the Support of Industrialization, which provided working-capital loans free of interest and monetary correction to companies that invested in new manufacturing projects or in a 50 percent or greater expansion of their physical plant.[12] Also, all companies based in an industrial district established by the Industrial Districts Company were exempted from municipal real-estate taxes for a period of ten years (INDI, 1978: 129–33). Finally, the state also granted import credits for a broad range of industrial inputs to investors in heavy industry.

Not only did the Minas state government create a favorable climate for investment, but public capital also constituted the lion's share of new industrial investment – 64 percent – from 1970 to 1977.[13] All totaled, federal

12 Monetary correction adjusts the value of a loan to account for inflation, which in the Brazilian case has been enormous. Though stable at about 20 percent per year from 1967 to 1973, inflation rose suddenly after the first oil shock to 40 percent per annum, and climbed steadily thereafter under military rule to an annual rate of over 100 percent in the early 1980s and over 200 percent when the military relinquished power to civilians in 1985. From 1985 to 1993 prices rose on average by over 1,000 percent per year. Inflation finally appeared to be brought under control in 1994.
13 Two giant steel projects, Açominas and Usiminas, together accounted for 49 of the 57 billion cruzeiros the state invested in this period (30.7 billion and 18.3 billion, respec-

Table 3.2. *Minas Gerais: Industrial investments, 1970–77 (in %)*

	Private national	Foreign	State	Total
Nondurable consumer goods	76	24	–	100
Intermediate goods	12	13	75	100
Capital goods and consumer durables	10	80	10	100
Total	16	20	64	100

Note: Only projects in operation or with installation begun by December 31, 1977.
Source: SEPLAN, 1978, 8: 23, 97.

public investments accounted for 33 percent of the Minas manufacturing gross internal product during these boom years (SEPLAN, 1978, 8: 82). The state also contributed capital through joint ventures to major industrial projects with significant multiplier effects; in the most celebrated of these ventures, the state of Minas in 1974 provided 44 percent of the start-up capital for the establishment of the Fiat automobile factory in Betim, an industrial suburb of Belo Horizonte.

State capital was augmented by foreign and non-Minas private capital. Multinational firms financed ninety-two projects, seventy of which represented new industries, and twenty-two the expansion and/or modernization of existing plants. Foreign capital, concentrated mainly in the capital goods and consumer durables sectors, represented 20 percent of the investments of the 1970s (Table 3.2). In 1976, after many of these investments would have come on line, two-thirds of the net assets of the 1985 existing principal industrial corporations in the state were foreign- and state-owned (SEPLAN, 1978, 8: 95). Private national capital played a clearly subsidiary role, contributing 16 percent of total investment in the period.

This strategy was quite successful in propelling industrial growth. Between 1960 and 1977, Minas Gerais underwent a metamorphosis from an agrarian state to one in full industrialization. In 1960, the agrarian economy contributed one-half of the state's income. (BDMG, 1968, I: 140), and employed three out of every five Mineiros (SEPLAN, 1978, 7, I: 171). From that date to 1977, annual industrial growth rates averaged 11 percent and the manufacturing sector bettered its share of the Minas gross internal product 10 percentage points and nearly doubled its payroll. By far the most striking gains were achieved during the 1970s, when the industry-wide

tively). The other investments made by federal public enterprises in the period from 1970 to 1977 were Acesita (4.1 billion); Usimec (816 million); Valefertil (3.1 billion) and Forjas Acesita (292 million) (SEPLAN, 1978, 8: 83). (All figures are in constant 1975 cruzeiros.) A complete list of principal industrial enterprises with shareholding participation of the state of Minas through June 1978 can be found in SEPLAN (1978, 8: 89–90).

average growth rate was 16.5 percent per annum, and nontraditional industries scored especially impressive growth: capital goods and consumer durables expanded by more than 27 percent per year, and chemicals, by 34 percent (SEPLAN, 1978, 8: 5). Minas also outperformed all other Brazilian states but São Paulo in industrial investment. Its investment rate (the ratio of liquid investment to industrial product) was nearly 50 percent, twice the national rate in the same period (SEPLAN, 1978, 8: 54). In fact, the state captured fully one-quarter of the value of all fixed investment in Brazil in projects approved by the Industrial Development Council (CDI/ MIC) for the years 1971 through 1977 (SEPLAN, 1978, 8: 47). In 1982, Minas Gerais produced 40 percent of Brazil's steel (IBGE, 1984: 202).

The impressive alliance between the state and foreign capital that made this development possible, however, did not pull in as partners a truly local bourgeoisie. In Minas Gerais, "private national" capital constituted 16 percent of industrial investment, but much of it derived from non-Minas industrialists, principally from the state of São Paulo. Many firms relocated or set up new operations in Minas because industrial overcongestion had restricted opportunities for physical plant expansion in the environs of São Paulo. The fiscal incentives offered by the state of Minas induced investors who could otherwise have transferred operations elsewhere in the state of São Paulo to settle instead on the South of Minas. Nearly half of all domestic investments in new plants and existing plant expansion and/or modernization in the South of Minas contracted before 1975 that benefited from fiscal incentives were made by corporations headquartered in São Paulo.[14] Although the private national capital component of all industrial investments recorded in the state Department of Planning does not distinguish local from other national capital, this type of breakdown does exist for the industrial projects assisted by INDI, about nine-tenths of all investments in industry during the 1970s (Table 3.3)[15] If the (2:1) ratio of national to Mineiro capital in the INDI figures is used as a guideline, the share of local capital could be as low as 5 percent.

Even with state fiscal incentives, state development bank financing, and foreign technology, moreover, private entrepreneurs in Minas were unable to launch nontraditional enterprises. Of those capital goods and consumer durables industries installed after 1970, only one, short-lived, microelectronics firm, Transit, was the venture of local Minas entrepreneurs. The

14 Data on the ownership and headquarters of the forty firms that invested in the region according to the records of the Fundação João Pinheiro (FJP) were available for only twenty-six (*Visão*, 1981) (*Visão* catalogs in its "Who's Who" only firms whose net assets meet an established minimum and are incorporated); of these, five were foreign-based. At least eleven of the twenty-one national firms were known to be headquartered in São Paulo.

15 Because of the lack of comparability between the various measures of investment (e.g., years in which the investments were undertaken, base years used to calculate investment capital), it is extremely difficult to arrive at a more exact figure. The nine-tenths figure used represents an accurate percentage of employment generated by new industry. The INDI-assisted investments might represent more than 90 percent of the number of projects.

Table 3.3. *INDI-assisted projects: Distribution by controlling capital, 1980*

	N of projects	% of investment	N of new jobs	% of new jobs
National	145	30.0	39,836	33.0
Mineiros	204	15.8	32,464	26.9
Foreign	90	45.7	45,465	37.7
State	5	8.5	2,903	2.4

Note: The measure of controlling capital tends to understate the role of state capital, much of which entered into joint ventures with foreign capital as a minority partner.
Source: INDI, 1980.

Minas bourgeoisie was also apparently unable to form joint ventures with state and foreign capital. In Minas, local entrepreneurs did not participate in the spate of projects that sprang up around Fiat. Among the many supporting industries in the metals, plastics, and other sectors that the establishment of an auto industry in Minas generated were joint ventures between foreign firms and the state government, such as the FMB foundry in Betim and Forjas Acesita in Santa Luzia; fully foreign firms, such as Formin of Italy in Sete Lagoas; and Paulista firms such as Commander and Plásticos Mueller in Contagem.[16]

The lack of direct and even indirect participation in the industrialization of Minas Gerais by the local entrepreneurial class contrasts sharply with the prominent role played by the predominantly São Paulo–based national bourgeoisie in Brazil's development in the 1970s. Peter Evans's seminal work (1979) found private national capital to be an active partner in a "tri-pé" of state, foreign, and national capital. Evans (1979: 281) judged the ability of local firms to build alliances with multinationals and the state to be at least as, and perhaps more, significant than entrepreneurship. Certain São Paulo–based groups – Matarazzo and Antunes, for example – were able through these partnerships in joint ventures to build extremely powerful positions, gaining "benefits quite out of proportion to their contribution of capital or technology."

Why Minas entrepreneurs did not negotiate their way into lucrative joint ventures with foreign and state capital, and why they could not take advantage of dependent development more generally, are probably attributable to their relative weakness at the time of the industrialization drive. The "most surprising and impressive" strength of the national bourgeoisie was perhaps abetted by its long establishment: the Paulista entrepreneurial

16 This partial list of firms is drawn from SEPLAN (1978, 8: 99), which distinguishes the national ownership of firms. The specific characteristics of capital identified as Brazilian were determined by data provided by *Visão* (1981).

class came into existence prior to World War I (Cardoso, 1965), and was fully formed by 1945.[17] In Minas Gerais, where the local bourgeoisie began from a less well established position and the state's role in regional economic development was more pervasive, native industrialists were weak, dependent on the state, and marginal to industrialization.

In the early 1960s, private Minas capital was concentrated in the "traditional" industrial sector, a plethora of small-scale, family-run production units with outmoded managerial practices; low growth rates, low levels of technology, productivity, and efficiency; obsolete equipment; and less than optimal plant locations (BDMG, 1968, I: 23, 180–83); Campolina Diniz, 1978). In contrast, local capital in the "dynamic" industrial sector, which accounted almost exclusively for the industrial growth registered in Minas in the 1950s and 1960s, was limited to a few nonmetallic minerals and construction industries, in a sector otherwise dominated by state and foreign capital.[18] In 1965, economic groups with headquarters in Minas Gerais were found by Queiroz (1965) and Martins (1965) to be practically nonexistent,[19] and the principal activity of the handful of groups that were locally based was not manufacturing industry, but banking and the export–import business.

The rudimentary character of Minas industrialists was brought to light in a survey of firm size, wages and salaries, and productivity of industry in five Brazilian states (Lamounier, n.d.). Of the five states – Guanabara (greater Rio de Janeiro city), São Paulo, Minas, Rio Grande do Sul, and Bahia – Minas's composite score on thirteen indicators of entrepreneurial structure was fourth, and the gap dividing first- and second-ranked Guanabara and São Paulo from the other three states was substantial.[20] Only Bahia, a relatively backward northeastern state, ranked lower on the composite scale. In 1960, average firm size in Minas was one-third

---

17 Two-thirds of the leading economic groups – sets of companies connected by links of shared ownership or multiple interlocking directorates – originated before World War I, and another 28 percent before 1930 (Evans, 1979: 105).

18 The industrial subsectors included under the grouping of "dynamic" industries were mining, electrical energy, civil construction, nonmetallic minerals, and metallurgy. Of these, mining and electricity were the preserve of state capital, and metallurgy, of both state and foreign capital (e.g., Usiminas, Belgo Mineiro, Mannesmann, Aluminas).

19 Of 83 groups (out of an estimated universe of 221) whose capital assets ranged from 1 to 4 billion cruzeiros, 54 were owned by nationals, and of these 54, only 2 were headquartered in Minas (Martins, 1965: 85). Of those 55 groups whose capital assets exceeded 4 billion cruzeiros, five had their own decision-making centers in Minas, but at least two were foreign-owned (Queiroz, 1965: 65).

20 The author acknowledges two complications in working with census data that would tend to understate the levels of industrial activity in the more industrially advanced states. First, the unit of analysis in the industrial census is the "establishment," not the "firm." The more powerful firms are subdivided into several establishments. Second, census data do not distinguish establishments located within a given state that are subsidiaries of firms headquartered in other states.

that of Guanabara's, and its average wages and salaries two-thirds the level paid in the city of Rio. Only 29 percent of Minas firms issued stock, as compared with 74 percent of Rio-based companies and 50 percent of those in São Paulo (Lamounier, n.d.: 22). In labor productivity, Minas firms ranked last.

Studies of state industry conducted by the Minas Gerais Development Bank (BDMG) in the early to mid 1960s cast the scornful impression that Minas industrialists were backward. They criticized the small scale, low wage levels, and low capital and labor productivity of Minas industrial establishments. They especially found fault with the low rate of private investment in productive sectors, "outdated managerial practices," and the persistence of family-owned ("traditional") enterprises as the primary organizational form in local industry. The bank's technocrats who wrote these studies largely blamed local entrepreneurs, whom they perceived to be incompetent, excessively conservative, undynamic, and too risk averse, for the failure of Minas to industrialize in the preceding decades. In 1968, in the *Diagnóstico da Economia Mineira* (BDMG, 1968, I: 42–43),[21] the technocrats concluded that "The conduct of the entrepreneurial sector . . . is not characterized by the degree of aggressiveness typical of the so-called 'entrepreneurial spirit,' which, in other contexts, has characterized the modernizing behavior of the entrepreneurial elite." Minas entrepreneurs did staunchly support state efforts to establish basic industry in the region – in the 1950s they lobbied for the creation of the state development bank, the BDMG; the state electric company, CEMIG; the mining and metals corporation, METAMIG; the meat-processing plants in the North and Northeast regions of Minas; and the giant Usiminas steel project (Dias, 1960–69: 122–23).[22] But the state technocrats only accused Minas entrepreneurs of "demanding and not participating" (BDMG, 1969, I: 42), encouraging the state to undertake the task of industrialization on its behalf. In their view, local entrepreneurs had, by their inability to carry out a project for industrialization, in effect forfeited their claim to lead this process.

If the economic weakness of the local industrialists indeed situated them poorly to capitalize on the incentives offered and opportunities presented by the state's industrialization drive, then the experience of Minas entrepreneurs under state-led capitalist development was probably not atypical, and

21 The *Diagnóstico da Economia Mineira*, a six-volume document drafted by a group of technocrats served, in the view of most observers, as the ideological justification for the replacement of traditional politicians with technocrats, and the expansion of the state in the economy during the administration of Governor Rondon Pacheco (1971–75). Grossi (1977) has called it the "Magna Carta" of the technocrats.

22 In a context of deficient capital markets, the proposal was for the BDMG to provide long-term finance capital for industrial projects within the state as the Banco Nacional de Desenvolvimento Econômico (BNDE – the forerunner of the BNDES) did nationally. CEMIG figured prominently in then governor Juscelino Kubitschek's program to furnish energy and transportation.

was most likely more representative of Brazil as a whole than that of the Paulista economic elite. Indeed, Chilcote (1990: 296) found a pattern of industrial ownership under military rule in two cities in the Northeast of Brazil – Juazeiro, Bahia, and Petrolina, Pernambuco – similar to that of Minas Gerais. There, as in Minas, the state was primarily interested in attracting outside national and multinational capital to the region, and local capital was rarely incorporated into these ventures.

One important implication of the state and foreign capital playing the leading role in industrialization in Minas Gerais and in the Northeast was that politicians per se were not challenged by industrial interests. As Chilcote (1990: 314) put it in writing about the industry that located in Juazeiro and Petrolina, "Enterprise from the Center-South constituted little political threat, because its managers lacked political power." In fact, local politicians even benefited from the location of industry perceived to be a gift of the public sector. With a playing field clear of exogenous political challenges, local political elites were unencumbered in their quest to reinforce their dominance amid an economic upheaval.

THE STATE AND THE POPULAR SECTORS

The manner in which economic development unfolded in Minas Gerais in the 1960s and 1970s restructured the labor market and rearranged the lower end of the class scale. Economic development is conventionally expected to diminish the economic and political roles of the peasantry and enhance those of an urban, industrial working class or proletariat. In Minas Gerais, state sponsored agricultural modernization produced half this equation: it reduced the size of the peasantry, and substantially increased the urban population. Yet, despite fairly robust levels of job creation, private industry proved incapable of absorbing new, migrant labor, and entry into the ranks of the industrial proletariat was limited. Instead, many former, full-time agricultural workers that migrated to urban areas divided their time between urban employment and temporary, seasonal agricultural labor. Others, who became permanent urban dwellers, were for the most part confined to temporary, unskilled, and poorly remunerated jobs in the construction and service sectors.

The modernization of agriculture

State-supplied capital investment revolutionized traditional agriculture in Brazil in the 1960s and the 1970s. Fiscal incentives attracted private industrial, financial, and commercial capital to agricultural production, supplementing direct state financing. The National Credit System created in 1965 made capital widely available to rural enterprises at real negative interest rates.[23] From 1969 to 1979, the government allocation to finance agriculture and livestock raising rose in real terms five times from 6.5 to 33 billion cruzeiros (Spindle, 1983: 10–11). Easy access to capital made possible the widespread introduction of machinery, especially tractors, fertilizers, and pesticides, into Brazilian agriculture. The consumption of fertilizers, for instance, rose from 221,000 tons in 1959 to over 2.3 million tons in 1976 (Silva and Gasquez, 1982, cited in Spindel, 1983: 11).

The modernization of agriculture also entailed a major production shift from traditional cash and subsistence crops – coffee, corn, beans, and rice – to livestock raising and dairy production, crops for export, and products for domestic food processing (soy, cotton, sesame, cotton), and other industries (e.g., sugarcane for alcohol (Sorj, 1980: 115; IBGE, 1977: 409; Spindel, 1983: 13). In Minas, the most pronounced trend in land use was toward livestock raising and dairy production; land devoted to pasturage increased by nearly 40 percent from 22 million hectares in 1960 to 30 million in 1980 (IBGE, 1977: 401, 435: IBGE, 1980a: 20, 26), at the same time that land in cultivation declined by about one-third.

These changes in traditional agriculture reduced substantially the agricultural labor force. Mechanization made many workers redundant, and the conversion of cultivated land to pasture expelled subsistence activities and lowered the overall demand for rural labor, since animal husbandry was far less labor intensive than crop tillage (Spindel, 1983: 13). In Minas, between 1960 and 1977 the number of persons employed in agriculture declined steadily from 1.8 to 1.5 million, or from 60 percent of the work force to 39 percent (SEPLAN, 1978, 7, I: 171).[24] This decline was even more precipitous relative to other sectors: in 1980, 1.5 million agricultural workers represented only 32 percent of the work force (IBGE, 1980b, 5: 10).

Economic change in the countryside also transformed much of what remained of the rural work force from subsistence farmers into landless laborers. The number of workers employed on a *permanent* basis declined both in absolute terms and in relation to temporary workers. The process of conversion to temporary labor advanced more quickly in Minas Gerais than in many other Brazilian states (Gomes Silva and Rodrigues, 1982, cited in Spindel, 1983: 7). According to official estimates, the number of temporary workers exceeded in 1970 the number of permanent workers by 52.7 percent in Minas Gerais as opposed to 25.2 percent in São Paulo (IBGE, 1977: 409).

23 In 1970, interest rates on government agricultural loans were 11.3 percent while the rate of inflation was 19.3 percent; a decade later, average agricultural interest rates of 20 percent were far below the official inflation rate of 110 percent.

24 These numbers differ slightly from those reported in the official census for 1970 (1.97 million), but they represent the most complete set of figures, and the trend is in the same direction and at approximately the same rate of decline. According to 1980 census figures, there were 1.5 million agricultural workers in the state, which represented only 32 percent of the work force (IBGE, 1980b, 5: 10).

One factor contributing to swelling the ranks of temporary laborers was the subdivision and proliferation of *minifundia*. *Minifundistas*, owners of bare subsistence plots, hire themselves out as day laborers on large farms to supplement their meager earnings (Sorj, 1980: 130). The number of *minifundia*, especially at the lower end of the scale, rose sharply in Minas Gerais in the 1960s and 1970s (Table 3.4). Farms of less than five hectares tripled from 25,000 in 1950 to 74,000 in 1980, and increased one and a half times as a percent of all farms. Crop conversion also played a small part in this change; cane, soy, and fruits (especially oranges), whose production doubled during this period, require substantially more workers during the harvest than during other stages of production.

The shift from the use of permanent to temporary labor was also accelerated by a political development – the passage of the Rural Worker Statute (Estatuto do Trabalhador Rural) in 1963 and the Land Statute (Estatuto da Terra) in 1964. The first extended labor rights to rural workers, the second some security of land tenure (Martinez-Alier and Boito Júnior, 1978: 294). Although legislation had been on the books since 1943 granting rural workers such labor rights as a minimum wage, annual paid holidays, and compensation if fired for "unjust causes," this coverage afforded little real protection, because the government created no means for its enforcement. Moreover, since rural unions were illegal in this period, there were no channels through which workers could articulate grievances. The Rural Worker Statute redressed the shortcomings of the earlier legislation, introducing a battery of laws that governed such aspects of work as the length of the workday and the work of women and minors, extended social security to the countryside through the creation of FUNRURAL (Malloy, 1979: 120), and established an arbitration council to hear cases of workers' grievances (Spindel, 1983: 14–15). The statutes' aims were to provide permanent workers residing on rural estates with the same benefits that their urban counterparts enjoyed. Their effect, however, was quite different.

Estate owners responded to rural labor legislation by expelling resident agricultural workers to avoid their obligations as employers, and rehiring those same workers on a temporary basis (Sorj, 1980: 127). Employers in the state of São Paulo cited the Rural Worker Statute as a factor impelling them to change over to temporary labor, not so much for the economic costs associated with permanent employees – minimum wage, thirteenth month salary, paid holidays – as for the advantages this statute gave workers in labor disputes (Spindel, 1983: 15–16). Rural workers won the majority of court cases brought against their patrons, for which they were awarded sizable compensation (Spindel, 1983: 16). This two-tiered labor market structure was formalized in 1973. Acknowledging that temporary workers had no de facto rights, new legislation formally withdrew legal recognition of rural workers who were not regular, permanent employees of a single estate.

Table 3.4. Minas Gerais: Farm size, 1950–80

Farm size (in hectares)	1950			1960			1980		
	N	% farms	% land	N	% farms	% land	N	% farms	% land
Less than 1	2,025	.8	--	4,437	1.2	--	8,631	1.8	--
1 - 1.99	4,068	1.5	--	8,819	2.4	--	12,767	2.7	--
2 - 4.99	19,440	7.3	.2	39,726	10.7	.4	53,113	11.1	.4
5 - 9.99	26,108	9.8	.6	47,875	12.9	1.0	63,293	13.2	1.0
10 - 99.99	149,130	56.1	16.0	199,658	53.7	19.6	252,353	52.5	19.9
100 - 999.99	59,776	22.5	44.7	66,500	17.9	46.7	83,357	17.3	47.0
1000 - 9999.99	4,889	1.9	29.7	4,727	1.3	26.3	5,260	1.1	23.6
>10,000	120	--	8.6	100	--	5.9	173	.1	8.1
No data	3	--		17	--	--	1,684	.4	--
Total	265,559			371,859			480,631		

Source: IBGE, 1980a: 2–4.

The decline in permanent agricultural employment and the relative abundance of readily contractable labor contributed to the passing of traditional production relations in the Minas countryside and throughout most of southeastern Brazil (IBGE, 1977: 411).[25] Sharecropping, for instance, once the prevalent form of labor in Minas agriculture, began to disappear. In 1960, there were 238,248 sharecroppers in Minas Gerais working on 54,427 farms. In 1970, there were only 123,182 sharecroppers on 11,209 farms, a decline of 79.4 percent in the number of establishments based on sharecropping and a 48.3 percent drop in the number of persons employed under this system (IBGE, 1977: 408).

In the place of traditional labor institutions new relations of production emerged in the countryside based on contracted, wage labor. The most important group of temporary workers were the _boiás-frias_, so-called for the cold lunches that these workers carry to work in the fields. Unlike _minifundistas_, who live on their own farms, and "itinerants," casual laborers under contract to a foreman who live on and move from one large farm to another (thus circumventing the Rural Labor Statute), the _boiás-frias_ typically live on the outskirts of cities and commute to the fields where they are employed on a contract basis as day laborers (D'Incao, 1975: 66, 87–88; Sorj, 1980: 125; Spindel, 1983: 1, 6, 21–22). _Boiás-frias_ journey as much as 20 to 50 kilometers to work, and, during harvest periods, employers recruit workers from as far away as 80 to 100 kilometers (Spindel, 1983: 20). These desperately poor rural laborers suffer acutely from job insecurity; they are to all intents and purposes unemployed for a period of from 90 to 100 days between harvests (D'Incao, 1975: 88–94). During this time, according to official accounts, they must eke out a living in the informal urban sector, usually as street vendors, but also in various menial jobs (IBGE, 1977: 409, 412–13).

Changing labor relations in the countryside, an overall contraction in the rural labor force, and the growing importance of formal credit and the lessening of informal credit (Sorj, 1980: 132) diminished the size of a peasant class that owed its survival to landlords, and thereby reduced the potential for rural elites to dominate this class politically. But the disappearance of traditional rural domination alone did not imply an escape from clientelistic politics, either for those workers who left agriculture or for

25 Even with the fall in agrarian employment _and_ rural population, the supply of labor still outstripped demand throughout the state for many years. The ratio of agrarian employment (the demand for agricultural workers divided by the supply, measured in labor hours), though increasing from 43.6 percent in 1970 to 55.4 percent in 1980, shows that there was an unmistakable excess of rural labor even as late as 1975 and the projections for 1980. While there are exceptions, in the fourth trimester (the harvest) in Planning Regions III, IV, and V in 1980, and III and IV in 1975, only in Region III (the South) in 1980 was the demand for agricultural labor greater on a yearly basis than the pool of available labor (SEPLAN, 1978, 7, I: 183, 185, 186–209).

those who remained. In the rural towns and the larger cities, the state presence in the labor market and labor relations laid the structural basis for a different sort of political clientelism.

The urban labor market

The exodus from agriculture contributed to Minas Gerais's convulsive population migrations of the 1960s and 1970s. Certainly urbanization was underway earlier: in 1940, 25 percent of the population resided in cities, in 1950, 30 percent, and in 1960, 40 percent. But after 1960 the rural population began to decline in absolute terms and the momentum toward the cities accelerated. Minas's urban population outnumbered the rural after 1970, and by 1980 comprised two-thirds of the total population (IBGE, 1983: 76, 78). Over these two decades, the rural population fell by one million inhabitants, while five million more Mineiros resided in cities in 1980 than in 1960. Although official figures tend to overstate the urban population,[26] the process of urbanization was nonetheless intense: the 1980 population census found that 364 predominantly rural municipalities of the state's 722 had fewer residents in 1980 than in 1970 (Estado de Minas, 2/1/ 81: 7), and 41 cities accounted for 90 percent of the state's population growth in the decade (SEPLAN, 1981: 13).

Agricultural modernization and rapid urbanization, when coupled with population growth, hurled more than two million workers onto the urban labor market in Minas Gerais between 1950 and 1980, one million alone from 1970 to 1980. The official census office reported that "the decline in the primary population . . . was not accompanied by a growth in the active population in industry and services at a pace that would make possible the complete absorption of the labor force" (IBGE, 1977: 178). Popular conception and official accounts hold that these workers were forced into marginal employment in the service sector. Vilma Faria (1984: 119, 1986: 80–92) has disputed this belief and accompanying claims that the development process in Brazil gave rise to a greater concentration of the urban population, an insufficient growth in the creation of industrial jobs, and the concentration of poverty in the metropolitan zones of the country. He argues that overall new job creation in Brazil was able to keep pace with population growth – almost 27 million new jobs were created between 1950

---

26 The definitions of urban and rural population in Brazil differ somewhat from internationally accepted criteria. In Brazil seats of municipal and district governments are automatically considered urban, regardless of their size. In 1950 the IBGE counted as urban 30 percent of the population, but only 17 percent of the population resided in centers of 5,000 or more inhabitants. In 1970 the official census registered 53 percent of the Minas population as urban but only 42 percent lived in communities of 3,600 or more inhabitants (SEPLAN, 1978, 5: 17–21).

and 1980 – and, while acknowledging that the largest increase in employment was in the service sector, he also stresses that the secondary sector was quite dynamic, generating as much as 30 percent of the new jobs created in those three decades. Faria also questioned the view that service sector employment is mostly marginal, pointing out that much employment growth in the tertiary sector took place in the transportation and social service sectors that offered stability of employment, reasonable pay levels, and legal protection.

If most Brazilians were not engaged in makeshift employment in the postwar period, the economic model pursued by the military regime did depress the labor market for well-paid industrial and service sector jobs. In Minas Gerais the new capital goods and consumer durables industries established by state, foreign, and Paulista industry did not provide enough new jobs to compensate for those lost in traditional agriculture in the 1970s and in traditional industries that survived the economic crisis of the mid-1960s. Between 1970 and 1980, nearly 200,000 jobs were lost in the agricultural sector. In the industrial sector, the policies of the new military governors to combat the economic crisis, especially the restriction of credit and the reduction of wages (and therefore demand), resulted in the bankruptcy of many firms in the nondurable consumer goods sector throughout Brazil.[27] At a competitive disadvantage, Minas factories were especially hard hit.[28] The state federation of industry estimated that the "traditional sector's" contribution to the gross domestic product declined sharply from 74 percent at the beginning of the decade to 46.4 percent at its end (FIEMG, 1980: 13).[29] The traditional labor-intensive industries that survived in the competitive sugar, dairy, and textile sectors of the economy, moreover, became more productive by replacing antiquated plant equipment and especially by trimming labor rolls. When the recession was over and growth resumes, productivity rose 52 percent from 1970 to 1977 among nondurable goods producers (T. Andrade, 1980: 25). At the same time that productivity rose in the textile industry by 79 percent from 1970 to 1977, only less than 1,000 new jobs (a 3 percent increase in employment) were added (T. Andrade, 1980: 28). Even in those industries that survived the recession of the 1960s and invested in expansions of their plants in the 1970s, the introduction of more technologically sophisticated equipment reduced the need

27 Perhaps the best accounts in English of the stabilization policies of the military government undertaken from 1964 to 1967 are Fishlow (1973, 1989) and Skidmore (1988).
28 The streamlining of Minas's traditional industries is most evident in the textiles and food processing sectors, which in 1960 had represented over half of the Minas industrial product. In the 1959–60 harvest year, 30 (of a total of 36) sugar mills were operating; in 1975, only 15 remained in operation. The number of dairy-producing enterprises was reduced from 601 in 1960 to 450 in 1970, a decline of 25 percent. Bankruptcies also hit the textile industry, where 15 of 98 firms failed between 1965 and 1970, and another 11 after that date (Campolina Diniz, 1978: 123, 126, 128–30, 133; SEPLAN, 1978, 8: 105–7).
29 Unfortunately, "traditional" in this context is not precisely defined.

Table 3.5. *Structure of employment in Minas Gerais, 1950–80*

Sector	1950 N	1950 %	1970 N	1970 %	1980 N	1980 %
Primary	1,618,491	67.4	1,717,333	49.6	1,518,442	32.1
Secondary						
Manufacturing	135,233	5.6	249,987	7.2	562,858	11.9
Construction	76,597	3.2	200,824	5.8	457,310	9.7
Other industry[a]	53,705	2.2	61,249	1.8	95,456	2.0
Total secondary	265,535	11.1	512,060	14.8	1,115,624	23.6
Tertiary						
Distribution[b]	173,444	7.2	349,987	10.1	587,583	12.4
Services	234,999	9.8	492,834	14.2	816,850	17.2
Social services and public admin.	94,036	3.9	280,866	8.1	486,408	10.3
Other[c]	16,307	.7	79,243	2.3	101,109	2.1
Total tertiary	518,786	21.6	1,231,222	35.6	1,991,950	42.0
Looking for work[d]			28,292	.8	110,174	2.3
Total active pop.	2,402,812		3,460,615		4,736,190	

[a]Includes mining and public utility services (electricity, gas, water, and garbage removal).
[b]Includes commerce, transportation, and communication.
[c]Includes real estate and "badly defined" activities.
[d]This category was not distinguished in the 1950 census from "without occupation," and in 1970 it encompassed only those looking for work for the first time. Thus, the data are not comparable across those decades.
Sources: IBGE, 1950: 34–35; 1970: 74–78; 1980b, 5: 29–34.

for new labor.[30] Thus, although the manufacturing sector generated the largest percentage increase in employment in the 1970s, it did so on a significantly smaller base than other sectors (Table 3.5). Even with a 50 percent increase in industrial employment, only approximately 150,000 new manufacturing jobs were created between 1970 and 1977 as a result of the local economic miracle (Table 3.6). The service sector by far absorbed more workers; by 1980, it employed 43.9 percent of all economically active persons in the state.

30 This argument is made by T. Andrade (1980: 22–28). The author's data on the contributions to the industrial product, productivity, and employment of each industrial group (nondurable consumer, intermediate, and capital and durable consumer goods) and economic sector confirm that employment varies inversely with productivity, and that overall growth rates were based on the greater value of the industrial product of low labor-absorbing sectors.

Table 3.6. *Minas Gerais: Employment by economic sector, 1960, 1970,*
1977

Sector	1960		1970		1977	
	N	%	*N*	%	*N*	%
Agriculture	1,819,516	60.4	1,714,109	50.4	1,539,696	39.1
Mining	31,551	1.0	43,088	1.3	47,555	1.2
Manufacturing	192,223	6.4	283,803	8.4	429,841	10.9
Construction	110,100	3.7	197,078	5.8	307,112	7.8
Services	857,454	28.5	1,157,850	34.1	1,614,914	41.0
Total	3,010,844		3,395,928		3,939,118	

Source: SEPLAN, 1978, 7, 1: 171.

The service sector, as Faria correctly asserts, includes a number of well-paid and secure scientific and liberal professionals (physicians, technicians, journalists). Yet, much other service sector employment is marginal. Fully one-quarter of service sector workers are poorly compensated domestic and personal service workers (maids and beauticians). Nearly 60 percent of workers in personal services in 1980 earned less than the monthly "minimum salary," the legally defined margin of subsistence, whereas in all economic sectors that proportion was approximately 40 percent (IBGE, 1980b, 5: 57–60). Between the two extremes, the service sector encompasses a diverse range of jobs in commerce (20 percent of the sector), transportation and communication (10 percent), food and repair services (5 percent each), finance (5 percent), and various public administration and public services (25 percent) (IBGE, 1980b, 5: 29–34). While some of these jobs are quite attractive, others are not.

State-led capitalist development that produced a labor force of poorly integrated and remunerated workers, did not, however, merely dump displaced workers into an amorphous "informal sector" that eluded state regulation and control. To the contrary, it pushed the urban labor force into a condition of dependence on the state in multiple ways. First, the state generated a significant amount of employment during the period of military rule. In the nation as a whole, employment directly or indirectly related to nonproductive state functions increased almost five times in thirty years (Faria, 1986: 92). This tendency was particularly accentuated in Minas Gerais. The two sectors registering the highest growth in employment from 1970 to 1980, in relation to national averages and past state trends, were "social services and public administration" and construction. The social services and public administration sector generated more new jobs than did the manufacturing industry, and construction employment in-

Table 3.7. *Distribution of new employment opportunity:*
Minas Gerais versus Brazil

Sector	1950-70		1970-80		1950-80	
	MG[a]	Brazil	MG[a]	Brazil	MG[a]	Brazil
Primary	9.3	22.8	-11.6	.2	-6.2	10.7
Secondary						
Manufacturing	10.8	13.1	24.5	25.4	18.3	19.7
Construction	11.7	9.1	20.1	10.1	16.3	9.6
Other industry[b]	.7	.8	2.7	2.3	1.8	1.6
Total secondary	22.3	23.1	47.3	37.8	36.4	30.9
Tertiary						
Distribution[b]	16.7	14.7	18.6	17.6	17.7	16.3
Services	24.4	17.2	25.4	22.2	24.9	19.9
Social services and public admin.	17.7	14.2	16.1	15.3	16.8	14.8
Other[b]	5.9	7.9	1.7	6.9	3.6	7.4
Total tertiary	64.7	54.1	61.8	62.0	63.1	58.4

[a]Percentages do not sum to 100 because of unemployment.
[b]For explanation of categories, see Table 3.5.
Sources: Table 3.5; Faria, 1984: 149.

creased in the state at double the national average (Table 3.7). Construction employment in Brazil, upon which Faria placed great weight in his interpretation of the structure of employment opportunity and which accounted for 10 percent of new jobs in the country as a whole and one-third of secondary employment in the period from 1950 to 1980, is not always secure, well-remunerated employment. Often, it is created on a temporary basis by state public works projects.

In Minas Gerais, the federal, state, and municipal governments directly employed large numbers. One-quarter of all service sector employment was formally state employment, representing a diverse range of state jobs including administrative workers, personnel specialists, doctors, teachers, and transportation workers. Five areas of public employment (government, public education, public health, sanitation, and communication) accounted for 10 percent of total employment in the state in 1977 (Table 3.8), more than double the amount employed in these same professions in 1960. The number of persons employed as public school teachers (186,000) particularly stands out.[31] Moreover, nearly one-fifth of the state's industrial employment is in

31 Throughout the developed Southeast (the states of Minas Gerais, São Paulo, Rio de Janeiro, Espírito Santo, and Guanabara), the census reports that the growth in the tertiary population employed in teaching rose 281.5 percent between 1950 and 1970.

Table 3.8. *Minas Gerais: Public sector employment, 1960, 1970, 1977*

Areas	1960		1970		1977	
	1,000 persons	%	1,000 persons	%	1,000 persons	%
Government	69.0	2.3	98.0	2.8	123.1	3.2
Public education	54.0	1.8	112.0	3.3	186.4	4.8
Public health	12.0	0.4	18.0	0.5	23.6	0.6
Sanitation	13.0	0.4	20.0	0.6	25.9	0.7
Communication	10.0	0.3	14.0	0.4	17.7	0.4
Total	158.0	5.2	252.0	7.6	376.7	9.7

Source: SEPLAN, 1978, 6, 2: 259.

state enterprises.[32] By the late 1970s, therefore, the number of direct public employees (approximately 445,000) exceeded that of industrial workers in the private sphere (approximately 343,000). Where intermediate-sized communities hosted state and federal agencies and new state-owned or assisted industries, the impact on local economies was considerable.

State spending also generated an impressive number of indirect jobs. How much indirect employment can be attributed to public expenditure in Brazil is hard to ascertain,[33] but the example of the construction sector is instructive. Construction encompasses housing, government buildings (schools, hospitals, bus stations), and civil engineering. In Minas Gerais, where 457,310 persons were employed in construction in 1980 (an increase of 50 percent with respect to 1977), at least 73,000 new jobs in the sector were officially credited to state spending on housing in 1980 alone (SEPLAN, 1981: 97).[34] The contribution of the national housing program to the substan-

32 The number of workers in the state enterprises was obtained by counting employees in those federal and state public enterprises headquartered in Minas Gerais (55,268), as reported in Visão (1981), plus some of those employed in federal state enterprises headquartered in other states but known to employ vast numbers of Mineiros, such as the federal railway authority and the Rio Doce Mining Company (CVRD). This should be interpreted as a minimum figure, for at least 20,000 workers in the public utility companies (e.g., 7,671 in the state telephone company, and 11,311 in CEMIG) were not included because of the possibility they might have been counted as "communications" workers in Table 3.8.

33 In calculating this measure for the United States, O'Connor (1973: 17) estimated that when production organized by industries under contract with the state (such as highway construction) was added to the state sector, the percentage of the civilian labor force employed by the state rose from about one-eighth to perhaps as much as one-third. Given comparable levels of direct state employment and the more pervasive presence of the Brazilian state in the productive sectors of the economy, indirect employment generated by state spending may have been at least as much.

34 Chubb (1981) also reports a high percentage of employment in construction in Palermo, Sicily, due to state spending.

tial increase in construction employment between 1950 and 1970 in southeastern Brazil was acknowledged officially by the IBGE (1977: 184).

Finally, the state assumed responsibility for cushioning the blows of precarious employment through supplemental programs. These are discussed in Chapter 5.

INDUSTRIAL CONCENTRATION AND UNEVEN DEVELOPMENT

The rapid industrialization of the 1970s exacerbated a preexisting pattern of uneven, concentrated spatial development. On the eve of the economic boom, economic opportunity and industrial employment was concentrated in Planning Region I (for planning purposes, the state has been divided into eight regions, which correspond closely to state zonal divisions accepted by popular convention). Region I encompasses the metropolitan region of the capital city, Belo Horizonte, and lying 200 kilometers to its northeast, the "Valley of Steel," so called for the giant steel enterprises of Usiminas and Acesita in the city that now bears the latter's name (formerly Timóteo). Region I was home to slightly more than one-quarter of the state's population and produced over half of the gross domestic product and almost three-fourths of the industrial product in 1970 (L. Andrade, 1980: 123; *Estado de Minas*, 2/1/81: 8; SEPLAN, 1978, 5: 99). The only other regions that hosted any industry of note were the Mata and the South. For the most part, these were traditional textile and food industries serving the Rio and São Paulo markets. Region I received over 80 percent of all new industrial investment from 1970 to 1977, the lion's share of which was targeted to the area's steel industries and the increasingly dense cluster of manufacturing plants in the metropolitan region of the state capital.[35] Metropolitan Belo Horizonte alone acquired one-third of all investment channeled through the Industrial Development Institute from 1969 to 1980 (INDI, 1980: 3–4). Only two other regions, III and VI, made significant strides toward industrialization during the decade. Region III was host to many relocated Paulista industries. Region VI became a preferred site for industrial location because of the double fiscal incentives it could offer investors: in addition to the state fiscal incentives available to all investors, new industrial investors in this region qualified for a second set of federal economic incentives because the region fell within the jurisdiction of the Superintendency for the Development of the Northeast (SUDENE).[36]

35 The Usiminas and Açominas steel plants were both located in Region I.
36 Officially recognizing the plight of the underdeveloped Northeast, the Brazilian government created SUDENE in 1959 to foster and coordinate economic development in the region. SUDENE expected to attract industry to the Northeast with a program of fiscal incentives that enabled companies already located in Brazil to apply 50 percent of their income tax liability to investments in projects approved by SUDENE, which in turn qualified for low-interest financing from the Bank of the Northeast (BNB) and the North-

Industrial development was even more concentrated than regional-level data would lead us to believe. A strategy of "dispersed concentrations"[37] carried out by the state Industrial Districts Company favored the successful development of new industrial centers, such as Poços de Caldas, Varginha/ Três Corações, Itajubá, and Pouso Alegre in the South of Minas; Montes Claros in the North, and Uberaba and Uberlândia in the Triângulo. All but 18 percent of new industrial jobs created in Minas from investments contracted during the height of the investment binge between 1971 and 1974 were located in about twenty-five municipalities (Table 3.9). One-third of all new employment was generated in the metropolitan region of the state capital.

The Minas industrial explosion was more accurately a series of isolated eruptions, confined to what may be termed industrial enclaves. Vast tracts of Mineiro territory were cordoned off from industrial growth; hundreds of Minas Gerais's 722 *municípios* were left virtually untouched by industrial transformation. The industrial work force that did form was clustered territorially. Indeed, as of 1980, concentrated industrialization and uneven spatial development had resulted in more continuity than change. The spatial pattern of industrial development accorded to traditional elites the opportunity to retain their power bases in more cities and towns than had industrialization proceeded in a more spatially diffuse manner.

CONCLUSIONS

The economic development of Minas Gerais in the 1970s confirms what by now should be an obvious conclusion: where state capitalism bolstered by foreign capital is the prevailing form of economic organization, industrialization may not engender the two great industrial classes – bourgeoisie and proletariat – upon whose political roles much social science theory bases its understanding of the transition to industrial society. Even if these classes emerge, their resources, and hence political role, may differ from that

east Investment Fund (FINOR). Companies located in this region also benefited from an exemption of up to 80 percent of the import duty for new equipment and a rebate of up to 60 percent on the ICM (value-added tax) (INDI, 1978: 152–54). For an early evaluation of the program, see Hirschman (1963). As a result of these added incentives and the ability of the state's industrial investment institute to package the Minas territory included in the SUDENE region as that closest to major southeastern Brazilian markets, the number of industrial projects submitted to SUDENE for location in Minas Gerais rose from only 2 as of 1967 (Campolina Diniz, 1978: 148) to 120 in 1978 (INDI, 1978: 152).

37 "Dispersed concentrations" is a term used by a superintendent of the Industrial Development Institute to describe the spatial pattern of Minas development (author's interview with Eduardo de Mello Cruz, Belo Horizonte, January 23, 1981). It appeared, based on a reading of correspondence between the Industrial Districts Company and the Industrial Development Institute, that the CDI and INDI persuaded various foreign and national investors to locate their plants in these districts.

Table 3.9. *Minas Gerais: New industrial employment by município, 1971–74*

	N of projects	New jobs created	
		N	%
Region I			
Belo Horizonte	50	7,188	5.3
Betim	17	17,323	12.7
Contagem	60	11,150	8.2
Santa Luzia	18	4,501	3.3
Vespasiano	7	1,249	.9
Pedro Leopoldo	6	1,248	.9
Lagoa Santa	2	417	.3
Metropolitan region	165	43,076	31.6
Ipatinga	5	6,057	4.5
Timóteo	2	1,583	1.2
Monlevade	2	1,800	1.3
Belo Oriente	1	3,700	2.7
Itabírito	4	2,069	1.5
Itaúna	7	4,640	3.4
Sete Lagoas	9	1,106	.8
Region II			
Juiz de Fora	21	6,765	5.0
Region III			
Varginha	4	2,225	1.6
Três Corações	3	1,396	1.0
Pouso Alegre	7	4,155	3.1
Poços de Caldas	13	2,579	1.9
Itajubá	8	3,689	2.7
Region IV			
Uberlândia	12	2,557	1.9
Araxá	2	1,700	1.3
Region V			
Morada Nova	1	10,000	7.4
Region VI			
Montes Claros	25	8,918	6.6
Pirapora	5	862	.6
Várzea da Palma	4	1,138	.8
Others and under study	167	25,387	18.7
Total	467	135,402	

Source: Pacheco, 1975: 64–85.

anticipated by historical precedent and conventional theory. As Cardoso (1989: 310) recently reflected on the development model which over twenty years ago he called "associated-dependent development": "the society which associated-dependent development wrought broke in significant aspects with the images which the sociological literature elaborated to describe the 'effects of industrialization' and of capitalization of the periphery." In restructuring patterns of economic ownership and redrawing the lines between public and private economic activity, state-led capitalist development produced a distinctive constellation of classes, class interests, and class power, all defined in relation to the public economy.

The industrialization of Minas Gerais, conducted as part of the military's economic program, reinforced patterns of traditional regional politics to a greater extent than it transformed them. Led by an interventionist state and foreign investors, the economic upheaval bypassed the local bourgeoisie. This class, whose prior failure to spark industrialization is presumed to have necessitated state capitalism, remained weak economically even after industrialization was well underway. Despite every advantage the state could offer – financing, the purchase of already sound enterprises, or joint ventures – local industrialists could not participate meaningfully alongside foreign capital and the state at the cutting edge of local industrialization. The entrepreneurs that did participate and grow stronger – other national and foreign investors – did not have the political means with which to intrude upon local politics. As Cardoso (1989: 310) has argued, "big foreign capital appears socially as an international bureaucracy, made up of professional administrators, with a strong 'structural presence,' but with enormous difficulty in becoming a class for itself at the level of local politics." The absence of a strong class of local industrialists left a political vacuum in which incumbent political elites benefited not only from the lack of formidable foes but also from taking credit for the new investments. In the two northeastern municipalities studied by Chilcote (1990: 314), development projects that were state and foreign, not locally, funded "brought local power holders both prestige and economic advantage." Because the lower-income people who stood to gain from an increase in jobs were incorporated into the local political machinery, "the participation of the state in local government projects . . . tended to reinforce the position of the local ruling class." Similarly, in the most dynamic communities in Minas Gerais traditional local elites turned industrialization to their advantage, as we shall see in Chapters 5 and 6.

The highly capital-intensive industrialization strategy adopted by new and expanding industries in advance sectors generated fewer jobs than did extensive state investments in production and physical and social infrastructure. Mechanization, crop conversion and new systems of labor relations led to the expulsion of estate laborers and the shrinking of both the dependent and independent, property-owning small peasant. Unable to find work in the modern-sector labor market, they by and large became a seasonally employed agrarian wage-labor force that resided in urban areas and lived in precarious circumstances. The extreme, if not uncommon, spatial concentration of industry made the political upheaval manageable.

If the primary economic beneficiaries of the industrialization of Minas Gerais were foreign investors and Paulista entrepreneurs, the *political* beneficiaries were state elites. The expansion of state resources and clients augmented the power associated with holding elected and appointed positions in the Brazilian state. Where the state is intricately involved in the economy, political demands tend to cluster around what the public economy has to offer, and political success depends upon access to state resources. Similar to prebendary and patrimonial systems, state positions are not merely honorific but significant sources of economic and political power. Their value, moreover, only increases as more citizens are integrated into the public sector economy and look to state elites to deliver the social services, public works programs, and other state benefits on which they come to depend. For a class such as the traditional political elite that had demonstrated its skill at converting state resources into political resources, maintaining its place in the state was both its major challenge and opportunity.

4

Bureaucratic authoritarianism and the state elite

In the early 1960s, the traditional political elite was anchored in and dominated the state. It commanded the executive, legislative, and judicial branches of federal, state, and local governments, as well as the state militias. In 1964 when it perceived a threat to its hegemony, it conspired with military and other civilian elites to overthrow the constitutional regime and safeguard oligarchical privilege. While politicians in the UDN, the party of the "outs," hoped to gain more from the military coup than did their rivals in the PSD, the traditional political elite as a whole fully expected to share power with the military. Members of the elite anticipated that a caretaker military government would demobilize autonomous mass movements, purge Communists and other political undesirables from government and the arena of formal politics, and then promptly restore to them the reins of state.

The military did, as the traditional elite hoped, swiftly and decisively dismantle the populist coalition that had supported the deposed President Goulart. But instead of restoring power to Goulart's civilian rivals in the parties of the oligarchy, it excluded them from power. The military reserved governing power for itself, balked at adhering to a timetable for new presidential elections, and began an assault on the practice of politics within the state. The new rulers centralized economic policy making in the national ministries, strengthened the executive in firm military hands, and purged key federal state posts of traditional as well as populist politicians and replaced these with uniformed military officers and civilian economists, engineers, educators, and professional administrators – the core of a new technocratic elite. Slowly, the shape of a bureaucratic-authoritarian state took form.

In the states, where traditional politics and regional oligarchies were rooted, the military interrupted the normal processes of competitive politics in order to assure the selection of compliant governors, who, in turn, were entrusted to carry out similar changes in the executive branch of the state governments. In Minas Gerais, after the governor loyal to former president Juscelino Kubitschek, Israel Pinheiro, exited from office, Rondon Pacheco, a trusted confidant of the military, was named his successor. Pacheco brought with him to office a technocratic team and launched a local version of the national development program. Focusing largely on his administration, many works postulated that traditional political elites in Minas had been dislodged from key posts by technocrats (L. Andrade, 1980; Campolina Diniz, 1978; Cintra, 1979; Grossi, 1977,1979), and that the slide of one was directly proportional to the rise of the other.

The military's attempt to transform significantly the Brazilian state deprived the oligarchy of much of its formal state power. For the Minas traditional political elite in particular, whose private economic base was too heterogeneous to wield economic power and concentrated in sectors inappropriate for exercising dominance in an urbanizing, industrializing region, bureaucratic authoritarianism seriously challenged the basis on which it had organized its power. The state positions and control over patronage resources that had underlain traditional elite power in Minas Gerais during the populist era became only more valuable with the rising stakes in controlling a state leading economic development. The future prospects, indeed survival, of the traditional political elite depended on the ability of its members to maintain or regain their positions in the state.

This chapter explores the scope and effect of the military's political project to displace traditional politicians from power and to reconstruct the state on a basis of technocratic governance. It examines the place of the traditional political elite in the state government of Minas Gerais from 1964 to 1982, the extent to which the executive branch of the state was penetrated by a technocratic elite, and the balance of power within the state between politicians and technocrats. It also considers if there were discernible shifts in the type of technical experts and politicians who held office, that is, if indeed a "technocracy" achieved power, and if the "oligarchy" survived the change of regime. What it finds is that the ambitions of the hard-line factions of the military were never fully realized. A sharp increase in the presence of technocrats in state government did not mean that a "technocracy" had grabbed power and that the state's traditional political elite suffered an irreversible erosion of its power and position in the state. Politicians returned in greater numbers to prominent positions in the state cabinet of Minas Gerais very shortly after scholars had noticed their absence, and state office was parceled out in such a way that permitted both technocrats to be effective and the traditional elite to conduct political business as usual: those parts of the state that controlled economic policy, of special concern to the military, were the first given to and the last taken away from technocrats, while those that controlled political appointments and patronage were under the control of politicians for most of the period of military rule.

On closer examination, the bureaucratic-authoritarian regime eventually not only restored politicians to the state, but also resurrected the most traditional elements of the state oligarchy. Within the ranks of the political class, the *traditional* political elite survived in the state to a greater degree than did "ordinary" politicians. From the beginning of the regime, the military was forced to look to the traditional elements of the political class when it needed civilian support (cf. Linz, 1973: 238). For a brief period between 1969 and 1971, during the administration of the hard-line president Emílio Garrastazú Médici, that support appeared expendable. But around 1974 the economic miracle began to slow and technocratic efficiency transparently failed in one crucial area: generating political support for a regime that kept open channels of mediation between state and society. From that time, the soft-line faction of the military, once again in control, abandoned the political project enshrined by President Médici and worked to resurrect the military-traditional political elite alliance.

Even if bureaucratic authoritarianism did not permanently impair the functioning of traditional politics, the Minas elite as a whole was subtly reconfigured in the ebb-and-flow process by which members of the political elite, and especially traditional politicians, regained their power base in the state. The political elite of a more developed region and complex state was better educated and qualified at the end of the authoritarian regime than it was as its outset; sons of oligarchical families became engineers, and traditional politicians were willing to work with the technical elite to manage the affairs of the state. The elite, like clientelism, underwent some necessary degree of "modernization."

THE BUREAUCRATIC-AUTHORITARIAN REGIME

The heterogeneous coalition of civilian and military forces that assumed power in 1964 proceeded on its political course without consensus on who should govern the new regime and what its priorities should be. The legalistic wing of the military, the *sorbonistas,* and its civilian allies in the UDN, who first emerged in command of the "Revolution" intended in a limited term in office only to institute the reforms necessary to rationalize the bureaucracy, raise productivity so as to allow capitalism to flourish, and restore "free" political competition to the electoral arena, which in practice meant enabling the UDN to achieve the victories that had eluded it through most of the postwar period (Velasco e Cruz and Martins, 1984: 18 – 19; Skidmore, 1988: 40).[1] The new president Humberto Castello Branco, who headed this coalition, eventually succumbed to pressure exerted by hard-line factions of the military that preferred to retain power in order to implement the military's own political agenda rather than hand it back to civilian elites. The hard-liners hoped to cleanse the state of the blight of

---

1 According to Velasco e Cruz and Martins (1984: 19), the perception was that because the PSD and PTB controlled the state apparatus, and thus state patronage, the UDN never had a fair chance to win national office.

"corrupt" politicians, clientelistic practices, and politics that they believed stood in the way of development (Sarles Jenks, 1979: 321). An early sign of their intentions came in June 1964 when the political rights of former president Juscelino Kubitschek were stripped. As Skidmore (1988: 26) has written of this watershed event, "Kubitschek's . . . 1956–61 presidency had been the last triumph of old-style politics. The hard-line military wanted to pronounce those politics a thing of the past. Turning Kubitschek into a political non-person certainly sent that message."

The divisions within the military and the slow-developing nature of military rule produced a measurable degree of ambiguity in the form the regime took. On the one hand, it was the prototypal "bureaucratic-authoritarian regime." In an effort to depoliticize important areas of economic and social policy, the military appointed to prominent governmental positions technical experts who previously had successful careers in complex and highly bureaucratized organizations (such as the armed forces and the public bureaucracy) (O'Donnell, 1973: 91). The military favored these technical experts, who are most commonly referred to by their term of opprobrium, technocrats, to steer the economy through the turbulent course of stabilization both because they had the necessary skills and experience and because they were unencumbered by political and electoral pressures.[2] By contrast politicians, the military believed, were incompetent and weak-willed. Military hard-liners were scornful of the alliance of traditional elite and populist politicians (embodied in the PSD-PTB electoral coalition) that had governed Brazil for most of the postwar period for such displays of weakness as calling off the stabilization program in 1959 and acquiescing in the months leading up to the coup in 1964 to workers' demands for what they perceived as inflationary wage increases. Technocrats were quite willing to serve the military, readily abandoning any allegiance to political democracy, because they could be more influential and their policies more effective in an "excluding" authoritarian political system (O'Donnell, 1973: 85; Skidmore, 1973: 17, 19–20, 46).

On the other hand, the Brazilian regime was also an "atypical" bureaucratic-authoritarian regime in that it did not completely depoliticize society and the state. Even at the height of the dictatorship, this regime did not eliminate classic representative institutions (Lamounier, 1980: 18). It permitted regularly scheduled elections; the convening of national and state legislatures for all but two brief periods;[3] and the direct election of mayors

---

2 I have used the term "technocrat" not in the pejorative sense but because the alternative, "technician," is inadequate to describe those experts who are alleged to have accumulated political influence.

3 The national Congress was recessed in December 1968 until well into 1969 for its refusal to lift immunity for Márcio Moreira Alves, a deputy whom the military wished to prosecute for a speech "insulting military dignity" (he urged military wives in an "Operation Lysistrata" to withhold their sexual favors from the men in uniform until the government ceased its

in all but state capitals, "national security" areas, and, inexplicably, tourist cities known as *"estâncias hidrominerais."*[4] It created two political parties, the progovernment National Renovating Alliance (ARENA) and the opposition Brazilian Democratic Movement (MDB), which had no real chance of winning elections but whose presence in the political system was nonetheless symbolically important. By designing an "artificial and unrepresentative party system quite appropriate to protracted authoritarian rule," it provided an "institutionally democratic facade and . . . domesticated semi-opposition . . . without imposing any serious restrictions upon executive power" (Schmitter, 1973: 211).

The military governed in an arbitrary fashion typical of authoritarian regimes, but it attempted to mask that rule within a legal framework. Seventeen "institutional acts" and more than 100 "complementary acts" – unilateral declarations on the part of the military governors – established the parameters for military rule. They dictated electoral laws and juridical practice, and they modified and superseded the existing constitution. The first institutional acts declared the military "Revolution" and parried challenges to military rule. Institutional Act Number 4 brought into being a new constitution in 1967. In December 1968 the notorious Fifth Institutional Act, which laid the foundation of the authoritarian regime and inaugurated the harshest years of the dictatorship, strictly curtailed opposition to the regime by empowering the president to suspend constitutional guarantees, including the writ of habeas corpus, indefinitely, canceling the mandates of select, rebellious officeholders, stripping citizens of their political rights, and imposing military censorship on the press.

To depoliticize policy and permit the technocrats autonomy, the bureaucratic-authoritarian regime first strengthened the authority of the executive and institutionalized its independence from elected representatives in the legislature through a series of constitutional changes that restricted the possible initiatives and responses of Congress in formulating budgets and enacting legislation. The size of the congressional majority required to approve presidentially proposed amendments to the constitution was decreased from two-thirds to a simple majority. Congress had thirty days (later changed to forty) in which to consider these proposed constitutional amendments and other executive-initiated bills; the lapsing of this period, known as the *decurso de prazo,* resulted in their automatic enactment into law (Brazil, 1981: 40–45). Only the president could initiate finance bills; Congress could not even increase the expenditure levels for items submit-

repression), and again in April 1977, when the regime enacted a package of electoral measures designed to preserve government party majorities. In the first six months of 1969, many state legislatures, including those of São Paulo and Rio de Janeiro, were also suspended (Skidmore, 1988: 79, 82).

4 *Estâncias hidrominerais,* or spas, are resort or tourist cities with fountains and natural mineral water springs that allegedly possess healing properties.

ted by the executive (Roett, 1984: 128). In the first two and one-half years of military government, the executive sent to the legislature 733 bills, 11 constitutional amendments, and a new constitution (Schmitter, 1971: 251). During the Médici presidency, 100 percent of executive-initiated bills were passed (Wesson and Fleischer, 1983: 82).

Second, the executive was empowered to enact legislation by decree, which bypassed the legislature altogether. In the first three years of military rule, Castello Branco issued 19,259 decrees and 312 decree laws (Schmitter, 1971: 251); his successor, Costa e Silva, issued more than 4,000 in his two years in office (1967–69) (Schmitter, 1973: 190). Typically, executive decrees were employed for unpopular measures in order to spare government deputies from future electoral peril.

Whenever the Congress displayed initiative, attempted independent action, or appeared to rebel against executive will, institutional procedures could be and easily were rewritten. Moreover, the repressive arm of the state was invoked to punish acts of defiance; individual senators and deputies who dared to challenge the regime openly were expelled from the Congress and stripped of their political rights, above all the right to stand for office. Between 1964 and 1967, Institutional Acts Numbers 1 and 2 were invoked to cancel the mandates of 76 members of Congress, and after 1968, under the draconian Institutional Act Number 5, 113 senators and federal deputies, too, lost their mandates (Alves, 1985: 96).[5] Such acts of censure were known as *cassações,* and their victims, the *cassados.*

Within the executive branch of government, control of the economy was concentrated in a select group of ministries of the federal cabinet, banks, and interministerial councils – the Ministries of Planning and Finance, the Central Bank, the Bank of Brazil, the National Economic Development Bank, the Price Council, the Industrial Development Council, and the National Monetary Council. From the outset of the regime, President Castello Branco (1967–67) entrusted the direction of these ministries, banks, and state councils to civilian and military technocrats such as Roberto Campos (Ames, 1973; Bresser Pereira, 1984; Malloy, 1979; L. Martins, 1977, 1985; McDonough, 1981a, 1981b; Mendes, 1980; Roett, 1984; Schneider, 1971; Skidmore, 1973; Stepan, 1971: 185), and the technocratic presence in government became even greater with the ascension of the hard-line military to power. Costa e Silva appointed ten military and nine civilian ministers to his cabinet (Schneider, 1971: 205). The new team's leader, a thirty-eight-year-old economics professor from São Paulo, Antônio Delfim Neto, became known as the "czar" of Brazil's "economic miracle" of the 1970s.

After 1969 the technocratic presence in the state reached its zenith.

5 Invoking Institutional Acts Numbers 1 and 2, the Castello Branco government also purged 100 state legislators, 11 city councillors, 10 state governors, and 27 mayors between 1964 and 1967, and under Institutional Act Number 5, canceled the mandates of 190 state deputies, 38 city councillors, and 30 mayors (Alves, 1985: 96–98).

President Médici appointed more technocrats, administrators, and political unknowns to top national cabinet positions than any previous Brazilian president (Sarles, 1982: 49; Skidmore, 1988: 106). Whereas from 1946 to 1964 60 percent of federal cabinet ministers had had legislative experience and only 26 percent technical experience, between 1964 and 1974 only 29 percent had served in the legislature but 52 percent had had technical careers and 11 percent were military officers (Nunes, 1978: 61). Not only professional politicians but also representatives of economic and social interests who typically had held such posts as finance minister in previous governments were excluded formally from the inner circles of power (Nunes, 1978: 63). The president's key advisers were almost exclusively military and technobureaucratic elites. According to Skidmore (1988: 106), "the Médici government claimed it was a state rising 'above' its society, with technocrats and military ruling in the best interests of the nominally unrepresented social sectors. As Médici explained in October 1969, he had chosen his ministers while 'immune to pressures of any kind . . . whether political, military, or economic.' "

Technocratic penetration of government extended deep into the federal administration. The "political" heads of the Retirement and Pension Institutes (IAPs) of the social security system, for example, were replaced with "apolitical" technocrats who had risen through the social insurance system, thus cutting off an important source of patronage from pro-Goulart populist labor leaders – the *pelegos* (Malloy, 1979: 124–25). Substantial turnover within the upper echelons of the bureaucracy, moreover, suggests that after 1964 the bureaucracy became vulnerable to the change in national political command. All 107 top state administrators (directors, superintendents, and department heads) – 66 in state enterprises and 41 in government – surveyed by Martins in 1976 had assumed their posts after 1964 (Martins, 1985: 197). This group was also made more responsive to the military: practically all the top state administrators who had taken courses at the Superior War College or belonged to the college's alumni association (ADESG) (less than 25 percent) had established those connections after the coup. The expansion of the state and particularly the state enterprises created more opportunity for technocrats. Sixty percent of the administrators entered their departments or agencies only after 1964, and two-thirds assumed the post they held in 1976 after 1974 (when General Geisel assumed the presidency) (Martins, 1985: 197–98).

Brazil was hardly the first country in which technocrats were present in high levels of government. Running the modern state has everywhere long depended on public administration, and, as Meynaud (1968: 72) claims, "the establishment of an absolute separatism between the political and administrative sectors has never been more than a simple piece of legal fiction." The ever increasing complexity of the administration of state services heightened even further the influence of professional managers and experts in government who hold the monopoly on technical knowledge (acquired through education or longevity in a particular department) needed to write legislation, model economic planning, and otherwise "run the state." Nor was the presence of technocrats in the Brazilian state novel to the period of recent military rule. Technocrats served in high office in the 1930s under Getúlio Vargas and again in the 1950s under both Vargas and Juscelino Kubitschek. Kubitschek in particular enhanced their effectiveness as economic managers and "insulated" them from political pressures by appointing them to new state agencies that he endowed with independence from legislative and ministerial interference in recruitment and funding (Geddes, 1990).

The role of technocrats in government during military rule in Brazil allegedly differed from instances of technocratic influence and decision making both in the more modern, more complex societies of Europe and North America and in the recent Brazilian past in one critical respect. Whereas in democratic regimes technocrats are, by and large, not allowed to implement their plans above the policy guidelines laid down by elected political representatives, under bureaucratic authoritarianism they were perceived as encountering no such limits on policy choice and law making.[6] If this perception is true, by granting technocrats autonomy from political elites in a broad range of departments and functions, military intervention would have provided them with the opportunity to achieve maximum influence, what Meynaud (1968: 30) calls the "open dispossession" of politicians, or pure technocracy.

By their very essence, then, bureaucratic authoritarianism provided both support for and a challenge to the traditional political elite. In sharply restricting "public contestation," in revoking the political rights of challengers to elite hegemony, and in using the state apparatus to depoliticize organized labor, the regime benefited virtually all elites. But, on the other hand, by empowering civilian and military technocrats and emasculating the legislative branch of government, the bureaucratic-authoritarian regime challenged the foundations of politics as traditionally organized in Brazil and so threatened to exclude the traditional political elite from arenas of power. A regime that restricted the functions of parliament and the political parties, Cardoso (1975: 206) claimed, undermined federalism and transformed the bases of political representation and recruitment. Politics had to be transacted through new channels of particularistic representation via functionaries recruited from public and private enterprises: technocrats, planners, economists, engineers, and firm managers. "Not only the

6 Bresser Pereira (1984: 64–65) alleges that even during the democratically elected governments of the populist era, "Brazil was unlike the majority, if not all the rest, of the capitalist countries, in that its public sector technocrats and professional administrators became a true technocracy – that is, they assumed a considerable part of the decision-making power – well ahead of their counterparts in the private sector."

political party system but all other forms of political action . . . became dependent on contacts and alliances with the military and technocratic groups that alone controlled the state apparatus" (Cardoso, 1973: 147–48). And the vehicle for political advancement shifted from the political parties, the classic instruments through which social groups and particularly the traditional political elite achieved power, to the state, the Brazilian "Modern Prince" (Cardoso, 1975: 200).[7]

POLITICAL RECRUITMENT IN MINAS GERAIS

It has been documented that national cabinets became the preserve of the military-technocratic alliance in the Costa e Silva and Médici governments, but whether the military evicted traditional politicians from the state altogether and in particular from the state governments that were their traditional redoubts is an open question. Some authors have alleged that the political class lost control over the process whereby gubernatorial "candidates" were selected. Schneider (1971: 319–20) in particular has argued that state political machines lost the ability to impose their preferences in the selection of the state chief executives, especially in 1970.[8] In fact, however, in sharp contrast to their eviction from the federal cabinet, politicians were not generally supplanted in the highest offices in their states. Santos (1971) and Sarles Jenks (1979) have shown that the military appointed primarily politicians to state governorships across Brazil. All but two of the first cohort of twelve appointed governors who assumed office in 1966 were politicians, and even those two had had at least some political experience (Table 4.1). Even in 1970, the most intensely authoritarian

7 Cardoso is of course referring to Gramsci's (1971: 129) revision of Machiavelli's concept of the Prince. For Gramsci, the "Modern Prince" was the political party.

8. According to Schneider (1971: 319–20), the president handpicked the candidates for succession at the state level after the military intelligence agency, the SNI (National Information Service), had explored the possible alternatives and "vetted" the candidates; the presidential staff had studied the problems, needs, and priorities of each state; and ARENA head Rondon Pacheco had paid a flying visit to consult in the state capital with leaders of factions in the ruling party and to talk with the would-be governors. New faces were favored particularly "when there seemed to be an impasse looming between the ex-UDN and ex-PSD leaders within the government party." Schneider also claims (1971: 320–22) that in Minas Gerais in 1970, Rondon Pacheco was the personal choice of President Médici to "replace the entrenched ARENA gerontocracy with its continuing feuds between UDN and PSD patriarchs." Rondon Pacheco's ascendancy in Minas could, however, also be interpreted as evidence that the Minas elite was well connected with upper military circles – Pacheco had been head of the civil cabinet in Costa e Silva's government and later national president of ARENA – and that the UDN faction of the Minas political elite (of which he was an "insider") retained substantial state autonomy in this period in the selection of governors. Pacheco and each of the governors who followed him had no apparent difficulty in choosing their successors. Sarles Jenks (1979: 364–65) also inferred from the selection of politician governors in Minas, São Paulo, and Rio Grande do Sul that the federal government felt that it could not safely ignore the political leadership in those important states.

Table 4.1. *Political experience of state governors, 1965–74*

	1965		1966		1970		1974	
	N	*%*	*N*	*%*	*N*	*%*	*N*	*%*
Training[a]								
Law and medicine	6	55	8	66	11	50	12	55
Economics and								
engineering	3	27	0	0	11	41	7	32
Military	1	9	1	8	0	0[b]	1	4
Other[c]	1	9	3	25	2	9	2	9
Channel of access								
Political	11	100[d]	11	100	15	68	16	73
Administrative	0	0	0	0	4	18	6	28
Military	0	0	0	0	3	14	0	0
Electoral experience								
Previously elected	9	82	11	92	14	63	14	63
Former senators	2	18	0	0	1	4[b]	4	18
Former fed. deps.	6	54	6	50	9	41	10	45
Former state deps.								
or lieut. govs.	2	18	8	66[b]	7	32[b]	9	41
Former mayors	5	45[b]	6	50	4	18	5	23
Old party affiliation								
UDN	5		4		11		4	
PSD	5		6[b]		2		4[b]	
Total	11		12[e]		22		22	

[a]I have regrouped the categories under "training" from Sarles Jenks's tables, and recalculated the percentages. In 1970, the number of governors trained in these fields (24) appears to exceed the number of governors appointed in that year (22) because two governors were schooled in two disciplines – José Cortes Pereira (Rio Grande do Norte), in law and economics; and Colombo Sales (Santa Catarina), in engineering and public administration.
[b]Figures represent recalculated percentages (from those reported in Sarles Jenks, 1979: 385) based on raw data provided in Sarles Jenks (1979: 335, 351, 362, 380).
[c]Includes accounting, business and public administration, education, and the priesthood.
[d]Although Alacid Nunes (Pará) had a military background, Sarles Jenks attributes his rise to the governorship to politics, because he, like all governors in 1965 who owed their office to direct elections, by definition was chosen through political channels.
[e]Twelve governors were appointed in 1966 because in 1965 in Alagoas, the top vote getter received only a plurality of the vote. The president then appointed an interventor and called another election for 1966.
Source: Sarles Jenks, 1979: 335, 351, 362, 380, 385.

period when Médici, the military president most obsessed with efficiency, designated four technocrats and three military men as state governors, 68 percent of the governors were politicians. In both 1970 and 1974, fourteen of twenty-two governors had held elected office; the 1974 governors, according to Sarles Jenks, were even better connected than their 1970 counterparts, and not one of the later cohort was drawn from the ranks of the armed forces.

The findings of studies that have examined the attributes of the governors of the military period raise doubts about the veracity of some claims of the demise of politicians, but they alone are inconclusive for answering the broader question of whether authoritarian centralization transferred power and resources away from traditional elites to technocrats in the states. Unfortunately, no study to date has extended its investigation of the patterns of political recruitment during military rule to the state level, nor considered if and when these patterns of recruitment to state office were revised after the Médici government.

Politicians, technocrats, and cabinets

To determine whether postcoup recruitment patterns differed from precoup patterns, this study compares the career paths of officeholders before and after the 1964 coup d'etat (a period of nearly three decades). It encompasses members of the administrations of all military-appointed governors (1965–82), but of only two gubernatorial administrations of the precoup period: those of Magalhães Pinto (1961–65) and Bias Fortes (1956–60). By beginning the study of political recruitment in 1956, I was able to include as broad a cross section of the precoup elite as possible – secretaries from both the old PSD (Bias Fortes was Minas's last PSD governor) and the UDN and PR (Magalhães Pinto, a UDN governor, rewarded many allies in the Republican Party for their support) – but had the limits of the study been pushed back any further, the task of monitoring the fate of the precoup political elite would have been complicated excessively by introducing a cohort that would have been for the most part too aged to survive into the 1970s.

The study targets for examination the career paths of occupants of positions within the executive branch of Minas state government at or above cabinet rank. It begins with the state chief executive – the most powerful position in state politics in Brazil. The governor appoints the cabinet secretaries, bank presidents, and agency heads who make state policy, and serves as de facto leader of his political party. He is, moreover, his state's most influential representative in national politics; bargaining with the congressional votes of his state's delegation to the Chamber of Deputies, he negotiates on his state's behalf with the president. Who filled the posts of state governors was so consequential that when the military-backed

UDN candidates failed to win victories in the gubernatorial elections of 1965 in such key states as Minas Gerais and Guanabara, the military responded by issuing Institutional Act Number 2; the Second Institutional Act gave military presidents the real if unofficial prerogative of naming the heads of the state governments (officially governors were "nominated" in Brasília and ratified in government party-dominated state legislatures). However critical the importance of who occupied the state governor's palace, how state resources were appropriated, how policy was formulated and implemented, and whether traditional politics and traditional political elites ultimately survived depended on the composition of the state cabinet and top administration. Thus the study extends to cabinet secretaries, state bank presidents, and the appointed mayor of the state capital. Recruitment to legislative posts – the typical focus of elite studies – is, however, not examined. If federal and state legislatures had indeed been stripped of all meaningful functions and jurisdictions by the military-technocratic alliance, then tenure in top legislative posts would carry little "real power" after 1964. A complete list of posts included in the study is provided in the appendix.

To distinguish the "political" from the "technical" elite, I first identified defining characteristics of both groups. I classified as politicians those officials who in their backgrounds either had held elected (local, state, or federal) office or had been members of the executive committee of a political party (or its local or state branches), and as technocrats those officeholders who had: an economics degree; an engineering degree; or a record of service in the following public sector enterprises: CEMIG, the state electric company; Usiminas, the federally owned steel company located in Minas; DER, the state highway division; and the BDMG, the state development bank. In including as members of the "technocratic-bureaucratic" elite those individuals with education or (preferably public sector) job experience that appeared to qualify them for their *particular* cabinet job, I expanded on the practice of most scholars, following Meynaud (1968), to define technocrats by the possession of a particular degree.[9] Because a degree in itself may not have been an officeholder's ticket into the cabinet, more than one type of common degree may have served to qualify technical specialists, and job experience – not education – may have provided either the skills or connections necessary for a technocrat to rise, I also judged professionals such as agronomists in the Department of Agricul-

---

9 Meynaud (1968: 27) included under the rubric of those who possess technical knowledge both those whom he describes as experts, who have a thorough knowledge of a particular field or subject, and "generalists" – general managers and administrators, who "have the ability to control various stages or sectors of operation and see them all as a whole." Suleiman (1977) has shown that it is rare that technocrats actually possess technical skill, at least in France. There, such an ability is viewed with scornful derision by top civil servants who take pride in their ability to see things whole and make well-reasoned decisions.

ture, physicians in the Department of Health, and university professors in the Department of Education to be technocrats.

These criteria proved adequate for readily classifying most officeholders, but some decision rule needed to be adopted for those that exhibited attributes of *both* technocrats and politicians. Following Suleiman, who in his study of French bureaucrats (1974: 378) argued that "technocrats" who stand in elections should be considered "politicians," I classified technically qualified elites who rose through the ranks of party and legislative service as politicians. An example of such a politician is Aureliano Chaves, a civil engineer who became governor of Minas in 1974. In practice, relatively few high-ranking state and federal cabinet appointees with economics and engineering degrees also participated in electoral politics in authoritarian Brazil (cf. Nunes, 1978: 63).[10] More common were technically qualified secretaries who had managed the political campaigns of others and/or affiliated with political parties (Nunes, 1978: 63). These secretaries were identified as technocrats. Generally, officeholders were classified according to the *primary* route they followed to the high-ranking offices included in this study, a determination that in turn required a working knowledge of the considerations that influenced the appointment of a particular secretary to office. When officeholders could offer to the executive votes from their native regions, or the allegiance of entire political factions that were loyal to their families, I concluded that they rose by political means. When technocrat-secretaries offered technical competence but little else, I judged that they had been chosen for their technical expertise.

It was also the case that some members of traditional families opted for technical careers, raising the question of whether the son of a traditional family who holds an economics degree rose into the state elite as a member of the traditional elite or as a technocrat. A descendant of the Minas oligarchy who had engaged in no known political activity but who had a long and distinguished career in public administration and enterprises was presumed to have gained his job on other than political grounds and judged to be a technocrat. The effect of this procedure was to set stringent conditions for the label of technocrat, but one that is justified if we are to learn the extent to which political elites in Brazil were deprived of their access to state resources and whether political recruitment was based on political criteria and service.

Most, but not all, members of the state elite fall into these two broad categories. A few belong to a third: the officeholders who rose from private industrial and banking circles. The state-led capitalist development model pursued by the military regime and the Minas state administration was sufficiently ambiguous that there are theoretical reasons to

10 This changed after 1985, when former technocrats of the military period stood for election to various federal and state posts, with reasonable success.

expect either that representatives of the business and banking elite should be well represented in the cabinet (if local development indeed privileged this class) or that they should be excluded from top state positions (in favor of a technocratic elite as autonomous from particular private economic interests as it was "apolitical"). Businessmen often entered public service after careers in the private sector, and many politicians joined the boards of large corporations after many years in elective office. For those officeholders who had served in both political posts and the private sector, the *order* of posts was taken as the best indicator of the route to power. If an officeholder held top management positions in the private sector before entering politics or appears to have been in a position to offer primarily the support of the local business class, then he or she was included in this category.

The relative representation of technocrats and politicians in the state elite are examined according to two measures of office holding. The first classified members of the cabinet from 1956 to 1982 according to the career path (political, technocratic, private sector) they traveled to high-level state office. The second measure represents the percent of total time (the sum of the number of months each cabinet post was in existence within the time frame of this study) cabinet offices were occupied by secretaries falling into these categories. The second measure was included to eliminate any potential distortions caused by weighing equally secretaries who served an extremely brief time in office (in many instances no more than one to two months) with those who completed full terms. Results are grouped according to gubernatorial administration.

The Minas state elite

The political elite of Minas Gerais traditionally controlled the highest levels of state government. The first governor in the sample from the precoup period, José Francisco Bias Fortes (1956–60), was from one of Minas's most illustrious families; his father, Crispim Jacques Bias Fortes, was a former governor of Minas Gerais (1894–98) and president of the Minas Republican Party. His career path was typical of a leading politician of his time: he was schooled in law; he served a stint as local councillor in his native Barbacena; he next was elected state deputy and rose to become president of the state Legislative Assembly; he joined the state cabinet as secretary of public security; he then entered the arena of federal politics as a member of the Minas delegation to the Chamber of Deputies; after the end of the Vargas dictatorship, he helped to found the Minas chapter of the PSD; and finally, he achieved the post of governor. The lineage of his lieutenant governor, Artur Bernardes Filho, was no less distinguished: Bernardes was the son of Artur da Silva Bernardes, governor of Minas (1918–22) and president of Brazil (1922–26). Bernardes perhaps more than any other politician kept the Minas Republican Party alive in the postwar period.

After the coup, at no time did Minas politicians cede this post. The first governor to assume office after the 1964 coup d'etat (and the last by direct election) was Israel Pinheiro, elected in 1965. The son of former governor João Pinheiro was initiated into politics through the old Minas Republican Party and the Liberal Alliance. Through a propitious alliance with Vargas's federal interventor in Minas, Benedito Valadares, Israel Pinheiro embarked on a long and distinguished career in state and national politics that traversed posts in the state cabinet (1933–42), the state enterprises (as president of the Rio Doce Valley Company in 1942), and the Congress (as president of the Finance Commission in the Chamber of Deputies). At the invitation of President Juscelino Kubitschek, Pinheiro played a leading role in moving the federal capital from Rio de Janeiro to Brasília, first as the president of the company that laid the groundwork for the construction of the new capital, NOVACAP (Cia. Urbanizadora Nova Capital), and later as Brasília's first mayor.

Israel Pinheiro's successor, Rondon Pacheco, who became governor of Minas at the height of technocratic power in 1971, too, was a politician. Although he enjoyed President Médici's confidence, he was hardly an outsider to the state and national political party machines. First in state politics and later as a federal deputy, Pacheco had held important posts within the UDN. He was its leader on the floor of the Chamber of Deputies in 1960, and he also served as a member of Magalhães Pinto's cabinet from 1961 to 1962. After the coup Pacheco rose in national stature, becoming secretary-general of the new ARENA in 1966, Costa e Silva's head of the civil cabinet (one of the most powerful cabinet positions in the national government) in 1967, and national president of ARENA beginning in 1969, a post he held until Médici nominated him to be governor of Minas Gerais. Pacheco's successors, Aureliano Chaves (1975–78) and Francelino Pereira (1979–82), were also politician-governors, as well as high-ranking national figures in ARENA; Pereira, like Pacheco, had served as national party president immediately preceding his ascension to the state's highest office.

Politicians did not, by contrast, monopolize the state cabinet. Before the coup, most cabinet secretaries did rise in Minas politics because of family connections or through political channels. Sixteen of the eighteen men who served in the cabinet of the Bias Fortes administration (including the lieutenant governor) rose by these means. Only one had had substantial administrative experience (Table 4.2). A similar pattern is evident during the administration of Bias Fortes's successor, Magalhães Pinto. Magalhães Pinto appointed forty of fifty-eight cabinet secretaries from political ranks, and only nine from the public bureaucracy. Politicians from the UDN and several minor allied parties occupied state cabinet offices for four-fifths of Magalhães Pinto's term. Political elites overshadowed representatives of

Table 4.2. Routes to power for the state elite: Composition of the cabinet, 1956–82

Gubernatorial administration	Political			Technobureaucratic			Private sector			Insufficient data			N[a]
	N	%	% time	N	%	% time	N	%	% time	N	%	% time	
Bias Fortes (1956-61)	16	89	96	1	6	2	--	--	--	1	6	1	18
Magalhães Pinto (1961-65)	40	69	80	9	16	12	3	5	4	6	11	3	58
Israel Pinheiro (1966-71)	23	61	58	11	29	33	2	5	7	2	5	2	38
Rondon Pacheco (1971-75)	8	40	47	11	55	47	1	5	5	--	--	--	20
Aureliano Chaves (1975-79)[b]	12	52	49	9	39	48	1	4	1	1	4	2	23
Francelino Pereira (1979-82)	14	64	70	3	15	17	2	10	9	3	14	4	22
Total	99	62		41	26		8	5		13	8		161

Note: State cabinet posts include the lieutenant governor and all state secretaries for each administration, except military portfolios. The post of the mayor of Belo Horizonte is included during the terms of the postcoup governors, Israel Pinheiro, Rondon Pacheco, Aureliano Chaves, and Francelino Pereira, when it was an appointed position.

[a] Column does not total because secretaries who occupied posts in more than one administration were counted only once. Each administration is considered as a separate unit in the rows, but the duplicates have been removed from the columns.

[b] Ozanam Coelho, the lieutenant governor during the administration of Aureliano Chaves, became governor in 1978 when Chaves resigned his post to "run" for vice-president.

the business community in the administration of the banker Magalhães Pinto, but private sector elites were no less prominent than they were during the bureaucratic-authoritarian regime.

After the regime change, the participation of technocrats in the cabinet increased, peaked during the administration of Rondon Pacheco (1971–75), and then declined. The rise of this group to the state cabinet began during the administration of Israel Pinheiro. Like his father, João Pinheiro, the positivist governor of Minas Gerais at the turn of the century, and his political mentor, Juscelino Kubitschek, Israel Pinheiro promoted economic development in Minas. For this purpose, he invited into his administration several technically qualified persons, who together accounted for approximately 29 percent of the state cabinet. The technocratic presence in the cabinet rose to its highest level (55 percent of the cabinet posts and 47 percent of "cabinet time") during the administration of Rondon Pacheco. Near the end of Pacheco's tenure as governor, politicians and technocrats shared fairly equally state office. Aureliano Chaves, who assumed office in 1975, maintained the technocratic presence in state government at approximately half his cabinet. Politicians were even more clustered toward the end of his term, which was served out by his lieutenant governor and an old stalwart of the PSD, Ozanam Coelho. His successor, Francelino Pereira (1979–82), clearly favored top vote-drawing politicians over technocrats for cabinet appointments. Pereira named ARENA's second most voted federal deputy, Maurício Campos, mayor of Belo Horizonte; the party's sixth top vote getter, Carlos Eloy, the secretary of public works; and the seventh, Gerardo Renault, the secretary of agriculture. In all, four federal and three state deputies, but only three technocrats, were initially appointed to Pereira's cabinet.[11] Also rewarded with a cabinet portfolio for his party service was Fernando Fagundes Neto, a former deputy who had sacrificed a congressional seat to run unsuccessfully against heavily favored MDB candidate Tancredo Neves in the 1978 direct senatorial election. Such an appointment was not unusual. Based on the political careers of all Minas federal and state deputies from 1946 to 1975, Fleischer (n.d.: 45) has observed that defeated candidates typically received high-level jobs in the state bureaucracy, enabling them to increase their "prestige," and run again.

When the trend in Minas office holding is extended to include the gubernatorial administrations of Aureliano Chaves and Francelino Pereira, a very different picture of the composition of the state elite emerges from that which might have been projected from scholarly claims and the empirical record at the height of the authoritarian period. Office holding by the

11 In an interview with the *Jornal da Casa,* João Marques de Vasconcellos, the deputy leader of ARENA in the state Legislative Assembly and the top-ranking ex-PSD legislator in the house, cited his nomination as lieutenant governor as proof of Francelino Pereira "fulfilling his promise to govern Minas with the 'political class.' "

two groups adhered to a curvilinear pattern; their positions merged in the mid-1970s, but then diverged sharply, presenting a near mirror image of the precoup years (Figure 4.1). The picture is illuminating, if crude: political elites were demoted but not evicted from the state at any point, not even during the apogee of technocratic office holding in the 1971–74 period, and the relative loss of their positions to technocrats was not permanent. Viewed from 1974, it was evident only that political elites had slid dramatically from their precoup highs: it was not obvious that their fortunes would soon reverse themselves. What appeared in 1974 to be an end point or only slightly better, the midpoint of a unidirectional slide, was actually the nadir of a longer curve that rebounded with the passage of time. What is striking when the whole picture is taken into account, indeed, is how brief the period of technocratic ascendancy was.

To know that the presence of technobureaucratic elites in the executive branch of the national and state governments increased in the early 1970s and then waned, however much it tells us about the accuracy of the political models of bureaucratic authoritarianism, tells us little about how disruptive the presence of technocrats was to politicians, how much power technocrats acquired, and the extent to which traditional patterns of politics within the state were altered. In order to answer these questions, we must examine the distribution of power and positions *within* the state.

POWER, POSITION, AND THE STATE

The technocrats that colonized the federal and state cabinets challenged the position of traditional political elites and the foundations of traditional politics, it was claimed, in two ways: by seizing positions formerly occupied by politicians, and by expanding the power of those positions and reducing the power of those that politicians retained. Fernando Reis, Rondon Pacheco's state secretary of finance, for example, has been credited with reducing the public deficit by reclaiming control of state coffers from free-spending politicians, an effort hailed by one observer as a "Copernican revolution" (L. Andrade, 1980). Technocrats, moreover, were viewed as particularly powerful and threatening to politicians because of their alleged independence and cohesiveness. Unlike previous career public servants who were well educated, experienced, and faithfully executed the policies of elected politicians, the technical experts who occupied federal and state offices in the 1970s were said to be lacking political obligations and accountable only to their military patrons. They purportedly coalesced as a technocratic elite, as students of bureaucracy generally claim, because they had common socializing experiences – technical education, training in public and private sector management, and advancement through the state administration, parapublic agencies and state enterprises – that led to a shared purpose, a uniform set of beliefs, and a coordinated pattern of behavior. To

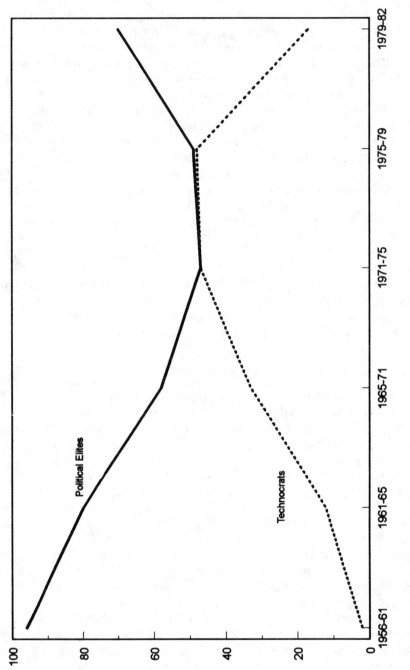

Figure 4.1. The state cabinet, 1956–82.

assess the validity of these claims and grasp the true significance of the increased presence of technocrats in the state requires a determination of which positions within the state were removed from the grasp of politicians, and whether a "pure technocracy" coalesced under military rule.

The two sides of the state

The term "technocracy" is often employed in the Brazilian context to connote a superelite stratum of national economic ministers and central bank officers. At other times, it refers to a far larger public and semipublic bureaucracy that includes but is not limited to the staffs of state agencies and enterprises. The former group in particular earned a reputation of being powerful during authoritarian Brazil among both Brazilians and those who studied Brazilian politics because the positions they occupied carried great economic decision-making authority.[12] In that the ministers of planning and finance had the authority to set budget priorities and even the power to veto expenditures in other state departments, and state enterprise managers administered enormous budgets (in extreme cases exceeding the funds available to many state governments), their reputations were deserved. Yet, however powerful these positions were, they did not control an entire range of other important state decisions and resources. Perhaps as early as the 1950s when the Kubitschek administration created "pockets of efficiency," a select few departments insulated from congressional oversight (Geddes, 1994), both the central and subnational governments of the Brazilian state had two "sides": one that coordinated developmental functions, and one that organized state clientelism. Before the 1964 coup, it was in the second side of the state – in those branches of the central and subnational governments that distributed state patronage – that traditional political elites based their power.

After the coup, the economic development model accelerated the bifurcation of state power. Just as state-led capitalist development augmented the decision-making power of the economic ministries, so too did it enhance the resource base and therefore the political power that accrued from serving in state positions responsible for administering patronage. Various departments of subnational governments supervised large discretionary budgets from which various regional and community development

---

12 Thus Brazilian technocrats superficially qualified as "powerful" according to all three criteria used in elite studies to determine who is powerful – reputation, position, and decision-making authority – criteria that, as Smith (1979: 318) shows, all have shortcomings. In Brazil, where hearsay about the composition of the power structure has been accepted as fact, the reputational method tends to reinforce existing stereotypes. In McDonough's (1981b: 98) study, for instance, "elite" informants most often cited the president of the republic and Delfim Neto as the most powerful personages in Brazilian society during the Médici government. To accept their reputations, in this case, as confirmation of their power is tantamount to accepting unverified gossip.

projects were funded. The state Departments of Education and Public Works were among those that freely distributed public employment and resources. The education portfolio in Minas Gerais, for instance, carried with it the right to appoint tens of thousands of schoolteachers, and the Public Works Department made decisions about roads, bridges, and other elements of physical infrastructure crucial to agricultural areas that needed to market their produce during rainy seasons.

For regionally based political elites in a clientelistic system, maintaining control of what McDonough (1981b) derided as only the state's powerless "underside" was at least as crucial as retaining the prerogatives to grant exemptions on import duties and to set prices or even controlling such large budget ministries as mines and energy.[13] Technocrats would need to have penetrated the "underside" of the state in order for traditional patterns of politics to be altered or undermined. The former minister of justice under Castello Branco and later governor of Bahia, Luiz Viana, questioned that they were able to do so in the national arena. In a 1988 interview with Scott Mainwaring (1991a: 23), he ventured the opinion that the military tolerated less efficiency in the "secondary parts" of government than in the "essential parts."

In Minas Gerais, the reach of technocrats was by and large limited to the ministries that formulated economic policy, and the technocratic presence in government did not long divorce politicians from their sources of patronage. In the early 1970s, technocrats were assigned to administer the Departments of Planning, Finance, Industry and Commerce, and Agriculture (Table 4.3). Political elites at no time controlled the Department of Planning, and after losing control over the Department of Finance during Israel Pinheiro's government, they did not regain it until 1985. But even during the height of technocratic influence, the administration of Rondon Pacheco, they retained the patronage Departments of Interior and Justice, Administration, and Government, and they quickly recovered others that returned to them the instruments of their patronage: Education, Health, and Public Works. In the administration of Francelino Pereira, they won back the Department of Agriculture from agronomists. Even departments such as Labor and Science and Technology afforded ample opportunity for patronage. At various times during the authoritarian period, politicians shared with technocrats and representatives of the business community a job that was a particularly attractive source of patronage, the mayor of Belo Horizonte.

Politicians not only held on to and regained state cabinet posts, but they even invaded the terrain of the scientific experts with some success. Former governors were handed control of some of the most important federal state

---

13 In 1985, the budget of the Ministry of Mines and Energy was four and a half times that of the next wealthiest, the Ministry of Industry and Commerce.

Table 4.3 *Political elite control of state office, 1956–82 (% of cabinet post time)*

Cabinet office	Administration[a]					
	I	II	III	IV	V	VI
Economic departments						
Finance	88	70	60	0	0	0
Agriculture, Industry, and Commerce (1956-63)	100	100	--	--	--	--
Agriculture (1963-82)	--	41[b]	78	0	0	73[b]
Planning (1970-82)	--	--	0	0	0	0
Industry, Commerce, and Tourism (1972-82)	--	--	--	0	77	0[c]
Economic Development (1964-66)	--	63	0	--	--	--
Patronage departments						
Education	100	98	86	0	17	100
Interior and Justice	87	100	100	100	100	100
Public Works	100	88	29	0	100	73
Administration	--	82	65	100	100	100
Government	--	64[b]	77[b]	100	17	100
Health	100	66	86	0	83[b]	58
Mayor, Belo Horizonte	0[c]	100	39	100	0	100
Others						
Public Security (1965-70)	100	63	14/mil	mil	mil	mil
Science and Technology (1977-82)	--	--	--	--	0	73[b]
Labor (1963-82)	--	39[b]	11	100	100	100
Social Action Affairs (1964-66)	--	100	100	--	--	--
Rural Credit and Supply Affairs (1964-66)	--	100	76	--	--	--

[a]For cabinet administrations, refer to Table 4.2
[b]Minimum estimates – officeholders included in total for whom data were insufficient to determine career path.
[c]Officeholding shared by technocrats and business elites.

enterprises. On leaving the office of governor, Rondon Pacheco became the president of Usiminas. Moreover, if politicians ceded control over economic planning to technocrats, they were hardly excluded from the state banking sector. To the contrary, following public service many members of the political elite found lucrative state bank directorships awaiting them. In all, more than one-quarter (27.2 percent) of the members of the political elite throughout the three decades of this study served at some point as directors, presidents, or board members of state banks.

Technocracy?

A fully informed conclusion about the relative power of politicians and technocrats in authoritarian Brazil requires an answer to the second question previously identified: were technocrats in office a loose amalgam of career bureaucrats or a pure "technocracy" whose power was enhanced by a solidarity forged through common socialization and independence from politicians? An analysis of the educational backgrounds, job experience, and political connections of those cabinet secretaries who rose to office via the technobureaucratic route failed to identify such a monolithic technocratic corps in Minas Gerais. If there was a "technical" route to office holding in Minas that circumvented and devalued traditional political channels for attaining state power, it was not a single one (Table 4.4). Brazil has no equivalent of the kind of national schools that in France and elsewhere infuse their graduates with a technocratic ethos and esprit de corps (the Ecole Nationale d'Administration and the Ecole Polytechnique),[14] and the formal educational experiences of technocrat-secretaries in Minas varied widely: only fifteen, or 37 percent, held economics or engineering degrees. Seven schooled in medicine became secretaries of health, and four agronomists headed the state Department of Agriculture. While four-fifths of the technocrats had had job experience that prepared them for their posts in state government, their experiences were not uniform. Two state agencies – the state development bank (BDMG) and the state electric company (CEMIG) – did groom a number of economists and engineers for cabinet duty.[15] Fernando Reis began his public career as an economist

14 McDonough (1981b: 67) asserts that in Brazil no single university dominates higher education for civilian elites. Although the Federal University of Rio de Janeiro (UFRJ) and the University of São Paulo (USP) graduated nearly half (43 percent) of the 251 business, political, labor, and religious elites included in McDonough's study, these two institutions do not provide civilian elites with a common socializing experience. The Superior War College (ESG), however, carries out the function of socializing military elites-to-be in the habits of command that is fulfilled by Oxbridge, Tokyo University, and the Ivy League in Britain, Japan, and the United States, respectively. See Stepan (1971) for the most complete study of the common background of the military elite.

15 The BDMG was created in 1962 to fund small and medium-sized industry in Minas, but it soon took on the functions of the state body responsible for economic research. It created a Department of Studies and Planning and hired a new technical team to prepare first a series of sectoral studies (e.g., sugar, textile, and meat processing industries), and later the major work, the *Diagnóstico da Economia Mineira,* published in 1968. This document enhanced the position of its authors, the so-called Prophets of Catastrophe: one Minas observer has claimed that it legitimated their rise at the expense of the "political class" (Campolina Diniz, 1978: 143). This same observer alleged that in the 1970s, "practically all the key posts of decision making in the state's economic sphere were under the control of the group originating from these two institutions [BDMG and CEMIG]."

for the BDMG, where he rose from a deputy in the Project Analysis Department to director of the bank in four years. But most technocrats followed a different route to state office. During the entire period from 1956 to 1982, only 37 percent of the technocrats rose in the state enterprises (as distinct from the fully public bureaucracy); at the height of their influence during Rondon Pacheco's administration, that figure rises only slightly to 45 percent. In Pacheco's government most technocrats were educated and trained for their specific posts, but in Chaves's government, the schooling of only one-third of the technocrat-secretaries was related to the requirements of their posts, and just over half had had related job experience.

The second ingredient that may be necessary for a "technocracy" to coalesce, to impose a single vision of state policy over the objections of political elites, and to build a power base is that cabinet secretaries owe their loyalty to each other and not to politicians, from whom they must rather acquire autonomy. Suleiman (1974) has painstakingly demonstrated that what prevents civil servants in France from coordinating their activities across ministries is that they owe their loyalty and attachment to their particular administration. Only when this loyalty breaks down and technocrat-ministers act in concert with their counterparts in other, rival ministries, he has argued, does an administrative elite become a "technocracy."

In Minas, neither were the technocrats an omnipotent, apolitical body nor did they appear to transcend loyalty to their own departments and to politicians. Many had been active in politics at some point in their public life. A small number early in their careers occupied such political offices as local councillor or *promotor de justiça* (district judge). Even more admitted to partisan affiliations. Over half (at least eleven of twenty-one) of those secretaries who rose through technocratic ranks claimed membership in or identified with a political party. The technocrats, moreover, appeared to be above partisan calculations and not accountable to political elites for only a brief time. The secretaries of the administration of Rondon Pacheco were highly professional – only one (of eleven) had any political or partisan affiliation – but the technocrats of Chaves's administration had vast political connections, all but two either having extensive contacts with politicians or engaging directly in politics themselves. Some had served politicians in a personal capacity; private secretaries of cabinet secretaries who later became governors, for example, themselves became cabinet secretaries during their former patrons' administrations. All three technocrats in Francelino Pereira's government had political connections. One, secretary of planning Paulo Haddad, was related to Pereira's wife.

The more frequent political connections of the technocrat-secretaries appointed by Aureliano Chaves and Francelino Pereira suggest that as the recruitment to state government began to revert back to the political class and technocrats themselves began to display political attributes,

Table 4.4. *Technocrats: Education, job experience, and political and private sector connections, 1956–82*

Cabinet[a]	Education[b]							Public job experience[d]					Connections		N[g]
	Job related[c] Yes	No	Law	Medicine	Econ./eng.	Agronomy	Other	Job related Yes	No	Bureaucracy	Enterprises	Universities	Political[e]	Private sector[f]	
Bias Fortes (1956-61)	1 (100)	0	1 (100)					1 (100)	0			1 (100)	1 (100)	0	1
Magalhães Pinto (1961-65)	7 (78)	2 (22)	3 (33)	4 (44)	1 (11)		1 (11)	9 (100)	0	8 (89)	1 (11)		4 (44)	0	9
Israel Pinheiro (1966-71)	5 (45)	6 (55)	3 (27)		5 (45)	1 (9)	2 (18)	7 (64)	4 (36)	6 (55)	3 (27)	2 (18)	7 (64)	3 (27)	11
Rondon Pacheco (1971-75)	8 (73)	3 (27)	2 (18)		6 (55)	2 (18)	1 (9)	11 (100)	0	2 (18)	5 (45)	4 (36)	1 (9)	4 (36)	11
Chaves/Coelho (1975-79)	3 (33)	6 (67)	3 (33)		3 (33)	1 (11)	2 (22)	5 (56)	4 (44)	4 (44)	5 (56)		7 (78)	5 (56)	9
Francelino Pereira (1979-82)	2 (67)	1 (33)	1 (33)	1 (33)	1 (33)			2 (67)	1 (33)	2 (67)	1 (33)		3 (100)	0	3
Total	24 (59)	17 (41)	10 (24)	7 (17)	15 (37)	4 (10)	5 (12)	33 (80)	8 (20)	20 (49)	15 (37)	6 (15)	21 (51)	12 (29)	41

Note: Numbers in parentheses are percents.

[a] Included in cabinet positions are the lieutenant governor and secretaries of state for all portfolios except those which became military portfolios, and, after 1967, the mayor of Belo Horizonte.

[b] Education is the highest degree held before assuming office.

[c] When a secretary holds more than one post in the same administration, his or her education and job training are related to the position held longer or first, depending on which is more prominent.

[d] Public bureaucracy includes the administrations of the federal, state, and, in the case of Belo Horizonte, local governments. State enterprises, such as the state electric company, steel companies, development bank, agrarian enterprises, and department of roads, though strictly speaking part of the state bureaucracy, are distinguished by their semiautonomy. Secretaries identified as having job experience in the universities have occupied such high-level career positions as rector, and are thus distinguished from other technocrats who happen to hold university appointments.

[e] "Political connections" includes any one of the following: admission of a partisan affiliation, relatives in politics, and tenure in political posts. In most cases, these are elected, but I have also included such appointed posts as state interventor (federally appointed governor) and municipal chief executive (state-appointed mayor) during the years of the Vargas dictatorship.

[f] Secretaries may have been engaged in private enterprise either before, during, or after having held office. Low-level positions in private enterprises before entering public service are not included.

[g] The total number of secretaries does not total forty-four as it apparently should because three secretaries held posts in more than one administration. Each administration is considered as a separate unit in the rows, but the duplicates have been removed from the columns.

their selection appeared to satisfy political constituencies. The appointment of João Valle Maurício, a physician with an impressive background
in public health, as state secretary of health in 1981 mollified the politically important North of Minas, which felt it had been underrepresented
in Francelino Pereira's cabinet. Maurício had been the leader of the
Republican Party and city council in Montes Claros before the coup and
had briefly served on the local ARENA *diretório (Montes Claros em
Foco,* 1981: 5–7).

Finally, four of nine technocrats in Aureliano Chaves's cabinet were
descended from Minas's traditional families. The secretary of planning,
Paulo Camillo de Oliveira Penna, a chaired professor of planning and
public administration in the Economics Department of the Federal University of Minas Gerais and president of the state development bank from
1963 to 1966, was from one of Minas's most traditional families of the Rio
Doce Valley; he was a descendant of ex-president Afonso Penna and a
nephew of former governor Milton Campos (1947–51). The same branch
of the Minas oligarchy gave Aureliano Chaves his secretary of finance,
João Camilo Pena, who rose through the ranks of CEMIG. José Israel
Vargas, the first state secretary of science and technology, who earned a
Ph.D. in chemistry in England from Cambridge University and who had
worked on the French Atomic Energy Commission, was Oliveira Penna's
first cousin. Penna's successor in the Planning Department (he died in
office in 1976), Hélio Braz, had managerial experience in foreign firms
and technocratic training, but was also the grandson of Wenceslau Bras,
governor of Minas during the Old Republic (1908–10) and president of
Brazil (1914–18).

POLITICAL ELITES, TRADITIONAL ELITES

The rapid and full-scale return of politicians to high state office, the reten-
tion by the political elite of niches in the state from which it could manage
its patronage operations, and the failure of a technocracy to coalesce suggest that the ability of the political class in Minas Gerais to resist the
bureaucratizing tendencies of military rule has been severely underestimated. Of primary interest, however, is not merely that *politicians* returned to state posts, even under military rule, but whether a *traditional
political elite* persisted or was replaced by a "new" political elite.

Assessing the fate of the traditional political elite first requires that a
clear distinction be drawn between members of the traditional political
elite and their "nontraditional" counterparts. Because, as some of its leading members insist, the members of the Minas oligarchy earned their positions like most politicians – through the ballot box – then the difference
between "modern" and "traditional" modes of acquiring power ultimately
hinges on what constitute "modern" and "traditional" modes of contesting

elections.[16] The union leader who campaigns successfully in the industrial suburbs of Betim or Contagem by promoting the national platform of the Workers' Party and by making class or other collectively based appeals has unambiguously achieved office in a manner quite distinct from the son of a local political boss in the interior whose candidacy was aided by the endorsement of a high state official visiting a municipality on the occasion of the inauguration of a major state project. But unfortunately for the purposes of this analysis, in Brazil, where political clientelism has so permeated the political system, the campaign styles of "modern" and "traditional" politicians more frequently blur. Moreover, even if "traditional" political careers were readily discernible from "modern" ones, it would be very difficult, from a practical standpoint, to reconstruct the routes, endorsements, campaigns, and constituencies of each elected politician in the state over a period of thirty years.

A more feasible strategy is to focus on those personal attributes and political experience of the officeholders that are more readily available to the researcher. Members of the traditional political elite typically held a law degree (especially from the Federal University of Minas Gerais) and listed landowner (*fazendeiro*) as one of their occupations, although these were neither required to be classified as a member of the traditional political elite, nor would these in and of themselves be sufficient to qualify an officeholder for inclusion in this category. The fundamental criterion used in this study for classifying politicians as members of the "traditional" political elite is descent from a "traditional" family, in practice determined by having older relatives in politics. If a politician's father, father-in-law, or uncle was a political figure of some import, the young candidate "inherits" the "personal" votes of his or her political progenitor and progressively fills the seats vacated by the elder politician. Although the political support and protection of a powerful state political figure are most advantageous for establishing the careers of aspiring young politicians, even a local councillor may deliver enough votes (several hundred are often sufficient) to a young family member to launch a promising career. If a younger relation, such as a nephew, held a local elective office, and, given the regionally segmented nature of Brazilian politics, if a relative had a political career outside the state of Minas Gerais, I presumed that the officeholder had no "relatives in politics" who might have advanced his or her political career.

Conferring traditional status on any politician who has older relatives in politics raises a question and potential problem: how many generations of

---

16 Bonifácio de Andrada distinguished between family oligarchies based on popular votes, which he termed legitimate, and on appointment, which were, in his view, illegitimate. Murilo Badaró (who paradoxically won his Senate seat through appointment as a "bionic" senator) boasted: "If the so-called 'governing families of Minas' have a title of nobility, it has not derived from wealth or blood, but by their public behavior which has earned them the respect of Mineiros" (*Estado de Minas,* 1/18/81).

family participation in politics does it take to qualify as a "traditional political family"? To address this problem, I divided the traditional political elite into two tiers. For the upper traditional elite, or the "oligarchy," the answer is many. Members of the oligarchy, strictly defined, belong to a branch of one of the twenty-seven "governing families" that were boldly identified in a classic work by Cid Rebelo Horta (1956). Since the time of the Brazilian independence movement, these families controlled municipal politics in dozens of important cities in the state, including Montes Claros, Teófilo Otoni, Itabira, Lavras, Leopoldina, Patos de Minas, Ubá, Guanhães, and Ponte Nova, and they dominated state politics as well: thirty-three of fifty-five presidents of Minas when it was a province under the empire and 80 percent of its republican governors were descended from one or more of these families. To classify traditional politicians in the second tier, I took one generation of political patrons as sufficient. Even if their family roots in politics do not go back for several generations, in most cases having "older relatives in politics" was adequate to establish a pattern of political recruitment and competition distinctive from that of a "modern" political elite.

If the definition of traditional political elite is based primarily on family lineage, it cannot be exclusively. If it were, the only divide within the elite would be that drawn between families, and all politicians not belonging to a traditional family would belong to a residual category – the "middle class" – all else notwithstanding. This study, then, would be of mere sociological interest, offering little insight into the workings of the political system. What is needed to complete our profile of the traditional political elite is a guideline for including those of its members who did not belong to traditional families but who nonetheless played a significant role in keeping closed the political system. Before 1964, political recruitment was controlled primarily through the political parties: high posts in parties were dominated by members of the traditional elite and places on the party tickets were awarded only with their advice and consent – they promoted politicians who supported them and vetoed the candidacies of those who did not.[17] Anyone who belonged to the cliques that founded the two major elite parties of the postwar era, the PSD and UDN, and who signed the *Manifesto dos Mineiros,* were surely high-ranking members of the precoup generation of the Minas political elite, as were those politicians related to these party founders, and they are accordingly classified as traditional in this study.

Was the military able to dispense with the "traditional" politicians of the

17 In 1982, Bonifácio de Andrada, for instance, vetoed the "candidacy" for lieutenant governor on the ARENA ticket of Crispim Jacques Bias Fortes, his arch-rival in Barbacena politics. The elder Andrada, who was about to retire from politics, argued that if Bias Fortes were allowed to hold such a high position, he would gain a firm upper hand over Andrada's son, who had less prestige at that stage of his career in the continuing feud between the two most famous families of Minas politics.

precoup period and effect a general renewal of the political class? An investigation into the fate of members of the pre-1964 political elite reveals that the state's political elite before the 1964 coup fared quite well in circumstances of military governance. In some cases, they made their way to quite powerful posts; in others, quite lucrative ones. Even at the height of technocratic influence, Rondon Pacheco handed two former presidents of the state Legislative Assembly in the 1950s, José Augusto Ferreira Filho and Francisco de Castro Pires Júnior, directorships in the state banking system, and another high-ranking politician from the Bias Fortes era, Juarez de Souza Carmo, the presidency of the state's housing department (COHAB). Of all eighty members of the political elite who occupied the state and federal posts this study has targeted for investigation before the change of regime,[18] forty-four (55 percent) "survived" politically after the regime change: thirty-two (40 percent) did so in the executive branch, and twelve maintained their political careers in legislative or party service. Eighteen "survivors" among the precoup political elite served after the coup as governor, vice-president, state and federal cabinet ministers, or state bank presidents (identified in Table 4.5 as high-level posts), and in many cases, they also filled lower-ranking positions before or after their service in higher office. A total of eighteen politicians of the precoup period at one time filled the positions of presidents of parastatal agencies or directors of state banks (lower-level posts), and twenty-six served in the state and federal legislatures or in the top echelons of ARENA. When the potential field of elite survivors excludes thirteen cabinet members who died before 1974 (see note b, Table 4.5), the percentage of the precoup elite whose careers extended beyond the regime change rises to two-thirds.

The *traditional* subset of the precoup elite was well represented among the survivors. The Coelhos of Ubá, the Bias Fortes and Andradas of Barbacena, and the Oliveira Pennas were conspicuously prominent in the high echelons of the state. Of the forty-four members of the precoup political elite who survived in high-level, lower-level, and legislative posts, members of the traditional political elite comprised twenty-eight (64 percent), of whom eighteen were descendants of the twenty-seven "governing families" (Table 4.6). What is striking is that surviving traditional elites dominated the highest ranks of posts included in this study. Half of the top layer of executive branch posts (high-level) that were filled by members of the precoup political elite were occupied by members of the oligarchy, and two-thirds by the traditional political elite as a whole. The traditional political elite, moreover, fared better after the coup than the "nontraditional" political elite. The "survival" rate of the entire precoup elite was 55 percent (Table 4.5), but that of the "traditional" segment (61 percent) and the

---

18 Including the legislative leaders (president and majority party leader of the state Legislative Assembly) of the precoup period.

Table 4.5 *Minas Gerais: Precoup elite, postcoup careers*

	Total attained		Highest attained[a]		Potential field[b]
Political office	N	%	N	Cumulative %	Cumulative %
High-level executive[c]	18	22.5	18	22.5	27.0
Lower-level executive[d]	18	22.5	14	40.0	48.0
Legislature and ARENA[e]	26	32.5	12	55.0	66.0
Subtotal			44		
None	36	45.0			
Total			80	100.0	

Note: I allowed only until 1982, when the direct election of governors changed the political rules of the game, for the political careers of the precoup elite to be resurrected.

[a] The cumulative number and percent of those members of the pre-1964 state political elite who had postcoup political careers eliminates duplication across categories of posts. Officeholders are counted only in the category of the *highest* office they attained.

[b] "Potential field" subtracts from the total of the 80 politicians of the precoup elite 13 members who had died by 1974 – 4 before 1964 and 9 others between 1964 and 1974 (N = 67). I chose 1974 as a cutoff to calculate the percentage of members of the precoup elite who might have "survived" politically the coup because it seemed reasonable to expect that they might have served in state office before their passing (since in 1974 politicians returned in force in the federal and especially state arenas). In the absence of knowledge about the state of their health and readiness for public service, I included the 6 other politicians who died after 1974 but before 1982 in the "potential field."

[c] High-level executive posts include state governor, vice-president, federal and state cabinet posts, and presidents of state banks.

[d] Lower-level executive posts include officers of state banks, and presidents and directors of state agencies. Omitted are federal and state judicial posts, and the chief of the national mission to the United Nations, which has the effect of excluding five members of the precoup elite.

[e] Federal and state deputies, and members of the national and state executive commissions of ARENA. This category excludes two MDB deputies who were *cassados* by Institutional Act Number 5, but includes one who was not. All pre-1964 politicians had a choice about whether to join ARENA and side with the government.

oligarchical subset (58 percent) is substantially higher than that for the "nontraditional" contingent (47 percent).[19] Members of the oligarchy were also more likely to survive in high office (50 percent in high-level posts)

19 Although I did not study the composition of the postcoup legislatures, there are indications that family connections abetted political survival in federal and state houses. In the first decade after the coup, from 1965 to 1975, 87.5 percent of ARENA deputies and 63. 6 percent of MDB federal representatives had relatives in politics (Fleischer, 1981b: 109). And in 1981 at least sixteen federal deputies and twenty-eight state representatives belonged to the twenty-seven "governing families" (*Estado de Minas*, 1/18/81).

Table 4.6. *Political survivors, 1964–82*

	High-level		Lower-level		Legislature and party		Total		Survival rate	
	N	%	N	%	N	%	N	%	%	N[a]
All traditional	12	67	8	57	8	67	28	64	61	46
Oligarchical	9	50	4	29	5	42	18	41	58	31
Other traditional	3	17	4	28	3	25	10	23	67	15
Nontraditional	6	33	6	43	4	33	16	36	47	34
Total	18	100	14	100	12	100	44	100		80

Note: Highest post achieved.
[a]Number of all precoup politicians in each category.

than other traditional politicians (30 percent) and their nontraditional counterparts (38 percent).

The staying power of the traditional political elite and the ability of its members to control recruitment after the coup produced a dramatic effect on the composition of the political elite after 1964: a larger segment of the elite *after* 1964 can be classified as "traditional" than can its counterparts before the bureaucratic-authoritarian coup.[20] Over the entire period from 1956 to 1982, 64 percent of the state elite of Minas Gerais who followed a distinctly political route to power either belonged to a "governing family," had older relatives in politics, or had organized an "oligarchical" political party (Table 4.7). Virtually three-fourths of the state cabinet members, lieutenant governors, and mayors of Belo Horizonte (or older relatives in politics who enjoyed such careers) after 1964 were "traditional" politicians, as compared with 57.5 percent before the coup. Although a slightly higher proportion of the precoup political elite are known to have been descended from the twenty-seven "governing families" (38.8 percent) than of the postcoup elite (34.3 percent), over 37 percent of the postcoup elite had other relatives in politics as compared with 17.5 percent of the precoup group. Moreover, at least seven of fourteen, or half, of the fathers, fathers-in-law, uncles, and older brothers of the precoup cabinet secretaries and ten of twenty-five (40 percent) of the postcoup cohort who did not belong to the oligarchy had taken their political careers to the state level. The sixty-seven politicians in the state elite after the coup were impressive not only for their distinguished origins but also for their own precoup political

20 This is not true, however, of the lower ranks of the elite. David Fleischer (1981b: 109) estimates that 97 percent of the PSD federal deputies and 100 percent of their counterparts in the UDN and PR who held office from 1945 to 1965 had relatives in politics (for PTB deputies, it was 71.4 percent). As we have seen (note 19), rates are lower after the coup.

Table 4.7. *The political elite in Minas Gerais, 1956–82*

	Precoup cohort		Postcoup cohort		Total	
	N	%	N	%[a]	N	%
Traditional						
Members of "27 families"	31	38.8	23	34.3		
Other relatives						
in politics[b]	14	17.5	25	37.3		
State/federal	7		10			
Local	5		7			
Insufficient data	2		8			
Party-political						
activity	1	1.2	2	3.0		
Subtotal[c]	46	57.5	50	74.6	92	64
Nontraditional	34	42.5	17	25.4	51	36
Total	80		67		143	

[a]As percent of the political elite.

[b]Relatives who made their political careers in other states were omitted.

[c]These should be interpreted as minimum percentages; because of incomplete data, it is impossible to know if all traditional members were discovered. 46 + 50 = 92 because the careers of four members of the traditional political elite spanned the two periods.

experience. In addition to the fifty traditional politicians, eleven had had political careers in state politics, two in local politics, and two had some political but primarily state-level administrative experience prior to the change of regime. In other words, *only two members of the postcoup political elite who were the first of their families to enter public life had apparently done so after the coup.*

With most members of the traditional political elite and an even narrower oligarchy well represented in top state posts in Minas Gerais, the parties and political class were thus not "renovated," or at least not to the satisfaction of the military and not to the extent anticipated by scholars. Nonetheless, although political recruitment was regulated during the authoritarian regime more so than in the period from 1945 to 1964, politics in Minas was not closed to all but the oligarchy after the military coup of 1964 any more than it had been during the Old Republic (cf. Wirth, 1977). Rather modest politicians such as João Marques de Vasconcellos and Ibrahim Abi-Ackel who had begun their political careers in the early 1960s were able, with the blessing of traditional politicians, to rise to high-ranking state and federal posts during the dictatorship. But "new" political elites who owe their positions to oligarchical patrons also owe them their allegiance, and old elites are more likely strengthened than weakened by the controlled acceptance of a limited number of new members (and their votes) to their ranks.

CONCLUSIONS

The bureaucratic-authoritarian state that was created by the Brazilian military was not purged of traditional politicians. The traditional political elite of Minas Gerais in particular was not eclipsed irreversibly by a centralizing military regime, and the announcement by scholars of the death of this class was premature. This study of state office holding in Minas Gerais suggests that in Minas shifts in power holding from politicians were less abrupt, longer in the making, more reversible to political control than on the federal level, and not as complete as has been commonly assumed. For a brief time, technocrats displaced politicians in many high state offices and those technocrats had few ties to politicians or to political parties. But the political elite regained most of these posts very soon thereafter. Even in the early to mid-1970s, moreover, political elites and technocrats "shared" the state. Under the guidance of politician-governors, economic and fiscal policy was planned by technically qualified personnel. These secretaries of departments overseeing the economy, however, did not pursue a single route to power, they did not rise through institutions that might have replaced political parties as an elite recruiting ground, and they had extensive partisan attachments and worked well with politicians, including members of the oligarchy.[21] The technocrats, moreover, barely nudged politicians from those posts in the "underside" of the state that distributed state patronage. Generally, while patterns of elite recruitment changed in the states, they did not do so in the same way, and to the same degree, that they did in the federal government. The design of macroeconomic policy by the federal government and state development programs by state planners did not structurally deprive political elites in the states of the means with which to conduct traditional politics.

By the mid to late 1970s, moreover, the ability to marshal support for the regime, largely but not exclusively by drawing votes, was once again highly regarded and rewarded, and political criteria once again determined career advancement. Political parties resumed their roles as vehicles for political advancement – "Modern Princes." This change poses a paradox: at precisely the moment in time when the regime was the most successful and invincible, it shifted course and accepted the return of politicians to powerful state posts. Most observers now agree that this was so because the military could not govern indefinitely in a technocratic style and, accord-

21 No politician that I interviewed in 1981 or 1982 complained of an inability to work with technocrats.

ingly, it brought back politically adept governors first to gain the support of the state legislatures and subsequently to help ARENA candidates win increasingly competitive elections (Nunes, 1978: 60; Sarles Jenks, 1979: 367–71). The military, these observers argue, traded a loss of efficiency in exchange for a significant gain in political support, something it was willing to do since the costs associated with retaining politicians as chief executives in their states were reduced by the transfer of policy making to those extragovernmental branches and agencies of the state whose administrators were not elected, and the potential benefits were considerable in a system in which political processes continued to function normally.[22] Politicians recruited from the legislature could bridge the interests of the national leadership and the state political machines, minimize dissension, and prevent defections from the promilitary coalition. After President-elect Ernesto Geisel and his chief political advisor, General Golbery de Couto e Silva, embarked on a course of political liberalization in early 1974 that restored many civil liberties and a greater degree of contestation to the political arena, these needs became all the more urgent.

The evidence presented in this chapter is consistent with the view that politician-governors were needed to compensate for the inability of technocrats to mobilize mass support. But it also suggests that the appointment of politician-governors alone was inadequate for marshaling political support for, or despite, the policy decisions of an authoritarian regime, and that the military was not free to dismiss and rehire politicians, traditional or otherwise, at its whim. The regime's ability to accomplish its immediate political and developmental objectives and longer-term development aims depended as much on consolidating its support among sympathizers in the political class that controlled the "underside" of the state, which conducts "low politics" and organizes consent, as it did on seizing the "upper side," which conducts "high politics," makes macroeconomic decisions, and executes particular development projects.

Arguments for the return of politicians that view military choices as essentially unconstrained, moreover, do not explain why the most *traditional* members of the Minas political elite should have enjoyed the success that they did. Presumably, if the return of politicians were due only to the largesse of military patrons, then the military would not have chosen the segment of a political class most capable of exercising power independent of its patronage. Yet, this is precisely what the military did, which suggests that it was unable even to sponsor a new political elite more to its liking than the populist and clientelistic politicians that it scorned. This elite was in fact more closed than in the competitive 1956–64 period, and it was led by its most traditional elements. Despite national regime change, oligarchs

22 Nunes (1978: 60) also points out that there was, moreover, no proof that technocrats were more efficient or less corrupt.

retained a measurable degree of influence over the political system that their forebears created a century ago.

Why this should have been the case dominates the two chapters that follow. Chapter 5 explores the causes, patterns, and consequences of the restoration of clientelism along with political elites to prominent positions within the state, and Chapter 6, why *traditional* elites in particular were able to survive and sustain traditional politics.

5

Back to patronage: State clientelism in Minas Gerais

A cornerstone of the military's economic project was to gain control of the levers of the economy through fiscal centralization. Traditionally in Brazilian politics, fiscal federalism had enabled the administration of public programs to become entangled with party politics in a clientelistic political order that blurred the divisions between public resources and private power. By transferring control of fiscal resources from the states to the federal government, the military hoped both to ensure financial stability and to remove the blight of political clientelism from state administration. In that the fiscal dependence of impoverished municipalities had left local elites, and their subjects, in a position of political subservience to whoever controlled the public purse, the military project also entailed shifting the focal point of municipal dependence from the states to the union and, ultimately, weakening the regional oligarchies.

Clientelism soon proved to be less retractable than the military had anticipated, however, and eliminating it was no more politically feasible than dispensing with traditional political elites. The measures introduced by the authoritarian regime to centralize finance – primarily centralizing tax collection and pegging transfers to federal guidelines – did not complete the anticipated fiscal centralization, and as such were grossly inadequate measures to defeat clientelism. They did not transfer control over patronage from regional traditional political elites to the federal government and technocratic policy makers. Even during the period of strained relations between traditional political elites and military reformers, the Minas state oligarchy was capable, through state, transferred, and borrowed resources, of sustaining its patronage operations.

But a more important reason for the failure of the military to eliminate clientelistic practices from the state had to do with the constraints of its own political strategy. Shrouding its seizure of power in legality, the Brazilian military had allowed a political market to operate and the political process to continue throughout the authoritarian regime, albeit with restrictions; it retained elections and the trappings of constitutional procedure. In the harsh, first decade of bureaucratic authoritarianism, these restrictions were sufficient to contain the regime's opponents. With the first crack of political liberalization in 1974, however, the regime suffered a major electoral setback in congressional elections. Its first attempts to combat electoral decline that tried to rekindle the economic growth rates of the "miracle" and manipulate electoral laws to its advantage were an inadequate formula for salvaging military rule. The military recognized that if it were to preserve its primary accomplishment of dismantling populism and remain in power without resorting to generalized and extreme coercion, it would have to abandon its project to achieve a depoliticized state administration and find a means to generate support.

Within the constraints of its political strategy and the opportunities created by the economic policies it implemented in the first decade of bureaucratic-authoritarian rule, the military revised its political project after 1974. State-led capitalist development that had multiplied the spaces for state–society interaction made a resort to clientelism an attractive option to bolster support for a regime that suddenly found itself engaged in contested elections. At a time when public sector expansion transformed clientelism and agricultural modernization, mass urbanization, and capital-intensive industrialization caused an explosion in the number of clients dependent on the state, increasing the amount of state resources earmarked for pork-barrel spending was all the more possible and potentially effective. A patronage-based strategy for mediating state–society relations also made sense given that voters used their ballots traditionally to solicit state patronage and increasingly to protest government policy. Since the politically effective *distribution* of state resources held the key to success at the polls, moreover, the regime's strategy for coping with electoral disaster eventually came to rest on channeling state patronage resources through civilian politicians, in many cases the most traditional of the political elite that had been restored to top-level positions in the state. In the second decade of bureaucratic-authoritarian rule, state patronage resources expanded dramatically, state agencies and programs to distribute them proliferated, and social development funds were increased and distributed under the guidance of governors through individual ARENA deputies and local politicians for maximum political punch.

National policy making by technical experts notwithstanding, the channels by which state resources reached municipalities and citizens remained in the hands of governors and deputies and hence were highly politicized. Despite its "statification," clientelism remained a political elite-driven and managed system that buttressed traditional politics. Fiscal and political centralization only transformed the patronage system into an oligarchical monopoly. As long as Brazil remained in the grip of an authoritarian regime, controlling state office became a self-perpetuating political resource.

THE INCOMPLETE CENTRALIZATION OF STATE RESOURCES

In the twentieth century, the Brazilian central government was weak relative to the states, by design of the regional oligarchies. In the heyday of the regional oligarchies, from 1907 to 1930, federal government revenues as a share of total public sector income fell from 65.8 to 51.2 percent, and the central government ran budget deficits every year from 1910 to 1926 (FJP, n.d., I: I-6). The constitution of 1934, centralizing in its spirit and effects and implemented during the previous height of central government authority, Vargas's Estado Nôvo (1937–45), only partially reversed this trend; the federal government increased its share of public sector revenue from 51.2 percent in 1930 to 55.7 percent in 1945, but at the expense of the *municípios,* not the states.

After 1964, the military sought to strengthen the center at the expense of the states.[1] As part of its larger economic project to wrest control of state spending from the regional oligarchies and concentrate fiscal authority in the hands of the federal government, it initiated a program of fiscal centralization. It enacted a sweeping tax reform package in 1966 (later incorporated into the constitution of 1967), which enhanced central government revenues. Under the new system, the union collected nearly all direct taxes and over half of all indirect taxes (Baer et al., 1976: 71). It reserved to itself the most important source of revenue in Brazil, the income tax (Imposto de Renda), while leaving to the states the lesser value-added tax known as the ICM (Imposto sobre a Circulação de Mercadorias), and to the municipalities a tax on urban property (Imposto Predial e Territorial Urbano, IPTU).[2] The federal government, moreover, set the rates and granted exemptions on state and locally collected levies. As a result of fiscal reform, between 1965 and 1975, the federal government increased its share of public sector revenue from 63.9 to 72.9 percent (Table 5.1). State-collected revenues especially declined after 1969, while the municipalities were left with virtually no tax base. In 1975, municipal government in Brazil collected only 2.6 percent of all tax revenue.

As part of the same 1966 reform package, revenue-sharing funds were established to transfer funds to states and municipalities to help meet operating expenses. Transfers from both the municipal revenue-sharing fund, the Fundo de Participação de Municípios (FPM) and the state fund, the

---

1 L. Martins (1977: 6) argues that this centralization of power in the federal government appeared to be a movement for the political control of *territory,* unlike the previous centralizing episode in the 1930s, when the government's intention was to unify the national market.

2 In all, the federal government authorized itself ten taxes and two apiece to the state and municipal governments. In addition to the ICM, the states were permitted to collect the ITBI, a transport tax. Of the two, the ICM was by far the more important, accounting for more than 95 percent of state-collected tax revenue in Minas Gerais in the 1970s. The municipalities were also allowed to levy a tax on social services.

Table 5.1. *Brazil: Federal, state, and local tax revenues,*
1965–75

Year	Federal	State	Municipal
Gross			
1965	63.9	31.2	4.9
1969	65.3	31.7	3.0
1972	69.5	27.6	2.6
1975	72.9	24.5	2.6
Net[a]			
1970	51.2	36.5	12.3
1971	50.8	37.1	12.1
1972	48.5	33.8	17.7
1973	49.5	33.3	17.3

[a]Net tax revenues = revenues after transfers.
Source: FJP, n.d., I: II-3, II-4.

Fundo de Participação de Estados (FPE), were allocated on an automatic basis and calculated according to population size. Additionally, transfers to states were inversely related to per capita income, thereby serving as a territorially redistributive fiscal instrument. Municipal governments also benefited from state revenue sharing: 20 percent of the state-collected ICM was returned to the municipalities in which the tax revenues originated. While transfers considerably augmented state and municipal revenues, how the subnational governments could use these monies was predetermined by guidelines set by the central government. Twenty percent of the transfers derived from the FPE had to be allocated to education, 10 percent to health, 10 percent to rural extension, and 10 percent to development funds (FJP, n.d., I: II-5). Similarly, 20 percent of municipal FPM funds was earmarked for education, 10 percent for health and sanitation, and at least 50 percent of FPM monies was to be channeled into capital investments (30 percent for smaller, poorer *municípios*) (IBAM, 1976). At least one respected observer and his colleagues (Baer et al., 1976: 74) argued that the imposition of ceilings on state and municipal revenues and restrictions on the use of transferred funds by the federal government undermined state and local autonomy. Moreover, the concentration of fiscal authority and resources in the hands of the central government threatened to transfer municipal dependence from the states to national authorities, and to deprive the regional oligarchies of independent sources of revenue and hence patronage.

Virtually across the board, fiscal centralization did not produce the kind of dramatic change in Brazilian federalism that the military hoped for and many scholars had anticipated. First of all, it is doubtful that the restric-

tions placed on state government revenues by federal constitutional legislation curbed state spending. Minas Gerais supplemented its tax base with
external funds. In the 1970s the state regularly borrowed at least 10 percent
of its total revenue and in some years much more (up to one-fourth of the
state budget in 1972) (SEPLAN, 1978, 6, 2: 355, 356). This trend continued
into the 1980s: perhaps as much as 24 percent of state income in 1980 and
19 percent in 1981 derived from borrowed monies.[3] Imaginative negotiations with foreign development banks produced matching federal grants,
thereby augmenting further the state's resource base. Borrowed money
eased state dependence on federal government transfers. In Minas Gerais,
transfers accounted for less than one-fifth of the state's budget from 1965 to
1975 (Table 5.2). In 1982 they represented 19.2 percent of state revenue
(Ministério da Fazenda, 1984: 18). Transfers similarly did not constitute a
large proportion of state income in other Center-South states (Table 5.3);
they mattered most to small states of the Northeast (e.g., Sergipe, Piautí)
and the northern and western "frontier" (e.g., Rondônia, Acre).

Second, centralization was not irreversible, nor were state governments
powerless to halt its march. In fact, state governments by 1980 regained
some ground lost over the preceding decade. The Center-South states,
including Minas, which relied least on the FPE, for several years complained vociferously of fiscal centralization and the loss of state autonomy;
they assailed the tax system, and especially federal government control of
the ICM, for depriving states of their rights to raise needed revenues.[4] In
1980, they successfully petitioned the federal government to adopt a series
of measures intended to enhance state revenues.[5]

Third, while the strings attached to federal transfers implied that the
national government had the authority to direct spending, substantial evidence from the municipal level suggests that federal guidelines had little
impact on local spending patterns.[6] A detailed study of the pattern of

3 These figures are taken from raw data (in graph form) from the state Finance Department
(Secretaria da Fazenda do Estado de Minas Gerais).
4 These states, Minas Gerais, São Paulo, Rio de Janeiro, Rio Grande do Sul, Santa Catarina,
and Paraná, worked for several years in a common effort to wrest concessions from the
federal government. As the wealthiest states in Brazil, they also protested that through
their FPE quotas they were in effect subsidizing the poorer states of the Northeast and the
developing regions of the North and West. A more detailed statement of their positions can
be found in Secretaria da Fazenda do Estado de Minas Gerais (1979).
5 Requested were measures to rescind several exemptions to the ICM, to revise FPE quotas,
and to lift federal restrictions on foreign borrowing. The federal government agreed to
extend the ICM to cigarettes and to transfer the minerals tax to the state governments. It
rejected the states' petition to subject liquid fuels to the ICM, and to permit states to
borrow freely without federal approval.
6 For advanced industrial societies, Tarrow (1978: 12) has similarly argued that the "empirical
case that fiscal centralization has robbed subnational governments of their vitality has yet to
be made." His claim rests on three factors: (1) though national spending has increased,
subnational spending has increased still more; (2) whereas numerous categorical grants tie

Table 5.2. *Minas Gerais: State revenue by source, 1965–75 (in %)*

Year	Transfers	Taxes	Credit	Other
1965	12.1	58.3	7.0	22.6
1966	14.3	59.5	--	26.2
1967	10.6	73.1	--	16.3
1968	15.8	69.0	6.5	8.7
1969	15.1	78.7	1.3	4.9
1970	13.0	80.7	.9	5.4
1971	14.1	68.8	12.6	4.5
1972	12.6	54.6	26.5	6.3
1973	18.5	57.8	16.5	7.2
1974	18.5	61.1	11.9	8.6
1975	17.6	58.7	16.3	7.3

Source: Ministério da Fazenda, 1981: 210, 236.

expenditures of eight Minas *municípios* from 1967 to 1972 (IBAM, 1976)[7] revealed that local spending did not conform to predicted levels on specified government services, in some cases well exceeding government minimums, in others, not satisfying legally prescribed levels. For instance, while nearly all the *municípios* spent well in excess of the amount stipulated by law on the broad category of "education and culture" (IBAM, 1976: 48), in more than half of the possible cases (8 *municípios* for 6 years = 48) the *municípios* failed to allocate the required funds to primary education (IBAM, 1976: 51). Instead, the money was spent on a medical school in one municipality, a television transmission tower in another, and new sports facilities in several others. Similarly, most of the 10 percent of FPM

down the activities of many local governments, the general revenue sharing that is more common leaves them far more freedom; and (3) there is apparent a continued high level of variation in spending across subunits within industrial nations, in many cases closely linked to local political factors. Tarrow's first factor may be inconclusive for Brazil, where although subnational spending did not increase at a faster rate than national spending from 1966 to 1988, it did increase in real terms. His second and third factors do have merit and are examined in the text.

7 Four pairs of *municípios* were chosen systematically from four categories of population size to illustrate the relationships between municipal size, degree of urbanization, revenue collection, and public expenditure. Minduri and Sardoa represented two extremes of urbanization within the category of the smallest municipalities; Bocaina de Minas and São João Evangelista, with a similar percentage of their population residing in urban areas, were at opposite ends of the second population size category; São João do Paraíso and São Lourenço, with roughly the same population total, exhibited maximum variation in their degree of urbanization; and Itajubá and Conselheiro Lafaiete, in the category of the largest of Minas *municípios,* with similar population sizes and similar degrees of dependence on transfers from the federal revenue sharing fund, exhibited very different degrees of dependence on the ICM (IBAM, 1976: 22, 24, 26, 28).

Table 5.3. *Brazil: State revenues, 1982 (in %)*

State	Transfers	Taxes	Credit	Other
São Paulo[a]	12	77	4	7
Rio Grande do Sul[a]	16	65	12	7
Rio de Janeiro[a]	18	61	7	14
MINAS GERAIS[a]	19	68	7	6
Paraná[a]	21	69	4	6
Santa Catarina[a]	23	58	15	4
Espírito Santo	23	68	3	6
Amazonas	24	49	13	14
Bahia	25	55	9	11
Pernambuco	25	64	6	5
Mato Grosso do Sul	28	50	19	2
Goiás	29	62	4	5
Pará	34	58	2	6
Ceará	35	51	10	4
Alagoas	36	53	2	9
Rio Grande do Norte	43	35	14	8
Paraíba	45	38	12	5
Mato Grosso	47	35	9	9
Maranhão	51	27	18	4
Sergipe	53	37	3	7
Piauí	63	29	5	3
Rondônia	76	17	1	6
Acre	83	14	-	3

[a]Center-South states.
Source: Ministério da Fazenda, 1984: 14–19.

funds mandated to be spent on health and sanitation was spent on sanitation (water, sewerage, and paved roads) alone. As municipalities typically disbursed more than this amount on sanitation,[8] federal efforts to attach 10 percent of the FPM for this end were purposeless. On the other hand, spending on health did not rise, despite the federal directives, since in most instances the states and the private sector ran medical posts (IBAM, 1976: 57), and most municipalities could not afford to pay the salaries of highly skilled medical professionals. The federal government was apparently unable to induce compliance in its priority areas where local authorities either could not or would not spend, despite the fact that the penalty for noncompliance with prescribed spending minimums was suspension of the quotas (at least until the irregularities were corrected). Only municipalities with

8 Water and sewerage are most often municipally provided services. Over 92 percent of Brazilian municipalities, for example, were responsible for delivering local sewerage services (IBAM, 1976: 53–54).

Table 5.4. *Brazil: Municipal expenditures by region, 1971 (in %)*

Services	Brazil	North	Northeast	Southeast	South	Center-West
Government and general administration	12.3	19.2	17.1	10.4	13.3	18.0
Financial administration	11.5	8.9	17.8	11.0	8.8	9.1
Defense and security	.6	2.0	1.3	0.4	0.4	0.7
Natural and agricultural resources	.8	.6	1.8	.4	1.5	1.7
Transportation and communication	14.1	19.4	10.4	11.6	23.2	30.3
Industry and commerce	1.3	.6	.3	1.6	1.5	.1
Education and culture	13.8	9.9	15.5	13.1	15.7	13.0
Health	4.5	3.6	6.0	4.6	3.4	3.6
Social welfare	7.9	7.1	5.9	7.9	10.3	2.8
Urban services	33.2	28.7	23.9	39.0	21.9	20.7

Source: IBAM, 1975: 53. Original source: *Finanças Públicas,* no. 317, 1974, Subsecretaria de Economia e Finanças.

more than 25,000 inhabitants (one-fifth of Brazilian *municípios)* were required by law to furnish their balance sheets to the federal government (IBAM, 1975: 60). As of 1975, less than 7 percent had had their quotas suspended.

Subnational governments, moreover, exhibited widely divergent patterns of spending on public services by region (Table 5.4). In one of the more extreme cases, Center-West municipalities spent nearly three times the amount on transportation and communication (30.3 percent) as their counterparts in the Northeast and Southeast (10.4 and 11.6 percent, respectively), while municipalities in the Southeast spent nearly double the amount on urban services (39.0 percent) as those in the Center-West (20.7 percent). Even within Minas, there were considerable fluctuations in spending levels on various services.

A more significant constraint on local spending than federal directives was the absence of state aid. In the eight *municípios* studied in detail by the Brazilian Institute of Municipal Administration (IBAM, 1976), the most urbanized spent approximately 10 percent of their total budgets on education, while the more rural spent nearly double that amount. Because the state is primarily responsible for urban education, the more urbanized a municipality, the more state funds it receives for this purpose and the less it needs to spend of its own resources. Similarly, in one *município* that had no federal and state highways in its territory, the local government was forced to construct and maintain its own road network, for which it spent on average more than three-fifths of its municipal budget (IBAM, 1976: 35).

Without special federal and state funds, local governments were forced to pay their own way and divert resources from discretionary funds to the provision of basic public services. The only and best alternative for poor municipalities of the interior was to seek to complement automatic transfers with discretionary grants of public works, employment, and social services programs from higher levels of the state.

Thus fiscal centralization produced at best a standoff between state and federal elites, and municipal dependence presented a political opportunity for both to exploit. If the military's project stumbled over fiscal centralization, it fell flat in its aim to depoliticize the distribution of state resources.

POLITICAL CONSTRAINTS ON THE MILITARY PROJECT

For the first decade of the authoritarian regime, the military's political strategy of maintaining the facade of representation and elections while distorting their true meaning through various manipulations of electoral law worked reasonably well. With the MDB barely functioning as a party, ARENA won resounding victories in the congressional elections of 1970 and the municipal elections of 1972. In many rural areas, ARENA candidacies went unchallenged by the MDB. In 1974 amid a fragmented polity, an economic miracle, and a demoralized and disorganized opposition, military leaders permitted more competitive elections to take place in what they believed to be very auspicious circumstances.[9] Part of the reason for doing so, as Lamounier and Moura (1986: 183) have argued, was that they were anxious to revitalize representative institutions – "in a context in which absolutely no one doubted that anything could occur but a tranquil victory for ARENA." In particular, the military, which should have otherwise reveled in its crushing victories at the polls, hoped to bring down abnormally high abstention rates. In the city of São Paulo, more than one-third of the votes cast in the senatorial and state deputy contests in 1970, and nearly 40 percent of those in the federal deputy elections, were either blank or spoiled (Lamounier, 1980: 72). In the Minas capital of Belo Horizonte, nearly one-half of all votes cast in the 1970 federal deputy elections were either blank or null (TRE-MG, 1970). A second, less widely cited reason for why the military permitted relatively free elections in 1974 may have been to challenge traditional elites. According to Sarles (1982: 45, 70), "the technocratic-oriented military, disgusted with traditional corrupt electoral practices, systematically purged the electoral lists of phantom voters, disproportionately depriving ARENA of many voters," in some Northeast states, by as much as 25 to 50 percent.

The regime's self-confidence, which prompted it to loosen electoral re-

9 Velasco e Cruz and Martins (1984: 48) report that Golbery even believed the opening to be a bit late: he would have preferred it to have been initiated during the height of economic success in the Médici administration.

strictions in the 1974 congressional elections, was abruptly proved to be overinflated. The government suffered an unanticipated defeat in those elections of a magnitude that stunned both the regime and the opposition (Kinzo, 1988: 157–59). Beginning from a base of 7 of 66 senators and 87 of 310 deputies, the opposition MDB won 16 of the 22 contested seats in the senatorial elections, and it increased its share of the seats in the Chamber of Deputies from 28 percent to 44 percent (it elected 172 deputies as compared with 192 for ARENA). It also took control of five additional state legislatures (prior to the election it held the majority of seats only in Guanabara) (Roett, 1984: 146–47; Alves, 1985: 144–45). The most frequently cited reasons for the regime's defeat were the effective media campaign waged by the MDB (a reason cited by military intelligence [Alves, 1985: 144, 147]) and the turn of the opposition to protesting bread and butter economic issues. As the Senate president and ARENA senator Paulo Torres lamented on his defeat: "I showed graphs and statistics on television, showing that in 1963 there were so many illiterates and today there are only so many. I spoke of the accomplishments of the Revolution, principally the Rio-Niterói bridge. Then they come and say that 'it takes so many hours of labor to buy a kilo of meat,' and that a bridge doesn't fill a belly" (Kinzo, 1988: 157). Indeed, in its television commercials in the state of Pernambuco, the MDB showed films of sugar workers cutting cane with the message "a day of labor in the *zona da mata* is worth 8 cruzeiros; a kilo of jerked beef costs 26, more than 3 days of work" (Kinzo, 1988: 156).

In its "victory," the MDB capitalized on a strong undercurrent of protest, capturing the allegiance of voters who previously had stayed home on polling day, cast blank votes, or spoiled their ballots.[10] In the city of São Paulo, null and blank votes in the Senate race decreased from 33.7 in 1970 to 10.9 percent in 1974 (Lamounier, 1980: 72). The rates of decline are less dramatic in the deputy races – one-fifth of the electorate still opted to register their protests in the form of a blank or null ballot – but significant nonetheless. In Minas Gerais, too, blank and null votes declined from two-fifths to one-quarter of the turnout in the federal deputy elections. Moreover, a shift occurred in the party vote; nationally, the vote for MDB candidates for the Chamber of Deputies rose from 30 to 48 percent, while that for ARENA candidates declined from 70 to 52 percent. In São Paulo, the shift was even more dramatic: the percent of the party vote captured by the MDB soared from 30 percent in 1970 to 71 percent in 1974. This shift prompted Lamounier (1980: 38–39) to argue that an electoral realignment had taken place between the 1970 and 1974 elections.

The regime responded to this "defeat" not by canceling its liberalization program, but by attempting to manipulate the results of future elections as

10 For more information on the elections of 1974, see the essays in Cardoso and Lamounier (1978).

much to its advantage as possible. It acted decisively to minimize the impact of reduced majorities in the Congress, to ensure that the government would not lose its majority in the Senate, and to safeguard the electoral advantage of ARENA. In April 1977 it recessed Congress and decreed an "April package" of fourteen amendments to the constitution, three new articles, and six decree laws. The "package" extended the presidential mandate from five to six years and reduced the quorum necessary for voting on constitutional amendments from two-thirds of both houses of the Congress in a joint session to a simple majority (after the 1974 elections, the government could no longer muster a two-thirds majority); it created "bionic" senators (one senator from each state would thenceforth be elected "indirectly," as the military euphemistically described the manner in which these posts were appointed by the federal executive but officially "ratified" by state electoral colleges, which included local councillors); and it extended the use of the "Lei Falcão," to include future state and federal elections (Velasco e Cruz and Martins, 1984: 55). The 1976 law, named for then Justice Minister Armando Falcão, had limited the use of the mass media by political parties in the 1976 municipal election campaigns to displaying a candidate's name, curriculum vitae, and still photograph. This restriction harmed the electoral prospects of the opposition more than the government. To enhance even further its probability of retaining control of both chambers of the legislature, the regime carved new states from old and gave premature statehood to territories where the government had reason to believe it held the political advantage. Thus, for example, Mato Grosso do Sul was subdivided from the state of Mato Grosso and recognized as an independent state.

The military did not stop at constitutional engineering and electoral manipulations; it also sought to devise a strategy to build more active support for ARENA. Part of that strategy entailed priming the economy to avoid recession, even when that meant borrowing abroad heavily to compensate for the effects of the first and second oil shocks (Lamounier and Moura, 1986). Equally significant was a profound shift in spending priorities toward neglected constituencies. During the presidential administrations of both Geisel and Figueiredo, military and transportation budgets were reduced while federal government spending was increased on agriculture, education, and welfare. Spending increases were most pronounced in election years (Ames, 1987: 175). And after years of squeezing wages to attract foreign investment, promote growth, and combat inflation, the Geisel and Figueiredo governments attempted to increase real wages for the working class.[11] The Geisel initiative fell short, but Figueiredo in 1979 enacted a wage

11 The labor union–supported research association DIEESE calculated that "the labor time required to earn the cost of a basic food ration soared from 88 hours in 1965 to 163 hours in 1974," as cited by Ames (1987: 194).

readjustment law that in fact redistributed income from the higher income brackets to the lower (Ames, 1987: 198).

As a strategy for arresting the trend of declining support for the military regime, the resort to general redistributive measures and programs was flawed. Massive wage increases placed too great a strain on the economy and particularly on antiinflationary efforts. Such a strategy, moreover, was virtually impossible to implement politically for a regime whose supporters, in class terms, were those most likely to pay the costs of redistribution. Land reform, for instance, a potential centerpiece of any redistributive strategy, floundered because land redistribution on deferred compensation, the only way a real reform could be carried out, would have directly injured the interests of the large landowners in the Northeast whose political support was crucial to the authoritarian regime (cf. Ames, 1987: 163–65). The regime needed desperately to find a more cost-effective strategy to target voting blocs than the expensive big-budget programs that were so damaging to the government's antiinflationary policies (cf. Ames, 1987: 206).

CLIENTELISM RESTORED

Operating under severe financial and political constraints, the military opted to reverse course and return to a time-honored tradition in Brazilian politics – appealing to the electorate through patronage. Although clientelism, especially personal clientelism, had at no time disappeared from local politics, not even during the Médici administration, the federal government after 1974 signaled the acceptability, indeed, desirability, of practicing patronage politics on a massive scale at all levels of the Brazilian state. The regime's revised political strategy was made feasible by its own economic model and, in particular, by those economic programs that had inflated state resources and the ranks of state clients. State-led capitalist development enhanced the need for patronage programs, the state's capability to fund and administer them, and their potential electoral value.

Such a strategy was all the more compelling in a political system in which societal interests were most often mediated in clientelistic networks, especially at election time. Generally, where state resources are allocated to communities on a discretionary basis, the potential for political gain is very high. But where entry to state employment is subject to civil service examination and state transfers are allocated to individual citizens on an automatic basis, there is little political gain for program administrators. In Brazil, the distribution of even automatic social services such as social security and medical care was at times politicized, and *both* automatic and discretionary spending were perceived by individual program recipients as well as elected local representatives as gifts of the state or particular politicians (cf. Sarles, 1982: 55).[12] And despite a competitive civil service examination (known as the *concurso),* securing employment in the federal bureaucracy remained highly dependent on political contacts. With the exceptions of the Bank of Brazil, Petrobrás (the state oil company), the National Economic and Social Development Bank (BNDES), and Itamaraty (the Foreign Ministry), the *concurso* was a farce (Mainwaring, 1991a: 6–7). At the local level, public employment was secured almost exclusively through political connections.

Brazilian voters, conditioned by years of patronage-based appeals on the part of candidates to elective office, were predisposed to cast their ballots to influence the distribution of resources but not necessarily the enactment of policies. In Minas Gerais, a survey conducted in 1968–69 of most (seventy-three of eighty) of the Minas Gerais state deputies at the time revealed that four-fifths of ARENA and 93 percent of MDB deputies were most frequently asked by their constituents to provide jobs for their political supporters (Table 5.5). The construction of educational and medical units was the second most frequently voiced demand. Whether shaping or responding to voter expectations, deputies appealed to electors on the basis of their ability to deliver state patronage. When the deputies were asked to name their most important campaign appeal, their most frequent response was a combination of development (e.g., road construction) and assistance (funds for schools, hospitals, and so forth) (58 percent), followed by just "assistance" (18 percent). Only 4 percent responded that "ideological" appeals were most important (Bastos and Walker, 1971: 146). In 1974, itinerant rural laborers – the *boiás-frias* – of the Campinas region of the state of São Paulo expressed the expectation that municipal government maintain unpaved streets (to guard against erosion), hold the line on municipal taxes, and provide them with piped water, electrical energy, medical supplies, and, above all, tangible benefits in return for their votes, but not enact an agrarian reform that did not interest them because "these days you need lots of resources to till the land" (Martinez-Alier and Boito Júnior, 1978: 251, 254). To the *boiás-frias,* a "good mayor" was one who "did things for the poor" – paid their medical bills and made good on his promise to provide them with shoes in exchange for their votes.

The regime's strategy, moreover, was as well suited to responding to the challenges posed by the changing basis of partisanship and electoral choice in Brazil as it was to capitalizing on the incentives of traditional electoral politics. Like other political parties in Brazilian history and consistent with the "artificial" means by which it was created, the MDB, as well as ARENA, did not evoke sharp, strong, and durable partisan attachments by

12 Sarles (1982: 71) reports multiple incidents from her own fieldwork where various education and health services, which were the state's obligation to provide, were nonetheless perceived by local residents as brought by local politicians and state deputies.

Table 5.5. *Most frequent demands made of state deputies in Minas Gerais, 1968–69*

Demands	Yes	No
Jobs for political supporters		
ARENA	45 (80.4%)	11 (19.6%)
MDB	14 (93.3%)	1 (6.7%)
Total	59 (83.1%)	12 (16.9%)
Construction of educational and medical units for municipal districts		
ARENA	25 (44.6%)	31 (55.4%)
MDB	2 (13.3%)	13 (86.7%)
Total	27 (38.0%)	44 (62.0%)
Support for construction of municipal projects		
ARENA	9 (16.1%)	47 (83.9%)
MDB	2 (13.3%)	13 (86.7%)
Total	11 (15.5%)	60 (84.5%)
Establishment of financial institutions or enterprises controlled by the state in municipal districts		
ARENA	2 (3.6%)	54 (83.9%)
MDB	0 (0.0%)	15 100.0%)
Total	2 2.8%)	69 (97.2%)

Note: Deputies were asked to identify the two most frequently made demands of them.
Source: Bastos and Walker, 1971: 147.

class (cf. Cardoso, 1978: 74).[13] Aside from important concentrations of MDB voters in the nation's largest urban centers, survey research suggests that partisan attachment did not differ by income level,[14] though there did

13 Created by the military as official progovernment and opposition parties, it is hardly surprising that they should have more closely resembled heterogeneous political clubs than parties with well-defined constituencies. With such disparate politicians in the two parties, party platforms never really coalesced nor were they effectively presented to the electorate.

14 In Juiz de Fora, the MDB did not have substantially more adherents among the poorest segments of the population, their "natural" constituency, than did ARENA. In a survey, 33 percent of respondents at the lowest end of the income scale in that city identified themselves as ARENA supporters and 36 percent as MDB sympathizers (with 26 percent preferring neither party and 5 percent not responding); in the next highest salary range, the margin of difference was even slighter: 36 percent preferred ARENA to 37 percent for the MDB (Reis, 1978a: 227). Similarly, within the highest income strata were found both

exist a positive relationship between levels of education and support for the MDB, and a curvilinear relationship between occupation and party identification. When lower classes did vote for the MDB, and upper classes for ARENA, moreover, their votes by and large did not follow from an accurate identification of and support for the ideological content of the preferred party's message (Reis, 1981: 216). The content of the two parties' programs did differ, but there is little indication that the electorate could distinguish those differences;[15] all but the best-educated, urban voters had little awareness of the MDB's positions on substantive policy issues (Lamounier, 1980: 39–41, 78).

After a decade of military rule, however, a substantial segment of the electorate began to identify with an MDB that had evolved from a token opposition party in the early years of the authoritarian regime into a genuine opposition party. On the national level and in some metropolitan regions of the more developed southeastern states, the MDB became what Shefter (1977: 415–17) calls an "externally mobilized" party, or one established by outsiders who, because they do not enjoy access to state patronage, must organize a mass following by other means – the greater the resistance the party must overcome to gain power, the stronger the tendency to eschew the use of patronage. Structurally blocked from attaining power, the party did not appeal to the electorate as Brazilian parties had traditionally – along personalistic or clientelistic lines (outside of Rio de Janeiro, where MDB governor Chagas Freitas headed his own political machine, it had no resources to distribute).[16] Yet, it did not mobilize its supporters along clear ideological or even issue lines like the socialist and labor parties in Europe described by Shefter. Instead, but no less damaging

the most frequent expression of opposition to the authoritarianism of the regime *and* the largest contingent of *"arenistas"* (Reis, 1981: 205). In Presidente Prudente, a predominantly rural *município* in the western part of the state of São Paulo, Lamounier (1978: 48–49) found a high party identification with ARENA and high levels of progovernment voting among the lower *and* upper classes; some middle classes identified with the MDB. Only rural upper classes appeared to consistently identify with one party (ARENA). In Niterói, the city across the bay from Rio de Janeiro, lower classes, particularly those with low levels of education, were as likely to support ARENA as were the upper classes (Lima, 1978: 142).

15 Especially beginning with the 1974 elections, the MDB leadership (Ulysses Guimarães and Pacheco Chaves) solicited the support of leading intellectuals from the São Paulo-based research institute CEBRAP (Centro Brasileiro de Análise e Planejamento) to edit the party's electoral platform. According to Fernando Henrique Cardoso, these intellectuals (including Paulo Singer, Francisco Weffort, and Maria Hermínia Tavares de Almeida) advocated that the party discuss democracy, salaries, distribution of income, union organization, and the participation of women and blacks in Brazilian society. When the top leadership of the MDB approved these ideas, they wrote the Campaign Manual of 1974 (Kinzo, 1988: 154–55).

16 The relative absence of personalism from the MDB is dramatically evident in Lamounier's 1978 survey of the São Paulo electorate: approximately 70 percent of voters in the city of São Paulo could not remember for which candidates they had voted in 1974 (1980: 77–78).

to the military, the MDB forged an identity as a strong, if vague, opponent of the military regime that successfully inspired the allegiance of millions of voters.

Military rule thus created a new foundation for partisan identification in Brazil – party image. In time, for the electorate the only really meaningful divide between the two official parties was that ARENA supported the government and the MDB opposed it (Lamounier, 1980: 78). The electoral fortunes of the progovernment party and the political careers of its candidates were pegged to regime performance: when, where, and as long as voters scored government performance highly, ARENA politicians and the government could approach elections with confidence. But when, where, and among those voters for whom memories of the 1970 World Cup soccer victory had faded and the "economic miracle" had ground to a halt – or never reached – the party of the regime was spurned. Statements from survey respondents in São Paulo illustrate in a particularly vivid fashion the dichotomous views: "The MDB is against the government, and ARENA is the party of the government. Everything is okay, I am studying, I have work, I lack for nothing. I vote for ARENA. As they say on the radio, protest against what?" (Lamounier, 1980: 41); and, on the other side, "ARENA is on the side of the government, it supports everything the government does, the MDB always tries to be on the side of the people"; "I've heard that the MDB could benefit the workers, but not ARENA." "The MDB is linked to the people. ARENA is linked to the government, and no one is satisfied with the government" (Lamounier, 1980: 40).

In this context, the regime turned to disbursing patronage in order to counter the growing perception that ARENA represented the "rich" and the MDB the "poor," to disassociate somewhat the electoral prospects of ARENA candidates from unpopular government policies, and to convert the association in the public mind of ARENA with the government into an electoral asset. Working to the regime's favor, the new partisanship was weak and conditional.[17] In Campinas, the poorest and most marginal segments of Brazilian society – itinerant rural laborers – expressed more interest in whether local candidates could deliver state and personal services than in their partisan label: "Our concern is with the mayor, not the party" (Martinez-Alier and Boito Júnior, 1978: 250). It didn't matter if a "good mayor" was from ARENA, despite the fact that the *boiás-frias* in this region believed ARENA to be the party of the rich.[18]

The electoral realignment announced by Lamounier, moreover, was in-

17 Lamounier's survey questions do not appear to have measured intensity. In the absence of panel data to that time, it is difficult to know how strong the attachment of first- or second-time opposition voters to the MDB really was.

18 They readily identified ARENA as the party of the government and of the president, but doubted that the MDB represented them. They also doubted the authenticity of the MDB's platform (Martinez-Alier and Boito Júnior, 1978: 259).

complete. The MDB dominated the balloting in the *senatorial* contests throughout Brazil in 1974, winning sixteen of twenty-two contested Senate seats, but ARENA candidates polled well in the federal deputy, state legislative, and local elections. What explains this bifurcation of the vote is that some Brazilian electors reconciled an ambivalent attitude toward military rule – by and large they disapproved of authoritarianism and government policy yet hoped that elected representatives could bring home the pork – by splitting their ballots: when they wished to secure state assistance, they voted ARENA; when they wished to protest government performance in such areas as the high cost of living (a salient issue for the poor whose adjustments to indexed wages lagged up to six months behind double- and later triple-digit inflation), they voted for the MDB. The government was more likely to elect deputies, mayors, and local councillors, whom voters expected to intercede on their behalf to deliver state programs, public works, and jobs, than senators, whom they did not.[19] Senatorial races instead became referenda on the regime and took on a plebiscitary quality. Although the direct popular Senate vote became an embarrassment, the appointment of bionic senators secured the government majority in the upper house. Majorities in the federal and state legislatures and local councils – the foundation of government majorities in the electoral colleges that ratified regime choices for executive positions – could not, however, be taken for granted. Patronage as a strategy to abet government candidates was necessary to win these races.

After 1974 the federal government stepped up federal programs and contributions to state programs to benefit state clients. Less so under Geisel than under Figueiredo, the military administration reversed spending priorities on social programs, redirecting their benefits to the lower classes. During the Figueiredo presidency, there was a concerted effort to shift spending priorities within the Ministry of Education from university to primary education, a shift that would have brought the resources of the ministry to a broader political base had it been successfully effected. The reach of other social programs was, in fact, extended. Agricultural credit after 1978 was increasingly meted out to small farmers (Ames, 1987: 157), and under both the Geisel and Figueiredo administrations, there was a significant expansion of public housing for the poor and the near poor. In 1974, only 7,831 low-income units were constructed – a meager 12 percent of the resources of the national housing program (down from 40

---

19 Diniz (1980: 355–56) found that the strength of the *"chaguista"* faction in the Rio MDB rose in elections for state deputy and local elections at the same time it declined in federal deputy elections. She postulates that electors distinguish between federal races in which they may wish to identify with the opposition, and state-level contests in which they tend to vote according to clientelistic calculations. This pattern was not in evidence in Minas Gerais. It might be the case that Rio is somewhat exceptional because the state government and federal government were on opposite sides of the fence.

percent in 1970); in 1980, nearly 200,000 units were built (Ames, 1987: 168).[20]

Increasing state programs for the poor in itself is, of course, an insufficient electoral strategy; without effective political distribution, even if such a strategy is less costly than awarding increases in wages and social security benefits, it will likely be no more effective. The military addressed this problem by funneling the resources it made available for patronage through the mediating structures of traditional politics. The analysis of Brazilian national budgetary outlays and the distribution of federal programs across policy areas conducted by Ames (1987) suggests that the regime reached out to voters along regional, not class lines. The distribution of program resources was biased toward the regions of steady political support for the regime – especially the Northeast, where the government party routinely trounced its opposition by a 3 to 1 margin in electing two-fifths of the government's representatives in the Congress and nearly half in the state legislatures (Table 5.6). Agricultural credit was lavished upon the Northeast after 1974, and politically important, smaller states received more credit per farmer than did larger ones (Ames, 1987: 160). The distribution of low-income housing benefited both regions and classes equally in the 1970s. Complementary infrastructural investment (sewerage, water, etc.) of the National Housing Bank, however, became more evenly distributed among states but not on a per capita basis within states (Ames, 1987: 170). Large increases in direct transfers to state governments also flowed toward the Northeast, especially in election years: in 1982, half of all transfers to states went to the region (Ames, 1987: 176).[21] Although these policies were intended to appeal to particular regions, "the regime never fine-tuned these programs to its political needs" in that "politically marginal states did not gain at the expense of solidly progovernment and hopelessly antigovernment states" (Ames, 1987: 205).

If the regime favored the backward corners of the Northeast with agricultural and housing assistance, it did not forsake as opposition turf the rapidly growing urban areas of the Southeast. Recognizing that its well-being rested on capturing the support of voters and their patrons in urban areas, it sponsored an expensive urban housing program and invested generously in complementary infrastructure.[22] Minas Gerais, part of the advanced

20 Part of this increase may be due to the revision of the definition of poor and near poor in 1974. This category originally included families whose household income fell below three times the monthly minimum salary; after 1974, the ceiling was raised to five times the minimum salary.

21 Although the Northeast undoubtedly benefited disproportionately, it should also be noted that the federal funds created to distribute transfers to the states and municipalities were intended to be redistributive. As the Northeast was a relatively poor region, it was entitled to receive more resources than it contributed in taxes.

22 While not denying its existence, Lamounier (1980: 34–35) has cast doubt on the relative importance of clientelism in accounting for regime victories. Based on survey data from

Table 5.6. *Brazil: Party seats by region, 1966–78*

Region	1966 ARENA	1966 MDB	1970 ARENA	1970 MDB	1974 ARENA	1974 MDB	1978 ARENA	1978 MDB
Senate								
North	2	1	6	0	2	1	3	0
Northeast	8	1	18	0	4	5	8	1
Center-West	1	1	4	0	1	1	2	1
Southeast	4	1	7	3	0	5	1	3
South	3	0	6	0	0	3	0	3
Total	18	4	41	3	7	15	14	8
Chamber of Deputies								
North	20	7	12	6	11	10	17	11
Northeast	107	29	73	17	82	25	92	34
Center-West	14	7	13	4	14	7	18	10
Southeast	91	66	83	40	55	82	62	94
South	45	23	42	20	37	41	42	40
Total	277	132	223	87	199	165	231	189
State Legislative Assemblies								
North	62	24	30	15	31	23	39	27
Northeast	325	94	184	54	204	69	221	81
Center-West	48	21	37	14	40	21	50	30
Southeast	198	159	126	107	108	141	100	143
South	98	47	91	43	74	76	77	72
Total	731	345	468	233	457	330	487	353

Source: Lima, 1984: 66–68. Original data from Tribunal Superior Eleitoral, *Dados Estatísticos*, vols. 8, 9, and 11.

Southeast, was neither securely in the government column nor was it an opposition stronghold as were the states of São Paulo and Rio de Janeiro: the MDB elected its popular candidates for senator in 1974 (Itamar Franco) and 1978 (Tancredo Neves), but ARENA retained majorities in the state legislature and the federal deputy delegation to Congress (Table 5.7). As a sometimes conservative, sometimes electorally marginal, region, the state benefited especially from the national regime's policy of industrial deconcentration. Minas received ample shares of the loans granted by both

São Paulo, and particularly on the basis for allegiance to the MDB voiced by respondents that identified with the party of the opposition, he claims that the appeal of clientelism to the electorate in the urban areas of the Southeast was diminishing. In so doing, he discounts the importance of Miyamoto's (1980) contribution to his own important volume, which shows that top vote getters in São Paulo used clientelism to get elected.

Table 5.7. *Federal and state congressional elections: Minas Gerais, 1966–78*

	1966			1970			1974			1978		
	Seats won	% turnout	% party vote	Seats won	% turnout	% party vote	Seats won	% turnout	% party vote	Seats won	% turnout	% party vote
Senate												
ARENA	1	42.5	59.5	2	51.1	79.7	–	41.7	53.3	–	37.4	49.0
MDB	–	28.8	40.5	–	13.0	20.3	1	36.5	46.7	1	38.9	51.0
Blank		21.8			32.4			13.9			14.7	
Null		6.9			3.5			7.9			8.9	
Chamber of Deputies												
ARENA	37	63.6	77.0	28	48.5	80.4	18	46.7	61.6	23	46.2	58.8
MDB	11	19.0	23.0	7	11.8	19.6	11	29.1	38.4	16	32.3	41.2
Blank		12.8			29.2			16.9			15.1	
Null		4.6			10.5			7.3			6.4	
Legislative Assembly												
ARENA	63	64.0	76.8	47	49.9	79.7	31	47.4	61.2	35	46.8	59.3
MDB	19	19.4	23.2	12	12.7	20.3	19	30.0	38.8	24	32.1	40.7
Blank		12.0			28.2			15.5			14.7	
Null		4.7			9.2			7.0			6.4	

Sources: TRE-MG, 1966, 1970, 1974, 1978.

the Bank of Brazil and the National Economic and Social Development Bank. In the late 1970s, Minas increased its share of Bank of Brazil loans to become the fourth most-favored state, and in 1980 it tied with Rio Grande Do Sul as the third. From the National Economic and Social Development Bank, only São Paulo received more loans, on average, in the thirteen-year period from 1970 to 1982 (Ames, 1987: 186–87, 190–91).[23] The state government also complemented federal programs with the state's own funds.

Within regions, the regime distributed resources through individual politicians that could act effectively as political brokers, which in practice most often meant traditional regional politicians. Not only did the regime acknowledge and attempt to rectify the political error committed during the Médici years of shunning the state oligarchies by ending its direct attacks on their positions in the state, but it now cultivated the personal vote of clientelistic politics by targeting federal allocations to state and local political bosses. The research department of the Ministry of Planning (IPEA) confirmed that state and local elites were able to influence the distribution of federal "controllable transfers" (Rezende, 1982, as cited in Ames, 1987: 176). Based on this case and others, such as the distribution of National Housing Bank resources – which he discovered to have been tailored to advance the political ambitions of the minister of the interior, Mario Andreazza – Ames (1987: 205) concluded that the military's spending program to maximize support was "more a response to the claims of powerful northeastern supporters than a calculation of the political needs of Brasília itself."

To expand its local political bases and broaden the government coalition, the regime also employed a strategy to co-opt local bosses with personal political followings. It offered such material inducements as housing programs and construction projects to opposition but essentially nonpartisan mayors with apolitical followings to join the governing party (a phenomenon known as *adesismo*) (Cammack, 1982: 68). After the local elections of 1972, ARENA attracted to its ranks as many as half to two-thirds of the 466 MDB mayors elected throughout Brazil by offering state resources in exchange for the partisan switch (Banck, 1974, 1978, as cited in Cammack, 1982: 68). Although the phenomenon of *adesismo* was especially marked in Espírito Santo, it was not limited to backward states with weak partisan identification for the opposition party. Between 1976 and 1982, Governor

23 Trends in the allocation of BNDES loans are difficult to establish because the breakdown of loans in any single year was distorted by the disbursement of resources associated with major projects (such as the massive Itaipú hydroelectric project in Paraná). To gain a sense of how Minas Gerais and other states fared over the thirteen-year period as a whole, I assigned a value of three for each year in which a state captured percentagewise the highest value loans from the bank, a value of two for a second-place finish, and a value of one for a third-place finish. Unfortunately, Ames (upon whose data I have relied in this section) does not disaggregate by state investment for projects approved by the Industrial Development Council (CDI/MIC).

Paulo Maluf of São Paulo induced 78 of 101 mayors elected in 1976 (as well as 16 state legislators) to switch to the progovernment party (Mainwaring, 1991a: 18).

Once the military committed itself to winning the votes of a mass electorate by targeting transfers for distribution through the clientelistic networks of individual politicians, the bargaining position of the traditional political elite within the governing alliance was enhanced. Politicians at all levels were now able to press more effectively their claims for patronage resources. The military had an added incentive to favor personalistically delivered state patronage over an "impartial" variant. After the 1974 election, it became concerned with not only maintaining itself in power for as long as it could, but also with influencing Brazilian politics after its own departure. Bolstering the popularity and electoral prospects of civilian politicians opposed to populist and radical politics was an excellent way of doing so. As Ames (1987: 149) put it, "to the degree they could induce the population to support conservative politicians, and to the degree the military commanded respect, civilian rule held less danger."

MINAS GERAIS: THE EXPANDING SCOPE OF STATE PATRONAGE

When the return to patronage was signaled nationally, the state of Minas had the financial and institutional capacity to distribute federal monies and launch its own programs. As we have seen, public expenditure levels in Minas Gerais grew annually from 1947 to 1969 by 6.5 percent and from 1971 to 1977 by nearly 17 percent (FJP, n.d., I: IV-13) and, as a share of gross domestic product, reached 28.9 percent in 1977 (SEPLAN, 1978, 6,2: 255); in real terms, state expenditure per capita nearly tripled between 1960 and 1977 (FJP, n.d., III: 141, 145) (see Chapter 3). The incursion into new branches of the economy and the provision of new social services by the state allowed for a marked expansion in the mid to late 1970s of traditional patronage programs and the creation of new ones. These programs paralleled federal programs; some were heavily endowed by federal monies, others were genuinely state programs. Reflecting the evolving priorities of the state elite, the national regime, and even international creditors who contributed amply to state programs,[24] the state of Minas after 1974 shifted resources away from development-oriented projects toward social programs to subsidize the urban poor. In 1959–60, at the close of the decade in which Juscelino Kubitschek committed Minas to developing its physical infrastructure, energy and transportation garnered one-

---

24 Many of these loans were forthcoming from the World Bank and the Inter-American Development Bank.

Table 5.8. *Minas Gerais: Per capita state expenditure, 1959–77*
(in 1977 cruzeiros)

Services	1959-60 Amount	%	1972 Amount	%	1977 Amount	%
Administration	11,884	3.5	14,837	2.3	14,852	1.1
Legislature	2,917	0.9	6,996	1.1	14,614	1.1
Judiciary	9,651	2.9	13,153	2.0	33,286	2.5
Public security	40,320	12.1	71,735	11.0	91,420	7.0
Finances[a]	35,280	10.6	51,325	7.8	42,091	3.2
Health	23,472	7.0	19,518	3.0	45,021	3.4
Education	32,396	9.7	157,363	24.0	239,245	20.6
Welfare and social security	24,122	7.2	50,319	7.7	139,813	10.7
Commerce	11,422	3.4	15,875	2.4	32,889	2.6
Transportation	89,745	26.9	106,260	16.2	222,579	17.0
Communications	920	0.3	1,285	0.3	4,940	0.4
Planning	8	0.0	3,866	0.6	20,027	1.5
Regional development	--	--	5,648	0.8	2,918	0.2
Industrial development	5,196	1.5	56,304	8.6	86,707	6.6
Urban development	75	0.0	--	--	80,030	6.1
Environment	68	0.0	3,924	0.6	2,574	0.2
Statistical and research services	4,985	1.5	11,687	1.8	26,502	2.0
Agriculture	16,992	5.1	22,125	3.4	52,833	4.0
Energy and mineral resources	24,340	7.3	6,579	1.0	108,050	8.2
Culture	156	0.0	1,191	0.2	3,138	0.2
Financial services and tourism	186	0.1	32,980	5.1	9,811	0.7
Modernization of public services	95	0.0	732	0.1	8,650	0.7
Total	334,230		653,702		1,281,990	

Note: Includes direct administration and parapublic agencies and foundations, but excludes state enterprise, federal, and municipal expenditures.
[a]Debt service and transfers to *municípios*.
Source: FJP, n.d., III: 141, 145.

third of state expenditure (Table 5.8). In 1972, during the height of the state's industrialization drive, infrastructural spending declined sharply while spending on "industrial development" rose from 1.5 to 8.6 percent of the total state budget. Between 1972 and 1977, as the rural areas emptied and urban agglomerations grew, state resources earmarked for "urban development" were increased more than for any other significant government service.[25]

Of all urban development programs, perhaps the most important was housing construction. In 1980, the state in Brazil, through the National Housing Bank and the federal and state savings institutions known as Caixas Econômicas, furnished nearly three-fourths (73.8 percent) of the capital in the housing mortgage market (IBGE, 1983: 902). Additionally, federal and state governments occasionally organized special housing programs to benefit the low-income population. In Minas Gerais, such a program was successfully launched on a somewhat modest scale in the first year of Francelino Pereira's government (1979), and later expanded into a major development project. In sharp contrast to the four years of Rondon Pacheco's governorship (1971–75) when the state of Minas built only 1,340 housing units (Chaves de Mendonça, 1978: 326), the state government from 1979 to 1982 built 107,343 new residential units. These represented a substantial share of a 7.8 billion dollar program to build 130,000, mostly low-income, residential units. In the following year, the governor promised 300,000 more units would be constructed by the end of his term in office in 413 *municípios* (more half the state's total) (SEPLAN, 1981: 97–99). If implemented, the state's housing program would have provided shelter for roughly 15 percent of the state's population.[26] In the 1983–86 period, an additional 78,890 units were planned for 100 *municípios* (Pereira dos Santos, 1983: 345), but a cutback in National Housing Bank funds amid general economic austerity rendered meeting this target unfeasible (Garcia, 1985: 248–49).

Other urban development funds were channeled through large-scale, comprehensive projects like the federal and state Intermediary Centers Programs, backed by the World Bank and the Inter-American Development Bank, respectively. The state program expanded on a federal project to develop midsized "dike" cities that could serve as receptacles for migratory flows that would otherwise move into the burgeoning metropolitan regions of the state capitals of the Southeast already straining to provide city services to recent migrants. Minas extended the benefits of the program from the two "dike" cities in the federal program (Montes Claros and Juiz de Fora) to fourteen other midsized cities within the state. The programs delivered basic sanitation (sewerage and water), infrastructure (in-

25 Of the twenty-two categories of government functions, only spending on planning accelerated more rapidly than on urban development. Whereas state resources earmarked for urban development rose from 100 (base year) in 1959–60 to 106,706.7 in 1977, those targetted for planning rose to 250,337.5. Yet, nominal levels of spending on planning were substantially lower than on urban development – 1.5 percent as opposed to 6.1 percent (FJP, n.d., III: 145).
26 My estimate (430,000 × 5 [average household in Minas Gerais] = 2,150,000/14,000,000 (state population) = 15.3 percent).

cluding public transportation), health and education, labor training, credit, and income-improving opportunities such as subsidies for artisanry to two million low-income inhabitants (one in seven of the state's population) between 1981 and 1985. The "Intermediary Centers" Program was perhaps the most ambitious of all state development programs.

While the state accelerated its program for urban dwellers, it did not neglect those who remained in agriculture. It extended its traditional support for small (as well as large) agrarian producers by extending them credit:[27] in 1980 90 percent of all agrarian credit in Minas Gerais was disbursed by public entities (IBGE, 1980a: 52). In the late 1970s and early 1980s, after years of relative neglect, small agrarian producers were once again privileged in state budgetary priorities.[28] The state Program for the Promotion of Small Rural Producers, "MG-II," which targeted a 264.2 million dollar investment to at least 30,000 small farmers and their families and 1,000 small entrepreneurs in 102 *municípios,* had by the end of 1982 reached over 17,000 of its intended beneficiaries. A second program, PRODEMATA (Program for the Integrated Development of the Mata Zone), intended to reach 128 *municípios* in the Mata Zone and 25,500 sharecroppers and small farmers (*Estado de Minas,* 1/20/82: 11), delivered credit and technical assistance to 25,000 families, 97 percent of its goal (Pereira dos Santos, 1983: 47). The reasonably good success of the most important of the state's programs for the rural areas augured well for the government's ability to reach its targeted 70,000 program beneficiaries, one-fifth of all small agrarian producers in the state of Minas Gerais (*Estado de Minas,* 5/21/81: 14).[29]

Not all effective state patronage programs were expensive. PRODECOM, the state Program for the Development of Communities, a low-cost, "self-help" program for low-income communities, was initiated in 1979 as a form of "participatory planning." In theory, the community was invited to define areas of community need and to contribute to meeting those needs

27 Forty-four percent of the Bank of Brazil loans in 1974 were allocated to agriculture, as opposed to only 15 percent of private commercial bank credit (Baer et al., 1976: 75).
28 State expenditure on agriculture fell from 5.1 percent of the total in 1959–60 to 3.4 percent in 1972, and then began to rise again. In 1977, it represented 4 percent of state expenditure (FJP, n.d., III: 145), even before the well-financed array of agrarian programs launched during the administration of Francelino Pereira.

　　According to the state secretary of planning in 1981, Paulo Haddad, state programs for agrarian producers were reaching the population marginalized in the process of industrialization in Minas in the preceding twelve years, a process that had accentuated regional disparities, increased pressure on large urban centers, and transformed Minas into an importer of foodstuffs (*Estado de Minas,* 5/21/81: 14).
29 Other programs for the rural areas include the integrated rural development projects for the northwest region (Planoroeste II) and the upper Rio Grande and Gorutuba Valleys (PDRI-ARG and PDRI-Gorutuba), and rural development schemes for the Jequitinhonha Valley (Prodevale), the Minas Northeast (Project Sertanejo), and the scrublands region (Polocentro). See Table 5.9 for a program summary.

in conjunction with the state. The program's spokespersons proclaimed that it would substitute for the actions of the "paternalistic state" (Haddad, 1980: 115). In practice, regardless of the source of program initiatives, PRODECOM brought public goods to vast numbers of Mineiros at little cost to state government. Moreover, in many cases, this program tied already existing neighborhood associations directly to the state.

Of the program's priority areas, "nutritional improvement" and the construction of "popular" housing soon became the services most in demand. Nutritional improvement, which encompassed operating community markets, raising farm animals and gardens, aiding small farmers, and even granting land titles to peasants, was aimed at alleviating malnutrition among the poor. Since food accounted for 70 percent of the family budget of the poor (*Estado de Minas,* 2/22/81: 16), better diets could be attained only by reducing food costs. The establishment of community markets was a step in this direction. Goods sold in community market stalls were as much as 60 percent cheaper than those purchased through normal retail channels (*Estado de Minas,* 12/27/81: 6). Animal farms were also introduced to improve nutritional levels; animals such as goats required little attention and yielded milk to supply entire communities.[30]

The aspect of PRODECOM's "nutritional" program most in demand was that of granting land titles to peasants.[31] In his request of May 1981 for a $17 million aid package for PRODECOM to the World Bank, Minas governor Francelino Pereira included funds to grant legal title to lands claimed by 25,000 families in 1983 (*Estado de Minas,* 5/21/81: 13). As of September 1981, 2,300 persons had been served by the program (in six communities). At least thirty-four other communities had already applied by December 1981 for the land title project. Another 56,000 hectares were due to be awarded to about 2,000 families during 1982 (*Estado de Minas,* 12/27/81: 6). In all, the "nutritional" programs underway in late 1981 were to have benefited 261,000 persons.

The housing programs administered by PRODECOM brought instant and largely unanticipated success. PRODECOM financed them by tapping a credit line secured by MinasCaixa, the state savings institution, from the National Housing Bank for low-income housing construction in the state. In February 1981, PRODECOM set a provisional goal of erecting 5,000 houses for persons who earned less than three times the monthly minimum salary. The interest rate for eligible buyers was an affordable 3.2 percent. By August, after only eight months, 15,000 homes had been built or were in con-

---

30 In the *município* of Patrocínio, one farm was to feed 300 schoolchildren and their families (*Estado de Minas,* 2/22/81: 16), and in Funilândia, an initial investment of fifty goats and two breeders were expected after three years of operation to meet the dairy needs of 7,500 persons (Haddad, 1980: 119).

31 This facet of the program was executed by a state foundation, RURALMINAS, and the rural unions; the average land plot was 29.15 hectares.

struction (*Estado de Minas,* 8/30/81: E6). The program was successful in making itself visible to the needy; by that same August, there was already a demand for 24,000 units on the part of community associations (*Estado de Minas,* 8/30/81: E6). Responding to demand, Francelino Pereira, in November 1981, negotiated an agreement with the Caixa Econômica Federal, the federal savings institution, to build 20,000 additional houses in 150 different municipalities (*Estado de Minas,* 11/15/81: 3).

A broad array of state programs was geared to reach target groups in every corner of the state (Table 5.9). While essentially providing economic assistance, these large-scale state urban and rural development programs and more modest initiatives had far-reaching political effects. By providing indirect employment, shelter, basic amenities, and other necessities, they integrated most low-income citizens into the public economy, and the political orbit of the state elite.

THE POLITICS OF PATRONAGE: DISTRIBUTING STATE RESOURCES IN MINAS GERAIS

In Minas Gerais, the major infusion of funds for state programs for the poor and needy and transparent tolerance for public patronage activities on the part of the federal government reactivated the state networks for the distribution of political favors and state resources that had functioned at less than full capacity in the first decade of military rule. In the 1970s, and especially after 1974, the state clientelistic machine in Minas was revved up to administer the patronage programs that were expected to rescue the declining fortunes of the government party.

Program grants were distributed in a politicized if sporadic fashion in the late 1970s. While the Minas state government no more efficiently targeted state spending to electorally marginal areas in such a way as to maximize its electoral support than Ames found the Geisel and Figueiredo administrations did nationally,[32] the governor did use in a highly visible fashion his

32 There does not exist a positive and linear relationship between levels of voting for ARENA in state and federal races and the allocation of state aid over which state elites could exercise some discretion – "other capital transfers," "other current transfers," and "credit" (as opposed to automatic transfers that form part of the federal and state revenue-sharing programs). Thirty-eight percent of the 98 *municípios* who received per capita levels of discretionary state spending – "other capital and current transfers" – above 2,000 cruzeiros per capita in 1982 gave between 40 and 60 percent of their vote to ARENA federal deputy candidates in 1978, a proportion only slightly higher than that for all 722 *municípios,* 34 percent. Nearly two-fifths of the 48 *municípios* that received the very highest levels of per capita state support (above 3,000 cruzeiros per capita in 1982) were in planning Region I, and half of those were either historical cities, part of the metropolitan region of the capital, or sites of iron and steel investments. Another sizable group (43 percent) were in Regions III and IV, the more prosperous agricultural regions. Only 10 percent of the *municípios* in this most highly favored category were located in the poorest regions of the state: the Jequitinhonha and Rio Doce valleys, the region of Minas included

vast discretionary power to allocate state resources to bolster the local administrations of his supporters, to keep potential malcontents from defecting, and to show *municípios* with opposition leaders the futility of their continued resistance to the state oligarchy. Throughout the interior of Minas Gerais, accounts by local elites in the early 1980s support the view that the state resources associated with the programs listed in Table 5.9 were allocated according to political criteria. The vice-mayor of Varginha, a dynamic center of the state's southern region, for one, spoke about his city's inclusion in the "dike cities" program, which had brought a bonanza of public works to the city. He revealed that Varginha had not appeared on the preliminary list of municipalities, but that the city's mayor, Eduardo Otoni, had fought for and won Varginha's inclusion in the program. The risk of incurring an accusation of patronage in a World Bank–financed program was not a sufficient disincentive for the vice-mayor to brag of the weight the mayor punched with the state administration. The gift from the state administration had had the desired effect. When questioned about his partisan affiliation, the vice-mayor responded: The party of the government has always helped us. We can't even think of changing parties, out of gratitude."[33] When a dissenting faction of the local traditional elite in Varginha contemplated bolting from the government party, Governor Pereira swiftly threatened to inundate the *município* with even more special projects, something that would certainly have benefited politically that faction's rivals, then the local leadership.

Local elites from cities in northern Minas Gerais interpreted programs specially designed to benefit the North as a gift from the governor. They distinguished two periods in the recent history of their relationship with state government: "before [Governor] Francelino [Pereira], and after." (Pereira assumed office in 1979.) In their view, prior administrations had overlooked the North, but Pereira, who built his political career based on support from northern politicians, showered the region with such public works projects as the Projeto Sertanejo, the Integrated Rural Development Project for the Gorutuba Valley (PDRI-Gorutuba), and a water project (Recursos Hídricos) (see Table 5.9). The mushrooming *município* of Montes Claros particularly benefited from this "northern strategy." Long a mere stopover on the migration route from Brazil's Northeast to the wealth-

in the Brazilian Northeast under the jurisdiction of SUDENE (Region VI), and the Minas Mata, combined.

The selection of *municípios* to be included in the rural development program known as MG-II was no more predictable on the basis of aggregate voting data. After eliminating the 208 municipalities that would not have qualified for MG-II funds under any circumstances, I compared the voting patterns of the 103 municipalities that were included in the program, and the remaining 411 that were not. There was virtually no variation in the percentage of the vote for ARENA in the 1978 elections between communities receiving the benefits of the agrarian program and those which did not.

33 Interview with Ronaldo Venga, Varginha, Minas Gerais, October 13 and 14, 1981.

Table 5.9 *State development programs in Minas Gerais*

Program	Purpose	Beneficiaries
Centros intermediários (1981-85)	Reorient migratory flows	2 million low-income inhabitants of 16 mid-sized cities
Crédito rural (1982-84)	Rural credit	30,000 small producers
Prodemata (1976-82)	Rural development in Mata region	25,500 small rural producers and landless sharecroppers
MG-II (1980-85)	Rural development	30,000-35,000 low-income farmers
Planoroeste II (1981-85)	Integrated rural development	Low-income population and small rural producers
PDRI-ARG (1982-85)	Integrated rural development	7,000 small rural producers in Alto Rio Grande Valley
Polocentro (1976-82)	Development of scrublands	Rural property owners in 44 *municípios* of Triângulo
Geoeconômica de Brasília (1975-82)	Reduce migratory flow to Brasília	Low-income population in 13 northwestern *municípios* of Minas Gerais
Prodevale (1979-84)	Rural development	Needy population in the Jequitinhonha Valley
PDRI-Gorutuba (1979-82)	Integrated rural development	5,000 rural producers in northern *municípios*
Projeto Sertanejo (1976-84)	Rural development in Minas Northeast	Small rural producers in six *municípios*
Reflorestamento (1982-84)	Increase wood and charcoal supply	Private firms
Saneamento básico	Metropolitan Belo water supply	Shantytown residents of capital
Energia elétrica (1981-84)	Connect 1,043 small communities	1.8 million inhabitants over 70 percent of area of Minas
Recursos hídricos (1979-84)	Minimize effects of drought	Rural population in 42 *municípios* of Minas N East
Transportes carvão e álcool (1982-84)	Improve transportation from fuel alcohol and charcoal-producing regions	Jequitinhonha, Rio Doce Valleys, Triângulo, Alto Paranaíba, Northeast, North, and Mata regions
Prodecom (1979-)	Community participation in improving shantytowns	750,000 residents in capital and interior

Source: SEPLAN, 1981: 33–71.

ier South, and especially São Paulo, Montes Claros in the 1970s began to benefit from state policy fashioned to prevent migratory flows from advancing farther south. Francelino Pereira's administration seized upon the federal government's decision to make Montes Claros a national "dike" city and built up the area with its own development aid programs.

By contrast, communities that supported the opposition were transparently discriminated against. Jairo Magalhães Alves, the mayor of Itabira, a large mining town and opposition bulwark, explained: "In March, 1977, I negotiated for the installation of CARPE (primary school buildings). It was supposedly in the budget every year. Only in 1981 did it get installed. Maurício Campos was running for governor the next year – he came to inaugurate it. It was the first public work [in Itabira] in 20 years"[34] Another opposition stronghold, Sete Lagoas, a city north of the capital experiencing growing pains much like those of Montes Claros, was ignored by the state administration. Its industrialization, largely a bootstrap operation and one rare case of being fueled by local capital, was not abetted by the state in any way, except for the awarding of an early industrial district.[35] Its mayor, commenting upon the question of state aid, voluntarily compared the fortunes of his *município* with those of Montes Claros: in relation to Montes Claros, "Sete Lagoas," he jested, "does not even get crumbs." Afrânio de Avellar Marques Ferreira was essentially correct in his allegations: whereas Montes Claros received 2,593 cruzeiros for every inhabitant in 1982 in "discretionary state aid," Sete Lagoas received less than one-tenth that amount, only 219 cruzeiros per head (Ministério da Fazenda, 1984). "The *município* grows with its own resources," was the pronouncement of the mayor of Sete Lagoas.

Whereas Afrânio de Avellar Marques Ferreira was able to withstand the punishment of state government for his transgressions with his political fortunes intact, and Sete Lagoas was able to prosper, the same was not true for less developed municipalities. In Curvelo, a popular opposition mayor serving a third (nonconsecutive) term was unable to resist the governor's overtures, and bribes, to cross over to the progovernment party. His *município* was dying, from a once powerful agrarian center, to a city left behind in the state's industrialization. Its rural population had declined from 14,322 in 1970 to 10,961 in 1980, and overall, its population had increased by only an average of 1.16 percent per annum during the 1980s – surely less than the natural rate of population growth. When the mayor was

---

34 Interview with Jairo Magalhães Alves, Itabira, Minas Gerais, October 16, 1981. Maurício Campos, a federal deputy who had been appointed mayor of Belo Horizonte by Governor Francelino Pereira, ultimately failed to secure his party's nomination for governor due to factional squabbles discussed at greater length in Chapter 7.

35 Industrial districts, authorized and funded by the state Industrial Districts Company, provided prepared land to industry. The municipal contribution was normally to grant exemptions on local property taxes.

invited to the governor's weekend palace and promised an array of new public works projects including a new bus station and a low-income housing program on the condition he change his partisan affiliation, the poor mayor acceded. Almost immediately, he began to reap his rewards. Agreements for low-income housing, electrification, telecommunications, roads, bridges, and urban development to be provided by the state government to the municipality were drawn up virtually overnight. In response to the question, "Do you believe, as a mayor of the government party, that your administration has benefitted from the state and federal governments?," Olavo de Matos offered the following: "Yes, absolutely. There has been a radical difference [since joining the party]. If I had continued in the opposition, I would have received nothing. [My switch] facilitated the industrial district; I would not have gotten it [if I had not changed over]."[36]

While the governor coordinated major decisions for the allocation of state program resources, patronage was delivered to local communities by federal and state deputies. Deputies, long at the core of the political class in Brazil, were all but ignored after the onset of bureaucratic authoritarianism by scholars who saw them as token representatives in the powerless parliaments of an authoritarian regime. Although their legislative prerogatives may have indeed been pruned by centralized decision making and their once powerful budget committees stripped of authority over appropriations, they nonetheless remained key figures in the political system – intermediaries in the state clientelistic chain and heads of their own patronage networks.

Traditionally, career advancement for Brazilian politicians and for the *traditional* political elite in particular passed through the state Legislative Assemblies and national Chamber of Deputies. It was especially important to demonstrate electoral prowess and draw votes for the legislative slate of one's party over and above that needed merely to get elected because top vote getters of the party to win a majority at the state level were rewarded with two means of access to state resources to aggrandize further their personal careers. The first, for the "majority" deputy receiving the most votes in a municipality, was the "political command" (*comando político*) of that municipality, or the prerogative to fill virtually all public posts and make other public sector decisions.[37] The second means for a smaller number of politicians was appointment to the state cabinet. Once named a state department secretary, the politician used that position to build up his or her personal following for a later run at

36 Interview with Olavo de Matos, Curvelo, Minas Gerais, October 9, 1981.
37 In Minas Gerais, the "political command" of municipalities had been thus awarded to "majority deputies" for at least four governor's administrations. (interview with Roberto Martins, Belo Horizonte, Minas Gerais, August 16, 1985). According to Martins, this system has been in place at least since the administration of Israel Pinheiro (1966–71), but how far this system extended beyond Minas Gerais is unclear.

higher posts. A typical, if enviable, political career would move from state deputy to state secretary of state to federal deputy or even governor (Fleischer, n.d.: 45).

During military rule, federal and state deputies continued to build up their clienteles by winning with state patronage the support of local politicians who were just as dependent on state-level politicians for municipal programs and services as ever. Several mayors in Minas Gerais reported that the 1967 fiscal reform alleviated some of their fiscal crisis, but ultimately did not alter the dependent nature of their relationships with higher levels of the state.[38] In the words of one opposition mayor: "Because of the centralization of revenue, the *municípios* are slaves of the federal and state governments."[39] Throughout the interior of Brazil, mayors enlisted state support through the intermediation of federal and state deputies who, in turn, attempted to gain state projects for the areas of their greatest electoral support. Because of their key role in the distribution of state resources, deputies were the lifelines of mayors. The mayor of Curvelo, Olavo de Matos, once remarked that "a mayor would not find an open door without a deputy – deputies use mayors as *'cabos eleitorais'* [ward bosses]".[40] Because the ability of local elites to govern, provide employment and basic services, and retain their dominance depended on the quality of their connections to the sources of state patronage, local elites sometimes gambled on early endorsements of state politicians;. an early endorsement of a victorious candidate netted more substantial gains from the state administration than a last-minute show of support. It was not uncommon for municipal leaders, for example, to caucus to select a candidate for governor months or even years in advance of party nominating procedures. In the coffee-growing center of Varginha, a full year before the 1982 gubernatorial election, the local PDS chapter favored the candidacy of Gerardo Renault, state secretary of agriculture, for the state's top post.[41] While patronage networks were most efficient in the hands of mayors, they also extended to local councillors, and even deputies cultivated the support of individual voters through constituency service, Brazilian-style. The most important service a deputy could render to individuals was to secure them public employment through the appropriate department of state government. To secure an appointment as a public schoolteacher, for example, a young woman of the interior needed to enlist, either directly or through the

38 In interviews conducted in Minas Gerais in October–November 1981.
39 Interview with Afrânio de Avellar Marques Ferreira, Sete Lagoas, Minas Gerais, October 19, 1981.
40 *Cabos eleitorais* are generally ward bosses, election organizers, or political brokers who, as Mainwaring (1991: 10) points out, serve the function of connecting candidates to the people as the literal translation "electoral cables" would suggest.
41 Interview with José Fernando Prince, President, Varginha PDS, Varginha, Minas Gerais, October 14, 1981.

intercession of her city councillor, the support of her state deputy who then obtained the appointment from the state secretary of education.

THE REWARDS AND LIMITS OF CLIENTELISM

Did the military strategy of resorting to clientelism successfully halt the precipitous erosion of support for its rule? Mainwaring (1991a: 13, 22) has argued that in the 1980s, as a strategy for governing, clientelism was counterproductive and, for garnering electoral support, it was bankrupt. As president, for instance, José Sarney was able to co-opt enough people to govern as long as he could retaliate against political adversaries, but as soon as he became a lame-duck executive, his support deserted him. In a context of broad political participation, moreover, attempting to buy off everyone produces economic effects so deleterious that they more than offset whatever electoral gains clientelism might produce. After 1980, the parties that most heavily relied on distributing patronage successively suffered devastating electoral defeats. In the 1970s, the results may have been different.

A resort to patronage did not raise the vote for ARENA but it did arrest its decline, stabilizing it at its 1974 level. In the 1978 national elections, the ARENA *legenda* received approximately 55 percent of the seats in the federal Chamber of Deputies, enough to retain its majority, and 58 percent in all state Legislative Assemblies. Fleischer (1980b: 72–81) has demonstrated that this would have been true even without the electoral measures that tampered with the composition of the Chamber – changing the basis for representation from the size of the electorate to the size of the population, increasing the size of the house, and limiting the number of representatives from any one state (which deprived São Paulo of twenty-six seats) – although ARENA would not have had the same results without extending the *Lei Falcão* restricting candidate access to the media. The success of the candidates for the federal Chamber and state Assemblies did not, however, spill over to the Senate races. Without "indirectly" electing one-third of the Senate in 1978, the MDB would have won majority control of the higher body. This pattern generally holds true for Minas Gerais. The vote for ARENA candidates for federal and state deputy was practically the same in 1978 (46.2 and 46.8 percent of the turnout, respectively) as it was in 1974 (46.7 and 47.4), although the MDB in 1978 with 32.3 and 32.1 percent of the turnout improved upon its 1974 showing of 29.1 and 30 percent. In the Senate races, the MDB's majority of the party vote declined slightly from 53.3 percent in 1974 to 51 percent in 1978.

The aggregate national decline of parties of patronage in the 1980s, moreover, masks whether patronage helped or hurt them in the short to medium term. A more accurate test of the effectiveness of clientelism as an electoral strategy would be to examine the effects of clientelism at the state or local level, where it was effectively directed. In much of Brazil clientelism was applied in a context in which a pattern of support and opposition to military rule in the federal and state legislative races and local elections corresponded roughly to levels of development and urbanization: the MDB tended to do well in the more industrialized regions of the country, such as São Paulo, whereas ARENA enjoyed a decided advantage over its opponents in the thousands of small, predominantly rural *municípios*. In an extreme case, there was only one opposition mayor in the western state of Mato Grosso, which had a total of eighty-four *municípios*. Within states, less developed, rural, and smaller cities of the interior tended to favor ARENA, whereas large cities and industrial regions swung toward the opposition. Sarles (1982: 58–59) found a very strong correlation between the size of a *município*, rates of urbanization, and the vote for the federal and state deputies in the old state of Rio de Janeiro (excluding the city of Rio) in the 1974 elections in which the opposition MDB polled quite well (n = 63 *municípios*). The smaller, rural *municípios* supported ARENA in significant numbers: the correlation coefficient for the ARENA vote for the Chamber of Deputies with municipal size was −.708, and −.741 for the same election correlated with percent urban. Sarles's study also demonstrates significant correlations between the percentage of workers employed in agriculture and the vote for the government party (r = .744); wealth (r = .713); and migrants with rural, rather than urban, origins (r = .572). There is a strong, negative correlation between areas of in-migration (from urban and rural settings) and voting for ARENA (r = −.771). Faria (1978: 219–23) found similar patterns in the state of São Paulo in the same 1974 election. The most efficient predictors of the ARENA vote in the state's forty-three "microregions" in bivariate correlations were rural employment (r = .666 in the Senate race; .624 in the federal deputy election; and .675 in the state deputy election), levels of schooling (r = −.825, −.704, and −.704, respectively) and electric lighting (r = −.798, −.718, and −.753, respectively). The direction of the signs indicates that the less developed a municipality, the more likely it was to vote for ARENA. The strength of these correlations led many observers to assume that the regime could not retain urban, industrialized *municípios* in its camp.[42]

42 Boosting the respectable correlations between municipal size and levels of urbanization with voting for ARENA is the close coincidence of voting for ARENA in small, poor, rural *municípios,* where the MDB often had no local *directório* – that is, no local organization – and where, even if it did, ballot boxes were often stuffed. Statistical tests that examine the entire gamut of *municípios* may be skewed by the strong correlation between levels of development and progovernment voting among the numerically significant *municípios* at the lower end of the population scale, and it seems worth asking how significant the correlation is between urbanization, municipal size, and industry with voting for the opposition when the very lowest end of the scale is omitted. Also, the direction and strength of the correlation in Faria's data for São Paulo may have been accentuated by taking the *microrregião,* a cluster of contiguous *municípios,* as the unit of analysis. In such

In Minas Gerais, where state and local elites forged effective urban patronage machines, municipal size and the degree of urbanization did not correlate as strongly with voting for the opposition as they did in the more advanced states of the Southeast. In Uberaba, one of Minas Gerais's most important and largest "dike" cities with a population of nearly 200,000, for instance, the two ARENA candidates for mayor combined received 52,000 votes in the 1976 municipal elections of a turnout of 65,000 (81 percent), whereas the MDB candidate received only 7,500. In another dike city, Pouso Alegre (pop. 57,000), the MDB candidate received 2,000 votes in 1970 but only 184 in 1972 and in 1976 the MDB did not even nominate a candidate, suggesting that where the MDB did poll well in midsized cities, its vote was volatile. The correlation coefficient for municipal size and vote for the ARENA federal deputy slate in 1978 in 721 *municípios* in Minas Gerais[43] was only a modest -.181, and for percent rural and the percent vote for the ARENA *legenda,* a moderate .457.[44] Despite the fact that the mean percent of the vote for ARENA in Minas was similar to that of Rio de Janeiro, the distribution of that vote broke down less neatly along urban–rural lines.

Numerous examples from state and local case studies suggest that outside the metropolitan regions of the state capitals of São Paulo and the Southeast, clientelism served as a basis for progovernment voting (Cammack, 1982; Sarles, 1982), and it was effectively employed to bring voters who had defected back to the government column. In Juiz de Fora, for example, a city of 300,000 in the Minas Mata, the ARENA party that had absorbed the old local elite rebounded in 1976 from a precipitous decline in the early 1970s to recapture city hall and a majority in the municipal council after receiving promises of federal support (Reis, 1978a: 221). In an opposition stronghold, the ARENA candidate for mayor in 1976 campaigned for four years leading up to the election on a platform calling for stronger ties with the federal government, which, he suggested, would bring more state funds and a renewal of industrialization to the area. A few days before the election, President Geisel personally dedicated a steel plant in a ceremony to which the local MDB administration was disinvited despite its role in the negotiations to bring the plant to Juiz de Fora. It appeared instead that the steel plant was

a cluster, political differences would tend to disappear and socioeconomic characteristics of a region to become more pronounced.

43 There were 722 *municípios* at the time in Minas Gerais. I omitted Belo Horizonte, the state capital, from the analysis because its size distorted the results.

44 Given that the opposition vote was roughly comparable in 1974 and 1978 (for the Chamber of Deputies, 48 percent in 1974 and 49 percent in 1978 nationally), if level of development is indeed the central independent variable in explaining voting against the government, then the correlation should have been *stronger* in the Minas figures based on the 1978 elections when these municipalities were *more* developed than in 1974. There is, moreover, nothing special or significant that distinguishes the 1978 from the 1974 election, and hence threatens the validity of such a comparison.

a gift from ARENA and the incumbent government, and placing ARENA in power locally would deliver more of the same (Reis, 1978a: 222).

This strategy, which was obviously effective in the 1970s, however, eventually bumped up against its limits. In anticipation of facing a united opposition in direct gubernatorial elections, the military government in 1979 eased the restrictions on the formation of political parties with the clear intention to split the MDB. ARENA leaders formed the Democratic Social Party (PDS), while the MDB split into five parties, including the Party of the Brazilian Democratic Movement, the PMDB (the core and largest bloc of the party), the elite Popular Party (PP), the Brazilian Labor Party (PTB), Leonel Brizola's Democratic Labor Party (PDT), and the Workers' Party (PT).[45] Despite the creation of a multiparty system, when governors were selected in 1982 in direct elections for the first time since 1965, clientelism alone could not deliver the vote for governor to the government column in the nation's most advanced states. Clientelism as a strategy worked only in "normal" economic times, as part of a larger authoritarian strategy. When genuine political competition expanded, clientelism could not rescue a regime in economic crisis.

If such a strategy was thus limited in bolstering support for the military regime, it reinforced the structures of traditional politics and guaranteed the persistent dominance of traditional political elites. Enhanced funding for the patronage system and a shift in national political priorities revitalized patronage networks and strengthened clientelism as a vehicle for state–society mediation by privileging it over other networks. It just as obviously afforded traditional elites entrenched in the state a means by which to preserve and expand their political support. Of all politicians, traditional political elites benefited most in elections and state appointments, as we shall see in Chapter 6.

CONCLUSIONS

The Brazilian military that set out to reform the administration of the state and the economy with an attack on traditional politics was soon constrained by the very structures it wished to dismantle. However much it may have wished to tamper with the system of distributing state and personal patronage in exchange for votes, it was thwarted from doing so. From the beginning the military had an inadequate understanding of the traditional role of those transactions in mediating state–society relations, and it failed to respond on any other basis to changes of its own creation. Fiscal centralization did not bring state spending under control; effectively constrain subnational governments from spending state revenues, from what-

---

45 Leonel Brizola, João Goulart's brother-in-law who returned from exile in 1979, attempted to reorganize his beloved PTB, but he lost the party label to Ivete Vargas, Getúlio Vargas's grand-niece.

ever source, as they wished; or transfer the allegiance of municipal bosses from the state governments to the federal government. While state patronage operations were funded primarily by the federal government, and the federal government appropriated broad policy-making prerogatives and set national development goals, federal authorities by and large did not directly allocate discretionary state benefits. With the exception of social security and a select few megaprojects, the administration of services and funds to implement priority programs throughout the dictatorship was entrusted to the state governments.

After 1974, when electoral competition intensified in a bipolar political game the military itself designed, the military regime struggled to retain legislative majorities. Having suffered the electoral consequences of allowing state–society relations to slip into dormancy, it did an about-face – from reviling traditional politicians, the military embraced them as allies in a conservative cause. In resorting to the traditional patterns of domination that had buttressed previous regimes, it was forced reluctantly to reestablish alliances with those state elites who predated its regime, abetted its coup, but who nonetheless did not share its vision for the nation.

Federal programs channeled through the state leadership benefited the national military leadership by helping to build ARENA majorities, but they also were perceived by voters as having been delivered by their *state* politicians. In Minas Gerais, after 1974 state clients and their communities secured employment, homes, loans for development aid, and other patronage programs through the mediation of elected political representatives. With policy implementation left to the discretion of these state political elites who perceived their functions in the same clientelistic terms in which they had traditionally operated, state resources were allocated through highly politicized, vertically organized networks that began in the governor's office and extended to deputies and mayors.

In reducing the number of channels through which state resources were allocated to a single political alignment, fiscal centralization, which was presumed to be the deathknell of state clientelism, actually strengthened traditional politics by transforming the patronage system into an oligarchical monopoly. With few exceptions, state governors supported the national government.[46] Local leaders were left with little practical alternative but to find sponsors well placed in the state elite. The concentration of national resources in the public sector provided a powerful incentive for municipalities with poor rates of success in garnering patronage projects to remain in the fold and press harder their case to the same state oligarchy that may have shunned them in the past. The penalty for noncooperation was to forfeit state aid, something most municipalities could ill afford. In the late

46 Only governors Chagas Freitas of Rio de Janeiro and Alacid Nunes of Pará belonged to the MDB, and, even then, Chagas Freitas generally supported the national government.

1970s the heightened importance of the links between each level of government offered both the state oligarchies and the national government an opportunity to construct durable political alliances based on the dispensation of state resources, thus bolstering one another's rule.

The most obvious question raised by the return to patronage in Minas Gerais in the 1970s is why the *traditional* political elite was able to take advantage of clientelistic politics, and why the system of patronage rewards and punishments could not be disengaged from the structures of traditional politics. Part of the answer is obviously due to the power of incumbency in a centralized, clientelistic system, but not all. State clientelism benefited traditional political elites above all in the context of an authoritarian political order that restricted political competition and reduced elite turnover. This subject is the focus of Chapter 6.

6

Authoritarian politics and traditional elites

When the military turned to the oligarchy to produce popular endorse-ments for the regime at the polls, it reluctantly accepted as allies members of the traditional political elite that its Médici wing had once hoped to replace. A new, perhaps more honest, competent, and above all loyal elite was an attractive prospect to hard-line military governors in the first de-cade of military rule. In choosing governors and national cabinet ministers from outside the state political machines, President Médici had tried to create just such a class. But with electoral majorities crumbling, his succes-sors abandoned those efforts. Why the military rulers did not back a new, more loyal political elite with more determination and less ambivalence, why the efforts they did make at replacing this elite were largely ineffec-tive, and why aspirants to a new political elite could not take advantage of the political disruption of an authoritarian regime are not self-evident. These questions are particularly puzzling since the military ultimately con-trolled state resources and, one might reasonably expect, should have been able to favor with federal patronage the candidacies of politicians of its own choosing.

The answer to why the traditional political elite and traditional politics persisted under military rule in Brazil is explored in this chapter in the context of the circumscribed nature of political competition during the authoritarian regime. Authoritarianism in Brazil did not "freeze" voter loyalties and the position of political leaders per se; party activity and participation in elections was actively encouraged by the Brazilian military. Because political activity was permitted in the context of elections, political repression was moderate, pre-1964 partisan identities were weak, and the authoritarian episode was long enough to allow for a substantial growth of the electorate, Remmer (1985: 269–70) and Lamounier (1989a: 43–44) believed that authoritarianism would permit and indeed did precipitate significant political change.[1] Remmer in particular identified Brazil as an

---

1 As Lamounier (1989a: 43–44) highlights, the political opening in Brazil led to a party system that differed completely from the one that existed under the previous democratic regime during the 1945–64 period. His surveys reveal new loyalties to the MDB and

"ideal case for the emergence of a democratic regime with minimal resemblance to its preauthoritarian predecessors," the most likely to experience major discontinuities in the party system and in political leadership from pre- to postauthoritarian rule.

However compelling the reasons to expect that elections would facilitate party system change in Brazil, the impact of restricted elections on political mobilization, elite turnover, and the formation of opposition was otherwise. The political arrangements, alliances, and rules of the bureaucratic-authoritarian regime in fact did not undermine, but rather prolonged, traditional elite dominance. To guarantee congressional majorities and loyal local officials, both of which an authoritarian regime required in a functioning political system, military governors purged from the political arena their keenest challengers and most dangerous opponents primarily through denial of political rights and exile; they appointed governors directly; and they created a two-party system in which one official party was guaranteed supremacy. With competition sharply reduced by law and practice, incumbents in state positions naturally advantaged in a clientelistic system became virtually invincible. This was especially so because the central appointment of state governors and the manipulation of party and electoral law narrowed the arena of political competition to a single, proregime party formed and dominated by the traditional political elite. Controlling ARENA allowed the regional oligarchies to extend their dominance over elite recruitment and to monopolize the distribution of state patronage. Elite competition became restricted by and large to those party leaders and elected representatives who had already entered the political game. In a territorially highly integrated electoral and political system distinguished by mutually serving if unequal alliances between local and state political elites, those changes that preserved the dominance of the traditional political elite at the state level locked into place traditional politicians at the local level. Local bosses, in turn, continued to nourish the traditional political system by mobilizing internal party and broader electoral support for their patrons in the state oligarchy. Given the high degree of personalism in traditional Brazilian voting patterns, moreover, the military dictatorship could neither appropriate the intricate and well-established personal political networks of traditional politics nor could it circumvent the traditional politicians who organized them.

This chapter draws heavily on statewide and local electoral returns and political party leadership data to determine the levels of local and state elite turnover. Disaggregated electoral data from a sample of twenty-five municipalities, and interviews in a subset of these, are used to examine local political organization, the stability of local political coalitions, and the

PMDB, and a massive realignment from 1970 to 1974 to the MDB in São Paulo, which he does not believe can be explained as the simple rebaptism of party identifications.

turnover of local political elites.[2] The chapter also examines the durability of elite-defined political cleavages. First, I review the contribution of political competition to elite turnover, and the limited nature of political competition in authoritarian Brazil.

POLITICAL COMPETITION AND ELITE TURNOVER

While Brazil has functioned as less than a full democracy and political competition has, with the exception of the late populist period, been limited to elite circles throughout the course of this century, the degree of competition *within* the elite, and with it the security of elite tenure, has varied from regime to regime. In the Old Republic, narrowly restricted political competition underpinned an archetypal oligarchical political system. The most successful state oligarchies used rigid centralization in the state, an iron grip on the dominant, indeed, sole party, and the diversion of state patronage through that party, the Republican Party, to so weaken their opponents that real competition was effectively curtailed and their power secured. Where the regional oligarchies were unable to ensure these conditions of competition, their grip on power was more tenuous; they had to face constant competition spurred on by federal intervention and local uprisings. The "Revolution" of 1930 displaced many entrenched state and local elites, but once the Vargas regime was consolidated competition was at least as restricted as during the Old Republic; the federal government had the authority, which it exercised, to replace elected with appointed state executives.

In the postwar party system, actors at each level of the political system had more freedom of choice than in the Old Republic, which in turn intensified political competition. Multipartism provided channels for discontented political veterans and new entrants in politics to contest office. Electoral coalitions helped otherwise weak candidates to attain office. A small party could barter its votes for the gubernatorial nominee of a major

2 This sample of twenty-five *municípios* includes small towns from traditional areas and large cities that received new industry and attracted significant numbers of migrants in the 1970s. They are geographically diversified as well: four are in Region I; three in Region II; seven in Region III; two in Region IV; three in Region V; four in Region VI; and two in Region VIII. Half (thirteen) were selected to determine if oligarchical families named by Rebelo Horta (1956) continued to dominate their *municípios*.

  Of this sample, I conducted field research in four *municípios* – Curvelo, Montes Claros, Sete Lagoas, and Varginha. Each had strong agrarian elites; Montes Claros, Sete Lagoas, and Varginha experienced substantial growth in the 1970s, as much as any *município* in the state outside the metropolitan region of Belo Horizonte. Montes Claros and Varginha did so under the government umbrella, abetted by foreign investment. Sete Lagoas, led by an opposition administration, industrialized with largely local capital. In these *municípios,* I augmented census and electoral data with interviews of local political and private sector leaders to investigate the effects of economic development and regime change in 1964 on local power structures.

party in exchange for support for one of its candidates for lesser office – state deputy or mayor. Schmitter (1973: 209–10) has called this post-1945 "Getulian" system that "permitted local-level competition on the basis of coalitional shifts, but ensured a stable [PSD-PTB] dominance at the national presidential level 'semi-competitive.' "

Because clientelism was the basis of the electoral appeals of all parties in both republics and lower levels of government were fiscally dependent on the higher levels and electoral intimidation was rampant, genuine political competition, and ultimately turnover of the political elite, required the real possibility of alternating in office. No opposition candidate, faction, or party could campaign credibly on promises to deliver state resources to starving municipalities without access to the state elite and patronage. For challengers at lower levels of the political system, gaining access to state clientelism was possible only if they could win the political favor of state and national incumbents away from local rivals in power; or if their allies at higher levels of the political system could displace the incumbent state and federal elites with whom their local rivals were allied. The first option was always open – however infrequent; even the hierarchical system of the Old Republic everywhere allowed for, and at times fostered, challenges to incumbent local political bosses.

In the rigid one-party system of the Old Republic, the second route to power was far less often successful. Especially where state oligarchies were strong, as in Minas Gerais and São Paulo, it was most common that the local "ins," or the *situação,* sided with state "ins" who dominated the national government. In those smaller states where the state and federal "ins" were enemies, however, local "outs" could choose to ally with federal "ins," state "ins," or their rivals. If an incumbent state group were to be defeated in state politics (possibly because the federal "ins" supported their adversaries), then the local elites under their protection would be left without their sponsors. The local elite's place was secure only as long as the state government to whom it offered its allegiance could stay in power. Otherwise, the successful state and local insurgents, their local rivals, would soon replace them as the local "ins." Only when a city had its own resources and was not dependent on the upper levels of government could a local group hope to occupy and retain office without powerful friends in state or federal government.

In the multiparty postwar system, it became less frequent that local "in" groups could be allied to both the federal and state incumbents. Many states elected governors during the period from parties opposed to that of the national executive; in Minas Gerais, the UDN elected the first postwar governor at a time when the presidency was controlled by the PSD. Particularly after Jânio Quadros was elected president in 1961 and João Goulart succeeded him later that year (after Quadros inexplicably resigned), it was more often the case than ever before that governors and presidents sat on opposite sides of the fence. In the 1962 elections, state and federal authorities backed opposing camps in several leading states with mixed results. In Bahia, Guanabara, and Pernambuco, candidates representing the PTB and other labor and socialist parties prevailed in gubernatorial contests over those favored by incumbent UDN governors (Sampaio, 1964: 44–45; Rios, 1964; Chacon, 1964). In Ceará, Rio Grande do Sul, and São Paulo, on the other hand, motley state coalitions formed to stop federally supported PTB candidacies were successful (Ribeiro, 1964: 99, 102; Ferreira, 1964). Generally, state governors exercised a more significant impact than federal authorities on the races for state and local office, and more on these races than on the races for federal offices. In the 1962 elections, twelve PTB candidates were successful in their bids for federal deputy (of twenty-four places) in Pernambuco despite the efforts of incumbent governor Cid Sampaio to block their election, but only one state deputy was elected as a candidate of the labor party (Chacon, 1964: 214–15, 224–25).

After 1945 the possibility that local outs could gain support from credible aspirants to state and federal office allowed more open contestation and set in motion a flurry of political activity at lower levels of the system. In Ceará, in 1962, the governor helped elect nine deputies running on the ticket of the Partido Trabalhista Nacional to the state Legislative Assembly; in 1958 the PTN had not fielded a candidate (Ribeiro, 1964: 102). In Minas the election of a UDN governor – Magalhães Pinto – in 1960 produced substantial gains for the party in the state Legislative Assembly and municipal elections that followed in 1962. The UDN more than doubled its representation in the Assembly from eleven (of seventy-four seats) in 1958 (15 percent) to twenty-six (of seventy-eight) (33 percent) in 1962 (Barbosa, 1964: 187–88). In the local races in 1958, with a sitting PSD governor (Bias Fortes), the PSD won outright 42 percent of the mayoral races and another 13 percent in alliance with other parties; the UDN elected less than 10 percent of its candidates directly and another 19 percent in alliance with other parties. By contrast in 1962 the UDN won an additional sixty-one city halls from the PSD, improving the percentage of UDN mayors to 22 percent while that of PSD mayors dropped to 35 percent. The electoral fortunes of PR candidates rose in 1954 and 1958 and fell in 1962 along with the vote of the PSD with which the party was allied (Barbosa, 1964: 189–90).

In this "semicompetitive" postwar regime designed to preserve PSD-PTB hegemony, the real if limited possibility of a national UDN victory and the party's frequent successes in state races allowed the system to become more competitive. It created a different set of expectations about local and state competition. Once Jânio Quadros demonstrated in 1961 that it was possible to break the PSD-PTB stranglehold on the presidency, the prospects of "out" parties coming to power became more realistic and the uncertainty surrounding the outcome of the next scheduled presidential election of 1965 was perhaps higher than ever before. As Schmitter (1973:

209) put it, a national opposition victory caused the parties to proliferate, alliances to shift, and the system to be transformed from "semicompetitive" to "truly competitive."

Just as this system approximated more perfect and unrestricted political competition, however, the coup of 1964 took place to put a halt to the expansion of contestation and participation. The revised rules of political competition ushered in by the authoritarian regime ossified personal and factional political alignments, sharply reduced elite turnover, and permitted the entrance of new aspirants onto the political scene only through avenues controlled by the state oligarchy. The new regime circumscribed political competition to a degree and in such a way so as to reshape dramatically the political and electoral systems to the advantage of its supporters.

RESTRICTING THE SCOPE OF POLITICAL COMPETITION

In a system whose lower levels were virtually blocked from independent political shifts, change tended to enter from the top and emanate downward. Because of the highly integrated nature of political competition across territorial lines, national political change, when it occurred, inevitably reverberated to the lowest levels of the political system. The impact of changes in national leadership on local politics depended on whether opportunities for the reorganization of clientelistic networks were created or denied at the state and federal levels. In 1930, Vargas's overthrow of the Old Republic disrupted existing federal, state, and local alignments. Splitting the ranks of the oligarchy offered a choice of sides to local chiefs. The power of the dominant *coroneis* allied with newly ousted members of the old guard in the state elite was undermined, in some towns only temporarily, in others on a more permanent basis. Local power studies document, if in a sporadic and descriptive fashion, the jolting of the rule of the "in" families after 1930 throughout Brazil.[3] In some *municípios,* one family replaced another; in others, there was a bifurcation of family control; and in yet others, traditional family rule was overthrown altogether (Murilo de Carvalho, 1968–69: 246). In the three decades that followed, the system became more competitive because federal and state races were opened up, and the effects of this competition spilled over into local races. But just as national political change could stimulate local and state competition, so too could it stifle it. In 1965, national political change produced just such an effect.

3 Local power studies conducted in Minas Gerais, Bahia, São Paulo, Piauí, Paraíba, and Alagoas by political scientists and anthropologists, although nonscientifically sampled (municipalities were often chosen for study by hometown authors), provide useful accounts of local politics, family rule, and the effects of economic change and other factors on traditional politics. In his review of this literature, Murilo de Carvalho (1968–69) conferred upon these studies a systematic dimension lacking when their findings are considered separately.

Political-electoral rules were revised in the wake of the first real popular test of the bureaucratic-authoritarian regime, the gubernatorial elections of 1965, when PSD candidates closely associated with former president Juscelino Kubitschek – whom the regime stripped of his political rights in June 1964 – won the gubernatorial contests in Minas Gerais and in Guanabara. PSD and PTB candidates were the victors in five states overall. The UDN, staunch allies of the military, achieved outright majorities in only three of eleven states. The military responded to what was widely regarded as its "defeat" by decreeing two institutional acts. To safeguard against any future embarrassments, Complementary Act Number 4 of Institutional Act Number 2 (October 27, 1965) abolished all existing political parties. New parties would be recognized and allowed to function only if they had affiliated at least 120 federal deputies and 20 senators. One purpose of this requirement was to curtail the number of parties, which in the years leading up to the 1964 coup had proliferated to thirteen. Another was to create a strong official party while keeping up the facade of democratic procedure. This decree effectively transformed what was by 1964 a "fragmented," multiparty system into a two-party system. Politicians were forced into either ARENA, which became the principal recruiting ground for government politicians, or the MDB, the refuge of government opponents, regardless of stripe or color. Following on the heels of the Second Institutional Act was Institutional Act Number 3 (February 5, 1966), which replaced the direct election of governors and lieutenant governors with "indirect" election by state legislatures, and that of mayors of state capitals with appointment by state governors.

Well positioned to dominate executive positions in the state and official party, the traditional political elite benefited immeasurably from these changes that restricted political competition. Nominees for governor acceptable to the military were often drawn from the traditional political elite; this was especially true in states such as Minas Gerais where regional elites remained powerful. The circumstances under which the two new "artificial" parties were created, moreover, left the "official" party in the hands of the oligarchy. When the military sounded the call to form a new, progovernment party, it fell to the oligarchy to organize it. All UDN senators and nine-tenths of the party's deputies flocked to the ARENA banner; a smaller percentage – 65 percent of PSD deputies and 74 percent of PSD senators – also cast their lot with the military government (Table 6.1). As the UDN had instigated the coup, members of the ex-UDN unsurprisingly assumed prominent roles in the new party nationally. In some states (Alagoas, Sergipe, and Guanabara) they dominated the regional ARENA branch, though in others (Minas, Goiás, Santa Catarina, and Piauí) they had to share power with members of the ex-PSD. Only in Maranhão and Rio Grande do Sul did the PSD clearly predominate (Roett, 1984: 67). While some members of the PTB joined with these two conservative par-

Table 6.1 *Brazil: Pre-1966 party affiliations of federal deputies and senators, 1966–71*

Pre-1966 party affiliation	N in 1983	Loss of seat[a]	1966-67[b] ARENA	MDB	Total	1967-71[c] ARENA	MDB	Total
Deputies								
PTB[d]	119	37	34	75	109	34	50	84
PSD	118	11	80	44	124	83	39	122
UDN	91	2	84	10	94	105	14	119
PSP	21	4	20	4	24	13	8	21
PDC	20	3	15	5	20	18	5	23
PTN	11	1	8	5	13	6	7	13
PST	7	5	3	1	4	1	2	3
PR	4	1	4	0	4	4	0	4
PL	5	0	3	0	3	4	2	6
PRP	5	0	6	0	6	4	0	4
PSB	5	3	1	2	3	2	1	3
PRT	3	0	2	2	4	1	0	1
Subtotal	409	67	260	148	408	275	128	403
Unknown	--	0	0	0	1	1	5	6
Total	409	67	260	148	409	276	133	409
Cassados	--	67	--	--	--	28[e]	66[e]	94
Senators								
PTB	19	1	6	13	19	3	10	13
PSD	23	1	17	6	23	18	5	23
UDN	16	0	16	0	16	19	1	20
PSP	2	0	2	0	2	3	0	3
PDC	1	0	1	0	1	3	0	3
PTN	1	0	0	1	1	0	1	1
PL	2	0	1	1	2	1	1	2
PRP	1	0	1	0	1	0	0	0
PSB	1	0	0	1	1	0	1	1
Total	66	2	44	22	66	47	19	66
Cassados	--	2	---	--	--	0[e]	4[e]	4

Note: PTB = Brazilian Labor Party; PSD = Social Democratic Party; UDN = National Democratic Union; PSP = Progressive Social Party; PDC = Christian Democratic Party; PTN = National Labor Party; PST = Social Labor Party; PR = Republican Party; PL = Liberator Party; PRP = Popular Representation Party; PSB = Brazilian Socialist Party; PRT = Rural Labor Party.
[a]*Cassados* removed by Institutional Act Number 1 (1964) and by Institutional Act Number 2 (1965–66).
[b]Realignment among surviving members of the Fifth Legislature, elected in 1962.
[c]Composition of the Sixth Legislature, elected in November 1966.
[d]Includes legislators of the Movimento Trabalhista Renovador, a progressive splinter of the PTB.
[e]*Cassados* removed by Institutional Act Number 5 after December 16, 1968.
Source: Wesson and Fleischer, 1983: 104.

ties in the states of Bahia, Pernambuco, São Paulo, Ceará, and Pará, most joined the MDB. Of the PTB deputies who were permitted to remain active in politics (PTB deputies had disproportionately lost their mandates and their political rights), 69 percent (seventy-five) remained in the opposition, and 31 percent (thirty-four) joined ARENA. At its inception, the MDB hardly qualified as a party: the government had to "loan" the party two senators in order for it to meet the newly established minimum of twenty. It suffered another blow after the issuance of Institutional Act Number 5. At least 40 percent of its deputies and senators were stripped of their mandates (Velasco e Cruz and Martins, 1984: 37).[4]

Most traditional Minas politicians joined ARENA and the government, as would be expected of an elite that prompted the regime change and was tied to the state. More than 80 percent of the members of each of the three most important elite parties, the PSD, the UDN, and the PR, who were in the state Legislative Assembly in 1968–69 joined ARENA (Bastos and Walker, 1971: 141). The affiliation of deputies was part of a larger movement of the entire traditional elite into the government camp. It followed upon the decisions of oligarchical leaders to back the "Revolution." Once the deputies moved into the party, lower-ranking members of the political class in the interior had little choice but to follow. Clientelism and centralization ensured compliance at every level of the system.

The creation of an "official" party represented a major shift in the terms of political competition, which favored the oligarchy. The certain outcome of the partisan affiliation of every postcoup governor threw up barriers to renegotiating state and local political alliances. In an authoritarian system operating under a system of state clientelism that reserved federal and state executive positions for the government and its supporters, state "outs" could no longer become state "ins," and the chances for federal "outs" ousting the military governors were even slimmer. Eliminating the customary means for successfully challenging local "ins" – riding the coattails of the state opposition to power at some future date – diminished considerably the incentives for local "outs," be they traditional bosses or newcomers, to ally with state and federal "outs." In contrast to 1930, when the replacement of the national leadership triggered the formation of new local coalitions, appropriation of the state executives and creation of a new party system with new electoral rules by the authoritarian regime in 1965–66 fixed the axes of conflict and froze standing alliances.

Thus the military monopoly of the national executive and its appointment of loyal governors limited the appeal of competition through opposition, and only with great difficulty could a challenge be mounted within ARENA, which was controlled by the traditional political elite. The coali-

4 The thinning of MDB ranks after 1968 forced the regime to relax the requirements for party registration in order to maintain its official opposition.

tional shifts that were previously a common feature of postwar Brazilian politics were all but ruled out. In the postwar republic when votes could be bartered and alliances renegotiated, competition for resources and for office was real. When authoritarianism took away this possibility, opposition became all but quixotic. Political alliances and divisions ossified, fixed alignments sharply reduced competition, and the oligarchy and local bosses were left in place at all levels of the political system. The brand of authoritarianism instituted by the military was even more rigid than the variant under which such states as Minas Gerais and São Paulo with powerful regional oligarchies and Republican Parties had lived during the Old Republic. Unlike its predecessor, the bureaucratic-authoritarian regime *could not become* truly competitive.

LOCAL POLITICS AND THE DEMISE OF INTERPARTY COMPETITION

In 1964 the political elite was as internally racked by factional divisions and rivalries as it was united behind its "Revolution." This posed a problem for a military that hoped to consolidate its local support among the traditional political elite in a single, progovernment political party. The military could not afford to allow local rivalries to drive away half of its strongest political supporters among the traditional political bosses and still hope to hold a comfortable advantage in the electoral arena. Naturally, being cut off from patronage was a powerful disincentive to defecting to the opposition. During authoritarian rule, even those who were willing to pursue a long-term strategy, betting that the regime could not endure indefinitely, had to face electors who, however poor and uneducated, understood that opposition *municípios* received next to no state aid above their meager, legally mandated transfers. Of course, many politicians, especially young ones who for the most part entered politics after the coup, affiliated with the MDB out of conviction and fought elections for the opposition not so much expecting to win but primarily as a means of galvanizing protest against the regime. Nonetheless, with political alignments fixed by authoritarian rules of competition that could be rewritten at any time (and often were based on the latest polls conducted by military intelligence) to guarantee the victory of the "ins," the best practical recourse for most local challengers who hoped to come to power was to join ARENA. This was especially true for weaker traditional politicians in very poor parts of the interior.

In more developed and richer municipalities, the military could not be complacent, however. Even in an authoritarian regime, politicians in a few select concentrated areas of heavy industry – Contagem, Betim, and the "Steel Valley" in Minas Gerais – and powerful local oligarchies in affluent *municípios* could challenge state and federal elites on the opposition ticket and maintain their local electoral dominance.[5] If uncomfortable in the party of their rivals, moreover, there were virtually no ideological obstacles preventing oligarchs from contemplating MDB membership. In Sete Lagoas, where members of the traditional local elite who had formed the PSD and the faction of the UDN that had been allied with Governor Israel Pinheiro and the former minister of justice Milton Campos joined the MDB, the opposition party had a competitive edge throughout the authoritarian era that it did not enjoy in most cities and towns. These and other powerful local elites who were in the best position to defy the military were precisely the ones the military would most want to keep as its supporters in order to maximize the progovernment vote – at the polls and in the state legislatures.

Accommodating powerful UDN and PSD politicians locally in one party was no easy task. As a first step toward fitting opposing factions who were bitter enemies into the same party structure, party leadership was shared. Places on executive commissions were alternated between the major parties of the postwar era. If the PSD was allocated the presidency, for instance, the general secretaryship was automatically assigned to the UDN, and so on with the first and second vice-presidents and other, lesser positions. Similarly, places on the party list for elections decided according to proportional representation (e.g., state and federal deputy elections) were made for members of each faction. But the regime's dilemma was only partially solved by conventional means of political compromise: who would contest various elections on the party ticket could not be settled as easily in the plurality races in which parties could field only one candidate. This difficulty, which would surface vividly in the gubernatorial contests of 1982, posed the greatest problems for the regime during the authoritarian years at the local level.

To make room for the entire local traditional political elite in its band of supporters, the military introduced a new electoral arrangement known as the *sublegenda* – literally "subticket." Employed in the elections for mayors and later for senators – the races decided by plurality vote – up to three candidates of the same party were allowed to contest the same office in general elections. The votes of each *legenda* were totaled and the office awarded to the highest vote getter of the party that polled best, even if a minority party candidate received more votes than the eventual winner. Three spots were generally sufficient to accommodate candidates of each of the party's rival factions.

The introduction of *sublegendas* successfully persuaded local bosses to fall into the government camp alongside their traditional rivals. In sixteen *municípios* in my sample, all local PSD, UDN, and PR politicians opted

5 In addition to the obvious and oft-cited reason for the electoral strength of the MDB in the most industrialized *municípios* – a proclivity on the part of industrial workers to vote opposition – these *municípios* had the highest levels of municipal revenue. *Municípios* were returned 20 percent of the revenue they generated by the collection of the ICM.

for ARENA immediately after the "Revolution." Ex-PSDers became "ARENA 2," and ex-UDNers, "ARENA 1," or vice-versa. Local enemies uncomfortably coexisted within the same party, occupying separate *sublegendas*. The *sublegenda* also proved to be an effective device for abetting government victories. With rival local bosses running for the same office on the same ARENA ticket, ARENA was sure to win most local offices. In the mayoral elections of 1972, ARENA candidates won 92 percent of the races in the country (Sarles, 1982: 45), and the MDB was able to run candidates in fewer than 2,000 of the country's 3,500 electoral districts (Schmitter, 1973: 211).

When there were breaks in the ARENA coalition, on the other hand, government vote totals suffered. In the 1972 municipal elections in Varginha, when ARENA ran only one candidate for mayor and one for vice-mayor, the ARENA nominee edged out his MDB rival by a margin of 1,246 votes (6,414 to 5,168 or 55 to 45 percent of the party vote). In the next municipal election, held in 1976, when a second candidate ran for mayor on the "ARENA 2" *sublegenda,* the two ARENA candidates combined received just over 15,000 votes, or 82 percent of the party vote. The lone MDB candidate ran a poor third with 2,897 votes. A similar pattern appears in Muriaé, where the ARENA *legenda*'s share of the vote for mayor rose from 51 percent in 1970 when it ran one candidate to 97 percent in 1972 when it ran two, and in Pouso Alegre and Dores do Indaiá, where the same circumstances produced an increase of from 69 to 94 percent and 65 to 95 percent respectively for ARENA in the same years. In all, in the ten *municípios* in the sample in which ARENA fielded two candidates in 1970, the nine in 1972, and the thirteen in 1976, the party commanded convincing majorities in local elections, receiving, on average, 77, 82, and 73 percent of the vote, respectively. By contrast, when it offered the electorate only one candidate (eleven cases in 1970, nine in 1972, and four in 1976), its majorities were significantly smaller: 57, 53, and 57 percent of the vote, respectively.[6]

Schmitter (1973: 210) recognized that the use of these "subtickets" would permit local conflict to continue. Logically, *sublegendas* should have transposed *inter*party competition into *intra*party competition. If they had, they might have accommodated new elites. But while a success from the regime's standpoint in maximizing its local support, *sublegendas* by and large did not make the system, especially locally, more competitive.

6 In 1966, before the MDB had organized branches in many municipalities, ARENA received most of the vote and the difference in the number of candidacies is less pronounced than in later elections: in eleven cases in which ARENA fielded two candidates, the party received an average of 78 percent of the vote, and in those twelve cases in which the party nominated only one candidate, it polled 67 percent of the vote. The number of cases in which ARENA fielded three candidates is so small before 1976 that it is difficult to generalize from the results.

Local competition and local elite turnover

Why vigorous and genuine intraparty competition on the local level did not develop through the mechanism of the *sublegenda* can be traced to the firm grip local party elites held over local party organization. The Organic Party Law left the process of party affiliation in the hands of local *diretórios,* which naturally advantaged incumbents. This was true everywhere in Brazil, both at the state level – in Rio de Janeiro, from 1969–75, the "Chaguista" group (that headed by and loyal to Chagas Freitas) controlled the admission of new members to the state branch of the MDB (Diniz, 1982: 90–91) – and especially at the local level. Since in most municipalities members of the UDN and PSD organized the ARENA *diretórios* and elected themselves their executive officers, members of the local oligarchy admitted new members, assigned places on the party tickets, and decided which state politicians to support. The local "in" parties were controlled by members of the local oligarchy. As on the state level, local bosses organized ARENA chapters in the cities and towns of the interior. These bosses could be the most powerful figures in their *municípios,* at times enjoying great stature in state politics.

The tightness of their grip on local party organization is reflected in the long tenure of members of local governing bodies. In Varginha, most members of the ARENA *diretório* over the years were semipermanent fixtures. Three-fourths of the members in 1975, the last elected *diretório* before the party's dissolution, had been members in 1972. Of these, all but two had been members at the time the local party branch was constituted in 1969. In Sete Lagoas, 86 percent of the members of the *diretório* of the MDB (the local "ins" – comprising the old PSD and half the UDN) in 1979 were carryovers from the previous election year, 1975. The executive commission in 1979 was reelected intact from 1975, and three of its four members were also on the local party's top body in 1972. Seven of eight of the elected delegates to the party's state convention had served on the party's *diretório* at some point; half were among the founders of the MDB in Sete Lagoas. Old elites even dominated the leadership of the PMDB in 1984.

With local party leadership posts divided between prominent figures from the two dominant, conservative parties of the precoup era, the PSD and the UDN, two places on the "in" party's *legenda* in each city and town were virtually "reserved" for old politicians from their ranks. New aspirants could enter the political arena on the side of the government through only one of two avenues: the ranks of one of the factions (in order to secure nomination on the *sublegenda* reserved for that group) or on a third subticket of ARENA, if open.[7] Mounting a viable challenge to local power on the third *legenda* was a formidable task. A third candidate could not

7 Securing a third *sublegenda* was difficult where either the PSD or UDN was divided into factions or the Republican Party had been strong.

count on the "prestige" and electoral support of the state elite; ex-PSD and ex-UDN politicians prominent in state politics campaigned in the cities and towns for "their own." Nor could the governor, who strove to be impartial in his dealings with the two sides, hope to maintain old oligarchs in the fold if he assisted local challengers from outside both camps.[8] The difficulties in "going it alone" within ARENA were compounded by the tendency of voters inclined to reject the local oligarchy to vote MDB, the natural party of protest. If a challenger did have a realistic chance of beating establishment candidates, the local *diretório* was under no obligation to nominate him for the city's top office (though this would be frowned upon by the state elite whose interest lay in maximizing the local vote).

Most often, young aspirants entered politics under the aegis of traditional local bosses. In Barbacena, state deputy João Navarro who began his political career in the PTB independent of the city's two oligarchical families (and went on to become the president of the state Legislative Assembly), joined the Bias Fortes faction. Once he did, he could immediately count on more votes for himself, and the votes he brought with him in turn strengthened Bias Fortes's position in the *município* and in the state. Only in 1976 in the last municipal elections held under bipartism did it become less than rare for three candidates to contest the same office on the local level. With nominations controlled by the party oligarchies, *sublegendas* allowed the oligarchy to confine competition to its own ranks and reduce elite turnover.

The oligarchical grip on the parties and the impediments to coalitional shifts reduced the number of candidates to local office, which in turn led to a low degree of turnover of local officials. In Três Corações, the mayor elected in 1962 was reelected in 1972; the mayor elected in 1970 was returned to office in 1976; and the latter's brother served as mayor in 1966 and was an unsuccessful candidate in 1972. In Varginha, Eduardo Ottoni, touted as an "outsider" and "proof" that "new leadership" had captured new migrant and worker votes and ousted the local elite, was actually from a prominent traditional family of Minas Gerais, well connected in state

8 In 1982 Minas governor Francelino Pereira, an ex-UDNer, sided with the ex-PSD faction of the progovernment coalition in Varginha at the time of the constitution of the local chapter of the PDS. When the ex-ARENA 1 faction threatened to bolt to the newly formed PP, Francelino Pereira sent for the rebellious group, in his private jet, and informed them personally that his response to such a desertion would be to shower the incumbent administration – their local enemies – with even more public works and state projects than he already had (interview with Dr. Marçal Paiva Figueiredo, Varginha, Minas Gerais, November 14, 1981). If carried out, this would have been a certain death warrant for years to come for the "outs." As de facto head of the party in the state, his primary concern was to galvanize the maximum vote total possible, and retain the greatest number of city halls and city councils in the hands of the PDS. Thus, it was important to back proven winners and, even more important, to keep the party together. Only by forcing the intransigent ex-UDN-PR faction to continue within the PDS could this be achieved.

elite circles, closely allied with the ex-PSD faction of ARENA in the *município,* and married to the great-granddaughter of Varginha's first mayor. In the *estâncias hidrominerais* in which the mayors were appointed by the state administration, the survival of the traditional political elite was more accentuated. In Poços de Caldas, the Junqueiras, long the dominant political force in the *município,* were named to head the city administration in virtually every "election." Whether elected or appointed, heading factions within ARENA secured a place for old elites in local political life. In Sete Lagoas, on the other hand, where the local oligarchy that controlled the *município*[9] was sheltered by the MDB rather than ARENA, the old elite faced a more serious challenge than elsewhere. The local business elite assumed leadership of the local ARENA branch, and local competition was real. But even on the MDB label, oligarchical connections were potent political weapons in the fight for political survival. In Teófilo Otoni, a "dike" city in the northeastern part of Minas Gerais with an electorate of 40,000, the MDB mayor elected in 1976 was a descendant of one of the branches of the Minas oligarchy: Sá. The vice-mayor elected in 1972 on the same MDB *legenda* "2" bore the surname for which the *município* was named: Ottoni.

At best, the use of *sublegendas* did not, as anticipated by Schmitter, stimulate or even permit local competition to take place. At worst, by allowing permanent factions to form within the party whose identities were formed in the precoup period, they contributed to maintaining elite-defined, precoup local and state cleavages.

The persistent personal basis of political alignments

Because coalitional shifts did not take place, pre-1965 political alignments superimposed on the post-1965 party system divided the political class throughout the postcoup authoritarian period, up to and including the 1982 elections. Starkly personal cleavages or ones filtered through the common partisan divisions of the precoup era continued to define factions within local branches of ARENA and the state party during the entire authoritarian episode. With partisan politics still divided by traditional rivalries, any emerging ideological cleavage, such as regime versus opposition, was naturally suppressed.[10]

9 The mayor Afrânio de Avellar Marques Ferreira (1976–82) was the grandson of João Antonio de Avellar and Teófilo Marques Ferreira. The two, according to the mayor himself, "ran" the municipality from 1900 by 1910 (author's interview, October 19, 1981). His predecessor, Sérgio Emílio Brant de Vasconcellos Costa, who was mayor from 1972 to 1976, was the son of the former political boss of Sete Lagoas, Emílio de Vasconcellos Costa. The elder Vasconcellos Costa was a descendant of the legendary Joaquina de Pompeu, matriarch of several branches of the Minas oligarchy (Rebelo Horta, 1956: 77).
10 Perhaps for this reason Castello Branco was opposed from the beginning to the introduction of the *sublegenda* (Sarles Jenks, 1979: 352).

Factional lines drawn during the Vargas dictatorship survived most visibly into the modern era in the municipalities, where traditional elites were strongest and politics was most often dominated by personal rivalries. Where politicians of the precoup cohort were aging, their sons and sons-in-law carried on their "political tradition." In Varginha, for example, the dispute pitting Vargas's local foes in the PR and UDN against his supporters in the PSD, which was as old as the Vargas dictatorship itself, was brought into ARENA after the coup and continued to constitute the most significant division among groups and the most important source of political conflict in the *município,* despite Varginha's impressive growth.[11] This political divide permeated most aspects of municipal life. The two major newspapers in town were owned and edited by the opposing sides.[12] When change did occur in 1976, only the group in power changed, not the composition of the contending factions. Even at the close of the authoritarian regime when the local PDS chapter in Varginha was being constituted, the arbitration of the state party was required for the warring factions to agree on the composition of the local party *diretório (Gazeta de Varginha,* 9/4/81). Throughout the state, when the political system opened for the first time in anticipation of the 1982 gubernatorial elections, the ex-PSD–ex-UDN divide resurfaced in Minas Gerais as if the coup had never happened and ARENA had never been formed.

Whereas the lines demarcating political rivalries after 1965 were drawn by and through individuals, in the precoup period they assumed the form of partisan divisions. Parties that were notorious for their weakness and ephemeral quality relative to their counterparts in more well-entrenched party systems in fact inspired intense and surprisingly enduring loyalty among their former elite members. As a former lieutenant governor and member of the PSD in Minas Gerais put it, "The regime abolished these parties [the PSD, UDN, and PTB], but not the feelings of loyalty people had to them."[13] Sixteen years after they had been suspended, the regional newspaper commented on the durability of the PSD–UDN schism: "The PSD and UDN evoke a deep longing in our politicians. What's more, after two party reforms [1965, 1979] they defy every law and threaten eternity" (*Estado de Minas,* 1/18/81). A peasant in a small town in the Alto Paranaíba region of Minas Gerais in the same year described the persistence

11 Municipal population had increased by 50 percent from 1970 to 1980, and significant new foreign and domestic industrial investments raised Varginha to the ranking of the twelfth most industrialized *município* (as measured by ICM collection) in the state.
12 The old PSD faction controlled the *Gazeta de Varginha;* the ex-UDN-PR alliance used as its mouthpiece the *Correio do Sul.* The editors of both (Armindo Paione Sobrinho and Mariano Tarciso Campos) had served as city councillors in Varginha representing the ex-PSD and the ex-UDN faction, respectively. This pattern of partisan ownership of television and radio stations is typical of the interior. A similar division of the media in Barbacena is described by Carvalho (1980).
13 Interview with Pio Soares Canedo, Belo Horizonte, Minas Gerais, August 1, 1989.

of this partisan divide in even starker terms, "As long as there is a world, there will be a PSD and a UDN."[14]

The residual divisions left by these proscribed parties continued to format political cleavages and intrude into representative politics in Brazil during military rule, even though the attachment of the *electorate* to these parties was weak and did not match that of the elite.[15] Political allegiance traditionally was directed not to parties but to individual, especially well-established, politicians. After the coup, there was little reason for voters to withdraw their loyalty to traditional politicians in favor of parties; as "artificial" agglomerations (cf. Cardoso, 1978: 67), ARENA and the MDB more closely resembled constellations of politicians than political parties that represented identifiable interests, ideas, or issues.

Because voters were less firmly attached to parties of the precoup era than they were to individual politicians, and because these politicians, and especially local elites, affiliated with the new parties after 1965 in an erratic pattern, levels of support for precoup parties are neither reasonable nor accurate guides to postcoup voting. In this context, the stability of political alignments would preferably be demonstrated not through an examination of the party vote, but of the *personal* vote. Yet, because individual politicians who as local bosses would have exercised considerable influence on electoral outcomes most likely did not contest every local election after the regime change, restricting an inquiry about political realignment to the electoral fate of individual politicians would unduly narrow its scope and might understate the influence of traditional elites on the fortunes of postcoup parties. To test whether precoup local political elites swayed votes for ARENA and the MDB, therefore, I traced the movement of local politicians in my sample of twenty-five *municípios* into the postcoup parties, and compared the outcomes of local elections in cases in which mem-

14 Personal communication with Elisa Reis.
15 In surveys conducted in the São Paulo *município* of Presidente Prudente, which was an ARENA stronghold, Lamounier (1978: 53–54) found no discernible pattern of support for the parties of the 1965–79 period based on pre-1965 allegiances, even among those who had a pre-1965 preference (only 26 percent of all respondents): 77 percent of those who identified with Adhemar de Barros's Social Progressive Party (PSP), 79 percent of ex-PTBers, and 81 percent of followers of both the PSD and UDN all backed ARENA. Lamounier also claims that pre-1965 party identification determined postcoup voting *less* in the interior, where parties might be more clientelistically oriented, than in the more politicized state capitals. In the city of São Paulo, among survey respondents who had a pre-1965 preference (one-third of those over the age of twenty-eight), 70 percent of the old PSD and PTB voters transferred their allegiance to the MDB, as opposed to only 43 percent of former supporters of the PSP and 32 percent of the UDN (Lamounier, 1978: 52). In the *município* of Caxias do Sul, Rio Grande do Sul, the state with the most ideologically based politics in Brazil, three-fourths of voters who identified with the PTB and PTR (Rural Labor Party) before the coup voted MDB, and an almost identical proportion of the old UDN–PL–PSD bloc in that state embraced ARENA (De Cew, 1978: 191).

bers of the traditional parties joined the opposition with those in which they did not. My study includes each of the four elections held during the authoritarian period (a total of ninety-four data points).[16]

How individual politicians aligned in the postcoup parties was more strongly correlated with the local MDB victories in the later years of the authoritarian regime, even *after* the "realigning" election of 1974, than more frequently cited factors such as municipal size and percent of the population residing in urban areas.[17] Opposition mayors were elected in thirteen of forty local elections in which at least one faction of the PSD, UDN, or PR joined the MDB in 1965 or subsequently defected to the opposition (32.5 percent), but in only five of the fifty-four cases in which all members of the precoup elite parties remained with ARENA (9.3 percent) (Table 6.2). Where the MDB began from scratch, and placed hopes on new leaders, its road to even local office was three and a half times more difficult than when it combined forces with politicians from the old populist and oligarchical parties. Where the MDB attracted a sizable percentage of voters in local elections in Minas Gerais, its leaders and candidates were often politicians of reputation before the coup. This trend is true regardless of the demographic characteristics of the *município*. Opposition mayors were elected in the relatively small municipalities of Unaí, Eloi Mendes, Várzea da Palma, and Santa Rita do Sapucaí, which were also among the least urbanized. The MDB elected mayors in ten of fifty-three elections in *municípios* that were at least 80 percent urban (18.9 percent), and a very similar percentage (19.5) in *municípios* that were less than 80 percent urban (eight of forty-one cases). When degree of urbanization is held constant, the results are even more illuminating. The opposition was more than twice as likely to elect a mayor in the more urbanized municipalities when members of the oligarchy defected to the opposition (six of twenty-two elections, or 27 percent, as opposed to four of thirty-one cases, or 13 percent), and nine times more likely to do so in the less urbanized *municípios* (seven of eighteen elections, or 38.9 percent, versus one of twenty-three elections, or 4.3 percent).

While the influence of the partisan affiliations of individual politicians was strongest and most readily detectable in local elections, it also spilled over into congressional elections. In Itajubá, Sete Lagoas, and Teófilo Otoni, three cases in my sample in which part of the local oligarchy moved into the opposition party, the MDB polled well in the state and federal races as well as in the local. As a general rule, votes followed the movements of the local and state politicians to whom they "belonged." In 1962, Joaquim de Mello Freire, then a young state deputy on the UDN ticket,

16 The total is 94, rather than 100, because no elections were held in Poços de Caldas and Patrocínio in 1970, 1972, and 1976.
17 These are among the factors found by Faria (1978) and Sarles (1982) to be strongly correlated with the MDB vote in São Paulo and Rio de Janeiro.

Table 6.2 Mayoral elections, select municípios, 1976, 1972, 1970, 1966 (% of turnout)

Município	Population 1980	% Urban	1970	Post-65 alignment[a]	1976 ARENA	1976 MDB	1972 ARENA	1972 MDB	1970 ARENA	1970 MDB	1966 ARENA	1966 MDB
Barbacena	86,388	83	73,905	IA	53	38	55	33	59	11	89	–
Con. Lafaiete	72,438	92	50,919	IA	80	13	52	40	64	24	45	45[c]
Curvelo	50,770	78	45,494	II	40	54[c]	50	44	61	30	44	47[c]
Dores do Indaiá	15,184	86	15,747	IA	89	6	95	–	65	30	44	47[c]
Eloi Mendes	16,986	55	14,712	IA	65	25	–	88[c]	78	–	78	–
Guanhães	22,781	60	22,489	IA	62	28	51	–	92	–	91	–
Itabira	71,115	83	56,394	IB	36	55[c]	27	61[c]	92	–	77	8
Itajubá	60,593	89	51,727	II	62	32	30	66[c]	58	33	77	15
Januária	71,941	35	62,615	IA	82	–	78	–	94	–	90	–
Leopoldina	42,118	74	41,337	IA	95	–	73	20	48	38	78	–
Montes Claros	177,308	88	116,464	IA	80	14	93	–	72	17	77	–
Muriaé	69,990	79	58,428	IA	95	2	97	–	51	35	91	2
Patrocínio[b]	44,373	70	35,600	IA.D-M							72	–
Pirapora	32,673	96	20,339	IA	86	10	97	–	89	5	91	–

				IA.[a]								
Poços de Caldas[b]	86,972	94	57,643	IA.	97	–	94	2	69	21	73	–
Pouso Alegre	57,364	89	38,141	II	33	61[c]	60	30	55	37	62	–
Santa Rita Sapucaí	22,212	68	18,927	II	35	56[c]	26	68[c]	47	40	70	–
Sete Lagoas	100,628	94	66,636	II	34	60[c]	34	59[c]	51	36	–	82[c]
Teófilo Otoni	128,827	68	132,960	II	40	54[c]	48	46	39	53[c]	53	38
Três Corações	44,382	81	35,244	IA	71	22	81	–	94	–	50	41
Ubá	53,311	82	44,663	II.D-A	81	11	94	1	57	34	87	4
Uberaba	199,203	92	124,848	IA.D-M	45	51[c]	50	47	48	48	61	29
Unaí	67,883	44	52,427	II	76	17	49	42	74	15	50	42
Varginha	64,906	89	43,707	II	44	46[c]	66	28	42	50[c]	50	39
Várzea da Palma	18,533	64	13,383	IA.D-M	44	46[c]	66	28	42	50[c]	68	–

[a]IA = candidates in 1962 from all precoup parties joined ARENA; IB = candidates from the MDB; II = candidates from PTB and/or MTR joined the MDB; II = candidates from the PSD, UDN, and/or PR joined the MDB; D-A = Defection to ARENA; D-M = Defection to MDB.
[b]As designated *estâncias hidrominerais*, Patrocínio and Poços de Caldas did not directly elect a mayor in the 1970, 1972, and 1976 elections.
[c]MDB victories
Sources: IBGE, 1970, 1980b, 3; TRE-MG.

won over 5,000 votes, or 52 percent of the turnout, in the city of Passos; in 1986, as a member of the state executive commission of the PMDB, he won more than two and a half times that number of votes, 32 percent of the turnout, and more than three times more votes than his closest competitor in the *município*. He also preserved electoral strength in the contiguous electoral districts of Cassia and Alpinópolis, where he garnered one-fourth of the vote.

The ability of local and state elected representatives to retain personal clienteles was enhanced by the "artificiality" of the political parties created by the military that reinforced and reinvigorated the clientelistic basis of Brazilian politics. By superimposing authoritarian limits on electoral politics in such a patronage-driven system, access to state resources could only be guaranteed by stable political alignments, which in turn enforced the allegiance of voters to incumbent elites, of local elites to the state oligarchy, and of the political class to the regime. The formation of new political identities and leaders on a wide scale was structurally blocked.

AUTHORITARIAN POLITICS AND THE STATE OLIGARCHY

In traditional Brazilian politics, the route to the upper reaches of the state – in particular, to state and national cabinets – for both members of traditional families and for aspirants to the state elite was an electoral one that wound through state and federal legislatures, the recruiting grounds for cabinet secretaries and governors. A strong showing in state and federal congressional elections, which was a sine qua non for membership in the state oligarchy of Minas Gerais, was, however, difficult to achieve without first capturing the loyalty of leaders of local party branches, who otherwise exerted little influence in state and national party politics. Traditional state elites were anchored in local politics: politicians from oligarchical families staked out bases in cities and towns of the interior that lasted a lifetime and transcended political generations;[18] the more secure their local bases, the stronger their positions in state and national politics.

Authoritarian politics restored to the state oligarchy the advantage of its local connections. In paving the way for the permanent residence of traditional bosses in the power structures of the cities and towns of the interior and in enforcing political loyalties in rigid electoral coalitions, authoritarianism secured the political dominance of the traditional political elite. If appointed governors provided stability, protection, and patronage assistance from above, entrenched local bosses supplied the support and allegiance from below to hold the state oligarchy in place.

18 Political elites by and large begin their careers in local politics (cf. Sarles, 1982: 51). According to data compiled by Fleischer (n.d.: 43–46), approximately three-fifths of all federal and state deputies elected in the years from 1946 to 1975 had previously served terms as either mayors or municipal councillors.

Electoral law and traditional politics

Federal and state deputies are chosen in Brazil according to an open-list proportional representation system. State party *diretórios* select the candidates to appear on their ballots (incumbents have the prerogative of running again under a rule called the *candidato nato* [the "birthright candidate"]), but do not predetermine their order – names do not appear on the ballot. Voters cast their ballots for only one candidate for deputy, and deputies run statewide (in effect, each state is a single, multimember district).[19] Which candidates will assume a party's seats in the legislature is based on individual vote totals. Election to the legislature thus depends not on faithful service to one's party but on personal vote-drawing ability.

When the vagaries of Brazilian electoral laws are combined with the predictable effects of clientelism, the proportional representation system, which elsewhere typically gives voters a greater incentive to vote for a party ahead of individual candidates, works in quite the opposition fashion. Few Minas representatives elected in 1978 to the Chamber of Deputies drew widely dispersed support as "ideological" party representatives might be expected to. Very prominent politicians, such as Magalhães Pinto and Tancredo Neves, attracted votes from all corners of the state – but they were exceptions that proved the rule: they were able to rise above the threshold only because their overall vote totals were so high. Most deputies in Minas Gerais drew their support instead from a geographically concentrated area. A hopeful deputy could launch his state-level political career from a single municipal base, especially if he was once mayor of a large enough city. More than half of the federal and state deputies elected on the ARENA ticket in 1978 drew at least 30 percent of their vote in contiguous cities and towns (Table 6.3). If we add as a measure of geographically concentrated support "solid vote totals in scattered districts," since even a deputy who was not a "district representative" strictly speaking might still have drawn support from specific *municípios* that he favored with state resources – even if they were found in different parts of the state – twenty-five of twenty-eight ARENA federal deputies (89 percent) and sixteen of nineteen MDB federal deputies (84 percent) in Minas exercised a form of what Cardoso (1978: 66) called "clientelistic-paternalistic" control.[20] It was even rarer for state ARENA deputies to gain election with only dispersed sup-

19 As in most any proportional representation system, the votes of each candidate of the same party are tallied, and the number of seats are awarded in both federal and state legislatures according to the proportion of votes the party polls statewide in that election, plus the distribution of the "leftovers" (the results of blank but valid ballots plus the votes won by a party that did not meet the electoral quotient).
20 Cardoso (1978: 66) has aptly pointed out that support for deputies who either represent a constituency that is not spatially concentrated or ideologically defined tends to be dispersed throughout a state. Conversely, where deputies' votes are concentrated in electoral zones, he suggests, it is safe to assume their vote is enhanced by paternalism and clientelism.

Table 6.3 *Minas Gerais: Patterns of electoral support for deputies, 1978*

	Federal deputies		State deputies	
	ARENA	MDB	ARENA	MDB
1. With more than or close to 50% of the vote in an electoral district	1	5	1	3
2. High vote percentage in a single district - but not enough to be elected in a district election	2	3	13	6
3. Around 30% of the vote in contiguous cities and towns which, if grouped into one district, might serve as a base for election	12	0	9	1
4. Solid vote totals in scattered districts	10	8	18	5
Subtotal - categories 1 through 4	25	16	41	15
5. Dispersed support - no zone with 30% of the vote	3	3	1	14
Total	28	19	42	29

Note: Minus those elected with most of their support in Belo Horizonte.
Source: Araújo, 1980: 51–64.

port. Presumably younger and with less established "prestige" which accrues from operating in the national political arena, all but one enjoyed geographically concentrated support. With limited access to state patronage, MDB state deputies were treated by voters less like "district representatives"; just over half (52 percent) had spatially definable constituencies.

Because of the powerful effects of state clientelism, Minas districts earned the reputation for being the most impermeable in Brazil (Ames, 1987: 124; Fleischer, 1976: 333–60). Individual deputies survived on the basis of their political resources and contacts – chiefly, the strength and reach of their personal electoral networks. The viability of these networks depended, in turn, on the extent to which their roots were nourished with patronage. Members of the traditional political elite had two advantages in retaining their personal votes: they more often joined the cabinet and could therefore draw from the state patronage bank, and they could depend on the loyalty of ward bosses with whom they had long-established personal relationships. Traditional elites especially prized the loyalty of their *cabos eleitorais*. Bonifácio José Tamm de Andrada, in a 1978 interview, claimed to have turned down an offer by an influential citizen of a *município* neighboring Barbacena (his home) of a number of votes two times greater than what he was being delivered by the then *cabo eleitoral* of the faction, on the condition he abandon his old ally. He preferred to stick with his old *cabo eleitoral,* who, year after year, had delivered to him a sure and steady vote (Carvalho, 1980: 92–93).

The party *diretórios* in the cities and towns of the interior heavily influenced the outcome of federal and state legislative elections. Despite the wide range of choice of candidates for deputy (ranging from a low of 19 candidates on the MDB side of the ledger in the 1970 federal deputy elections to a high of 141 candidates on the ARENA ticket for state deputy in 1966),[21] only three to five candidates normally captured from three-fifths to three-quarters of a community's vote.[22] To win such large blocs of votes, the aspiring deputy had to court members of local party *diretórios*. At times, a candidate might trade votes from his hometown or other areas of support for a federal deputy from a city whose vote he is soliciting, in exchange for that *diretório's* support for his run for state deputy. Local party endorsements, which carried with them anywhere from half the municipal vote for a native to 30 percent for a parliamentary candidate from another part of the state, were crucial if a deputy was to garner enough votes statewide to be elected.

Stable party leaderships such as those in Varginha and Sete Lagoas were likely to support incumbent deputies, especially those who had been good patrons to the cities they "represented." Long-standing loyalties and alignments were a powerful political bond, for good practical reasons, to both sides. Without electoral districts, were an incumbent deputy to lose, or

21 Parties in Brazil are allowed to present up to one and a half times the number of candidates as seats to be filled for federal and state deputy races (up to three times for local council elections) (Mainwaring, 1991b: 25). During the period of military rule, the size of federal and state legislatures fluctuated. In Minas Gerais, ARENA ran a list of 57 candidates for federal deputy in 1966; 46 in 1970 and 1974; 53 in 1978, and the PDS ran 54 in 1982. The MDB ran 38 in 1966; 19 in 1970; 29 in 1974; 43 in 1978; and the PMDB, 50 in 1982. In the state Assembly elections, ARENA nominated 141 candidates in 1966; 121 in 1970, 109 in 1974; 132 in 1978, and the PDS, 104 in 1982. The MDB presented a list of candidates for state deputy containing 128 names in 1966; 70 in 1970; 90 in 1974; and 112 in 1978, and the PMDB ran 111 candidates in 1982 (TRE-MG, 1966, 1970, 1974, 1978, 1982).
22 The results of the 1982 elections for the state Legislative Assembly in select municipalities of Minas Gerais are illustrative of this general rule: two candidates in Itabira captured 75 percent of the vote; three in Barbacena, Conselheiro Lafaiete, and Sete Lagoas polled 75, 62, and 73 percent of the vote, respectively; four in Curvelo and Varginha, 63 and 73 percent; and five in Montes Claros, 70 percent. In the races for federal deputy, the vote was a bit more dispersed, but the trend is similar. From three to five candidates won from a low of 50 percent of the vote in Conselheiro Lafaiete to a high of 74 percent in Barbacena.

were a municipality's 5,000 votes to be delivered to a "wrong" candidate – one who failed to get elected – a locality might have been left without "representation" altogether, something that no *município* could afford in a system that underfunded local government. Cities and towns of the interior were forced to supplement their revenues with state program funds and public works – pork barrel projects that were usually secured through political connections. The more traditional the aspiring political representative, and the better connected he was, moreover, the more state resources he could deliver. Even oligarchies in opposition could take advantage of old networks. The mayor of Sete Lagoas, according to the president of the Commercial and Industrial Association of Sete Lagoas (and member of the PDS *diretório*), was the best the municipality had had in twenty years, "very well connected" despite being from the opposition.[23] The local oligarchy, who founded the PP (Partido Popular) in Sete Lagoas, persuaded the local PDS to support the candidacies of two opposition federal deputies and one state deputy, "sons of the city," who would in exchange for their votes attend to requests from local members of the PDS in the state Legislative Assembly and the federal Chamber of Deputies. Where connections were at a premium, the only people worth supporting were those who could operate in state networks; in this exceptional case, local oligarchies best fitted the bill.

Authoritarianism and state elite turnover

These mutually beneficial if unequal alliances between local elites and state oligarchs resulted in high rates of reelection for ARENA deputies. Nationally, the turnover rates of federal deputies during the authoritarian regime declined visibly, if undramatically, from precoup levels (Table 6.4). Apart from the exceptionally high level of 1950, when 70 percent of the representatives in the Chamber of Deputies were "new," that is, they had never before occupied a seat in the federal Chamber, precoup turnover rates hovered around 50 percent. In the first election after the coup, this rate dropped to 41 percent, and did not appreciably rise thereafter.

Actual elite turnover may have declined even more sharply after the regime change than these figures initially suggest. Institutional Act Number 5, issued in December 1968, annulled the legislative mandates of 28 ARENA and 66 MDB deputies – 94 of 409 or 23 percent of the total – and prevented these representatives from standing for reelection in 1970 (see Table 6.1).[24] Though fewer legislators had lost their seats in 1964 and 1965 as a result of Institutional Acts Numbers 1 and 2, the cancellation of mandates nonetheless exercised an impact on the composition of the legislature

23 Interview with Taft Alves Ferreira, Sete Lagoas, Minas Gerais, November 9, 1981.
24 As Alves (1985: 96–98) uses a higher figure for the number of *cassados,* this figure should be considered a minimum.

Table 6.4 *National elite turnover*

Year	New representatives[a] (%)	Deputies (N)
Precoup		
1950	70.7	304
1954	51.8	326
1958	49.1	326
1962	46.9	409
Postcoup		
1966	41.3	409
1970	45.8	310
1974	43.4	364
1978	44.8	420

[a]"New" representatives are deputies who never before occupied a seat in the federal Chamber (as opposed to those who may have returned after a previous defeat or after serving in some other office).
Source: Fleischer, 1980b: 59.

elected in 1966 as well. Second, these rates represent the number of new legislators over the *total* number of seats. Yet, in both 1974 and 1978, the size of the Chamber of Deputies was increased. All other factors being equal, an increase in the number of representatives from 310 to 364 between 1970 and 1974 and from 364 to 420 between 1974 and 1978 should have produced corresponding increases in the percentages of new elites. Yet turnover stayed at practically the same level. Thus although these figures accurately inform us of the full extent of the opportunities the system created for new contestants, they do understate how secure incumbent elites were in office.

In Minas Gerais, elite turnover declined more sharply during the authoritarian regime from its precoup levels than it did nationally. Forty-one percent of Minas federal deputies and 54 percent of state deputies were elected for the first time in 1954, and 48 percent of federal and nearly 60 percent of state deputies in 1962 (Table 6.5). Shortly after the Second Institutional Act was issued, turnover rates slumped despite the *cassações* of many deputies. In the 1974 congressional elections, the first postcoup elections unaffected by the expulsion of deputies and generally regarded as the freest of the military term in office, turnover rates fell sharply to less than 30 percent in the federal deputy elections and 13 percent in the state elections; 1978 rates rose moderately with the sizable increase in the size of the legislatures but not to the levels of the 1950s. When the size of the legislature is held constant by counting only the deputies elected to previously existing seats, moreover, the rates remain significantly lower than their corresponding measures in the precoup years: in the state legislative

Table 6.5 *Federal and state deputy turnover, Minas Gerais, 1950–78*

	Chamber of Deputies				Legislative Assembly			
	N	New deputies			N	New deputies		
Election	elected	N	%[a]	%[b]	elected	N	%[a]	%[b]
Precoup								
1950	38	--	--		72	--	--	
1954	39	15	38.5	(41.0)	74	38	51.3	(54.0)
1958	39	18	46.1		74	40	54.0	
1962	48	14	29.1	(47.8)	82	41	50.0	(59.7)
Postcoup								
1966[c]	48	15	31.2		73	39	53.4	
1970[d]	35	15	33.3		59	22	37.2	
1974	37	9	24.3	(29.7)	61	6	9.8	(13.0)
1978	47	11	23.3	(46.0)	71	13	18.3	(32.3)

[a]This column represents the percentage of incumbent deputies elected to previously existing seats.
[b]This column represents the percentage of all nonincumbent deputies.
[c]If not for the *cassações*, there might have been 11, not 15, new deputies in the Chamber representing Minas Gerais, depressing the rate of new elite entry to a possible low of 22.9 percent.
[d]The figures for 1970, too, are inflated due to the *cassações* following Institutional Act Number 5. Seven Minas federal deputies and three state deputies lost their posts and their rights to defend them in the next elections.
Source: Araújo, 1980: 65–70.

races, approximately 10 percent in 1974 as opposed to 50 percent in 1962. The state returns are particularly significant because these rates had been higher in the precoup period than they had been in the federal elections, and it is at this level where politicians first rise from their local bases to join the state elite.

These two measures of legislative turnover, moreover, also understate the turnover rate of the elite because neither takes account of the family ties of "new" deputies. When José Bonifácio Lafayette de Andrada retired from politics before the 1978 congressional elections, his eldest son, Bonifácio José Tamm de Andrada, took "his place" on the *legenda* and was easily elected. The younger Andrada's brother, José Bonifácio Tamm de Andrada (José Bonifácio Filho), in turn, replaced his elder brother on the state deputy *legenda* and in the state Legislative Assembly. Both, as "new" deputies, contributed to the increase in elite turnover. Neither represented the infusion of "new blood" into elite ranks.

When elite turnover is calculated instead as a proportion of "old politicians" who win a statewide deputy race, and when it takes into account

Table 6.6 *Elite turnover recalculated: Deputy elections in Minas Gerais,*
1962–78 (in %)

	1966		1970		1974		1978	
	CD	AL	CD	AL	CD	AL	CD	AL
A. *Deputies in 1962*								
ARENA	92	62	82	36	74	24	61	17
MDB	73	21	57	17	29	8	21	4
B. *Ran in 1962*ᵃ								
ARENA	--	13	--	9	--	--	--	--
MDB	--	5	--	--	--	3	--	--
C. *Progenitors*								
ARENA	--	2	4	--	--	3	4	2
MDB	--	--	--	--	--	--	--	--
D. *Elected in preceding elections*ᵇ								
ARENA	--	--	7	24	28	54	28	43
MDB	--	--	29	33	28	42	37	52
"Corrected" incumbency (A + B + C + D)								
ARENA	92	77	93	69	100	81	93	62
MDB	73	26	86	50	57	53	58	56

Note: CD = Chamber of Deputies; AL = Legislative Assembly.
ᵃAnd achieved top alternate status.
ᵇPreviously elected as state or federal deputy or higher. For example, a former state deputy who wins election as a federal deputy is considered "reelected."
Sources: TRE-MG, 1962, 1966, 1970, 1974, 1978.

whether "new" representatives inherited the electoral machines of their political progenitors in the state oligarchy, the full extent of the closure of the political system is more starkly evident. In 1966, 92 percent of federal deputies elected on the ARENA ticket were incumbents (Table 6.6); in the state race, that figure was lower (62 percent). These percentages steadily declined as the authoritarian regime wore on: from 82 percent in the federal contest in 1970 to 74 percent in 1974, to 61 percent in 1978, and to 38 percent in 1982. Similarly, the rates for the state Assembly declined, from 36 percent in 1970 to 24 percent in 1974, and to 17 percent in 1978 and 11 percent in 1982. But, when to these percentages are added those who in 1962 were poised to cross the electoral threshold from high alternate *(suplente)* to regular deputy status, who were the sons or younger brothers of retiring deputies, and those who had been elected in preceding elections, the figures for 1970 rise to 93 percent and 69 percent respectively. In 1974, the year of the watershed election in which the MDB made an electoral breakthrough, 100 percent of the federal deputies elected on the ARENA ticket and 81 percent of the state deputies were not newcomers to the state elite; even the *top seven alternates* for federal deputy on the ARENA ticket had previously served as deputy or state cabinet secretary. This pattern continued in 1978, when 93 percent and 62 percent of elected deputies were not "new" to Minas state politics. On average, over 90 percent of federal and 72 percent of state ARENA deputies were members of the state elite, if not incumbent representatives.

As might be expected in a clientelistic system, there was less turnover among ARENA than MDB deputies. In the first two elections for the federal Chamber after the coup, 73 and 86 percent of the deputies elected, respectively, were "incumbents." After 1974, with the revitalization of the party that accompanied its new electoral success, a clear rise in turnover is visible; 57 percent of the deputies elected in 1974 and 58 percent in 1978 were "old." In 1966, the ranks of the MDB state deputies were decimated. It was entirely possible for new opposition representatives to emerge, at least when it was less apparent that the MDB was a good alternative both for voters and for those aspiring to build a political career.

Why some incumbents were able to cling to their positions in the oligarchy or "pass on" their votes to a personally groomed successor while others were eclipsed is attributable to their access to and ability to distribute effectively state patronage. Comparing the backgrounds of those deputies whose tenure in the legislature began before the regime came into being (or their sons) who "survived" several elections with those that did not reveals that "name recognition" in itself persuaded voters less than did the ability of a candidate to deliver state resources (Table 6.7). Systematically, the effects of three variables are examined: if candidates were elected by a "district" vote, a measure particularly salient for ARENA deputies whose access to state patronage was greater; if they had served in the state or federal cabinets; and if they were "traditional," or at least, part of the state "oligarchy."

In fact, surviving federal and state deputies were much more likely to have concentrated electoral support than nonsurviving deputies. Whereas three-quarters of surviving federal ARENA *and* MDB deputies drew a significant share of their support from single electoral districts (greater than 45 percent) and contiguous municipalities (at least 30 percent of their total vote), only 38 percent of nonsurviving federal deputies did the same. Conversely, only one-quarter of "surviving" federal deputies did not draw their electoral support from some form of district (district, contiguous A, and contiguous B), whereas over three-fifths (62 percent) of "nonsurviving" deputies did not. *Not one* state deputy survived whose votes were sporadic or dispersed around the state. The effects of state cabinet service on the electoral fortunes of incumbents is even more pronounced. Those federal *and* state deputies

Table 6.7 *"Surviving" versus "nonsurviving" deputies in Minas Gerais*

| | Federal deputies | | | | | | | | State deputies | | | | | | | |
| | Survivors | | | | Nonsurvivors | | | | Survivors | | | | Nonsurvivors | | | |
	ARENA	MDB	n/p[a]	Total	ARENA	MDB	n/p[a]	Total	ARENA	MDB	n/p[a]	Total	ARENA	MDB	n/p[a]	Total
Electoral support[b]																
District	-	-	-	-	2	-	1	3	9	-	-	9	9	1	2	12
Contiguous A	7	-	-	7	3	1	1	5	12	-	-	12	14	-	1	15
Contiguous B	3	1	-	4	3	1	1	5	9	1	-	10	9	1	3	13
Sporadic	2	2	-	4	10	1	5[c]	16	-	-	-	0	4	1	3	8
Dispersed	-	-	-	-	4	-	1	5	-	-	-	0	1	1	-	2
Subtotal	12	3	0	15	22	3	9	34	30	1	0	31	37	4	9	50
Cabinet service																
Yes	9	1	-	10	10	1	1	12	15	1	-	16	9	3	-	12
No	3	2	-	5	12	2	8	22	15	-	-	15	28	1	9	38
Traditional oligarchy[d]																
Yes	5	1	-	6	2	-	-	2	10	-	-	10	5	-	-	5
No	7	2	-	9	20	3	9	32	20	1	-	21	32	4	9	45

Note: Survivors, at minimum, were reelected at least three times, or served a combination of three terms in legislative and executive office (vice-president, governor, or lieutenant governor). The exception was when a family "teamed up." For example, the brothers Elias and Juarez de Sousa Carmo and Guilherme Machado and José Machado Sobrinho "split" the three-term requirement.

[a] n/p = party not identified; deputy did not contest office under either party label from 1966 to 1978.

[b] Key: "District" = more than 45 percent of the deputy's vote in a single *município*; "Contiguous A" = more than 45 percent of the vote in contiguous *municípios*; "Contiguous B" = more than 30 percent of the vote in contiguous *municípios*; "Sporadic" = at least 20 percent of the vote in 2–3 noncontiguous *municípios*; "Dispersed" = no more than 5 percent of the vote in any one *município*.

[c] Includes Sebastião Pães de Almeida, who was *cassado*.

[d] Incomplete data on all deputies mean that this measure can only be suggestive. Data on membership in the "oligarchy" are more reliable than that on "older relatives in politics."

who passed through the state cabinet were twice as "secure" as those who had not. Two-thirds of surviving federal deputies and 52 percent of surviving state deputies had served in the cabinet, as opposed to 35 percent of nonsurviving federal deputies and 24 percent of nonsurviving state deputies. Finally, the survival of "traditional" politicians grossly outstrips that of deputies with no family connections to the oligarchy. Forty percent of surviving federal and 32 percent of surviving state deputies were members of the traditional oligarchy, whereas only 6 percent of nonsurviving federal and 10 percent of state deputies were.

CONCLUSIONS

Brazil's unique elections under authoritarianism set the parameters for political competition, elite turnover, and, eventually, political change or its absence. Practically from the outset of its rule, the military in Brazil set rigid parameters for political activity in order to achieve a stable political infrastructure in the states and localities. The regime eliminated its opponents, removed the posts of federal and state chief executives from the electoral arena, and created a semiofficial political party. Possibilities for genuine mobilization from below vanished, as might be expected in a regime that deprived citizens of political rights. But the potential for opposition was also severely limited even for aspiring elites.

Political centralization and the monopoly of executive power conferred a stunning advantage on incumbent state and party elites that were allowed to monopolize the distribution of state patronage resources. The institutional advantages accorded ARENA in the electoral arena and the exercise of state clientelism within it rendered opposition, and with it interparty competition, effectively futile as a route to state positions – the MDB survived and eventually thrived as a party of largely symbolic protest. Oligarchical control of a single dominant party made intraparty competition just as illusory. Restricted political competition in a clientelistic, authoritarian political system congealed coalitions of national, state, and local political elites, fixed local party factions along the lines of precoup elite rivalries, and stifled the possibilities for the realignment of factions in local and state politics. Genuine realignment did not take place until 1985, after a new governor had been elected and *when it became apparent the system could change at the top*. By that time a new party system was in place, and bipartism – de facto as well as de jure – had ended.

Whatever its ambiguous political project, the regime was forced to rely on *traditional* political elites to support itself in power. While there were undoubtedly hard-liners in the military who would have preferred to go on alone and purge the political system indefinitely of its "corrupt politicians," in the end, they lost the day. Despite the fact that any state elite should theoretically have been able to generate its own political support by distributing state resources, in practice seizing the Brazilian state did not ensure being able to gain control over the separate clientelistic networks that composed its elaborate support system – these belonged to the persons who organized them. A tradition of personalism, so deeply ingrained in Brazil's electoral system and state–society relations, defeated any attempts to convert state clientelism into an instrument of an autonomous military elite.

By limiting political competition, the bureaucratic-authoritarian regime that had originally challenged the regional oligarchies not only did not evict oligarchical interests, but it helped traditional political elites retain their power and positions. In fact, with the artificial political support of the authoritarian umbrella, traditional political elites were possibly stronger as authoritarian rule drew to a close than they were in 1964 when it began. Weak state oligarchies now had federal government protection, which they lacked in the earlier period. State elites who never really lost their grip, like the Mineiro, had less to gain immediately but nonetheless profited from a more secure order in the long term. State patronage has, with rare exceptions, heretofore not been conceived as a stable power base of dominant elites.[25] The power inherent in the control of state resources has been underestimated because these assets are perceived to lack the durability of land and other forms of property.[26] What the Brazilian authoritarian experience demonstrates is that in circumstances of limited competition that diminish the likelihood of state elites being voted out of office, public assets can prove to be as durable a political resource as private assets in competitive political systems, which are sometimes subject to redistribution by reform or revolution.

The Brazilian experience with authoritarianism also suggests that reformulation of scholarly perceptions of the effects of authoritarianism on political change is in order. Most obviously, it shows that the staging of elections in itself does not necessarily stimulate the formation of new leaders.[27] But it also highlights that voter preferences for particular party labels

25 Even in a highly clientelistic society such as southern Italy, Christian Democratic Party patrons that control public jobs and works are scarcely viewed as a power elite. They are seen instead as political power brokers, subordinate to the hegemonic northern industrialists.

26 Scott (1972: 97–98) suggests that posts that confer on their occupants the "indirect control of the property or authority or others (often the public)," which are otherwise attractive because the resources connected with many of them are far greater than those which an individual can amass directly, are of limited value as a source of patronage. The availability of this resource is dependent on continuity in positions ultimately given or withdrawn by third parties, usually electors, and is thus a less durable source of power for a patron than land or other privately owned assets.

27 Another reason for the absence of new leadership formation was suggested by a member of the Minas oligarchy: in proscribing the associations of university students, authoritarian rule closed an important avenue by which new recruits traditionally had entered politics (interview with Pio Soares Canedo, Belo Horizonte, Minas Gerais, August 1, 1989).

can be an inadequate and even misleading indicator of political system change, especially where parties lack deep roots, voter loyalties, identifiable ideologies, and discernible constituencies. Where, rather, power is personalized, individuals create and dissolve parties at will, and elite-defined factions can easily reassemble under a new party label, the disappearance of a transient party may be stronger evidence of political *continuity* than of political change. It is certainly a less accurate guide to political system change than turnover of the elite and modifications in regime-distinguishing political practices, such as clientelism. It is also far less significant for political change than the survival of individual members of a closed political elite whose collective interests and internal rivalries determine most meaningful contours of politics. In federal political systems with strong regional and local components and identities, moreover, the omission of elite turnover at even the state and local levels may crucially understate the degree of continuity from a pre- to postauthoritarian order. When authoritarian rule provides a protective umbrella for entrenched elites such as these, the effect of the *length* of authoritarian rule, a key variable identified by Remmer (1989: 70) as leading to political and party change, lies in the opposite direction. To the extent that new political identities and cleavages grow up in an authoritarian regime, they may do so because of such exogenous factors as urbanization or industrialization, but not the political practices of authoritarianism.

In 1982, the authoritarian regime that safeguarded traditional elite interests began to unravel. This traditional political elite faced an accelerated opening of the political system, which produced a qualitative change in permissible political competition. What part the Minas oligarchy would play in that process would become crucial for its own survival and for the future of Brazilian politics.

7

The traditional political elite and the transition to democracy

The forward-looking, modern military regime that revived its rule by substituting politics for the technical rationality it had once prized came to a surprisingly abrupt close in 1985 when a civilian opposition candidate, Tancredo Neves, was elected president in an electoral college convened by the military. Only months earlier, Neves's victory would have seemed impossible. Although it had become clear as a result of the watershed election of 1974 that military rule could not be institutionalized, a form of authoritarian rule easily endured, and the possibilities for a permanent *"democradura"* were alive and well.[1] For a decade, political liberalization, the gradual restoration of civil liberties, and party reform had proceeded according to military plan, and the military was confident of handing power to a loyal civilian.

The deviation from military course began in 1982 with the first direct election of governors since 1965. In these elections the PMDB won nine governorships (of a possible twenty-two) and legislative majorities in the most developed states including São Paulo, Rio de Janeiro, Paraná, and Minas Gerais. The PDS failed to achieve an outright majority in the federal Chamber of Deputies, and the government was forced to enter into a coalition with the Brazilian Labor Party (PTB) of Ivete Vargas. Amid economic crisis, it soon became apparent that the military government could no longer be sure of the electoral majorities it had manipulated in the 1970s, and that the authoritarian regime could no longer be sustained at the polls. From that time, it became clearer that the military would have to abdicate power, and the military struggled to maintain control over the liberalization process. Although the men in uniform failed to handpick a civilian successor from among the PDS hopefuls who had supported military rule, the military did not resist abdicating power. Following a year of mass popular mobilization and elite bargaining, enough top officers were

---

1 O'Donnell and Schmitter (1986: 9) invented the term *democradura* to describe a limited democracy in which the freedoms of particular individuals or groups who are deemed "insufficiently prepared or sufficiently dangerous to enjoy full citizenship status" are restricted. Translating literally from the Spanish, a *democradura* is a "hard" democracy, as well as a cross between a democracy (*democracia*) and a dictatorship (*dictadura*).

prepared to exit that even the death of the president-elect did not impede the orderly transition from military to civilian rule in early 1985.[2]

The transition to democracy was a critical period for the traditional political elite. Lifting the lid on political competition posed a challenge more real than military rule to the oligarchy and local bosses that had thrived in a political environment in which such competition had been limited and regulated. When authoritarian restrictions on competition dwindled, the political game was thrown open and many opposition candidates waged successful campaigns that broke the highly centralized political order. The regime that traditional politicians had helped bring to birth and supported made an inglorious exit, and the electorate exhibited an emerging propensity to punish those who had supported authoritarianism. With the frenetic competition of four important elections to come in the following five years, moreover, this challenge to their dominance was likely to mount, not diminish, as time wore on. Perhaps, finally, without artificial political limits, socioeconomic change could transform politics and multipartism could break the hold of the traditional elite on party representation. Most important, electoral defeats could sever the traditional political elite from its power base in the state. Scott's (1972: 97–98) admonition regarding the tenuousness of "resources that ultimately belong to others" might finally have rung true for a traditional political elite that had long been able to defy this maxim.

In fact, although it fragmented and its ranks thinned, the Brazilian traditional political elite as a class remained strong through the transition. Like other inveterate oligarchies, it had the foresight to abandon in a timely fashion a decaying regime. When the *abertura política* gained momentum, traditional elites who had once embraced the 1964 "Revolution" and benefited from the authoritarian regime became strong advocates of a controlled liberalization. When the governing coalition began to crumble under the weight of its own corruption, personal rivalries, and petty ambitions, the politically astute joined forces with the advocates of regime change. By situating themselves squarely in the democratic camp, they placed José Sarney, a PDS leader during the military regime, in the executive coalition, and ultimately, by chance, in the presidency. In rising to meet the challenge of civilianization and democratization, and in scrambling to ensure its own survival, the traditional political elite also steered Brazilian democratization to its advantage; indeed, it placed its indelible imprint on the New Republic, at the cost of compromising the foundations of democratic politics in Brazil.

The cottage industry of studies about the transition to democracy in Brazil has debated amply whether the long-awaited opening was spawned by intraelite, and especially intraregime elite, divisions, or, propelled by

2 Tancredo Neves was hospitalized the day before he was to be inaugurated as president, and died shortly thereafter due to complications following multiple surgeries. José Sarney, the newly elected vice-president, was sworn in as president. For an account of the events of 1984, see *Veja*, 1/16/85.

resistance growing from within an increasingly restive civil society, from the hierarchy and grass-roots of the Catholic Church, leaders of the "new unionism," and even an amorphous lot of MDB voters.[3] It has devoted relatively less attention to the nature of alliances and bargains that defined the latter stages of the transition and influenced the posttransition distribution of power. In particular, it has not addressed why traditional politicians who had previously supported military rule were able to impose a relatively "conservative" outcome to a transition that mobilized millions.

This chapter examines the role played by the traditional political elite of Minas Gerais in the Brazilian transition to democracy by focusing on the resources this elite gained in the negotiations to bring about the change of regime, and what its influence has been on political institutions and political practice in the posttransition order. What the analysis suggests is that the traditional political elite, which entered the transition period in a strengthened position due to the economic policies and political strategies of the military, skillfully used its ample political resources to direct the process of regime change to its advantage. The chapter first lays out the challenge to dominance posed by the expansion of electoral competition in the waning years of the military dictatorship. It then details the negotiations that made the transition possible but that also ceded control of state and national cabinets, several major political parties, constitutional design, and policy to old regime elites. I argue that through the participation of the traditional political elite, traditional politics in general and clientelism in particular were considerably strengthened and political parties were weakened, unmistakably more so than would have been the case without this type of transition. If this argument is correct, then the traditional political elite influenced the design of political institutions, and not the other way around. Posttransition elections show change in the party system and the electorate, but also reveal the persistent influence of traditional political elite-organized machines.

Of all Brazil's regional oligarchies, the Mineiro stands out during the transition for its political genius and cunning for survival. One of Brazil's first regional elites to plot its escape from the sinking authoritarian coalition, it proposed the realignment of forces that made the transition possible and placed it under traditional political elite control. The manner in which it recovered its own state base after the 1982 elections and rescued its class nationally, at least through the perilous transition, closes yet another chapter of traditional elite resilience.

3 Because to some extent each of these views is correct, which version of the *abertura* one accepts becomes a matter of mere analytical emphasis and whether one is more centrally concerned with what precipitated the transition or what sustained it. See Cardoso (1989) for perhaps the most intellectually satisfying summary of functionalist- and modernization-based, state-centered, and grass-roots explanations for democratization in Brazil.

THE CHALLENGE TO DOMINANCE: OPENING STATE POLITICS, 1982 – 84

In Minas Gerais, the first direct election for governor in seventeen years resulted in a narrow but clear victory for the opposition PMDB. Tancredo Neves was elected governor with 45.8 percent of the vote;[4] Itamar Franco was reelected senator; the party elected twenty-seven federal deputies to the twenty-six of its rival, the PDS; and it captured a slim forty to thirty-seven majority in the state Legislative Assembly. A single representative to both houses was elected by the Workers' Party (PT) (Table 7.1). While the PDS won control of many more city halls and city councils than the PMDB – the PDS elected 461 mayors to 247 for the PMDB, and 4,662 city councillors to 2,788 for the PMDB – the PMDB won the local elections in the most important and largest cities in the state, including those in the metropolitan region of Belo Horizonte, the state capital, and ten of fifteen "midsized" dike cities into which the government had pumped considerable sums of money precisely in order to preserve victory in the 1982 elections.[5] In Montes Claros, which had been particularly showered with projects by PDS governor Francelino Pereira, Luiz Tadeu Leite, a twenty-nine-year-old PMDB city councillor, garnered 30,000 votes in the mayoral race to defeat the progovernment machine. In Varginha, the opposition took control of the local council for the first time. The mayor-elect, Dilzon Luiz de Melo, had no prior experience in local politics, yet he polled better than both candidates of the PDS who had previously served in local public office and who belonged by birth to the local elite. In Barbacena, the bastion of the traditional Minas oligarchy, voters for the first time elected candidates from outside the political machines of the two families that dominated local politics – the Bias Fortes and Bonifácio de Andradas. In that city, the PMDB won the races for mayor and vice-mayor, a majority of municipal council seats (eight to seven for the PDS), and, most significantly of all, 41.6 percent of the vote in the state deputy election went to Manoel Conegundes da Silva, a PMDB candidate whose vote total surpassed that of the candidates of the two families *combined*.

Although the 1982 PMDB vote has been logically interpreted as a rejec-

4 Tancredo Neves began his political career in the old PSD. As a cabinet minister in Goulart's government (indeed, he had been the prime minister in the brief parliamentary episode), he was part of a minority that did not accept the military incursion into politics and thus, in 1965, when the military offered politicians an exclusive choice of membership in either a pro- or an antigovernment party, he opted for the opposition MDB. He remained with the MDB until its dissolution by the party reform law in 1979, when he cofounded the PP. He rejoined the PMDB in 1982.

5 Of these ten cities, Montes Claros, Varginha, Uberaba, and Juiz de Fora were won by ARENA in 1976. Três Corações, Teófilo Otoni, and Unaí were won by the MDB, as were the three *municípios* in the "Valley of Steel," which were opposition strongholds. The mayor of the sixteenth "dike" city, the *estância hidromineral* Poços de Caldas, was appointed.

Table 7.1. *Minas Gerais: Party electoral strength, 1982*

Party[a]	Chamber of Deputies		Legislative Assembly		Mayors	Local councillors
	N seats	% of turnout	*N* seats	% of turnout	*N* elected	*N* elected
PDS	26	39.7	37	38.7	461	4,662
PDT	-	.2	-	.2	-	-
PT	1	2.2	1	1.8	-	16
PTB	--		--		--	--
PMDB	27	42.2	40	41.3	247	2,788
Total	54		78		708[b]	7,466

[a]PDS = Democratic Social Party; PDT = Democratic Labor Party; PT = Workers' Party; PTB = Brazilian Labor Party; PMDB = Party of the Brazilian Democratic Movement.
[b]Fourteen mayors from the state capital and "national security" areas were named by the governor, not directly elected.
Source: TRE-MG, 1982.

tion of the authoritarian regime, in Minas Gerais it represented only a partial and temporary defeat for the political elite that had backed authoritarian rule. Neves's lieutenant governor, Hélio Garcia, began his political career in the UDN and ARENA. Three-fourths of incumbent federal deputies that had last been elected on the ARENA ticket were reelected to the Chamber of Deputies, 62 percent of former ARENA state deputies were reelected to the state Legislative Assembly, and 10 percent of the state deputies were actually promoted by the voters to the federal Chamber. These rates at which ARENA deputies were reelected are higher than those for the MDB representatives – 68 percent of the opposition's federal deputies and 59 percent of MDB state deputies were reelected in 1982, with 7 percent of the incumbent state representatives being voted to the federal Chamber – despite the fact that the PMDB won the election and the electorate was weary of military-authoritarian rule. On average, moreover, the votes of both the federal and state ARENA deputies *rose* from 1978 to 1982, despite the declining popularity of the regime.[6]

The cohort of deputies elected in 1982, moreover, was dominated by veteran politicians and members of the elite. Ninety-two percent of federal deputies elected on the PDS ticket either defended their seats won in 1978, had been state representatives in 1978, or had previously served in a high-ranking office (Rondon Pacheco and Ozanam Coelho had both been gover-

6 Of the twenty-one federal deputies who were reelected, thirteen improved upon their 1978 votes. In the state races, twenty-four members of the Assembly raised their vote totals with respect to the previous election, nearly two and a half times the number (10) who lost votes.

nor, and Israel Pinheiro Filho, son and grandson of state governors, had been the second-best vote getter in the 1966 federal deputy election). Similarly, 70 percent of the PDS delegation to the state Legislative Assembly were incumbents; only about one-fourth of PDS state deputies were new to winning state office. Most striking perhaps about the PDS federal delegation in 1982 was that sixteen of twenty-six, or 62 percent, had been prominent in the state elite in 1962: nine had either been elected governor, federal, or state deputy in the last precoup election; three had stood as candidates in the state and federal races in 1962 but had narrowly missed election; and four were the sons, younger brothers, or nephews of members of the Minas oligarchy. Although a great deal of turnover took place in the lower ranks of the PMDB as might be expected given the rise in their numbers – 55 percent of the party's state representatives were elected to that body for the first time – only about one-fifth of PMDB federal deputies elected in 1982 were new to Minas politics. The ranks of the opposition's delegation to Brasília even contained traditional politicians. Joining Renato Azeredo in the federal Chamber of Deputies were José Aparecido de Oliveira, Jorge Carone Filho, Milton Reis, Anibal Teixeira de Souza, all of whom had not run for office since 1962, and Raul Décio de Belém Miguel, a state deputy in 1966. Tancredo Neves's victory was less accurately the culmination of an opposition sweep than the product of a sporadic coalition of opposition and once promilitary forces. His candidacy attracted the first wave of defections in what was to become a progressive detachment on the part of the traditional elite from the government coalition.

The traditional political elite in Minas Gerais was initially divided over how to approach the 1982 gubernatorial elections, the most important political contest since the coup. While most preferred to side with the apparent safe option, the eventual PDS nominee, some staked their hopes for maintaining power in a liberalizing political environment on the new "Popular Party" (PP). The PP, a primarily Minas- and Rio-based party (its leading officers – Tancredo Neves and former Minas governor Magalhães Pinto – were Mineiros) formed soon after the party reform of 1979 opened the door to a multiparty system.[7] For those abandoning the government party who had been staunch regime allies, such as Magalhães Pinto, the PP provided an opportunity to jump from a sinking ship and land on secure ground. For those moving from the MDB, such as Tancredo Neves, the PP

---

7 Leaders of the newly created PP were selected to submerge pre-1964 party divisions. With Tancredo Neves (national president) from the old PSD and Hélio Garcia (state president) and Magalhães Pinto (honorary national president) representing the old UDN, PP ranks would not be restricted to members of only one of the extinct parties. As a refuge for the traditional political elite, the PP was a welcome development to the architect of party reform, retired General Golbery de Couto e Silva. As a last resort, if the military had to accept defeat, better to concede to members of the traditional political elite than to the popular classes.

offered the possibility of constructing a winning coalition that the military would find nonthreatening. The PP in Minas Gerais was extremely successful at attracting traditional oligarchs anxious to shed the baggage of the government's economic failures, and an agricultural policy unpopular with rural elites, without what for many in 1980 was anathema – sharing a party slate with the PMDB. Their adherence gave the PP an impressive statewide network of local organizations.

This segment of the traditional political elite was forced to rethink its decision to contest elections on a third-party label soon after a government riposte of an opposition offensive undermined this strategy for controlling the transition. The decision to form the PP had been taken under standing electoral rules that permitted ticket splitting and electoral alliances among parties. It was reasonable under such conditions to expect that Neves, the strongest of the opposition candidates, would receive the gubernatorial nomination of more than one party. Because the PP was relatively new and not well established in every electoral district, Neves's hopes for winning the gubernatorial contest rested on capturing the votes of PMDB and PDS voters, who, in other races, planned to support their own party candidates, In late 1981, the military government abruptly changed the rules of the electoral game.

Electoral "reform" was set in motion earlier that year when Congress voted to abolish the *sublegenda* over the wishes of the government. With the coming gubernatorial elections, party discipline among the government majority could not be maintained because PDS politicians had crosscutting interests in the *sublegenda*. PDS members of Congress from the Northeast wished to retain it, while PDS representatives from the South, where this system benefited the PMDB, did not. These PDS defectors, together with the opposition, defeated the *sublegenda*. In the fall of 1981, military intelligence predicted that without the *sublegenda,* the government was in danger of losing the governor's races in more states than the military cared to tolerate. Accordingly, that November, it issued a decree known as the "November package" which, among its other provisions, banned electoral coalitions and prohibited ticket splitting. A reverse coattails effect was expected to enter into the elections: the military anticipated that voters' preferences in local races (determined by particularistic criteria and relatively immune from antiregime sentiment) would swing votes in the state races.[8] The reform intended to make successful opposition by new and especially small opposition parties more difficult. It also appeared to doom Neves's gubernatorial candidacy. Without the possibility of jointly nominating candidates, each party was forced instead to nominate its own candidates for every office, including that of governor. Moreover, the new

8 It turned out that the true electoral effect may have been in the opposite direction; Tancredo Neves's candidacy appears to have benefited politicians in local races running on the PMDB ticket.

legislation, by forcing electors to vote for a single party slate from governor to local councillor, ensured that voters could only cast their ballots for Neves at the cost of abandoning their own party's candidates in other races altogether.

Neves responded to the "November package" by dissolving the PP and instructing its members to join or rejoin the PMDB. The merger of the two parties in Minas Gerais and nationally was presided over by men loyal to Neves who placed his many supporters in a strong position in the new party.[9] From this organizational base Neves plucked the party's gubernatorial nomination from Itamar Franco, the PMDB's other senator, in large part because the veteran Neves, a masterful politician, was accurately perceived as the most electable candidate of the opposition.

Within the government party, intraelite rivalries that had been artificially contained for eighteen years were rekindled by the defeat of the *sublegenda* and Neves's candidacy. Use of the *sublegenda* could have accommodated competing oligarchical factions that coalesced along pre-1965 partisan lines: one *sublegenda* would have been occupied by a former member of the PSD, one by a member of the UDN, and one by either a technocrat or a member of the defunct PR. When the *sublegenda* was abandoned, however, the government could nominate only one candidate, inevitably exacerbating intraparty tensions and fracturing the party. The ex-PSD wing of the PDS was particularly embittered that every governor of the postcoup period had been an ex-UDN member with the single exception of Ozanam Coelho, who, as Aureliano Chaves's lieutenant governor, became the state's chief executive for eight months when Chaves had to resign to "run" for vice-president. Former PSD lieutenant governor Pio Canedo reflected that as a consequence of UDN predominance at the executive level, the ex-PSD members of the party had "always felt marginalized."[10]

When, in an effort to stop UDN–PSD feuding, the Planalto[11] intervened in the gubernatorial succession in Minas, nominating the engineer-technocrat Eliseu Resende as the PDS's candidate, it is hardly surprising that the government's attempted compromise failed. Many oligarchs not satisfied with President João Figueiredo's gesture flocked to Neves's camp; in Tancredo Neves they now had an alternative to the UDN and the MDB – one of their own. In the North of Minas, the sons and grandsons of regional

---

9 Hélio Garcia, who oversaw the state merger, had been a member of ARENA until 1969, when he became disgusted with the closing of Congress. He did not seek reelection as a federal deputy in 1970. "Out of politics," he was appointed by Aureliano Chaves, then governor, as president of the state *Caixa Econômica* in Minas Gerais, a post he held from 1975 to 1978. In 1979, he returned to politics under the PP banner. He was elected lieutenant governor in 1982, and jointly served as mayor of Belo Horizonte. Thus, the governor in 1984 had never been a member of the MDB. Affonso Camargo, the "bionic" senator from Paraná who presided over the national merger, was also from the PP via ARENA.

10 Interview with Pio Soares Canedo, Belo Horizonte, Minas Gerais, August, 1, 1989.

11 The Planalto, the presidential palace, also refers to the president and his advisors.

cattle barons threw their support behind Neves, partly to manifest their discontent with the PDS's candidate, and partly to protest recent agricultural policies, which they guessed would not change under a technocrat. The support the traditional political bosses delivered to the PMDB in the cities and towns of the interior, when combined with that mobilized by the left among a genuinely discontented populace, accounted for the narrow opposition victory.

At the top of state politics, those elements of the traditional political elite who were instrumental to Neves's victory, who had a place in his designs for governing, and who could further his political ambitions, profited from his victory. The state cabinet reflected both Tancredo Neves's personal political debts and his attempts to hold together an improbable coalition. To reconcile competing factions of the state oligarchy and sectoral interests, Neves assembled a hodgepodge of traditional politicians from both ARENA and the PMDB, young deputies who were initiated into politics through the MDB, and technocrat-economists. Politicians outnumbered technocrats by more than 3 to 1: of the thirteen politician-secretaries, seven were elected federal deputies, one failed to be elected, and four were successful in their bids for the state Assembly. Traditional elites were not excised from the cabinet, but in the cabinet's party-political dimension can be detected a subtle turn away from the incumbent faction of the state oligarchy toward Neves's trusted colleagues. The original cabinet included only three secretaries who began their political careers in the MDB and remained faithful to the party. Four PMDB secretaries traced their political origins, and a portion of their power, to pre-1964 parties dominated by traditional elites – the PSD, UDN, and PR (Table 7.2). After the traditional politician Renato Azeredo died and more portfolios were added, three more members of the PMDB (who had all followed Neves into the PP) were appointed to the cabinet. The remaining three politician-secretaries had belonged to ARENA during the dictatorship. At least four of the thirteen politicians in the cabinet – Renato Azeredo, Dario de Faria Tavares, José Aparecido de Oliveira, and Leopoldo Pacheco Bessone – were members of the traditional political elite. To mollify the state's agrarian elite, Neves named as secretary of agriculture Arnaldo Rosa Prata. Prata had been president of such powerful agrarian societies as the Brazilian Association of "Zebu" Cattle Raisers and the Rural Society of the Minas Triângulo, as well as the ARENA mayor of the important Triângulo city of Uberaba (1970–72).

The cabinet assembled by Tancredo Neves, an opposition governor, to steer the state through a period of transition from authoritarian rule ultimately included even some of the same secretaries who had served his military predecessors. Neves's choice for secretary of health, Dario de Faria Tavares, one of three brothers of a traditional family of Patrocínio prominent in state politics, had occupied the same position from 1975 to 1978 in the administration of Aureliano Chaves. Neves also left much of

Table 7.2. *Partisan origins of cabinet politicians, 1982–87*

Administration	Party background[a]				
	(1)	(2a)	(2b)	(3)	N/D
Tancredo Neves	3	3	4	3	
Hélio Garcia[b]					
(1984-86)	6	3	4	5	1
(1986-87)	2	1	1	2	

[a]Key: (1) PTB, MDB/PMDB only; (2a) MDB/PMDB w/PP; (2b) PSD, UDN, PR + MDB or PMDB; (3) PSD, UDN, PR + ARENA/PP, PDS, PFL/PMDB.
[b]Hélio Garcia's cabinet has been divided into two periods: 1984 to mid-1986; and mid-1986 to March 1987. Brazilian election law requires all officeholders to resign their posts several months before an election in order to be eligible to run for office. This special subdivision is justified because the number of resignations from the cabinet by aspiring candidates was much greater after 1985 than during the period of military government.
Sources: Minas Gerais, 1983–87; TRE, Election Reports, 1962–86.

the economic decision-making machinery to the technocratic secretaries and undersecretaries of economic departments in previous state governments who for all intents and purposes had masterminded economic policy in Minas during the authoritarian era: Luiz Rogério de Castro Leite (secretary of finance), Ronaldo Costa Couto (secretary of planning), and Márcio Garcia Vilela (president of the state bank, the BEMGE), all had worked for ARENA and PDS governments. The new administration of sectoral elites, technocrats of the authoritarian regime, and political representatives of ARENA did not threaten elite interests in the policy realm.

Preoccupied with broadening his own base of support among the political class for a future run for the Planalto and uninterested in political reform, Neves moreover governed in a manner that did not upset the state of traditional politics. The PMDB governor not only did not dismantle the clientelistic system that had long pervaded the politics of Minas Gerais, he hardly even redirected it. PMDB mayors in the interior that had risen through the ranks of the opposition without the benefit of family connections received few state benefits from the governor who had helped to elect them; rather, Neves used the spoils of the governor's office to co-opt, by and large successfully, PDS deputies. With few exceptions, there is little indication of opposition to Neves from the promilitary party and, indeed, less as time went on.[12] In fact, the more significant opposition came from

12 The vote in November 1983 to create the new Departments of Transportation; Sports, Recreation, and Tourism; Culture; and Special Affairs is one: the entire PDS delegation (thirty-seven deputies) voted against the governor.

within the PMDB. Neves routinely used PDS politicians to isolate his opponents on the left of his own party.

The considerable continuity of the Neves administration with the political past of Minas Gerais notwithstanding, the election of an opposition governor in Minas Gerais ushered in a period of true transition, one of flux, uncertainty, and new possibilities for loosening the grip of the traditional elite. First, electoral returns from the state's fastest-growing cities indicated that the local base of traditional politics might be eroding. Second, if some members of the traditional elite exercised sound political judgment in supporting Neves, other leading political representatives of the oligarchy, like kingmakers Bias Fortes and Bonifácio de Andrada did not; only four of twenty-eight PDS federal deputies defected to the PMDB in 1982. Despite being reelected, those who opted to stay with the PDS through the 1982 elections found their access to some of the most important bases of political clientelism cut off and their personal patronage machines under strain. They stood to lose positions in the state cabinet; the "political command" of the cities and towns that gave them their greatest vote totals (when the PDS lost its majority, the "political command" in many cities passed to PMDB deputies, even where venerable politicians in the PDS polled better); and the power to make high-level federal and state appointments.

The loss of patronage resources, if not recuperated, would cost future votes and spell certain doom for the medium- and long-term survival of the traditional political elite. Members of the traditional political elite understood well that their positions in local, state, and ultimately national politics were secure only as long as they could protect their access to patronage resources in the cabinet and as majority deputy. The opportunity for the old elite to recover the machinery of state patronage and secure its statewide dominance presented itself when it had something to trade: its support for the governor in the electoral college that would convene to elect the next president.

THE NEGOTIATED TRANSITION AND THE ROLE OF THE MINAS OLIGARCHY

In preparing the terrain for the transfer of power to civilians, the military had aspired to retain considerable control over the new government by guaranteeing a civilian president acceptable to itself. It intended to accomplish this by the "indirect" election of the first civilian president in January 1985; this election was to take place in an electoral college of national, state, and local politicians in which the military enjoyed a secure majority.[13]

13 The electoral college was composed of all senators, federal deputies, and 132 state delegates (a total of 680). After the 1982 elections, the partisan representation in the college stood as follows: PDS, 359; PMDB, 269; PDT, 30; PTB, 14; PT, 8 (Wesson and Fleischer, 1983: 119).

The opposition camp had for some time debated how to approach the "indirect" election for president. With a government victory presumed to be a foregone conclusion, many advocated boycotting the electoral college to be convened to ratify the government party nominee (and presumably handpicked presidential successor) rather than legitimize an electoral farce. This group galvanized public opinion in favor of direct popular elections. In early 1984 they led a Campaign for Direct Elections (the Diretas Já), a highly visible campaign abetted by the media, whose public demonstrations in Brazil's major cities drew millions of protesters to demand that Congress pass an amendment providing for direct popular elections for president later that year. Others in the opposition advocated focusing efforts on the electoral college. The most notable proponent of this position was Tancredo Neves. Never believing the Congress would approve the amendment for direct elections or that the military would permit them (he called the demonstrations "lyric"), Neves lent nominal support to the campaign while never losing sight of his candidacy within the electoral college.[14]

Once the amendment was defeated and it became clear that an electoral college would choose Figueiredo's successor, Tancredo Neves became the opposition's candidate for president. In a blatant display of the politics of *café com leite,* the governors of Minas Gerais and São Paulo, Neves and André Franco Montoro, took the decision that the rest of the party had little choice but to ratify. The opposition was disposed to participate in the electoral college because of the opportunity Neves's candidacy presented for a partisan realignment. Since PDS electors were the clear majority in the electoral college, any opposition candidate needed the backing of former military supporters among the political elite to win. Of all PMDB politicians, Neves, rooted in the oligarchy, stood the best chance of attracting votes from the government forces. His prospects for luring defectors were enhanced by the politically suicidal decision on the part of President Figueiredo to permit the government party to nominate Paulo Maluf – the governor of São Paulo who had more than a few enemies in high places – as the party's standardbearer.[15] Many PDS deputies, disgruntled with Maluf for personal reasons, genuinely apprehensive for their own political futures of electing a president so unpopular within the electorate, and recognizing an opportunity for securing their positions in the posttransition state, scrambled to line up behind Neves. A motley coalition of PMDB "radicals," PDS deserters later to become the Liberal Front (Frente Liberal, or FL) and dissident PDS

14 According to one member of the executive commission of the state PMDB, the idea of the campaign was discussed only once: a subcommittee of three was appointed to study the idea, and two members, being named, departed immediately for personal vacations (interview with Roberto Martins, Belo Horizonte, Minas Gerais, August 16, 1985).

15 Why Figueiredo behaved so passively has been the subject of much speculation. The reigning theory is that he, himself, wished to stay on as president for another four-year term (*Veja,* 1/16/85: 24–27).

governors of the Northeast coalesced rapidly in the months of June to September 1984 to ensure Tancredo Neves's victory.

To gain the support of the old regime's elite, Tancredo Neves was prepared to accept considerable constraints on his campaign and to concede several political achievements of the preceding two years. In exchange for the agreement to back the candidate of the PMDB in the electoral college, the Liberal Front of the PDS was assured that Neves would neither run as a representative of the "opposition" nor criticize the "Revolution" or the (incumbent) Figueiredo government; the vice-presidential nominee would come from the ranks of the Liberal Front or, if prohibited by electoral law, be someone who "supported the 'movement of April 1964' [the coup]"; and there would be an "equitable distribution of administrative posts" (*Istoé,* 7/25/84: 24). For vice-president and fellow Mineiro Aureliano Chaves, Neves even put in writing that all those who backed him would be repaid with posts in his government (*Veja,* 1/16/85: 36). This promise was extracted as a condition for not only the vice-president's support (and with it the votes of the hedging members of the Minas PDS delegation) but also for that of ex-president General Ernesto Geisel, which was critical if a preemptive coup were to be avoided.[16]

While a political settlement of this magnitude could be sealed in principle relatively easily on the national level – it was a fairly simple matter to promise federal cabinet posts to a handful of influential figures – in order to secure the votes of the deputies and other delegates in the electoral college, agreements had to be hammered out and implemented in the states. Careful, detailed, and explicit bargaining was conducted on a state-by-state basis between the two parties wherever such an accord was struck. The success of these state-level negotiations hinged on the mutually satisfactory division of state patronage between two uneasy allies. At stake was the distribution of 15,000 federal jobs. In many states, regional presidents of the PMDB and the FL drew up agreements stipulating explicitly which federal and state posts would be assigned to each party's pork barrel (these posts were of varying political worth) (*Veja,* 7/17/85: 20). Federal Deputy Oscar Alves of Paraná reported that Neves promised the Liberal Front in Paraná, if elected, a number of federal posts in equal proportion to the number of *frentista* votes in the electoral college. Since FL members had cast 25 percent of Neves's votes in the Paraná delegation, Alves calculated

16 The fear of a coup attempt was not irrational. Security forces had attempted in 1981 to sabotage the political opening by planting a bomb (which exploded prematurely in the lap of a saboteur) at the Riocentro theater complex in Rio de Janeiro during a music concert to benefit leftist causes on the eve of May Day. Between August and November 1984, once it became apparent that Neves had the votes to triumph in the electoral college, the PMDB steeled itself for a coup. Expecting it to originate in Brasília under the command of General Newton Cruz, it even planned in detail a resistance. *Veja* (1/16/85: 40–45) provides a full account of the events of these months.

they were owed the right to appoint one-fourth of these posts in the state (*Veja*, 7/17/85: 26–27). Israel Pinheiro, one of the FL's founders and most enthusiastic backers of what came to be called the "Democratic Alliance" between the PMDB and the FL, used the same rationale as a basis for proposing that the FL in Minas Gerais merited a one-third participation in state government (*Estado de Minas*, 9/7/84: 3).

In Minas Gerais, dissident PDS deputies drove their own hard bargain – the "Acordo de Minas," or the "Minas Agreement." The embryonic core of the new Liberal Front in the state agreed to support Neves, to "put a Mineiro in the presidency," in exchange for the return of the power of patronage they had lost in the 1982 elections. They were able to impose their preferences on each significant term of the accord. First, the new governor, Hélio Garcia,[17] reluctantly agreed to name two members of the Liberal Front into the cabinet (earlier in the negotiations, he had stated publicly that he would not do so [*Estado de Minas*, 9/4/84], only that he would review the firings in the interior of those primary school directors, regional school administrators, and police chiefs who were ward bosses [*cabos eleitorais*] allied with politicians formerly in the PDS but now associated with the FL). Crispim Jacques Bias Fortes, of the most famous family of the Minas oligarchy, was selected to head the Department of Public Security. Second, it was agreed that the "political command" of a municipality would be handed back to whichever deputy of the Democratic Alliance polled best in the municipality, irrespective of party; the PMDB had wanted "proportionality," or the sharing of the perquisites of majority deputy between the top-polling deputies of the PMDB and the FL in relation to their share of the municipal vote.

The third achievement of the accord for the traditional politicians who endorsed it was that Liberal Front federal deputies would regain another prime source of state patronage – the right to make appointments to seventy-two second- and third-echelon federal posts in the state (e.g., regional directors of the National Housing Bank and the Brazilian Coffee Institute).[18] Finally, the agreement called for direct elections for mayor to

17 When Tancredo Neves, according to Brazilian law, resigned as governor in order to run for president, the post devolved to the lieutenant governor, Hélio Garcia, in July 1984. Much of the negotiations with Aureliano Chaves and other FL leaders to seal the "*Acordo*" fell to Garcia.

18 The prerogatives to make these appointments were parceled out to dissident deputies according to the precepts of traditional politics. When the deputies could not agree among themselves on how to divide the spoils (different posts, of course, had different real and relative value), Israel Pinheiro is reported to have provided the solution. Recalling how such disputes were resolved during the Estado Nôvo by Benedito Valadares (Vargas's interventor and later governor of Minas Gerais), he suggested that the names of each post be put on separate pieces of paper, and the deputies pull these scraps of paper from a hat. Later, they could be traded among deputies seeking to strengthen their positions in different parts of the state (*Veja*, 7/17/85: 26–27).

be held in the state's thirteen *estâncias hidrominerais* in November 1985; at the same time, the mayor of Belo Horizonte was to be elected directly for the first time since 1965. As long as these posts were appointed by the governor and approved in the state legislature, the majority party was assured control over them. By having the schedule moved up, the PDS-FL dissidents hoped to recover by direct elections at least some of what they had lost for the first time in 1982. The "Acordo de Minas" was understandably opposed, albeit in vain, by those who stood most to lose from the agreement: local, recently victorious, PMDB politicians, especially those young mayors who after years of quixotic opposition in the MDB had finally made an electoral breakthrough in 1982.

The defection of seventeen members of the Minas PDS delegation set in motion a major realignment of political forces; as ever, in Brazil, once it is apparent that an "out" can win, the "ins" scramble to be sure to back the winning side.[19] The "Acordo de Minas" had the immediate effect of cementing Tancredo Neves's election as president in January 1985 in an electoral college composed of mostly old elites from the authoritarian regime. His untimely death, however, denied both sides in Minas Gerais that had made his victory possible the rewards of the presidency. As one news magazine (*Senhor,* 2/25/86: 43) summed up the "pure irony of history": "the Mineiros, who opened the authoritarian parentheses with the bayonets of the troops commanded by General Mourão Filho and the then governor Magalhães Pinto, had the glory of putting it out with the eraser of conciliation. But there was no opportunity to taste the appetizing flavor of power." Although Mineiros were immediately denied the full fruits of their national victory, the pact they arranged produced enduring benefits for the traditional elite.

STATE AND PARTY IN TRANSITION

Through negotiated state and national political pacts, traditional political elites secured their own place in the New Republic and smuggled into the new democracy antidemocratic political practices inherited from both the military regime and its civilian predecessors. With their forced reentry into the national and state cabinets, the regional oligarchies recaptured their access to state patronage resources and reestablished their domination of federal, state, and local executive positions, and they reproduced clientelism at each level of the political system. With their appropriation of the PMDB, the new party of government, they dramatically weakened

19 At the popular level, this has been called the "Flamengo effect," so named for the popular soccer club of Rio de Janeiro whose success in the 1980s spawned a new generation of loyal supporters. Among survey respondents polled in Presidente Prudente in the state of São Paulo in 1989, 71 percent of Collor's followers considered "the chance of winning the elections" to be an important motive for their choice (Kinzo, 1993: 327).

political parties. Ultimately, through their representation in the Congress elected in 1986, which doubled as a Constituent Assembly, they gained a position from which to influence heavily future constitutional arrangements and the design of political institutions. These developments, moreover, were self-reinforcing. Just as a realignment of forces in state politics during the transition to democracy triggered a major shift in national politics, once the regime had changed, the way in which power was exercised at higher levels shaped the political landscape at lower levels of the political system. Closure at the top of the system brought about by national negotiation constricted the space for local competition that had opened from 1982 to 1984, and made real political change harder to effect.

Cabinets and clientelism

The national agreement that accompanied state agreements placed remnants of the traditional elite and ARENA politicians in the national cabinet. For their crucial support for his presidential candidacy, Tancredo Neves awarded four posts to FL defectors, including the largest-budget Ministry of Mines and Energy to fellow Mineiro Aureliano Chaves, and the Ministry of Communications to Antônio Carlos Magalhães, the powerful PDS governor of the Northeast state of Bahia whose vitriolic opposition to Paulo Maluf helped to elect Neves president. Sarney, former president of the PDS, swore in the cabinet designated by Neves and, as time went on, increasingly filled the cabinet with uniformed military officers and members of the ex-PDS, even after the Democratic Alliance formally collapsed in 1987 (*Veja,* 8/3/88: 34–35).[20]

On the state level, the new governor Hélio Garcia did not substantially alter the recruitment patterns and the allocation of cabinet posts ingrained under the military and maintained by Neves. More secretaries were "authentic PMDBers" (nine in his first two years in office), but despite the opposition victory so too had more (five) once belonged to ARENA (see Table 7.2). Saddled at the outset with Neves's cabinet, Garcia was subsequently obligated by the terms of his agreement with the state's Liberal Front delegation to accept Liberal Front politicians into his cabinet. When to the number of ARENA politicians are added representatives of the old PSD, UDN, and PR, the representatives of these non-MDB/PMDB parties amount to half the politician-secretaries in Garcia's cabinet.

Garcia, moreover, did not upset the balance between politicians and technocrats in the cabinet struck in the late military and transitional periods of

20 Among the secretaries in Sarney's cabinet in 1988 who either belonged to the PDS or to ARENA or who supported the military coup of 1964 were: Prisco Viana (Housing and Urban Development), Borges da Silveira (Health), Aluízio Alves (Administration), Aureliano Chaves (Mines and Energy), Antônio Carlos Magalhães (Communications), and Hugo Napoleão (Education).

Table 7.3. *Routes to power in the state cabinet: Preauthoritarian,*
authoritarian, and postauthoritarian

Gubernatorial administration	Political			Technobureau.			Private			Insuf. data		
	N^a	%	% time	N^a	%	% time	N^a	%	% time	N^a	%	% time
Tancredo Neves (1983-84)	13	76	72	4	24	28	0	0	0	0	0	0
Hélio Garcia (1984-86)	19	73	83	5	19	8	0	0	0	2	8	10
(1986-87)	5	23	29	11	52	53	2	10	8	3	14	10
1965-82 average		55	56		33	35		5	6		6	2
1956-65 average		79	88		11	6		3	2		9	2

[a]Cabinet positions have remained fairly stable with respect to pre-1982 cabinets, with two exceptions. The secretary of public security was included in the universe of civilian cabinet positions after 1983 (it was not included for the 1970–82 period, when it was exclusively a military post). Also, the post of mayor of Belo Horizonte became an elected position again in 1985.

state politics. In the first two years of his administration, considerably more politicians were named to head state departments relative to technocrats than during the period of military rule as a whole, but not appreciably more than during the administration of Francelino Pereira (1979–82) (when 64 percent of the cabinet rose via political routes and these politicians occupied office 70 percent of the time) (Table 7.3). The percentage of cabinet positions occupied by politicians remained about the same as during the brief administration of Tancredo Neves, although the amount of time that they collectively dominated the cabinet (83 percent of the period) was greater. What gains politician-secretaries made with civilianization came in the posts they recaptured, not in their gross numbers. For the first time since the position was created, the secretary of planning, Luiz Alberto Rodriguez, was a politician – the third-leading vote getter of all candidates for state deputy representing the PMDB in 1982 (Table 7.4). And the return to the cabinet of Crispim Jacques Bias Fortes as part of the "Acordo de Minas" restored the post of secretary of public security, which had been in the hands of the military since 1970 (and a civilian judge in Neves's brief term), to the traditional political elite. Moreover, the "technocrats" of the 1980s differed from the technocrats of the 1970s in that they, even less than the earlier cohort, resembled a coherent group. They were not economists and engineers trained in the state enterprises and banks, but instead experts in their particular fields; a physician was named secretary of health; an educator secretary of education; and a distinguished judge and president of the Minas

Table 7.4. *Political elite control of state office, 1970–74, 1979–82, 1982–87*
(% of cabinet post time)

	Administration				
	Pacheco	Pereira	Neves	Garcia(1)[a]	Garcia(2)[a]
Economic departments					
Finance	0[b]	0[b]	0[b]	0[b]	0[b]
Planning	0[b]	0[b]	0[b]	57[b]	100
Industry	0[b]	0[c]	100	100	0[d]
Patronage departments					
Education	0[b]	100	0[b]	100	0[b]
Interior and Justice	100	100	100	100	0[b]
Public Works	0[b]	73[b]	100	100	0[b]
Administration	100	100	100	100	100
Health	0[b]	58[b]	100	100	0[b]
Government	100	100	100	100	100
Agriculture	0[b]	73[b]	100	100	0[b]
Public Security	mil	mil	0[b]	90[b]	0[b]
Science and Technology	--	73[b]	100	100	100
Labor and Social Action	100	100	100	100	n/d
New portfolios					
Culture			100	100	0[b]
Supply			--	100	0[b]
Mines and Energy			--	100	50[b]
Transportation			100	--	--
Sports, Recreation, and Tourism			100	100	50[d]
"Special Affairs"				n/d	
Administrative Reform and Debureaucratization				n/d	
Political Affairs				100	

[a]For explanation of division of Hélio Garcia's cabinet, see Table 7.2.
[b]Remaining time occupied by technocrats.
[c]Remaining time shared by technocrats and business/banking elites.
[d]Remaining time occupied by business/banking elite.

chapter of the Organization of Brazilian Lawyers secretary of public security. At the end of Hélio Garcia's term, the group of officeholders who I have
loosely called "technocrats" were, more accurately, by and large career
bureaucrats who, as the second-ranking officials of their respective departments, assumed the top posts much as they might have temporarily if the
secretary were to travel abroad or to return to the legislature for a crucial
vote.

Throughout Brazil, the ample participation of traditional, promilitary, and conservative elites in state and federal cabinets during the transition period provided a powerful foothold from which to influence policy. More subtle but perhaps more consequential in the long term, cabinet positions afforded traditional elites the resource base from which to mount and sustain their clientelistic operations. Scott Mainwaring (1991a: 27–29) has carefully chronicled the dramatic expansion of the public payroll for political purposes, a phenomenon known in Brazil as *empreguismo,* during the regime transition. In the years between 1979 and 1985, employment in public administration increased by 40 percent from 3.1 to 4.4 million people, or from 16.1 to 21.4 percent of the full-time formal sector labor force. Mainwaring believes most of this increase to have occurred at the state and municipal levels. Many governors packed their state bureaucracies with political appointees before resigning to run in the 1982 elections; in 1982 alone, the governors added 500,000 persons to the states' public payrolls.[21] This tendency was more marked in the "backward" North, Northeast, and Center-West regions of the country, where, by 1985, over 35 percent of the labor force was employed in public administration. If *empreguismo* was transparent in state and local government, it was also practiced widely at the national level. Aluísio Alves, minister of administration in 1985, estimated that, in the federal direct public administration, only 125,000 persons had been hired through the public service examination (1.3 million had taken the examination, and 400,000 who passed the examination were not hired), and 1.7 million "according to criteria I don't understand, because they are eminently political" (Mainwaring, 1991a: 6–7). During the transition to the civilian regime in the early months of 1985 alone, it was estimated that 42,000 politicians were nominated to administrative offices (Campello de Souza, 1989: 392).[22]

Access to national and state cabinets and state patronage resources was thus restored to the members of the traditional political elite who fled the government party. The redefinition of the *situação* then unleashed a torrent of defections and precipitated an elite partisan realignment, which until then had been systemically blocked.

21 The example of Maranhão is particularly vivid. Governor João Castelo increased the state bureaucracy from 26,000 to 52,000 in three and a half years in office. In São Luis do Maranhão, the outgoing municipal administration hired 14,500 people illegally in its last months in office (Mainwaring, 1991a: 27).

22 What makes this figure (drawn from *Veja,* 3/13/85) so striking is how high it is when compared with other countries. A study by David T. Stanley, *Changing Administrations* (Washington, DC: Brookings, 1965) (reported by Kurt Von Mettenheim) claims that the changes of administrations during the 1960s in England and the United States brought 100 and 2,000 politicians, respectively, to administrative posts (Campello de Souza, 1989: 392).

The party system

Bipartism ended as it began, by military decree to suit military purposes. With its party reform law of 1979, which had fostered multipartism to divide a maturing opposition, the military intended the traditional elite to prevent electoral victories by the PMDB and other, more radical parties by mobilizing the vote for the PDS, its new official party, and the PP, the "moderate" elite opposition party.

In the transition from authoritarian rule, the traditional political elite redefined the party system, but not as the military had intended. Rejecting the restrictions placed on their access to state power, Tancredo Neves and those traditional politicians who joined him in the PP dissolved their party and boosted the electoral fortunes of the opposition. When the close attachment of the PDS to the military regime became an insurmountable electoral liability, other traditional politicians began to abandon the former party of government for the new Liberal Front. Eventually, they forged a party out of the dissident elite movement – the Party of the Liberal Front (PFL) – which elected 133 federal deputies (10 in Minas Gerais) in the 1986 election in which the PMDB ran an especially strong race and participated in the federal cabinet until early 1987 as part of the Democratic Alliance with the PMDB. But more significant for the organization of the party system during the period of transition and beyond, previous supporters of the military regime also muscled their way into, and transformed, the new party of government, the PMDB. The traditional elite's takeover of the PMDB at the state, national, and finally local levels blurred the party's identity in government and transformed it from a "catchall" to a "traditional, clientelistic" party.[23] During the transition, the regime–opposition dichotomy within the political class faded, and just who represented the "ins" and "outs" was no longer discernible.

The faction of the PMDB loyal to the governor emerged from the party's 1983 elections in the state in undisputed control of the party commissions. His so-called *Constituinte* slate won all seats on the *diretório* but sixteen (of seventy-one), and all but sixteen delegates and sixteen alternates to the national convention (of fifty-eight for each). In exchange for these few seats, the "radical" group, Direct Elections (Eleições Diretas), had to cede pivotal posts on the executive commission, including that of president, to conservative and traditional politicians imposed by the governor who had only recently joined the party and whom many in the PMDB found distaste-

---

23 Cardoso (1985: 3) identified three types of parties: the catchall, typified by the PMDB; the ideological, of which the PT was the best example; and the traditional clientelistic, which accurately described both the PDS and the PFL. He admonished that the PMDB had to avoid evolving into what ARENA had been. Three years later, in an interview explaining why he had left the PMDB, he criticized the party precisely for becoming a machine to dispense government patronage (*Veja*, 6/29/88: 5–6).

ful. The *Estado de Minas* (11/17/83) wrote of the new executive commission: "The moderate wing [of the party], derived from the PP, prevails in the party command." A PMDB deputy commented, "If Governor Tancredo Neves is not thinking of creating a new party, as he declared in a press conference, at least he has succeeded in making the PMDB closer to the party of his dreams" (*Estado de Minas,* 11/17/83).

Soon thereafter, Tancredo Neves's loyalists gained control of the national party. In negotiations for the national command of the PMDB in November 1983 (just prior to the party's national convention), party president Ulysses Guimarães ceded half the posts on the executive commission and 43 percent of those on the national directorate to Neves's group. Guimarães's own group received 35 percent of the seats (17 percent were allocated to a third party faction composed of independents and first-time members of Congress). The complexion of the executive commission, too, changed. "Radical" Francisco ("Chico") Pinto was pushed out of his position of first vice-president by "moderate" senator Pedro Simon. In return for retaining the presidency, Guimarães allowed Neves to name the party's secretary-general, the post that controls the party's organization. Neves's choice, Affonso Camargo, the "bionic" senator from Paraná who had only recently joined the PMDB via the PP and ARENA, precipitated strong opposition from party regulars, including threats from the rank and file to organize a resistance, cancel the convention, and resign from the party. The threats were to no avail; Neves by this time was in extraofficial command of the party.

In Minas Gerais, a PMDB governor in the state house swelled the party with new recruits. Individual party membership more than doubled between 1982 and the end of 1984, while that of its old rival, the PDS, rose by only 35 percent (Table 7.5). This process accelerated most dramatically after the PMDB gained the presidency in March 1985. Between March and June 1985, party membership jumped from less than 200,000 to nearly 300,000, while that of the PDS began to decline. Once the party attracted much of the state oligarchy and established itself as a party of government, moreover, local elites and party bosses flocked to its ranks. Anxious to join the "ins" and not be excluded from state resources, at least 200 mayors and local party *diretórios* changed partisan affiliation virtually overnight in mid-1985 from the PDS to the PMDB.[24]

Recently converted mayors and party bosses for the most part shared little or nothing ideologically with the party's veteran national leaders. The

24 *Senhor* (2/25/86: 43) reports that "The number of mayors who have sought refuge in the PMDB is about four or five per month. Two hundred mayors have submitted to [Governor Hélio] Garcia's charisma." PMDB vice-president Roberto Martins suggested that the time in which these 200 mayors converted to the PMDB was shorter, and furthermore that they were accompanied by entire PDS *diretórios,* during the Brazilian winter (June–August) months of 1985 (author's interview, Belo Horizonte, Minas Geranis, August 16, 1985).

Table 7.5. *Minas Gerais: Individual party membership, 1982–85*

Party[a]	1982	1983	1984	1985(M)	1985(J)	1985(D)
PDS	163,501	163,007	221,298	235,272	231,847	228,572
PDT	11,796	13,656	22,692	27,103	28,468	30,788
PT	22,641	23,872	34,883	36,348	36,907	38,447
PTB	12,256	12,390	21,406	24,276	26,575	28,216
PMDB	91,530	105,125	190,939	199,097	297,413	319,657
PFL						5,775

Note: "Individual party membership" signifies those who are "affiliated" (*filiados*) with the parties, not those who are "members" (a term reserved for members of the local and state *diretórios*). (M) = March; (J) = June; (D) = December.
[a]PDS = Democratic Social Party; PDT = Democratic Labor Party; PT = Workers' Party; PTB = Brazilian Labor Party; PMDB = Party of the Brazilian Democratic Movement; PFL = Party of the Liberal Front.
Source: TRE-MG.

mayors were part of a cohort elected in 1982 that carried on Minas Gerais's political tradition. In a survey of 387 (of 708) mayors elected in Minas Gerais in 1982 conducted by the state Planning Department (SEPLAN, 1983), nearly 60 percent reported that they had "political tradition in the family," meaning that their fathers, grandfathers, uncles and/or brothers had participated in politics in an elected capacity. Thirty percent had been active in politics for more than twenty years, and another 25 percent from twelve to twenty years. Only one-fifth had entered politics within the preceding four years. Two-thirds had previously occupied political posts. Hand in hand with their "political tradition," approximately 30 percent identified themselves as *fazendeiros* by profession; nearly 60 percent were from families of *fazendeiros*. Well over half (58.9 percent) of the mayors sampled attributed their victories to "personal attributes"; 28.9 percent to "political tradition"; and only 8.3 percent to party program (3.9 percent not available) (SEPLAN, 1983: 43).

The migration of the old elite into the PMDB was not confined to the municipalities of Minas Gerais (though perhaps the process is most dramatically illustrated there). In other states, politicians who had supported the military regime were quick to change their partisan affiliation. One-third of all ARENA congressional representatives had, by 1987, joined the PMDB (Fleischer, 1987: 4). Forty-four percent entered the PFL, and only 15 percent remained with the PDS.

When the PMDB, which had sheltered opponents to authoritarianism and those who had suffered from it, opened its ranks to those who had supported and profited from the military regime, it fanned its electoral fortunes. The party scored a knockout victory in the 1986 elections, winning a majority in the Congress and Constituent Assembly, and 22 of 23 state governorships. Although this victory was undoubtedly purchased by the Sarney administration with the loose monetary policy and real wage increases of the Cruzado Plan, the "heterodox" program that relied on a new currency (the cruzado), deindexation of the economy, and price controls to fight inflation, it was also abetted by the entrance into the party of the bosses of the interior and their state patrons. In Minas Gerais, the PMDB candidate for governor, Newton Cardoso, won despite dissension within the party's ranks over his nomination. The party captured thirty-five seats in the Chamber of Deputies, three and a half times more than the number won by the coalition of the PFL and the Liberal Party (Table 7.6). The PMDB victory was not quite as convincing in the state deputy race, but the party nonetheless gained more than double the number of seats of the PFL-PL alliance, and a comfortable majority in the state Assembly.

The mass conversion that made the impressive PMDB victory in the 1986 elections possible, however, also clouded the meaning of the sizable PMDB majorities. Of the thirty-five members of the Minas PMDB delegation to the Chamber of Deputies elected in 1986, six had belonged to ARENA or the PDS, and seven had begun their careers in the PSD or UDN (Figure 7.1). Three who began in the MDB had detoured through the PP before rejoining the PMDB. Ony 54 percent could be considered "historical" PMDBers. In national terms, one-fourth of PMDB representatives to the Constituent Assembly elected in 1986 were once members of ARENA; slightly under half (47.3 percent) had been members of the MDB or PMDB. Fleischer's (1987: 2) research shows that in 1987 "the largest delegation in the Constituent Assembly [was] not [the 1986] PMDB, but in 1979 terms, it [was] ARENA." Two hundred seventeen members of the Assembly had been members of ARENA prior to 1980, as opposed to 212 who identified themselves with the PMDB. Thus, Fleischer (1987: 5) notes, the "real" PMDB was represented by only 40 percent of the Congress, not the 53.3 percent it appeared to have in name only. These data led him to remark wryly that in Brazil, politicians "change their party affiliations like star players change the shirts of their soccer teams" (Fleischer, 1987: 2). The traditional elite presence in the party disallows the interpretation of party electoral victories as a popular rejection of the old order, the future replacement of its elite, or the overhaul of its institutions and political practices.[25] It implies, moreover, that traditional and conservative forces were much stronger in the early years of the New Republic than the combined vote totals for the PDS and PFL would imply.

Realignment precipitated by the large-scale migration of traditional and authoritarian political elites into the PMDB confused the party's purpose.

25 Guimarães (1985: 41) aptly argued that PMDB victories in the 1985 mayoral races did not signal an advance of progressive and leftist forces in Brazil. He saw two (or more) PMDBs in place, and "in the majority of cities, the more conservative PMDB won."

Table 7.6. *Party strength in Minas Gerais, 1986–88*

	1986						1988
	Senate		Chamber		State Assembly		
Party[a]	Seats won	% of turnout	Seats won	% of turnout	Seats won	% of turnout	Mayors elected
PMDB	2	49.4	35	61.5	41	50.4	307
PFL/PL[b]		17.4	10	18.5	19	23.1	193
PT/PH[c]		8.3	3	6.6	5	6.8	7
PDI/PDS[d]		8.9	3	5.2	5	6.1	36
PDT		9.0	1	3.1	4	5.2	13
PTB			1	2.7	3	4.5	27
PDC							116
PSDB							7
PMB							6
PSC							5
PJ							4
PSB							2
Total			53		77		723

[a]PMDB = Party of the Brazilian Democratic Movement; PFL = Party of the Liberal Front; PL = Liberal Party; PT = Workers' Party; PH = Humanist Party; PDI = Independent Democratic Party; PDS = Democratic Social Party; PDT = Democratic Labor Party; PTB = Brazilian Labor Party; PDC = Christian Democratic Party; PSDB = Party of Brazilian Social Democracy; PMB = Brazilian Municipalist Party; PSC = Social Christian Party; PJ = Party of Youth (the forerunner of the Party of National Reconstruction); PSB = Brazilian Socialist Party.
[b]The PFL and PL allied in the 1986 elections. PFL representatives won all ten seats in the Chamber of Deputies and seventeen of nineteen seats in the Legislative Assembly. The parties ran separately in 1988; the PFL elected 176 mayors and the PL elected 17.
[c]The PT and PH allied in the 1986 elections. All three seats in the federal Chamber and all five seats in the state Assembly were won by candidates of the PT. The parties ran separately in 1988, and the PT elected all 7 mayors.
[d]The PDI and PDS allied in the 1986 elections. PDS candidates won the three federal and five state deputy seats. The parties ran separately in 1988, and the PDS elected all 36 mayors.
Sources: Minas Gerais (12/30/86: II, 17–35); TRE-MG, 1989.

In shifting the balance of conservative and progressive forces within the PMDB, realignment inevitably diluted the party's already weak programmatic message. Although most parties are not as ideologically coherent as textbook depictions of the highly disciplined parties found in parliamentary systems would lead us to believe, the ideological heterogeneity of the PMDB congressional delegation was easily greater than that characteristic of multiclass, catchall political parties. The eclectic character of the new

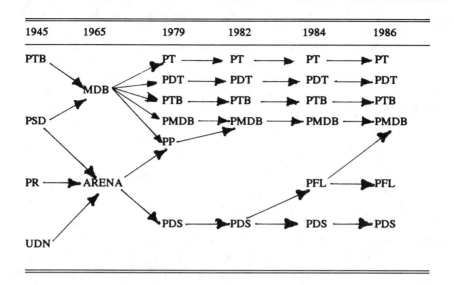

Figure 7.1. Party migrations: Partisan trajectories of Minas federal deputies, 1987.
   PMDB trajectories (35): MDB-PMDB (9); PTB-MDB-PMDB (2); PMDB only (8); MDB-PP-PMDB (3); PSD, PR, UDN-MDB-(PP)-PMDB (7); (UDN)-ARENA-(PP, PDS)-(PFL)-PMDB (6).
   PT trajectory (3): PT only (3).
   PTB trajectory (1): PTB only (1).
   PFL trajectories (10): PSD-ARENA-PDS-PFL (5); ARENA-PDS (3); PFL only (2).
   PDS trajectories (3): UDN-ARENA-PDS (2); ARENA-PDS (1).
   PDT trajectory (1): PDT only (1).

PMDB undermined the ability of the party to carry out in government the programs it had advocated while in opposition. Because many of the party's new leaders and federal representatives did not even endorse the party platform, it became practically impossible for the party to stake out coherent policy positions, and in the rare cases when it did, party discipline could not be maintained in legislative votes. Votes on key policies and constitutional issues instead cut across partisan lines, which were left little substantive meaning. Traditional political elites inside the party were in a position to veto any policies that they perceived to be not in their own interest or in the interest of their constituents. In large part for this reason, some of the most prominent leaders of the party in São Paulo – Fernando Henrique Cardoso, former head of the government in Congress, Franco Montoro, former governor of São Paulo, and Mário Covas, PMDB senator and the party's leading vote getter in the 1986 congressional elections – bolted from the PMDB in early 1988 to form a new, social democratic alternative, the Party of Brazilian Social Democracy (PSDB).[26] The new party immediately attracted 48 members of Congress to its ranks. In all, the PMDB registered a net loss of 105 deputies and senators between February 1987 and January 1990, a period in which no elections were held, mostly to the advantage of the PSDB and several smaller parties including the Liberal Party, the Christian Democratic Party, and the PDT (Mainwaring, 1995: 377).

Institutions and policy

Two of the most important policy issues immediately facing the New Republic were ones on which the PMDB had issued promissory notes to the workers and peasants of Brazil: reform of labor legislation, especially the right to strike, and agrarian reform. Party leaders had also staked out strong positions on the two most significant institutional issues that were to be resolved in the constitution: they favored a parliamentary system to replace presidentialism, and they advocated limiting the length of the term of the head of government to four years. The inability of the PMDB to enforce party discipline doomed these legislative and constitutional initiatives in the life of the Constituent Assembly.[27] In late 1987, traditional members of the political elite in the PMDB joined their counterparts from the PDS and the PFL to form a conservative group of 287 members of Congress, which cut across partisan lines and traditional rivalries, called the Centrão (literally, the "Big Center") to contest what they saw to be "excessively liberal" articles in the draft text of the constitution.[28] Their efforts paid handsome dividends. When the Constituent Assembly had finished its work, only labor had won qualified gains. Agrarian reform was defeated, the presidential system was retained, and the length of the presidential term was extended to five years at the behest of the incumbent president despite widespread public sentiment in favor of reducing it.[29] The

26　The party defined as its goals to fight for parliamentarism and to "reform the state," or reduce clientelism. Cardoso justified deserting the party whose candidates and government policies he had always backed, even when not to his liking, by claiming that the PMDB had changed, becoming a "rubber stamp to obtain government jobs" and "a machine glued to the government" (*Veja*, 6/29/88: 8).

27　The proponents of parliamentarism did have another opportunity to revise Brazil's presidential system. The issue was placed before the Brazilian electorate in an April 1993 referendum, but failed to pass. Only 55 percent cast valid votes in the plebiscite, of whom two-thirds voted to retain the presidential system. In June 1994, however, a successful constitutional amendment scaled back the presidential term to four years.

28　The group's greatest early victory was to change the procedure by which the Constituent Assembly would ratify the constitution from a single vote to a separate vote on each article, section, and amendment. In practice, this procedure gave the parliamentarians the opportunity to defeat certain measures and it made the adoption of others more likely.

29　The *Folha de São Paulo* (11/15/87) reported that 80 percent of those interviewed in the ten most important capital cities of Brazil wanted to reduce the presidential term and hold

stinging defeat of parliamentarism was a particularly bitter pill to swallow for party leaders. At one early point, given the support of prominent politicians and a majority of congressional representatives, the adoption of at least some form of parliamentarism had seemed almost inevitable.[30]

The voting records of the members of Minas Gerais's PMDB delegation to the Constituent Assembly on labor issues, agrarian reform, presidentialism, and the five-year presidential term illustrate particularly well the infidelity of the traditional elite migrants to the party's long-held positions. Whereas the average "labor ranking" of the state's PMDB deputies was 4.5 of a possible 10 (as compared to 2.0 for the PFL and 9.7 for the PT), the deputies who either began their careers in the MDB, that is, in opposition to military rule, or who had joined the PMDB as their first and only party voted more frequently in favor of labor (their "rankings" on these issues were 5.4 and 5.6, respectively) than those who had begun their careers in an "oligarchical" party (2.3) or who had served the military government in ARENA (3.0) (Table 7.7). Contrary to expectations, those with prior links to the PTB (Group 1B) did not have a higher score than those whose first affiliation was the PMDB, despite the fact that those who joined that party after 1982, and especially after it became the majority party in 1985, would not necessarily have held a historical commitment to party positions. Somewhat surprisingly, even those who had followed Tancredo Neves and Magalhães Pinto into the PP voted more consistently for measures granting labor rights (5.0) than those who had begun their careers in the PTB (2.4). The voting record of the Minas PMDB delegates was less favorable to labor than that of its counterparts in Rio Grando do Sul, São Paulo, Rio de Janeiro, and, more surprisingly, any state in the Northeast save Sergipe (Table 7.8).

The traditional elite presence in the party also contributed to the large bloc of fourteen votes opposing agrarian reform (eighteen members of the delegation voted in favor of agrarian reform, while three were absent for the vote). Half of those Mineiros in the PMDB opposing agrarian reform were recent converts to the party label. Seven of nine who had traveled from the MDB to the PMDB voted in favor of the reform. Similarly, all votes but one from the Minas delegation opposing presidentialism were cast by deputies whose partisan roots lay in the MDB, PP, and/or PMDB.

direct elections in 1988, and only 11 percent supported a five-year term for Sarney (cited in Campello de Souza, 1989: 386).

30 Mainwaring (1994: 9) has clarified that the proposed system was in fact a semipresidential system in the French mold, but with a strong prime minister. During the deliberative phase of the Constituent Assembly, this option was supported by the Subcommission on Executive Power, the Commission on the Organization of Powers and System of Government, and the Commission on Systematization. Even after the vote there was considerable support in the Congress for changing the system of government: 68 percent of 469 deputies and senators who responded to a survey conducted in June 1991 (80 percent of the Congress) declared themselves in favor of parliamentarism (Lamounier, 1994a: 213).

Table 7.7. *Voting records: Minas Gerais PMDB deputies,*
Constituent Assembly

| | PMDB | | | | | | | | |
| | "Authentic" | | | "Migrants" | | | | | |
	1A	1B	1C	2A	2B	3	Total	PFL	PT
Labor ranking[a]	5.4	2.4	5.6	5.0	2.3	3.0	4.5	2.0	9.7
Agrarian reform									
Yes	7	0	4	3	1	3	18	1	3
No	2	2	3	3	2	2	14	9	0
Absent	-	-	2	1	-	-	3	-	-
Presidentialism									
Yes	3	2	5	5	2	4	21	9	2
No	7	0	4	2	1	0	14	1	0
Abstaining	-	-	-	-	-	-	-	-	1
Five-year term									
Yes	6	2	6	4	3	5	26	10	0
No	3	0	3	3	0	0	9	0	3

Note: The labor rankings and votes on agrarian reform and the five-year term include the votes of the alternate Israel Pinheiro who replaced Deputy Luiz Leal while the latter served in the state cabinet. Leal returned to the Assembly for the vote on presidentialism. 1A = MDB-PMDB; 1B = PTB-MDB-PMDB; 1C = PMDB only; 2A = MDB-PP-PMDB; 2B = PSD, PR, UDN-MDB-(PP)-PMDB; 3 = (UDN)-ARENA-(PP,PDS)-(PFL)-PMDB.
[a]Labor ranking: The union group DIAP (Departamento Intersindical de Assessoria Parlamentar) "ranked" deputies by scoring "yes" votes in the first and second rounds of voting in the constitutional convention on job tenure, the forty-hour work week, the six-hour shift, the right to strike, vacation pay, (thirty-day) notice for firings, and job security for union leadership as either a .5, 1, or 1.5 and no votes, abstentions, and unexcused absences as 0. The maximum score a deputy could receive was 10.
Source: Calculated from DIAP, 1988: 261–318.

On the issue of a five-year mandate for President Sarney, twenty-six PMDB deputies from Minas voted for the five-year mandate, while only nine voted against. All nine deputies had begun their political careers in the ranks of the opposition, and seven subsequently defected from the PMDB to join the PSDB. The traditional elite representatives who remained in the PFL raised conservative vote totals: only one PFL deputy (of ten) broke ranks to vote in favor of agrarian reform, and all ten voted to give the sitting PMDB president a five-year term.

Where votes did not follow from ideological commitments, they were cast according to the operating principles of traditional politics. Victory for

Table 7.8. *Voting records: PMDB deputies, Constituent Assembly
(select states)*

State	N	Labor ranking	Agrarian reform (yes)	Five-year term (no)	Partisan origins[a]		
					1	2	3
North							
Amazonas	2	4.6	2	1	2	-	-
Northeast							
Alagoas	3	8.5	3	3	2	0	1
Pernambuco	14	7.5	11	9	11	-	3
Piauí	2	7.1	1	1	1	-	1
Paraíba	7	7.0	5	2	2	1	4
Bahia	23	6.1	14	16	13	4	6
Rio Grande do Norte	4	5.8	3	0	2	1	1
Ceará	12	5.7	8	2	6	-	5
Maranhão	7	4.9	5	1	4	1	2
Sergipe	4	2.7	1	0	3	-	1
Southeast							
São Paulo	28	5.6	16	13	22	3	3
Rio de Janeiro	12	5.0	7	6	7	2	2
Minas Gerais	35	4.5	18	9	20	10	5
South							
Rio Grande do Sul	17	6.6	14	9	15	1	1

[a]Partisan origins: group 1 = PTB-MDB-PMDB – for the purposes of this table, parties to the left of the PMDB (PDT, PSB, PCB) were also included in group 1; group 2 = PSD, PR, UDN (PDC, PRP)-MDB-(PP)-PMDB; MDB-PP-PMDB; group 3 = (UDN)-ARENA-(PP, PDS, PFL)-PMDB.
Source: Calculated from DIAP, 1988: 59–71, 79–162, 211–33, 261–318, 341–56, 393–536, 577–656.

the presidential system was purchased with the machinery of clientelism. The governor of Minas Gerais, Newton Cardoso, by this own admission swung ten votes from his state's delegation to presidentialism in exchange for a "torrent of appropriations" for the state from Sarney (*Veja*, 6/29/88: 50). The housing minister, Prisco Vianna (an ex-PDS leader), selectively committed nine billion cruzados worth of resources from his department to win votes. If the vote on presidentialism was influenced by offers of patronage, the issue of the extension of the presidential term to five years was settled virtually entirely by political opportunism. Sarney's ministers waged a public campaign to deliver the vote. Before providing resources, the Ministry of Planning requested deputies to sign a statement on behalf of a five-year mandate, and Antônio Carlos Magalhães, then the minister of communications, admitted publicly granting licenses for television and radio stations – coveted by politicians to bolster their standing and attack their adversaries – to those deputies who voted "correctly" (Mainwaring, 1991a: 20–21). Given the potential rewards for a yes vote, the five-year term was immensely popular in all regions, and in most parties. Most representatives from the Northeast in particular voted with the president; in his native Maranhão, only one deputy voted against the five-year term.

Local politics

At the outset of regime transition in 1982, local politics was forced ajar in those states which ran strong candidates for governor on opposition tickets. After partisan redefinition and the consolidation of a conservative, elite-dominated national regime, however, the system closed at the bottom. Local change, the foundation of any real political change, was thwarted by the reconstruction of the state's clientelistic machine by the oligarchy.

In Minas Gerais, the tight grip on state government and the parties of government exercised by the traditional political elite constricted local political competition. More traditional politicians emerged victorious in the local elections in 1988 than in 1982 when turnover at the state level was minimal but new mayors were elected in many of the largest municipalities of the interior. In Varginha, the young PMDB mayor who was elected on Neves's coattails in 1982 was turned out by the voters in 1988 in favor of a slate which ran for vice-mayor Marçal Paiva Figueiredo, the son of Jacy Figueiredo, a former mayor of Varginha and the grand-nephew of the local *coronel* who dominated politics in Varginha earlier in the century. In Muriaé, yet another Canedo made a triumphal electoral debut: Christiano Agosto Canedo was elected mayor, and his vice-mayor, João Braz, had twice been elected mayor of the municipality for ARENA. The party label on which they were elected – PTB – did not matter; both had PSD roots. Uberaba remained in the hands of the politicians who had backed the military, despite rapid industrialization and population growth, and in Barbacena, the mayor elected in 1976 on the ARENA ticket retook the city famed for its oligarchical politics. One-half of the mayors and vice-mayors of the sample of twenty-five municipalities who were elected in 1988 had previously held one of these local executive posts, that of deputy, or city councillor. Seventeen of the fifty victorious candidates (34 percent) had run on the ARENA ticket during the dictatorship, and two others had represented the UDN and PR in 1962. Twelve former mayors were elected to local executive office: seven as mayors, five as vice-mayors. Eight of the twelve had won on the ARENA ticket: one switched to ARENA during his tenure, one former MDB mayor ran in 1988 on a ticket with the ARENA candidate for vice-mayor in 1972; one had belonged to the UDN, and one had been a PSD councillor and a member of the regional oligarchy.[31]

That local politics echoed state and national trends is also visible in the reshuffling of local party *diretórios* in the interior. The PDS continued its precipitous decline. In mid-1989, only 209 established and 95 provisional *diretórios* remained attached to the decaying party of the military government, leaving 417 in the state with no party branch at all. In its place, new parties arose. The fastest growing was the PRN, the Party of National Reconstruction. In June 1989, there were but 20 established local *diretórios* of the PRN and the Party of Youth (Partido da Juventude, PJ, with which it merged) in Minas Gerais, but, in anticipation of the increasingly viable presidential candidacy of Fernando Collor de Mello, 252 had earned provisional status from the state's electoral tribunal, and 85 were in the process of formation.[32]

THE NEW REPUBLIC OF THE TRADITIONAL POLITICAL ELITE: ELECTIONS AND REFLECTIONS

If traditional elites emerged in a strong position in state and national politics in the immediate aftermath of the negotiated transition and the death of Tancredo Neves, were they able to maintain that position? In the face of an increasingly urban society and an electorate weary of political corruption and economic mismanagement, could they continue to manipulate elections through the use of political clientelism to preserve an elite-dominated, traditional order?

There is little question but that clientelism as a widespread political practice to contest elections and to govern survived the regime transition. Freer elections appear to have intensified political competition within much of the political elite, contributing to patronage inflation and a period of undisciplined or "wild" clientelism that Lamounier (1989b: 153) has called Brazil's "Jacksonian Age." Traditional elites in particular persist in using clientelism to make public appointments as a way to reward friends and gain new ones for future electoral contests, with dire fiscal consequences. The president of the National Accounting Court estimated that 100,000 new jobs in federal public administration were created between March 1985 and August 1987, and that between January 1984 and January 1988 personnel expenditures for employees of the direct public administration increased 90 percent in real terms (Mainwaring, 1991a: 28). State and municipal governments were even more profligate. In 1990, the payroll

---

31 Three ran on the ticket of the PMDB, three on that of the PFL, one on that of the PDS, and five on those of small parties.
32 Nationally, at the time of Collor's campaign, the PRN controlled outright only three municipalities and had only fourteen federal deputies (Ames, 1994: 99).

costs of the states and cities accounted for 7 percent of Brazil's gross domestic product, twice as much as the federal government. By the late 1980s, according to Mainwaring (1991a: 29), salaries and wages of public employees in several states of the Northeast accounted for over 100 percent of government revenue. In the period from 1988 to 1990, the cities' payroll spending went up 32 percent in real terms (*Economist,* 1991: 9). All together, Delfim Neto calculated that between 1984 and 1987, government payroll spending at the federal, state, and municipal levels rose by 67 percent in real terms, three times as fast as GDP (*Economist,* 1991: 7).

Clientelism has also been widely used in the New Republic to administer public programs, to structure governing coalitions, and to win congressional votes. In one blatant example of the politics of patronage, the Housing Ministry in 1987 awarded 520, 348, 210, and 154 million cruzados to the states of Amazonas, Goiás, Pará, and Minas Gerais – whose governors were supporters of President Sarney – but only 8 million to Rio de Janeiro and none to São Paulo, whose governors were not (*Folha de São Paulo,* 3/23/88, cited in Mainwaring, 1991a: 16). Access to patronage was a major negotiating tool in forming cabinets, even at the federal level. In April 1992, President Collor reshuffled his cabinet in order to strengthen the prospects of passing an economic reform in Congress (by assigning portfolios with the highest number of jobs to fill and discretionary resources to distribute to the parties with the most votes in Congress) (*Folha de São Paulo,* 4/12/92: 4, 5, 7). Bahian governor Antônio Carlos Magalhães had threatened during the negotiations, "There is not a *município* in this country that doesn't need a road or a bridge. If the government wants support in the Congress, it must open the state's coffers."[33] At this time and others, clientelism was used to influence the votes of state congressional delegations on major policy issues.

The widespread resort to clientelism was reinforced by the "new federalism," enshrined in the constitution of 1988. Under the guise of decentralization, the union restored substantial fiscal resources and autonomy to the subnational governments. The new constitution required that 21.5 percent of the income tax and ICM be delivered to the state and 22.5 percent to the municipal governments by 1993, with no strings attached (Baer and Paiva, 1994: 13; *Economist,* 1991: 9). With these provisions, the subnational governments accelerated the steady fiscal gains made since the mid-1970s (cf. Baer and Paiva, 1994: 13). The *Economist* estimated that in 1992 Brazil's

---

33 The reform that regulated the minimum wage and wage readjustments was opposed by the PT, PMDB, and PSDB (who favored more frequent wage readjustments amid galloping inflation). After receiving the promise of federal government resources for housing and other programs to those states whose delegations backed the legislation, governors pressured their state delegations to vote with the government in Congress. The day after the government won its vote, the president quite openly announced that the governors would receive the resources they had been promised (*Folha de São Paulo,* 5/8/92: 1–5).

states and cities would receive just over half of the country's main tax revenues, whereas in 1980 their share was 20 percent. In 1990, with 46 percent of total tax revenues, states and cities accounted for 60 percent of government consumption (*Economist,* 1991: 9). In the 1980s and early 1990s, it became the practice of many states to borrow from their banks; such borrowing became so unrestrained that many state banks became illiquid and required the Central Bank to rescue them (Baer and Paiva, 1994: 29). Within a very short time, state governments had rolled up a debt unofficially estimated to be between $52 and 57 billion, much of which the federal government was later forced to assume (*Economist,* 1991: 10). In 1993, state governments owed the federal government $36 billion (Baer and Paiva, 1994: 29). There was little doubt that most of this debt had been contracted for the political advantage of sitting governors.

But despite these obvious political resources which traditional politicians secured for themselves during the process of regime transition, the question remains whether the system of clientelism is in its death throes and the dominance of traditional politicians is being eroded by the advance of new electoral forces, as Lamounier (1989a) and others have alleged. Many students of Brazil believe that demographic change in the Brazilian electorate, which is now 77 percent urban and numbers over 95 million people, has disengaged many voters from personal and party machines. Some of these voters identify strongly with nonclientelistic parties of the left like the Workers' Party, which has fashioned a coherent ideological platform, forged ample ties to social movements, and undoubtedly come to represent something genuinely new in Brazilian politics. Others, largely disorganized, receive their political information primarily from the media and are susceptible to populist appeals. In either case, they now reject the corruption, favoritism, and privatism of the traditional politicians and politics as traditionally practiced in Brazil, and in their place, have sounded a cry for accountability and genuine democracy (Moisés, 1993: 575–76).

This observed trend toward change in Brazilian electoral politics and political culture is alleged to have been especially evident in the 1989 presidential elections, which, according to the consensus view as expressed by Maria D'Alva Gil Kinzo (1993: 316), did not take place "in a rural society in which clientelistic machines have control of a tame electorate, as used to be the rule in large parts of Brazil's countryside." On the contrary, in this election, "political weight was given to a massive electorate which lives in the cities" and "treated the election as a chance to protest against all sorts of deprivation." Indeed, voters did resoundingly reject the candidates of the two parties with the strongest electoral machines, the PFL and PMDB; Aureliano Chaves and Ulysses Guimarães together did not garner even 5 percent of the vote in the first round. The victor, the former governor of the small Northeast state of Alagoas, Fernando Collor de Mello, waged an unabashedly populist campaign. Consciously aping the master of populism, Juan Perón, Collor even overtly appealed to the group that Kinzo (193: 316) describes as "the dispossessed people who are continuously marginalized in society, but who are integrated in the political market and participate in elections" as the *descamisados* (the "shirtless" ones). Claiming the status of an "outsider," he promised to attack government corruption and sack the bloated bureaucrats he dubbed *marajás* ("maharajahs"). His opponent, former metalworker and union leader Luis Inácio "Lula" da Silva representing the PT, garnered 47 percent of the second-round vote. These two candidates, it is widely believed, capitalized on a groundswell of discontent in Brazilian society. Both, it is further claimed, benefited from media exposure (Straubhaar, Olsen, and Nunes, 1993), and Collor in particular from a carefully orchestrated campaign on the part of the Globo television network (De Lima, 1993).[34] Their strong campaigns of protest have been interpreted as proof that the party system of the military is dead, that voters are rejecting "the archaic remnants of Brazilian political tradition" (Moisés, 1993: 578), and that traditional politics, the politicians that practice it, and especially the electoral machines of the oligarchy, are in decline.

There is a very large grain of truth in the assertion that most voters in 1989 wished to protest poor government performance and a lack of democratic accountability. It is certainly the case that Collor and Lula captured the support of the dispossessed classes. Collor in particular won the majority support of the poorest and most disorganized segments of Brazilian society. In a national survey conducted by the Brazilian Institute for Public Opinion Research (IBOPE) in December 1989 on the eve of the presidential election, 51 percent of voters earning less than two times the monthly minimum wage expressed preference for Collor, along with 55 percent of those with only a primary school education (Singer, 1990: 137). Extensive surveys involving 600 respondents conducted by Maria D'Alva Gil Kinzo during the campaign in the *município* of Presidente Prudente in western São Paulo also suggest strongly that Collor won among unregistered workers (those without a labor card) and the low-income stratum, and Lula among the average wage earners (Kinzo, 1993: 324). Lula's supporters, the clear minority in Presidente Prudente, were also better organized – they were, by and large, union members and party militants, and were mobilized by the progressive church (1993: 327) – and they manifested a clearly ideological character. One of Kinzo's most significant findings is that, since the 1976 municipal elections, on which Lamounier (1989a) placed so much

---

34 Globo was allegedly influential by not only providing favorable and extensive coverage of Collor during the campaign, including tagging him as the front-runner months before the first-round elections, but also by broadcasting for several months in the run-up to the elections *telenovelas* (prime-time soap operas) that portrayed Brazil as a kingdom of political corruption whose problems could only be solved by an outsider (De Lima, 1993: 98, 103, 105).

stock in his forceful analysis of "modernizing" trends in the Brazilian electorate, party identification has lost its significance (1993: 320).

Careful studies of the 1989 election, moreover, throw into serious question the assumption that the electoral machines of the oligarchy are in disrepair. Ames (1994: 96) has found that outside the metropolitan capitals of southeast Brazil, party endorsements and the mobilizational commitments they represent had a powerful impact on the fortunes of the major candidates in the 1989 elections. Local organization remained critical to electoral success; all candidates polled significantly better in municipalities where the mayor represented their party. When socioeconomic and demographic factors are included in Ames's model, the effects of party machines sharpen (1994: 100–1). The results hold when partisan tendency is added to the model, though the ability of the PT to deliver votes to Lula in the second round is less than for other parties, in large part because the party drew its electoral strength in large cities and it lacked the kind of dominant local organization typical of small, rural towns (1994: 102–3). Organization was central to the electoral fortunes of even the Brazilian politician reputed to have the most "charismatic" electoral appeal, Leonel Brizola. Brizola scored well only where his political organization had been in place long before the 1989 campaign, and he failed to penetrate São Paulo (Ames, 1994: 106). Perhaps most interesting in assessing the survival of traditional politics, Ames found that, when local politicians that are vulnerable to the political influence of larger *municípios* must decide whether to endorse their own candidate for president of that of a powerful political figure of a contiguous area, they choose the latter, indicating that political careers are still determined at the state level (1994: 105).

Since that election, the strength of the parties and electoral machines of the traditional political elite has not diminished. Despite their dismal showing at the polls in 1989, the two parties that had sealed the transition to democracy, the PMDB and the PFL, remained Brazil's two largest parties. In the 1990 gubernatorial and congressional elections, when public disillusion with "establishment" politicians ran high (30 percent of eligible voters abstained, and 31.5 percent cast blank or spoiled ballots, a rate comparable with that registered nationwide in 1970 when the MDB encouraged such symbolic protest against the dictatorship), these two parties combined elected fifteen governors and 38 percent of the Congress. While the vote for the PMDB did decline between 1986 and 1990, that for the PFL held steady. To put their electoral performance in perspective, the PT and PSDB each elected only one governor. Even after doubling its vote from 3.4 percent in 1986 to 6.8 percent, the PT elected only thirty-five representatives to the Chamber of Deputies and one senator. The PSDB captured only thirty-seven seats in the Chamber of Deputies and ten in the senate, a reduction in its overall congressional representation (*Istoé/Senhor*, 1991: 11; Mainwaring, 1995: 366–67).

Traditional politicians have also enjoyed considerable success in elections for subnational governments and the legislature. In the 1990 elections, governors of the authoritarian regime were returned to their state houses in impressive numbers. Five governors elected by the PFL – Antônio Carlos Magalhães (Bahia), Agripino Maia (Rio Grande do Norte), João Alves Filho (Sergipe), Edison Lobão (Maranhão), and Anibal Barcellos (Amapá) – had served as PDS governors in the mid-1980s, (Rodrigues, 1984). At least two others, who had been governors for the PDS and PMDB during the late military regime – Geraldo Bulhões and Hélio Garcia – were elected on minor party labels (the Social Christian Party and the Party of Social Reform, respectively). In addition, turnover in the Chamber of Deputies, or the percent of nonincumbent deputies elected, has *declined* since 1986, from 75 percent to 65 percent in 1990 and 57 percent in 1994. Moreover, both incumbent and "new" deputies had a great deal of political experience. About two-fifths of the deputies elected in 1990 had served a prior term as a federal representative or senator, and about one-third as a state deputy. Just under one-quarter had been cabinet secretaries in their respective states. The level and type of political experience of members of Congress varied considerably along with their party label, reflecting their party's proximity to power. In 1991, 49 percent of PMDB and 51 percent of PFL deputies had previously sat in Congress, while 32 percent and 24 percent, respectively, had served stints as state cabinet secretaries. Although 31 percent of the PT delegation had served a previous term in Congress and 39 percent in the state Assemblies, not one Workers' Party deputy had had state administrative experience in any capacity (Câmara dos Deputados, 1991). Included among the ranks of the new deputies elected in 1994 were 42 former federal deputies and a number of ex-governors, state deputies, senators, and ministers. Only 152 deputies, or 30 percent of the Chamber, had not previously served in public office (*Veja,* 10/19/94: 31).

Perhaps most important, the influence of traditional political elites is also ever evident in the race for the largest prize in Brazilian politics: the presidency. In the 1994 elections, Fernando Henrique Cardoso won a convincing first-round victory as the candidate of the social-democratic PSDB, capturing 54.5 percent of the 63.4 million valid votes cast – more than double that of his closest competitor, Lula, who again represented the Workers' Party. This impressive electoral victory has been widely attributed to the popular endorsement of the antiinflation program, the *Real,* designed and implemented by Cardoso as finance minister in early to mid-1994, which lowered the rate of increase of consumer prices from more than 40 percent per month to about 2 percent per month in the last five months of 1994. While satisfaction with recovering the purchasing power of their wages obviously influenced ordinary Brazilians to vote for Cardoso, his election was also abetted, as was Collor's before him, by a network of alliances with traditional and clientelistic politicians.

In 1994 Fernando Henrique Cardoso sought and struck an electoral alliance with the PFL and the PTB in a style closer to that of Tancredo Neves than would be expected of a founding leader of a party that broke away from the PMDB of São Paulo governor Orestes Quércia because of excessive clientelism and that supported the candidate of the Workers' Party in the second round of the 1989 presidential election. Indeed, he was elected by roughly the same political coalition that elected his predecessors – the Collor–Franco ticket in direct elections in 1989 and the Neves–Sarney ticket in an electoral college in 1985. The parallel was not lost on Lula, who charged that the alliance smacked of attempting to "resuscitate the cadaver of the Democratic Alliance between the PMDB and PFL" (*Veja*, 3/16/94: 33). To secure the support of the traditional political machines, Cardoso agreed to accept a vice-president from the PFL. After his own designated running mate was forced to resign from the ticket because of irregularities in his personal financial affairs, Cardoso accepted as a substitute on the ticket the choice of the leadership of the PFL, the former governor of Pernambuco Marco Maciel. Maciel had the blemish of having served the military governments of Costa e Silva, Geisel (he helped to draft the infamous 1977 "April package"), and Figueiredo, but nonetheless was capable, as has been widely acknowledged, of leading the campaign for the ticket in the Northeast (*Veja*, 8/10/94: 31).[35] For its allegiance the PFL was also awarded the top posts in the Ministries of Social Welfare, Health, Environment and Irrigation, and Mines and Energy. Politicians from the PMDB, which did not cosponsor his candidacy but with whose support he hoped to govern, received the portfolios of Transportation and Justice.

Further evidence that the overwhelming vote for a social democrat and a socialist for president does not represent a partisan realignment and a broader rejection of traditional politics in Brazil is that the gains achieved by the programmatic parties of the left and center-left in presidential elections have failed to carry over in a sustained and systematic way to other races. Rather, there is evident a bifurcation of the vote between presidential elections (which have assumed a plebiscitary quality) and legislative contests (in which clientelistic criteria are still primordial) reminiscent of the electoral patterns of the late authoritarian period. The PSDB won the presidency and six governorships, including those of the most populous and richest states in Brazil – São Paulo, Minas Gerais, and Rio de Janeiro – but

35 As governor of Pernambuco, Marco Maciel exercised virtually unrestrained state clientelism. In three years, he hired 60,000 functionaries and opened fifty state agencies, most of which ran deficits. After his term, the Bank of the State of Pernambuco (BANDEPE) almost failed, and had to be taken over by the Central Bank (*Veja*, 8/10/94: 32–33).

still elected only about 13 percent of the Congress. The PSDB, moreover, continues to be primarily a parliamentary party and in Minas Gerais, the governor, Eduardo Azeredo, belongs to one of the most traditional families of the state – the Avellar Azeredos of Sete Lagoas. The only electorally significant party with a genuine grass-roots membership, the PT, elected two governors and increased its congressional delegation to forty-nine deputies and five senators. Yet, its members still comprise only 9 percent of the Congress and govern only about 6 percent of the population at the local level (Lamounier, 1994b: 51). If the 1989 vote for the Workers' Party represented part of a larger rejection of traditional political candidacies, the party should have made larger gains at lower levels of the political system. To the contrary, however, the public discontent that swelled the vote for Lula and a programmatic labor party for many years vanished suddenly with the abrupt fall in the rate of monthly inflation. This can be explained by the nature of the PT's electorate, which encompasses not only average wage earners in large cities organized by the church and labor unions, but also a largely unorganized electorate that is less aware of the party's positions on particular issues. If the former constitutes a growing core constituency for the PT, the latter, beyond the control of traditional political machines, has largely gravitated toward the party in order to register a protest vote and can just as easily desert it. By contrast, the parties of the traditional elite continue to be the largest in the Congress. The PMDB increased its delegation from 94 to 110 in the Chamber of Deputies, although it lost 6 seats in the Senate, and the PFL increased its overall representation from 99 to 110 deputies and senators. The PMDB also elected the largest number of governors of any single party, nine. Together, these two parties retained 39 percent of the Chamber and 49 percent of the Senate.

The strength of traditional elites in the cabinet, legislature, and state houses will have serious implications for the government's ability to fulfill its campaign pledges to improve the delivery of public services and reform the state. Whereas the government has been able to stabilize prices and secure enough support in the Congress to reform the constitution in order to attract foreign investment, it will likely have difficulty from this point forward in reducing the potential for state clientelism across agencies and programs. Traditional politicians of the PFL and PMDB in the Congress cannot be expected to support measures that imposed fiscal responsibility on profligate state governments; if they do, that support will most likely be purchased at a very high price. There is not even any assurance that the PSDB governors who campaigned as closest to the *situação* and best connected to the president-elect will permit the privatization of state government-owned enterprises needed to cancel out the debt of the state banks (*Veja*, 11/23/94: 31–32).

In sum, the election of an honest president with honorable intentions who has assembled an economic team that any country would envy for its talent and competence is insufficient reason to question that the dominance of traditional political elites and traditional politics is coming to an end. To the contrary, these politicians played a vital role in his election. In rural areas as well as midsized and large cities, local bosses and ultimately the political machines of the state-level oligarchies can still mobilize votes in sufficient numbers to influence the outcome of state and national elections, and they do so readily to support whichever candidates can keep them in powerful positions in the state. If Brazilian politics and society have traveled far from the days of the oligarchical republic and the military regime, Brazil is undeniably not past its period of traditional politics.

CONCLUSIONS

Periods of regime transition provide rare opportunities for rapid political change – including elite turnover, institutional reform, and party system realignment. In Brazil, the exit of the military and the transition from authoritarian rule created the possibility for the eventual eclipse of the traditional political elite and the traditional patterns of politics their domination engendered. By lifting the ban on real political competition, the new regime removed the obstacles to political participation and autonomous local politics and laid a new basis for competitive interest representation to supplant state clientelism. In the latter stages of the military regime, political competition had given opponents of the oligarchy in the PMDB an opening through which to attack the foundations of elite power.

However genuine the possibilities were for a fatal blow to be dealt to traditional politics and politicians in the process accompanying the transition to democracy and for new forms of political representation to emerge, traditional politics survived the regime change, and traditional politicians – who had been bolstered by military policies and strategies that reinforced the structural bases of traditional politics and kept alive the operation of patronage machines – were strengthened by the process of regime transition itself. At the end of military rule, these politicians controlled state houses, populated federal and state cabinets and the state delegations to the Chamber of Deputies, handed out jobs and appointments to political friends, and constituted the majority in the electoral college that was to select the president. Taking advantage of an enviable bargaining position, they secured policies beneficial to their constituents but, more important, preserved the resources and institutions that permit them to continue to practice traditional politics.

In Minas Gerais, a PMDB governor, Tancredo Neves, broadened his coalition by reaching out to his state-level opponents. Local bosses, and not their ideological and political rivals, inherited the mantle of the PMDB. Tancredo Neves pursued a strategy of *trasformismo,* with much the same effects that became apparent in Italy: immediate success for the government majority, the co-optation of opposition, and a long-term blow to political parties as vehicles of nonelite interest representation at precisely the moment they were most needed and held their greatest potential to advance democratization. The same script was acted out on the national stage very shortly thereafter.

Arrangements put into place during times of regime transition become self-perpetuating, even when their alternatives are not institutionally proscribed. In Minas Gerais, political bargains necessary to advance the transition returned to members of the traditional political elite their primary political resources – their positions in the state and access to political patronage. Traditional politicians also gained the leadership of nearly all potential parties of government, which afforded them the political structures through which to funnel state resources for clientelistic purposes. Local political bosses of the interior who rode the wave of partisan conversion to emerge with their political health intact in 1988 – the cogs in the traditional patronage machines – remain in place to serve the oligarchy from within whatever governing party they form or appropriate in the perpetual reconstruction of clientelistic networks. In a self-reinforcing circle, clientelism helped to maintain traditional elite dominance in federal, state, and local politics after the transition. It enabled traditional elites to defeat Lula in the presidential elections in 1989 and 1994, and traditional politicians to poll impressively in the state and congressional races in 1990 and 1994. In the early 1990s, it was still possible to speak of ARENA-dominated cabinets, constructed with the state's coffers. Even during the period of democratic consolidation, when state executives and federal and state legislators were chosen according to democratic procedures, they mediated the interests of Brazilian society as they had during the military and premilitary governments.

The traditional political elite used the prominent roles in the state and the major parties that it earned in the transition to civilian rule not only to preserve the structures of traditional politics, but also to thwart the emergence of new forms of political organization. First, and ultimately perhaps most consequential, most political parties remained vehicles for the exercise of political clientelism. The political realignment engineered by the traditional political elite redefined several party labels but not their programs, recruitment patterns, rules of internal organization, or especially styles of political competition. The ready and efficient mass conversion of traditional politicians reinforced the extreme ideological and programmatic weakness of parties. In democratic societies in which political parties realign, however infrequently, over salient, cross-cutting issues, the process of realignment broadens the possibilities for democratic representation by providing electors with the opportunity to express their preferences along a new axis of conflict in society. In Brazil, where realignment was precipitated instead by oligarchical factionalism – the PFL differed initially from its parent, the PDS, only in its preference for Tancredo Neves over Paulo Maluf – it actually *diminished* the potential of parties to represent a broader range of interests. Although ideological and substantive disputes did surface during the transition – most evidently during debates in the Constituent Assembly – and the PT today continues to wage an impressive ideological offensive of behalf of Brazil's workers, most major parties were robbed of the opportunity to process demands and to contest substantive and ideological issues during the partisan realignment that accompanied the birth of the New Republic. The migration of the traditional political elite in particular to the new party of the *situação*, the PMDB, converted the emblem of opposition to authoritarianism into an internally mobilized party, a claim with which the breakaway PSDB would not disagree. The diminished significance of party identification, an unstable party system, and a volatile electorate are the products of transition by *trasformismo*.

The renewed strength of the traditional political elite, moreover, blocked certain constitutionally governed policies, moderated others, and built an inherent conservatism into Brazil's constitutionally defined institutions. Although the democratic constitution ratified in 1988 is exceptionally strong on civil, social, and political rights,[36] it failed to provide for an agrarian reform (Article 185 of the final version exempts "productive property" from appropriation). And while its principal institutions are not undemocratic in theory, federalism and presidentialism obviously advantage the regional oligarchies and are consistent with what might be termed "oligarchical democracy."[37] In the past they were exploited by antidemocratic forces, and in the future they could just as easily hinder as advance the process of democratization. The new federalism enhances local control over government spending, but it also restores to regional political oligarchies the resources with which to grease their political machines. The

36 Article 5 grants equal rights for women, prohibits torture and censorship, and guarantees freedom from searches, of assembly, and the writ of *habeas corpus*. In all, it contains 77 sections. In the realm of social rights, the Brazilian constitution grants 120-day maternal leave, an eight-hour workday and forty-four-hour workweek; and thirty days notice for firings and layoffs. Article 9 of the constitution grants labor the right to strike. The constitution also consciously guards against authoritarian encroachments on democracy. It strengthens Congress – emasculated by the military regime – by granting it the right to review the national budget and the public debt, including any agreements about the foreign debt, and by abolishing the two main instruments of military government – decree laws and the *decurso de prazo* – it dismantled much of the *entulho autoritário* (authoritarian "rubble") of the document it replaced. Article 15 bears the imprint of a nation seeking to prevent future military abuses of political rights: it prohibits *cassações*.

37 Parliamentarism *was* opposed by some for other reasons. Leonel Brizola and his supporters in the PDT, hoping for victory in the 1989 presidential race, did not wish the powers of the office to be diluted. Parliamentarism, Brizola remembered, was used by the oligarchy in 1961 to weaken the hand of his brother-in-law, João Goulart. The PT also supported presidentialism.

strengthening of Congress notwithstanding, the potential for the Brazilian legislature to be an equal partner in government with the executive branch and for political parties to play a major role in policy formation and implementation is seriously limited by the Brazilian presidential system, which reinforces the excessive strength of Brazil's executive, its insulation from popular pressures, and its recourse to the wholesale distribution of federal patronage.[38] There was similarly nothing inherently undemocratic about a five-year presidential term, but in Brazil its adoption had distinctly undemocratic undertones. The sole rationale for the five-year term was a thinly disguised effort on the part of the sitting president to remain in office for an additional year. On ideological grounds, the measure's only supporters were the military and others who wished to postpone the transfer of executive power from incumbent president Sarney to any candidate whom authoritarian forces potentially could not control.

The political transactions that accompanied the transition from authoritarian rule in Brazil allowed the protagonists of the old regime to assume a commanding position at the helm of the central institutions of political life in the new, and traditional politics to survive at least the initial stages of civilian government. The latest regime creation of the traditional political elite is a hybrid that has been cleansed of abusive authoritarian rules but not traditional, undemocratic politics.

38 Mainwaring (1991a: 26) has pointed out that measures taken by the military government to limit congressional powers (paradoxically to undermine clientelism and enhance efficiency) actually reinforced the ability of presidents and ministers to use patronage in a clientelistic fashion in the 1980s. With the legislature virtually excluded from the budget process and congressional oversight of the executive branch nonexistent, the president and ministers could favor friends and discriminate against foes without restraint.

8

Continuity in change: Brazilian authoritarianism and democratization in comparative perspective

This study has been concerned primarily with explaining why the strategic state elite governing the Brazilian bureaucratic-authoritarian regime failed in its mission to recast the national political system, why traditional politics and a regional, traditional political elite survived rapid economic and social modernization and significant attempts at political restructuring, and what the consequences of the persistent dominance of this class have been for Brazil's new and future democracy. Whatever the expectations that regional political elites should have been easily able, in their own states, to survive a military project to "technocratize" the state, it was by no means assured that these elites could have withstood the regime's initial attacks on it to steer bureaucratic authoritarianism through its rocky second decade and the transition to democracy. It was even less apparent that traditional, clientelistic, and even oligarchical politics of the sort decried by Cardoso and Weffort in the opening passages of this book should have been restored after regime change.

Brazil's military governors initially proposed to rationalize the state, a project that was quite radical politically for it would have altered the historical patterns of decision making and elite participation in Brazilian politics. Backed by a new hegemonic alliance of foreign and domestic entrepreneurs and a technically competent state elite, the military attempted to centralize fiscal and political decisions beyond the reach of the regional oligarchies in the innermost circles of the federal state. It also set out to substitute technocratic rationality for clientelism in the state bureaucracies, thus depriving the regional oligarchies of their power bases in the state.

Ultimately, the military did not reformat patterns of politics ingrained in the fabric of Brazilian society for nearly a century. For a short while during the height of military repression (approximately 1969–73) traditional elite influence declined in national politics as the technocratic presence in government rose. Policy making was transferred from elected representatives to appointed technocrats, and the absence of direct elections for a strengthened national executive took important decisions out of politics. But attempts to revamp the subnational governments were far less successful than those that reformed the national state, and the military's goals of transforming the state and undermining the traditional political elite proved to be elusive. The regime did not permanently evict traditional politicians from the state or emasculate the positions they did occupy, purge local bosses loyal to the regional oligarchies from the subnational governments or make local incumbents allies of the federal military governors,[1] or remove the resource base for clientelism and disrupt irreparably the clientelistic chain.

In the vast expanses of Brazil where traditional political elites practiced traditional politics on the eve of the coup, they could still be found doing so at the close of military rule. Throughout the bureaucratic-authoritarian episode, members of the traditional political elite served as state governors, even when these posts were appointed. They also retained, at least on the state level, the means with which to keep their patronage machines operational. The centralization of revenue collection in the union notwithstanding, state governments continued to enjoy discretion in the implementation of national policies and the administration of federal and state programs. Traditional political bosses who owed their allegiance to regional oligarchies also continued to rule in thousands of municipalities in the interior of Brazil. While Minas is noted for its "conservative" and "traditional" politics, there are certainly indications that traditional politicians were well represented in the upper echelons of other state governments, and that despite political centralization, the practice of traditional politics persisted outside the major metropolitan regions in the Northeast, the North, the West, and even elsewhere in the Southeast (traditional politics was historically weak in the South). The traditional political elite may have been even stronger in the second decade of military rule than it was on the eve of the 1964 coup.

The fact that political change did not penetrate the lower levels of the political system during bureaucratic authoritarianism severely limited the ability of the military regime to consolidate itself and certainly contributed to its eventual demise. It also empowered traditional politicians to act as a brake on political change that might have otherwise followed from the many initiatives launched from civil society to challenge the authoritarian political order and the strong Brazilian state – among them the forceful advocacy of the economic and political as well as spiritual needs of the poor on the part of a Catholic Church morally outraged at the abuse of human rights and dignity (Bruneau, 1982; Della Cava, 1989; Mainwaring, 1986a, 1989a);[2] new forms of voluntary association, especially in large urban areas

1 Reis (1985) suggests that the military attempted to do precisely this in a small town in the Minas scrublands known as the *cerrado*.
2 Della Cava (1989: 154–55) has suggested that the Catholic Church has reversed itself, under great pressure from the Vatican (and due to the appointment of more conservative bishops), and is becoming once again a conservative force in politics.

(Boschi, 1983, 1987; Cardoso, 1984; Mainwaring, 1987, 1989b); a "new unionism" in Brazil's industrial heartland that aimed to supplant corporatist forms of labor organization (Alves, 1985; Humphrey, 1982; Keck, 1989; Martins Rodrigues, 1990; Moisés, 1979, 1982; Tavares de Almeida, 1981, 1983, 1987); and new opposition political parties – the Brazilian Democratic Movement and, after the party reform law of 1979, the Workers' Party. Since the transition to democracy, many potentially significant changes were not sustained and those that were have not permeated the whole of Brazilian society. With the important exception of the "new unionism," the new social movements of civil society fizzled in the New Republic (Campello de Souza, 1989: 354) – at least to the extent that their impact on Brazilian politics has been more limited than earlier analyses hoped. Political change that has transformed Rio de Janeiro and the "ABC triangle"[3] of São Paulo has been slow to arrive in small and midsized cities populated by recent migrants from rural areas, where instead traditional political domination endures and traditional elites exercise state clientelism. Despite obvious party-system change, there is a great deal of continuity in the political elite and political practices of the parties from the preauthoritarian to the authoritarian regime, and from authoritarian rule to the new democratic republic. Many major political parties are dominated at all levels of government by either civilian allies of the military or members of the pre-1964 elite.

Judged by the persistence of elections, political leaders, and the practice of political clientelism, Brazil exhibited more political continuity from its previous semicompetitive regime to the authoritarian regime than did any other bureaucratic-authoritarian regime, and its political system perhaps more closely approximates Charles Anderson's (1967: 104) famous metaphor of the "living museum" – where new power contenders may be added to a political system but old ones may not be eliminated – than that of any other Latin American country.[4] If, on balance, Brazil's enigmatic political system has exhibited a capacity to change, these changes have lagged behind economic change, even by the standard of a region in which substantial economic change in the postwar period has been met in country after country with sometimes subtle and sometimes harshly repressive attempts to keep political systems closed in real ways to broad segments of their populations. Although there are certainly countries in Latin America whose politics are

---

3 The "ABC Triangle" is named for the municipalities of Santo Andre, São Bernardo do Campo, and São Caetano. These municipalities host the auto industries and, hence, the largest concentration of Brazil's most militant workers: the metallurgical workers. The "new unionism" was born here.

4 In a "living museum," "all the forms of political authority of the Western historic experience continue to exist and operate, interacting one with another in a pageant that seems to violate all the rules of sequence and change involved in our understanding of the growth of Western civilization."

more closed, the extent to which politics in Brazil is controlled by elites, and operates on "traditional" principles, is perhaps extreme among the region's developed economies; rapid socioeconomic development has coincided with political stasis. The Brazilian political system has not so much resisted change as it has digested it, and while it has accommodated itself to change by developing new, hybrid forms of elite control that are neither strictly "traditional" nor "modern," the fundamental contours of the system have remained in place. The view that the political system has been saddled with traditional and authoritarian legacies challenges conceptions of Brazilian politics as fundamentally transformed by new political parties, electoral cleavages, and democratizing social movements, but is supported by a parade of events in the last decade. The 1980s began with a ray of cautious political hope, then witnessed a tide of political exuberance and euphoria, but ended in rude disillusion and political disaffection when it became apparent that the democratizing potential of the regime transition had been thwarted by traditional elites. Even in the 1990s, each advance of the political left has been matched by a comeback of the traditional right, culminating in a government headed by Fernando Henrique Cardoso that was elected with the support of traditional political chieftains.

Whatever Brazil's future, and whatever the future of the traditional political elite in a competitive political system, the survival until now of the traditional political elite and traditional politics deserves to be explained, not only to understand better what has and might have transpired in Brazil, as well as what might follow, but also to understand the broader question of how political systems accommodate, resist, and fail to resist change.

STATE – SOCIETY RELATIONS, REGIME STRATEGIES, AND POLITICAL CHANGE

This study has rejected explanations for political continuity that depend on economic determinism, especially since such arguments would suggest not continuity, but change, in the Brazilian case. Indeed, for decades scholars and practitioners have predicted that as Brazil develops further, its agriculture continues to modernize and its rural areas to empty, its regional oligarchies will eventually and inevitably be eclipsed. Virtually every study of the elections of the late military period stresses that the opposition vote was greatest in the largest cities of the most developed parts of the country, a point on which some otherwise astute observers (such as Sarles, 1982) seized to depict a picture of a shortsighted military whose immediate economic success would ultimately spell its political doom. Several analyses have collectively suggested that the democratization of the 1980s was built on a socioeconomic foundation that developed during the military regime; rural dislocation, urbanization, and industrialization bred newly militant urban workers who voted for the opposition and struck against the military regime, as well as urban popular classes who organized in neighborhood associations to press a variety of claims to the state. There predictions have been proved by events to be wrong, and so too by now it should be obvious that contemporary arguments that contend that the precepts of modernization theory were not wrong, only that they had been applied to Brazil and other countries like it prematurely,[5] are no more likely to provide an accurate basis for future theorizing about political change. Similarly, I have rejected the new institutional determinism. Despite its promise, it does not readily explain change in a constant institutional context.

This book has not disregarded either the economic or institutional context in which regime change takes place, but rather has focused on the "state–society relations" embedded in those contexts in order to explain which elements of political systems survive and which fail to survive regime change. In calling greater attention to the patterns of political association, competition, and representation by which political actors respond to old and new political challenges, it hopefully has strengthened our understanding of *how* economic models and state institutions influence or constrain political system change. Nonetheless, this framework does imply that politics enjoys partial autonomy from economic constraints, and the course of political change can proceed independently of economic change, even if it is set in motion by it. Although state–society relationships correspond to particular economic configurations, they are fundamentally brought into being by politics, and maintained, transformed, or discarded through the negotiation, renegotiation, and collapse of political bargains.

One need look only to the different political configurations arising from similar economic policies, class structures, and manifestations of social conflict in Latin America in the postwar period to appreciate this point. Brazil and Argentina both pursued import-substituting industrialization under the aegis of an excessively interventionist state in the postwar period, but in Argentina corporate groups predominated over parties as representatives of a praetorian civil society, which was itself stronger than the Argentine state, while in Brazil an elite-dominated political system succeeded in imposing various forms of state control, including corporatist controls, over a civil society with virtually no autonomous organization. Brazil and Chile both had a substantial peasantry on the eve of bureaucratic authoritarianism but ideological parties with identifiable class constituencies contested competi-

---

5 Huntington (1984) has hypothesized that the relationship between economic development and democracy is not linear, as postulated by Lipset (1960), but does exist at the lower and upper ends of the development scale: with the exception of India, poor countries are not democratic, and rich countries are. In an intermediate range of development, a "transition zone" encompassing the top one-third of middle-income countries, however, "political elites and prevailing political values can shape choices," and such authoritarian retrenchments as bureaucratic authoritarianism are possible. For a critique of "neomodernization" theory as an explanation for the transition to democracy, see Cardoso (1989).

tive elections for state power in Chile, whereas in Brazil a hegemonic coalition of a dominant clientelistic party and an inclusionary labor party restricted political competition.[6] Most significant, once in place the systems of mediation and representation between states and societies can change the political means and consequences of economic development, privileging some bases for societal organization while devaluing others, and they can themselves be changed – strengthened, weakened, or destroyed – by political and economic measures that impact directly upon them.

This work has suggested that the extent to which authoritarian political regimes were able to transform patterns of political association, competition, and representation – in other words reconfigure state–society relations – varies according to the cumulative effects of: (1) the design of preauthoritarian state–society networks that primarily structured and constrained the economic programs and political strategies adopted by bureaucratic-authoritarian regimes; (2) how the economic policies military regimes adopted to stabilize and restructure the economy and the political strategies they pursued to depoliticize society, keep themselves in power, or influence the political system after their departure from government, nourished, left dormant, or undermined these preexisting state–society networks; and (3) how various actors and institutions were privileged or injured during the transition to democracy.

From this framework follow several arguments to explain the heavy dose of political continuity in Brazil. First, because Brazilian clientelism was a more "workable" network for organizing consent than the channels of mediation in the other countries of the Southern Cone of South America, the military reserved it as an institutionalized alternative to check runaway populism and tempered its repression. Second, the ample resources generated by state capitalism and the regime's necessary political commitment to selectively targeted distribution to deter opposition victories in a functioning if authoritarian political system uniquely sustained personal–state clientelistic networks. And third, the organizers of state clientelism of the "old regime" were sufficiently strengthened by the authoritarian experience that at the close of bureaucratic-authoritarian rule they were able to negotiate their place in the posttransition order and to pattern state–society relations in the democratic regime after the traditional networks that had sustained oligarchical politics.

---

6 In making a claim for sharply divergent political configurations in Chile and Brazil, I depart from Collier and Collier (1991) who have identified as similar in the two political systems the strength of labor, the relationship of labor to the state, and the ultimate radicalization of politics and eventual demise of center-left presidents. Valenzuela (1978) has disputed that the constituencies of Chilean parties corresponded closely to distinct social classes, but I tend to agree with Stallings (1977) who has argued, based on various surveys conducted by the Chilean pollster Eduardo Hamuy, that at least until 1973 the constituencies of Chilean parties could be defined in class terms.

An assessment of the utility of this framework for adequately answering the question of why the Brazilian political system, even when captured by a "modernizing" authoritarian regime, was well suited to preserving the dominance of a traditional political elite and patterns of traditional political organization and practice now requires a broader test. A comparative analysis of the strategies, policies, and demise of the Brazilian and other Latin American authoritarian regimes should shed light on whether such a framework can account for the different rates and types of political change and continuity evident elsewhere. Brazil's regime strategies, representative networks, and regime transition are compared primarily with those of the other former bureaucratic-authoritarian countries – Argentina, Chile, and Uruguay – but contrasts are drawn to Mexico as well.

HISTORICAL LEGACIES AND THE REFORM STRATEGIES OF AUTHORITARIAN REGIMES

The authoritarian regimes that governed the Southern Cone of South America in the 1960s and 1970s had their origins in common patterns of democratic breakdown, were led by similar alliances of brutal militaries and professional technocrats, and initially offered broadly similar political and policy responses to a common set of economic problems. Yet, once in power, prodded by distinctive technocratic ideologies and economic constraints, military governors designed considerably different economic and political reform strategies. The economic policy solutions adopted by the Brazilian and first Argentine bureaucratic-authoritarian regimes in a time of expanding world trade – quasi-orthodox stabilization followed in the Brazilian case by an aggressive expansion of the state enterprise sector – contrast sharply with the later economic projects of the Uruguayan, Chilean, and second Argentine military regimes, which were showcases of neoconservative experiments in monetarist economics, trade liberalization, privatization, and currency overvaluation (Foxley, 1983; Schamis, 1991). Politics was also organized and practiced (or not practiced) quite differently in each of these regimes. The authoritarian regimes in Uruguay, Chile, and Argentina disrupted normal political processes, dissolved legislatures, and recessed political parties. In Brazil, in contrast, political society functioned within military-set limits. Political parties were allowed to contest elections, mobilize the votes of general electors, and fulfill their function to recruit leaders. Throughout the period of authoritarian rule with brief and limited exceptions, the federal Congress and state Legislative Assemblies were convened and even mayors and municipal councils were directly elected.

Just as economic strategies responded to different levels of inflation and opportunities for world trade, so, too, did the political projects of Southern Cone militaries vary according to the design of state–society relations that the militaries found when they came to power. Most obviously, each pursued repression with greater or lesser fervor, applied state coercion against distinct segments of the population, and cooperated with civilian elites to differing degrees in response to the extent to which channels of political mediation in each country had broken down – indeed, these militaries seized power in order to restore state control and reorganize the bases of consent. More fundamentally, the political strategies of these military regimes – what they set out to alter and with how much commitment – were tailored to the political systems they inherited and, in particular, the prevailing networks for organizing and mediating societal interests. Their political strategies – and, where they had political purposes, their economic policies as well – were designed with an eye toward breaking, bending, or reconfiguring in each country what Manuel Antonio Garretón (1989) has called the "backbone" of their political systems.

Occasionally regime strategies were zealously adhered to, but more often they were revised or discarded in response to the largely unanticipated needs for mediating relations with their societies that each regime faced. As Guillermo O'Donnell (1979: 294–98) insightfully argued, once the need for even bureaucratic-authoritarian regimes to mediate their relations with society became manifest, bureaucratic-authoritarian regimes that restricted citizenship were at a disadvantage in doing so directly.[7] Ruling through fear and naked domination alone was an uneasy and ultimately inadequate formula for the institutionalization of long-term rule.[8] Just as the original designs for both the "defensive" and "offensive" projects of each military regime (Garretón, 1989) were initially shaped by the state–society relations it inherited, so each regime's response to the challenge of mediating relations in an authoritarian setting could be more or less flexible, based on the reservoir of options it had available. In effect, the objects of the regime's ambitions for change became constraints on change, and eventually set the parameters within which its projects for reform would be rescued, revised, or abandoned.

The Brazilian military headed the least repressive of the bureaucratic-authoritarian regimes. Far fewer persons lost their political rights and

7 O'Donnell, who witnessed the legitimacy crisis of the Brazilian military in 1974, and anticipated those in Uruguay in 1980, Argentina in 1981–82, and Chile in 1983, argued that because the bureaucratic-authoritarian state restricted citizenship, its nationalistic appeals fell hollow. Since it excluded popular classes from participation in the political system and the fruits of economic development, moreover, it could not appeal symbolically to *lo popular*.

8 This was especially true because, as Mainwaring (1986b) has cogently argued, the Brazilian military failed to manipulate symbols effectively. Rather, the military regime initially constructed almost exclusively negative symbols – anticommunism, anticorruption, antichaos. Though attractive at first to a large part of the population, they were intrinsically unreliable in the long run, since, once the regime was successful at extirpating these evils, its raison d'être disappeared.

their lives than in Chile, Argentina, or Uruguay. According to the account of military repression compiled by the Archdiocese of São Paulo from the records of the military tribunals, *Brasil: Nunca Mais* (Never Again), the government was responsible for "only" 333 deaths from 1964 to 1981 (Skidmore, 1988: 269), a per capita death toll 100 times lower than that of neighboring Argentina (Stepan, 1988: 69–70) and 50 times lower than that of Chile.[9] Considerably fewer persons were detained than in Uruguay. The regime also displayed leniency: at the height of the repression (1969–73), military courts acquitted 45 percent of the cases brought before them and, for the entire period from 1965 to 1977, 68 percent (Skidmore, 1988: 132). Even the "moderate" repression of the Brazilian military was blunted against politicians – only about 500 politicians lost their political rights – and it was hardly directly against the traditional political elite at all. PTB politicians bore the brunt of the *cassações,* though such notable PSD politicians from Minas Gerais as former president Juscelino Kubitschek and his political ally Sebastião Paēs de Almeida were also stripped of their political rights. Especially in comparison with its counterparts in the other bureaucratic-authoritarian regimes, the Brazilian political elite as a whole was silenced only briefly.

Without denying that the Brazilian armed forces tempered repression because they were internally divided and because excessive authoritarianism violated their own values and those of a quasi-pluralistic society as well – the explanations most often offered for their moderation (cf. Lamounier, 1989a)[10] – this study would suggest that the Brazilian military restrained its attack on Brazilian society in general and the political elite in particular because it was constrained by the state–society relations it inherited. The backbone of the Brazilian political system was a strong state that controlled society through two avenues: functionally, through corporatism, and territorially, through clientelism administered by weak, nonideological parties. By the standards of the Southern Cone, these channels of state–society mediation had malfunctioned only slightly in processing economic crisis and forestalling political polarization and class warfare on the eve of the coups d'etat. Brazilian labor was not unique in being organized into state corporatist unions, but it was restrained through comparatively harsh corporatist labor legislation (cf. Collier and Collier, 1979: 972) and weakened by the absence of ties between union members and their leaders who were co-opted by the state. It was less of a threat to the established order than the more independent and militant workers' associations in the neighboring bureaucratic-authoritarian regimes. Labor's weak position in the

9 I have based the Chilean figure on the number of deaths reputed by the national Truth Commission (estimated to be in excess of 2,000).

10 In a similar vein, Skidmore (1988: 150) has written, the "incomplete dictatorial practices" of the Brazilian military "seemed to signal a lack of total confidence in their ideology and a lack of total commitment in applying it."

"populist" coalition was ensured by the pattern of political alliances negotiated by Vargas.[11] Though prices and exchange rates were set against agriculture to support import-substituting industrialization, Vargas included rural
oligarchs in his governing coalition, labor legislation was not extended to
the countryside, and agrarian elites were allowed to continue to dominate
their peasantries (Reis, 1989: 4). In 1964 the labor "strength" feared by
some and extolled by others was an illusion that became manifest when
minimal labor resistance to the coup was easily countered in the early years
of military rule (Erickson, 1977). Even at the height of military repression,
labor perceived the Brazilian state to be a "benevolent leviathan" (Cohen,
1982).[12] Traditional elite-dominated channels of clientelistic mediation functioned even more smoothly up to the coup. New clients welcomed whatever
state patronage benefits were directed their way, and state resources were
not strained. Economic growth was robust in the 1950s, and the coup-
instigating economic crisis of 1964 did not stem from structural stagnation –
in fact, the "deepening process" had advanced considerably in the late
1950s and early 1960s – but from an eminently curable inflation (Serra,
1979: 117; Wallerstein, 1980).

With a moderate challenge from labor and civil society more broadly, the
Brazilian military designed a strategy for change that was quite conservative by regional standards. It set out to weaken urban labor organizations in
order to contain labor costs, and herded independent-minded peasants into
new state-sponsored rural labor unions. Limiting its political agenda to
transforming the state through the centralization of finance and decision
making, it preserved elections, censured few politicians, and allowed political parties to operate with some restrictions. It did not at first, however,
confer upon them any advantage other than permitting them to contest
office.

After easily and swiftly dispensing with its manageable threat, however,
the Brazilian military found it considerably more difficult to carry out the
second part of its political project to cleanse the state of traditional, clientelistic practices. Its economic model brought the state into frequent
contact with society, and its early commitment to let politics and elections
go on handed society an opportunity to endorse or reject the military
project. Regime "defeats" in elections after 1974 tightened the constraints

11 John Johnson's (1958: 178–79) analysis of political change in Latin America, which excessively extolled the progressive role of the "middle sectors" in the economic, social, and
   political development of five major Latin American countries, in fact expressed some
   discomfort with applying the "populist" label to Brazil because the "vigorous middle and
   working element amalgams" present in such countries as Uruguay and Chile were missing
   in Brazil; rather, "the majority within the middle sectors has tended to associate itself with
   those elements in the P.S.D. and U.D.N. who look askance at the political emergence of
   the workers."
12 Recent research from the Northeast shows that this is especially true of rural unions
   (Pereira, 1991; Ventura de Morais, 1989).

that were already being applied on the military project by the defection of important segments of Brazilian elite society from the authoritarian coalition.[13] After several years of flouting its relations with society, the military needed to develop ways of mobilizing political support but found its options restricted. Having repressed corporatist labor unions outright, the other obvious existing channel of state–society mediation in Brazil was state clientelism. Neither the military nor its technocratic handmaidens, however, could operate patronage networks for effective electoral gain, nor could they structure new ones.

Lacking an alternative basis on which to organize consent and the means to channel patronage through political-organizational structures of their own, the military enlisted the support of regional, traditional political elites that it had initially demeaned to administer state patronage on its behalf. Traditional politicians had long dispensed state patronage through political parties linked to the state at each level of government, and they controlled the national network of the progovernment party – an impenetrable amalgam of private networks of local bosses and state oligarchs. Because they were best equipped to operate state clientelism on a grand scale in Brazil, they were the military's best option to secure the electoral victories needed to legitimize military rule and to prevent the radicalization of the polity and the development of class- or interest-based politics. Thus, the military restored to them the direction of those state institutions from which they had been temporarily evicted and made available to them ample public resources for patronage.

Uruguay, like Brazil, was dominated by clientelistic state–society relations exercised through political parties by career politicians. In Uruguay, the two "traditional" parties that held a virtual monopoly on government inspired firm loyalty in the electorate. Although Uruguay's multiclass parties played a more prominent role in organizing political identities and incorporating citizens into political life than their counterparts in Brazil (De Riz, 1989; Mainwaring, 1988), they, too, were amorphous and factionridden, and power within them was highly personalized.[14] With their ori-

---

13 The Catholic Church reversed its initial support of the coup because of human rights abuses, and the discontent of the bourgeoisie with military rule grew with each new state incursion into the private sector of the economy, and, perhaps even more important, over the state's regulatory actions (Stepan, 1985: 335). The leading sectors of the national bourgeoisie made plain their opposition to the state's economic policies, and their inability to influence (at least to their satisfaction) the processes of decision making in an authoritarian regime (Martins, 1986). In a highly visible campaign, they called for the state's withdrawal from the economy and then, later, for the liberalization of the regime.

14 As Jorge Domínguez has pointed out, however, the factions *within* the Uruguayan parties – lista 15 and lista 99 among the Colorados and Herrerismo among the Blancos, for instance – had more programmatic content than did parties in Brazil. Uruguay's leftist parties that eventually coalesced as the Frente Amplio were ideological, but before the 1973 coup they could not seriously challenge the two major parties.

gins in the nineteenth-century, the traditional Uruguayan parties emerged before, not out of, industrialism, and the party system was consolidated before the formation of the modern class structure; class cleavages went unnoticed and unrepresented by the party system. Party competition in this clientelistic system was dulled by an arrangement that removed potential partisan advantage over the distribution of state resources: the minority "out" party was allowed by the victorious "ins" to share in the allocation of patronage. Like in Brazil the state was stronger than civil society, but in Uruguay the state was a "state of the parties."

The Uruguayan military was more repressive than the Brazilian because clientelism in Uruguay had lost its purchase in mobilizing regime support. Why this is so was a legacy of the timing of the entrance of new groups into political life and the state distribution network more specifically. In Uruguay, the agrarian issue was resolved early and broad segments of society were incorporated by the "premature welfare state" erected by Battle y Ordóñez in the early part of the century. "Batllismo" made the benefits of state clientelism widely available decades earlier than in Brazil. Second- and third-generation "clients" came to see state benefits as entitlements rather than as favors from their political representatives that required reciprocity. When, then, economic stagnation set in and the "assistentialist" state was exhausted, party-administered state clientelism could not prevent the erosion of consent in the Uruguayan political system.[15]

In Uruguay, the military expressed even more political ambivalence toward traditional politicians, and more confusion about how to structure political life, than its Brazilian counterpart. Gillespie (1991: 53) characterized the early years of the authoritarian regime as plagued by "chronic uncertainty, disagreements, and improvisation as the structure and aims of military domination emerged." One year after the coup of 1973, the Uruguayan military confiscated the presses and arrested the leaders of the Socialist, Communist, and Christian Democratic Parties that composed the Frente Amplio, but only "suspended" the traditional parties – the Blancos and the Colorados (Gillespie and González, 1989: 220), which President Bordaberry said remained "the essence of democracy and the backbone of our nationality" (Gillespie, 1991: 52). Less than a year later, he insisted politicians "give up hope of once more 'using their perverted political apparatuses' " (Gillespie, 1991: 53). In 1976, he went so far as to propose the permanent abolition of all political parties and the eventual creation of a semicorporatist system. The military rejected this proposal, insisting that it "did not want to share historical responsibility for abolishing the parties" and that "sovereignty resides in the nation . . . as expressed . . . in the

---

15 Rial (1989) has argued quite convincingly that a good deal of the breakdown of the Uruguayan political system in the early 1970s can be explained by the incapacity of the two clientelistically based traditional parties to express social conflict and cleavages in Uruguayan society.

popular vote" (Gillespie, 1991: 54). Yet, it did not enlist politicians to marshal popular support for its albeit blurry efforts to remake the Uruguayan economy and society. Later that year, forgoing any attempt to co-opt notable conservative civilian allies, the military barred 15,000 former politicians from engaging in any political activity for a period of fifteen years.

Despite this obvious intention to undermine political leaders, the Uruguayan regime made few attempts either to build a party to mobilize support for the regime or to construct its own patronage networks (Gillespie and González, 1989: 222).[16] The inclusiveness of preauthoritarian clientelistic networks, and the "automatic" nature of state transfers in an "assistentialist" state, prevented the Uruguayan military from trading welfare-state programs for votes. Unlike in Brazil where the military successfully unleashed a torrent of state patronage programs to shore up its sagging support among a state client class whose ranks were swelled by peasants who willingly left, and were unwillingly evicted from, the land, "sophisticated Uruguayans had already come to see these as their birthright" (Gillespie and González, 1989: 223). Its attacks on politicians notwithstanding, the military did not press ahead fully in its efforts to rid the parties and the political system of traditional politicians. In fact, when forced to think about choosing successors, it actually abetted the return of traditional politicians and parties by manipulating electoral and party laws to their advantage, especially by lifting the limit on the number of permissible party subtickets known as *sublemas* (González, 1985; Rial, 1989).

In contrast to the Brazilian and Uruguayan militaries, the Argentine and Chilean militaries continued to shun mediation with their societies and their political classes. In Argentina, the interests of labor and capital were historically organized and represented predominantly along corporatist lines. Despite the superficial similarities in the rise of the populist leaders Juan Perón and Getúlio Vargas, the apparent simultaneous exhaustion of the "easy stage" of import-substituting industrialization, the weakness of parties in political life, and the coups of 1964 and 1966, the structure and legacy of populism in Argentina was quire different and led to a very different manifestation of bureaucratic authoritarianism. Unlike in Brazil, the populist coalition in Argentina had been organized as a truly urban coalition that squeezed agrarian exporters, with disastrous consequences for the economy and for political stability (Waisman, 1987; O'Donnell, 1973, 1988). Perón weakened the organization of his Justicialista Party relative to the unions, corporate groups became stronger than the parties, and civil society stronger than a state weakened by inflation and civil conflict (Cavarozzi, 1989: 312). Isolated politically by his own strategy of elite

---

16 Its failure even to attempt to mobilize citizens directly also perplexed Gillespie (1986: 223), given "the very large size of Uruguay's public sector and the number of civil-service jobs to be filled as alleged 'subversives' were fired."

confrontation, Perón came to be far more dependent on labor support than Vargas. As a consequence, Argentine labor gained an upper hand in its relations with the state and once Perón was overthrown and exiled in 1955, labor fell beyond the control of the state or any segment of the elite. At the time of the military coup of 1966, "mass praetorianism" ran deeper in Argentina than it had in Brazil two years earlier.[17]

With the Argentine state dangerously weaker than civil society, and labor strength perceived as hindering governability and national productivity, the Onganía administration (1966–70) tried to renegotiate state–labor relations. It attempted to elicit labor support while retracting bread-and-butter rewards – proposing no less than to harden the state's role in corporatist mediation and to tilt Argentine corporatism away from an "inducement" toward a "constraint"-based system[18] – but failed abjectly. What turned out to be only the first of two bureaucratic-authoritarian regimes ended in fiasco four years after the eruption of middle-class and worker protest in the industrial city of Córdoba in 1969 known as the *cordobazo*. When Onganía and his successors failed to repair channels of mediation between state and society, a second, more ruthless regime came to power only three years after its predecessor handed power to civilians to destroy and rebuild them on a new basis, and to put an end to what O'Donnell (1973) called the "impossible game." The hard-line military regime that seized power in Argentina in 1976 to end inept civilian rule made no effort to resuscitate corporatism and win labor support. To the contrary, it attempted to decapitate the labor movement with harsh economic policies and state-sponsored murder, unleashing an "unparalleled and effective" repression against primarily the left wing of the Justicialista Party; thousands of middle-rank union officials, party cadres, teachers, and student activists simply "disappeared" (Cavarozzi, 1986: 155). When the military lost its gamble in the South Atlantic to capture by force the British-owned Falkland Islands which Argentina claims as the Malvinas, it faced a united political opposition of the five leading political parties – the *multipartidaria* – that had come together in 1981 for the purpose of rejecting the military's timid offer of political dialogue (Smith, 1989: 255).

In the case of Chile, the backbone of the political system was "formed by the interlocking of base-level social organizations with the political party structure, both in tension with the state as the focal point for political action" (Garretón, 1989: xvi, 13). Programmatic parties with strong identities distributed across a wide ideological spectrum long competed ferociously for constituent loyalties on the basis of their issue of ideological platforms.[19] In Chile the parties, not the state, organized societal groups

17 Paradoxically, in retrospect, O'Donnell (1973) had once believed the "threat" in Argentina to be less grave than in Brazil, perhaps because Argentine labor did not oppose the coup.
18 I have borrowed the inducements–constraints dichotomy from Collier and Collier (1979).
19 There was some clientelism in local politics (Valenzuela, 1977) and in the administration of

and unions and they even helped to structure people's friendships and social lives (Valenzuela, 1989: 169). Intense and frenetic party competition led to the election of a Marxist president in 1970, opened a genuine contest for state power, and drove the political system headlong into class warfare.

When the Chilean military came to power, it zealously set out to fulfill its promise to excise the "Marxist cancer" from the farms, factories, and body politic. Its ambitions for reforming Chilean politics, however, extended far beyond eliminating its enemies. Hoping to diminish the roles of the political parties as the central organizers of political life and monopolizers of political representation,[20] the regime directed its most severe repression against the parties – their leaders, organizations, institutional arenas of operation, and web of relationships with social movements and individual constituents. The regime closed Congress, banned elected local governments, and disallowed all party and political activity (A. Valenzuela and J. S. Valenzuela, 1986: 185). Even elections within private organizations and associations were circumscribed or monitored by the authorities (Valenzuela, 1989: 159). Such drastic action was taken to reorient the entire basis for political association in a society targeted for a monumental cultural change. To root out every last vestige of socialism, and even any future potential for its resurrection, the Pinochet regime privatized state corporations and social services alike (Garretón, 1989; Remmer, 1989). To give time for its program to produce the desired changes in Chilean society, the military doggedly clung to its political course with near religious fervor, even amid financial collapse, a deep recession that caused real unemployment rates to soar to 30 percent, and an eruption of societal protest in 1983. Even after adjusting its economic model, it found itself without adequate popular support to survive a plebiscite held in 1988, just as it was extolled outside Chile for its economic wisdom and competence.

Ultimately, whether consciously and by design (as in Brazil and Uruguay), or to their chagrin (as in Chile and Argentina), the bureaucratic-authoritarian regimes eventually handed power to the party and social leaders whom they had once scorned. But, as Garretón (1989: 108) has argued, the failure of the historical projects of these military regimes "does not mean that the societies involved have not suffered changes and transformations. Nor does the transition toward democratic regimes imply that there is nothing new under the sun or that everything picks up where it left

agrarian reform (Kaufman, 1973), but it was submerged in national politics to the ideological competition of the parties.

20 Influenced by the "gremialista" philosophy of the regime's leading political strategist, Jaime Guzmán, the military regime believed that intermediate organizations such as neighborhood associations, labor unions, and business and professional associations had been politicized by their close association with political parties. In their view, party politicization had aroused these entities to exceed their specific and proper representational roles and, ultimately, contributed to the destabilization of democracy.

off before the dictatorship." The degree and nature of political system change that resulted from these regimes followed from the amount of political space these regimes left open, and which state–society networks were allowed to operate in those spaces.

REGIME STRATEGIES AND STATE – SOCIETY RELATIONS

The strategies of authoritarian regimes had an important impact on existing networks of state–society mediation. In some cases the effects of regime policies were intended, but in others the economic policies and political programs of military regimes ofter produced unanticipated effects that complicated their larger economic and political objectives. Below, the effects of military regime economic policies and regime strategies on different channels of state–society mediation are compared in different national contexts.

Authoritarianism and clientelism

The economic model pursued by the Brazilian military – above all, the expansion of the state's roles in production, regulation, and distribution – bolstered a form of clientelism channeled through the state and provided a new basis for traditional domination and the power of traditional oligarchies, namely, control of an economically interventionist state. This effect was especially pronounced in Minas Gerais, where state and foreign-led industrialization defied the customary social scientific expectation that in the course of industrialization, new industrial classes (bourgeois, middle class, and workers) will arise and put forth a democratic political project, and peasant laborers – offered the opportunity to leave the land and become urban, industrial workers – will escape their dependence on their former landlords, leading to either the outright disappearance of traditional elites as a political force or to their demotion to the status of lords of remote corners of backward regions. Agrarian classes did shrink in numbers and in political significance with the shift of national resources from agriculture into industry. Industrial classes, however, did not effect large-scale political change. The capital-poor bourgeoisie ceded the dynamic sector of the economy to foreign capital and the state, to whom it pledged economic and political allegiance. The proletariat, organized into corporatist networks, was easily repressed in the early years of military rule. To the extent that the organization of the working class improved in the 1970s and it became more independent of the state, particularly where it was geographically concentrated, its unions turned inward, to shop-floor concerns and to winning various labor rights. In the 1990s with eighteen million members unions have become more powerful than ever before, but the greatest electoral success of the PT in the 1989 presidential election was primarily not a conscious labor vote for a socialist platform but a protest lodged against the political establishment.

As a result of the ever larger economic burdens shouldered by the state during Brazil's transition from a largely agrarian to an industrial society, political clientelism, which had been used by traditional elites to deliver votes in the Old Republic and to survive the explosion in political participation accompanying the transition to democracy after World War II, was transformed from a fundamentally private affair between lords and peasants into a state-based system and, as a result, became more ubiquitous. The state sector provided permanent and temporary employment, basic sanitation and shelter, transfer payments, and credit to the growing number of semiurban, nonindustrial laborers, seasonal agricultural laborers, unskilled workers, and lower-middle- and lower-class service sector employees. For these state dependents who were not represented functionally through unions and other corporate groups, economic integration into the public economy structured interest representation along the same territorial lines by which state resources were distributed.

With state-led capitalist development in Minas Gerais augmenting the number of state clients, traditional elites who had earlier shifted their power base from land to the state were ideally placed to use positions of public power to preserve their dominance. The enrichment of the public sector enhanced the political value of occupying federal and state cabinet and other top administrative posts, and hence enhanced the power of the traditional oligarchy. Even during an authoritarian regime that excluded the vast majority of the population from participation in political life and economic gain, administering state patronage allowed the regional oligarchies and traditional local elites to win electoral victories in not only small cities and rural areas where they might be expected to poll well but also in many midsized cities experiencing rapid urban and industrial growth where they might not. With material resources concentrated in the public sphere, controlling the state and its distributional apparatus was as important a source of political dominance as land ownership in an agrarian economy.

The beneficial effects of the economic model for the traditional political elite were reinforced by the political strategy of the Brazilian military to permit contested elections in an authoritarian political system. Measures that sharply reduced political competition such as the military's monopoly of the national executive, the creation of a two-party system with a dominant proregime party, and the appointment of governors insulated the Brazilian traditional political elite from the punishment typically suffered by incumbents when they are unable to distribute enough resources to enough clients in a state patronage-based political system – being voted out of office (a fate that befell the Colorados in Uruguay in 1958). The traditional political elite was also sheltered from intraparty competition by virtue of its role in organizing and managing the official party, a position that enabled it to regulate the entrance of new contestants into the political arena. Across Brazil, the effects of authoritarianism and clientelism were mutually reinforcing: each separately would have been insufficient to guarantee political continuity.

Clientelism and a blunted authoritarianism were also the essence of the most stable political system in Latin America over a period of fifty years – the Mexican. In Mexico, as was true in Brazil during military rule, traditional politics is pervasive at the subnational levels of the political system, and a "soft" authoritarianism permits elections in which a governing party is guaranteed national and most state election victories. Yet, clientelism and authoritarianism in Brazil may have more effectively protected and better served the political elite than they have in Mexico, despite the greater degree of regime stability achieved by Mexico's governing Institutional Revolutionary Party (PRI).

The postrevolutionary Mexican political elite has exhibited considerably more permeability and suffered more turnover in its ranks than the Brazilian (Smith, 1979). In contrast to the territorially well-integrated system of political clientelism in Brazil, which, under military-authoritarian rule, precluded the possibilibty of rival factions coming to national or even state executive power, the Mexican system was "disarticulated." This permitted more fluidity. Purcell (1981: 200) aptly identified two clientelistic systems operating in Mexico, one, a "chain of vertical, personalistic ties that originate in the presidency," and the other, a basically stable "network of patron–client relationships that are manipulated by *caciques* [local bosses] with as yet relatively autonomous local power bases." Due to the prohibition against the reelection of the president and the changes in executive leadership every six years (which given the power of appointment in a one-party system means a massive shift in personnel in the entire system), this national-level system is unstable, and political loyalty to tomorrow's "outs" tentative. This feature has produced what Purcell (1981: 205) has characterized as an "extreme degree" of elite mobility, and a political system that can be conceptualized as "a rigid-looking authoritarian facade that overlays a hyperfluid clientelist interior composed of multistatus elites who are in perpetual motion."

Recent events in Mexico confirm that the central Mexican state enjoys more control over regional and local-level traditional elites than the Brazilian. The national antipoverty program known as PRONASOL (National Solidarity Program), which is under the direct supervision of the president of the republic, has strengthened the centralized clientelistic system at the expense of the regionally operated ones.[21] The Mexican

21 During the administration of President Carlos Salinas (1989–94), PRONASOL officials, perhaps with the participation of Salinas himself, decided the pattern of allocations, and they clashed with local PRI officials on numerous occasions in Oaxaca, Yucatán, and other states (Dresser, 1994: 157).

authoritarian regime has been able to do what the Brazilian military could not: promote a new structure of state clientelism and circumvent traditional local politicians.

In Uruguay a more repressive form of bureaucratic-authoritarian rule than that evidenced in Brazil was also imposed on a political system dominated by clientelism. But despite a roughly similar configuration of clientelism and authoritarianism, the impact of different authoritarian economic policies and political strategies on existing state–society relations played a major role in producing differential rates of elite turnover, and perhaps even different prospects for the survival of clientelism, in Uruguay and Brazil.

The policies of the Uruguayan authoritarian regime most probably undermined, rather than reinforced, the clientelistic nature of politics. In Brazil, the networks that bridged state and society remained open for business as usual, especially but not exclusively at election time. "Modified competition" enabled the traditional political elite to expand its influence at lower levels of the political system, which in turn made clientelism stronger even while unions and other civil organizations were also growing stronger. The full closure of the political and electoral arenas by the authoritarian regime in Uruguay, by contrast, left dormant clientelistic networks of mediation.

Unlike the Brazilian elite, which was able to sustain and then even expand its patronage operations with military support during authoritarian rule, the Uruguayan political elite was cut off from its sources of patronage during the military dictatorship. In Uruguay's cities, electoral machines ground to a halt; "without a raison d'être, they had no money or headquarters" (Gillespie, 1991: 62). Uruguayan party elites also suffered compared with their Brazilian counterparts in that their clientelistic networks were also starved of economic resources: although state expenditure grew by 3 percent per year, some limited privatization did take place and the public budget deficit was cut (Remmer, 1989: 175–76). As a result, many members of the old political elite in Uruguay were not rehabilitated after being held in "suspended animation." Elite turnover rates in the 1984 elections, the first to be held since 1971, were much higher in Uruguay than in Brazil: one-third of the Senate (ten of thirty), and 70 percent of (ninety-nine) deputies elected in 1984 had no prior parliamentary experience (Rial, 1986: 257). These rates do not vary by party nor within party by ideological faction: overall, 60 percent of the Blancos, 69 percent of the Colorados, and 70 percent of the Frente Amplio's legislators had not before served in the legislature. Rial (1986: 257–58) had little doubt that the displaced politicians were the old clientelistic leaders, especially from the provinces. With "many of the old *caudillos* no longer on the scene" and "the emergence of new political actors," he predicted that a strongly rejuvenated political class would be "less prone to clientelistic politics, even in the provinces," and that "although these new politicos might want to use the old methods, they will encounter severe limitations on the practice of traditional politics." In subsequent elections, the two coalitions of leftist parties – the Frente Amplio and the Nuevo Espacio – improved their electoral performance at the expense of the traditional parties, as we shall see.

In sum, clientelism is not a self-perpetuating form of state–society mediation that confers a permanent advantage on incumbents. Rather, the survival of clientelism and state incumbents in a clientelistic system depends on the economic and political strategies of a particular regime or government. Regime support for clientelism permitted traditional politics and politicians to adapt to change in Brazil. In Mexico, clientelism served to uphold the system, but not necessarily incumbents. In Uruguay, the disruption of patronage weakened the state clientelistic system, the political parties that distributed it, and the traditional elites who practiced it.

Authoritarianism and corporatism

Bureaucratic-authoritarian regimes displayed none of the ambivalence toward corporatism as a network of mediation that they did toward clientelism. Where labor was organized by the state along functional lines and linked to the state through corporatist channels, these regimes ceased to treat corporatism as a framework through which to negotiate with labor and instead turned it into a weapon with which to repress and demobilize the working class. In both Brazil and Argentina, where states spurned these historic forms of mediation, a dramatic change in the relationship between the state and the labor movement followed from state efforts to dismantle populism and deny labor leaders access to centers of state power. In Mexico, where this relationship was preserved by successive administrations in an authoritarian regime, corporatism survived even despite substantial economic liberalization.

In Brazil the essential ingredient of paternalistic co-optation that had kept labor leaders and rank-and-file unionists within the state corporatist fold was withdrawn and the illusion of state benevolence shattered by a regime that stole wages from labor by manipulating the inflation index to which wage and salary adjustments were pegged. As Keck (1989: 256–59) describes it, the "new unionism" was born when and because the form of union mobilization and organization that had previously won benefits for labor was no longer tenable. When the state turned its back on labor, labor leaders looked to the shop floor to build new bases of strength on the foundation of their relationship with their rank and file. When civilian democracy was reestablished, several large unions chose to break their links with the state rather than try to patch together the party-state-union coalition of the 1945–64 period (Campello de Souza, 1989: 380). Since the transition to democracy, the confederation of labor unions that most forcefully advocated the "new unionism," the CUT (Central Unica dos Trabalhadores), as well as the less militant Força Sindical, which also favors direct collective bargaining and shuns alliances with political parties and state bureaucrats, has grown stronger at the expense of the CGT (Central Geral dos Trabalhadores), the central union organization that attempted in vain in the 1980s to revive precoup forms of corporatist mediation.[22]

A similar split within the labor movement and the severance of state control over a new union movement took place during the first bureaucratic-authoritarian regime (1966–73) in Argentina. When the Onganía administration attempted to elicit labor support while retracting bread-and-butter rewards, the General Confederation of Labor (CGT) divided over the issue of what its appropriate relationship to the state should be. The new breakaway CGT de los Argentinos, which like the Brazilian new unionism was attentive to rank-and-file interests and unafraid of union democracy, adopted a more militant stance toward negotiation with both the state and employers than had been seen in Argentina since Perón reined in the union movement decades earlier. Responding to labor's exclusion from meaningful participation with the state, this group advocated political autonomy from and noncooperation with the military government even at the expense of abdicating labor's "privileged" position within the state. The smaller CGT de Azopardo, headed by the veteran Peronist leader Augusto Vandor, attempted instead to put the shattered Peronist state–labor coalition back together again. That this strategy was doomed by the regime's intention to harden the state's role in corporatist mediation was soon made manifest by worker protest in Córdoba in May 1969. After the *cordobazo,* "the state was truly 'floating' above social and class forces, but this autonomy betrayed not strength but profound weakness" (Smith, 1989: 185).

If the return of Juan Perón to Argentina in 1973 might have rescued the faltering corporatist system, his death and Argentina's relapse into mass praetorianism doomed such a salvage effort. The hard-line military regime that seized power in Argentina in 1976 made no effort to resuscitate corporatism and win labor support. To the contrary, state-sponsored murder completed the decapitation of the labor movement that the junta's economic policies had begun. After the transition to a civilian democracy, the Argentine state had so lost control of the unions that the Radical govern-

---

22 There is abundant evidence that corporatism in Brazil has eroded. In 1990, 70 percent of more than 28,000 collective bargaining processes initiated by urban, rural, and professional workers' unions were settled directly, either at the firm level or with employers' associations. More than half of all unions, moreover, reported that the state-collected union tax represented less than 20 percent of their total revenues, and only 7 percent that it represented more than 80 percent of their finances. Union members are also more active today than in the past. Also in 1990, 41 percent of all unions in Brazil, and 63 percent of urban unions, reported that between 80 and 100 percent of their members had paid dues (IBGE, 1993: 2–252).

ment of Raul Alfonsín shunned corporatist networks of mediation in the design and implementation of the Austral Plan for economic stabilization (De Riz, Cavarozzi, and Feldman, 1987). While a Radical president was not the most likely to woo and win the hand of labor, state-labor corporatist mediation has not been restored during the two governments of the Peronist Carlos Menem as it was. Rather, although Menem has consulted with labor leaders in pursuing economic reforms that include a pared-down role for the state in the regulation of labor markets, he has also split the labor union movement that helped to elect him in 1989. In perhaps the ultimate irony, a Peronist president is systematically dismantling the system of political representation that Perón erected five decades ago.

In contrast to Brazil and Argentina, corporatism in Mexico as a channel of state–society mediation was fully operative throughout the life of an authoritarian regime whose political strategy remained inclusionary, and it perseveres. In the late 1980s and early 1990s, the Mexican state used its open channels of communication with labor leaders to negotiate successfully over a period of several years an "economic solidarity pact" governing a range of economic issues crucial to its program of economic restructuring, including the minimum wage, public sector prices, and public finances (Whitehead, 1989; Zapata, 1994). The leadership of the Confederation of Mexican Workers conceded changes in the nature of work, compensation, and factory-level worker participation in order to resist reforming the federal labor law and maintain its monopoly of representation (Zapata, 1994: 2–5). While there are indications that the corporatist network uniting labor to the state is currently buckling under the weight of the economic adjustment required by the 1994–95 plunge of the peso, it is also most certainly the case that the life of the corporatist system has been prolonged by its central role in mediating state–labor relations.

Authoritarianism and parties

The ability of regimes with transformative ambitions to tamper with political parties varied according to the nature of the parties' appeals (individual-clientelistic or collective ideological), their relationship to the state and to their constituents under authoritarianism, and their relation to each other. Economic policies that sharply reduced the size of the unionized working class had a potentially greater effect on class-based labor and socialist parties than on multiclass parties that sustained their constituencies through state patronage. Clientelistic parties, in turn, were dependent for survival on whether the economic models of authoritarian regimes allowed them to commit resources to patronage operations and whether their political strategies created the incentive for them to do so. The electoral stock of particular parties rose and fell as a function of their relationships to military regimes, while all parties whose contact with their constituents and militants was through networks of mediation operating outside the state apparatus were weakened when those networks were severed by authoritarian decree.

As an outgrowth of the political strategy of the Brazilian military regime to sponsor controlled political competition, Brazil's party system suffered significant discontinuity. From the clientelistic PSD to the populist PTB, the parties that dominated the political landscape in the two decades following the restitution of democracy in 1945 did not survive two revisions of the party system. Yet, on the more significant question of the extent to which the parties have changed the manner in which they mobilize electoral support, compete with one another, and govern, the record is mixed. On the one hand, new parties such as the PT and PSDB are new in more than name only. The PT in particular is an outgrowth of the decline of corporatism and offers the model of a very different party-union-state relationship than did the PTB when it was the dominant labor party before 1964. There can be no question that the electoral advance of a genuine labor party with a coherent platform and disciplined congressional delegation marks a significant departure in Brazilian politics. Yet, on the other hand, parties remotely close to power continued to compete, mobilize supporters, and govern on the basis of state-sponsored clientelism during and after the authoritarian episode, and most parties then and now have been led at the national, state, and local levels by traditional political elites.[23]

In Argentina, where elections were strictly proscribed, repression harsh, and at least Peronist identities firm, perceptible changes took place in the parties during authoritarian rule. New leaders steered their parties in new directions and agreed to cooperate with one another. The Radical Civic Union (UCR) changed its internal organization perhaps more during authoritarian rule; Renovación y Cambio (Renewal and Change), a dissident movement within the party created during the first bureaucratic-authoritarian regime by Raul Alfonsín, used new methods of mobilization and a substantial modification in the traditional ideological focus of the UCR to reach out to new constituencies.[24] Party reform soon produced electoral realignment: in capturing the presidency in 1983, the Radicals won their first election in

23 The PDT, led by Leonel Brizola, constitutes an exception. It is neither a new-style, disciplined, and programmatic party nor one dominated by traditional politicians that competes and governs primarily along clientelistic lines. It is social-democratic in orientation, and although its leaders have resorted to using clientelism while in office (Weffort, 1989: 336), it is more accurately a populist party that relies on a heavy dose of personalism. Mainwaring (1995: 376) has placed it, along with the PSDB and two smaller parties, in an intermediate category between the parties he calls disciplined and programmatic (the PT, the Communist Party of Brazil [PCdoB], and the Popular Socialist Party [the successor of the Brazilian Communist Party]), and the loosely organized parties with weak programmatic commitments (virtually all the rest).

24 Palermo (1986: 50) has shown that more "authoritarian" means of promoting local leaders took place in the local assemblies of the Justicialista Party in Buenos Aires in 1983 than in those of the Radicals.

which a Peronist candidate was allowed to run (Cavarozzi, 1986; Mora y Araújo, 1986). In subsequent elections the UCR has seen its vote totals slide steadily in favor of a Justicialista Party that has radically reformulated its programmatic basis, as well as new electoral alternatives on the left.[25]

In Uruguay the traditional political parties reemerged after their "recess" for the reasons typically identified by students of electoral change: (1) their long duration and "solid roots" in society that made them the symbols of the "good times" of Uruguay's past prosperity, democracy, and social welfare, a powerful, appealing contrast to economic stagnation and dark authoritarianism; and (2) their freedom from competition – the military regime suspended the activity of all parties but named the traditional parties as its successors (Rial, 1989: 259–63). Rial (1989: 269) has observed that when the Uruguayan parties reemerged in 1980, however, they did so as coteries of notables without party organizations. His observation is supported by Gillespie's research (1991: 64); only 13 percent of the Blanco and 37 percent of the Colorado politicians that Gillespie interviewed had contacts with leaders of other party tickets under authoritarianism, and only 19 and 17 percent, respectively, with new activists. The traditional parties were also weakened by their inability to distribute patronage resources during military rule. Soon after the 1984 elections, in which the traditional parties garnered shares of the vote similar to their pre-1973 totals, the party system evidenced deeper change. In 1989 in only the second election held after the transfer of power to civilians, the parties of the left – those in the Frente Amplio and the Nuevo Espacio coalitions – raised their share of the vote from 18 percent in 1984 (and 1971) to 30 percent. These parties benefited from their relationship with their constituents under military rule. According to Gillespie (1991: 64), they enjoyed more contacts with civil society during authoritarian rule than did the other parties. Fifty percent of Frente Amplio politicians interviewed by Gillespie had had "frequent" contacts during the dictatorship with students and Christians, 38 percent with human rights organizations and trade unionists, and 25 percent with exiles. Blanco and Colorado politicians had more frequent contact with journalists (56 and 53 percent, respectively), but substantially fewer with the other associations of civil society.[26] Parties of the left also improved their position during the regime transition, as we shall see.

In Chile exceptionally strong parties that historically sustained themselves not by access to state resources but by the appeal of their world view to their

---

25 The center-left Frente Grande won a 38 percent plurality of the vote in the Federal Capital in 1994. In the 1995 presidential election, the Radicals won but 15 percent of the vote nationwide.

26 Only 27 percent of Blanco politicians had contacts with student groups, 21 percent with Christian groups and human rights organizations, and 7 percent with trade unions, exiles, and business associations. Fifty-three percent of Colorado politicians had contacts with students, but only 11 percent with Christian groups, human rights organizations, and trade unions (Gillespie, 1991: 64).

constituents were able to survive underground, separated from the state and in the absence of elections. But even the current Chilean party system bears the stamp of military economic policies and the military's blueprint for the posttransition political order. Parties of the left must replace constituencies lost to economic liberalization and social modernization, while those on the right stand to gain in the long run from the proliferation of independent merchants and the transformation of peasants into prosperous farmers. The party system has also been changed by the relationship of parties to the authoritarian regime. The military's rebuke of the Christian Democrats who had supported their coup forged a powerful opposition alliance between Chile's largest party and the left, an alliance that today has a firm grip on government. The electoral prospects of the right – divided between the National Renovation (RN), which sees itself as a loyal, conservative opposition, and the Union of Independent Democrats (UDI), which favors a continuation of the course set for Chile by Pinochet – were diminished by the public's association of these parties with an unpopular dictatorship. The "left," "center," and "right" blocs of parties still seem to command roughly a third of the electorate each, but two of the new parties to emerge on the Chilean political landscape, the centrist UCC (Unión del Centro Centro) and the UDI, together accounted for one-fifth of the vote in the municipal elections of 1992.

It is, moreover, possible to detect fundamental changes in Chilean political culture and particularly in the political parties that are the result of Pinochet's economic and political strategies, which pushed representative relations in new directions. Parties across the political spectrum are more internally democratic; most now directly elect their leaders, their central committees meet more often, and local branches have more say in the nomination of party candidates for Congress and municipal council. They are also more generally willing to concede autonomy to social organizations led by party militants, in part because social movements that learned to operate independently of political party initiatives when parties were banned during the dictatorship did not readily relinquish their independence when parties were reborn. Party identification is weaker than in the past, individual membership is comparable with or lower than in the pre-1973 period as a percentage of the electorate, and Chilean society shows signs of effective depoliticization.[27] The profound economic transformation that was the signature of the Chilean military regime has also set in motion

---

27 From 1969 to 1973 the Christian Democratic Party, for example, had approximately 100,000 militants and 1,000,000 voters, or ten electors for every militant. In 1989 the party had 40,000 militants to 2.2 million voters, or a ratio of 55 electors for every militant (Arriagada Herrera, n.d.). Moreover, in a poll conducted in 1992 in greater Santiago, 48 percent of respondents said they had "little interest" in the municipal election campaign, and 29 percent expressed "no interest" (Centro de Estudios de la Realidad Contemporanea, 1992: 5).

the ideological renewal of many of Chile's parties. The party that has traveled the farthest ideological distance is the Socialist Party, which has begun to realign party principles and programs to conform to the legacy of an open if deindustrialized economy.

Thus the economic policies and military strategies of military regimes exercised variable but significant effects on representative politics in the former bureaucratic-authoritarian regimes. Different conceptions of the state's role in the economy and different strategies of the Uruguayan and Brazilian militaries for marshaling support for military rule weakenend clientelism in Uruguay but enshrined it in Brazil as a semipermanent feature of the political landscape. Both the Argentine and Brazilian militaries sealed off the corporatist links joining state and society, and in both cases strained and perhaps snapped labor–state and business–state relations as well as the networks of corporatist intermediation that had been in place for nearly five decades. Such a result was not inevitable, as the Mexican case shows. Beneath the veneer of party system change and continuity, party-mediated networks of representation have changed more in those countries in which party identities were strong but parties were recessed during authoritarianism – Chile and, to a lesser extent, Uruguay – than in Brazil, where parties were weak and not well institutionalized but where they were allowed to operate.

Just as military policies directly threatened or dismantled some networks of interest mediation, moreover, they also indirectly privileged or undermined others based on the way their actions affected secondary options for political representation. In Argentina the decline of corporatism strengthened the hands of parties that had always been less important instruments of representation than business and labor organizations, whereas in Brazil both clientelistic parties and the PT benefited from the state's neglect of its corporatist constituencies. In Uruguay clientelistic parties, deprived of resources to distribute, declined, to the clear advantage of the nonclientelistic parties of the left. In Chile, where there was no practical alternative to parties for the intermediation of interests, parties were not replaced but their roles in society and government have noticeably diminished.

REGIME CHANGE AND DEMOCRACY

If the legacies of premilitary and military regimes weigh heavily on posttransition political systems, then the extent to which each of these shape the democratic political terrain may be influenced by the nature of the process of transition from authoritarian rule. The transition process serves most probably to reinforce the positions of various actors and institutions coming out of the authoritarian period, but it can also conceivably weaken them.

The ability of military regime supporters and premilitary, nondemocratic actors to design political institutions and procedures to their advantage is greater when they actively participate in the transition from authoritarian rule than when such a regime change takes place without or in opposition to them. In Brazil civilians who participated in the military government and mobilized support for it gained in strength during authoritarian rule. Because the traditional political elite was strong and most of its members were sufficiently prescient to jump on the democratization bandwagon in time to avoid being tarred with the authoritarian tag, it was able to play a leading role in a regime transition demanded by the masses of Brazil in the most significant public demonstrations in the country's history. Those who participated earned democratic credentials with a population weary of authoritarianism; as a result, they were allowed to retain top state and party posts and, in effect, to escape punishment for having long supported the repressive forces of an authoritarian regime.[28]

At the opposite end of the spectrum, in Argentina, authoritarian forces were defeated dramatically in war, and the democratic government that followed authoritarian rule put top generals on trial. By refusing to compromise and open the door to political notables until the very end, the old regime pushed away virtually all potential allies, except a handful of Peronists, and forfeited influence in the new.

In Uruguay and Chile, the outgoing militaries were able to bargain with their democratic opposition. Uruguay's transition to democracy was one of the few in Latin America to be based on an explicit agreement between the military and sections of the opposition – the Colorados and the Frente Amplio – rather than on uniting the opposition against the military (Gillespie, 1991: 159). The National Party (the Blancos) followed the more intransigent strategy of its leading presidential candidate, Wilson Ferreira, of not participating in the Naval Club Pact, which eventually provided the framework for a return to democracy. The strategy of the Blancos was not unconstrained by authoritarian politics: with limited links to social movements, the party had less leverage to force the military to capitulate (Gillespie, 1991: 135).

The Uruguayan military, defeated in a 1980 plebiscite, negotiated from a position of less strength than the Brazilian military but certainly more than its disgraced Argentine counterparts. Stepan's (1985: 328–29) interviews with members of the political secretariat of the Uruguayan armed forces revealed that the military did not feel under great pressure from civil society to withdraw from power, and that in the absence of impelling societal or corporate reasons to withdraw, it prepared a rather elaborate agenda of "participatory prerogatives" for the armed forces in any future democracy.

28 Many of those who remained in the military camp lost their legislative seats in the 1986 elections.

By following the lead of the army commander, General Hugo Medina, it secured, most importantly, immunity from prosecution for human rights abuses and, second, the electoral proscription of the Blanco politician Wilson Ferreira. The Colorados and the Frente Amplio each gained from their participation in the negotiations over regime transition. The Colorados won the presidency, but arguably, the left gained more. First, those parties that joined in the Naval Club Pact won legalization. Second, by reaching agreements with other parties in 1985, the left for the first time won allotted seats on the boards of directors of some industrial and commercial state enterprises, and it won back much of its former influence in the nation's largely state-run educational system (Gillespie, 1991: 230). Finally, it achieved an electoral breakthrough in 1989 when it gained control of the city hall of Montevideo.

In Chile, the military under the leadership of outgoing president General Augusto Pinochet retained considerably more prerogatives than its Argentine and Uruguayan counterparts. From his unassailable position as head of the army, Pinochet constrained the new democracy with such affronts as bionic senators. Yet despite the similar strong participation of the outgoing militaries, the outcome of the Chilean transition was less conservative than the Brazilian. By shunning *all* parties during authoritarian rule, the Chilean military gave occasion for most to join a single "Command for the No" to contest the 1988 plebiscite and, eventually, for sixteen to form the Concertación of Parties for Democracy that has governed Chile since 1990.

If the transition process generally serves to reinforce the trends toward renewing or dismantling prevailing networks of political representation that were set in motion during authoritarian rule, the question remains open of whether patterns of politics established now will become semipermanent features of the political landscape. On the one hand, in moments of transition and convulsion there may arise unique opportunities to discard the constraints of the organizational forms inherited from previous regimes, and political arrangements, once in place, may condition future political behavior and possibilities. On the other hand, it is not apparent why a system whose antidemocratic practices are not constitutionally bound cannot change. Clientelism is not a political right, and there are no structural obstacles to the formation of new, ideological parties. The prosperity of the PT in Brazil serves as an eloquent example of this possibility. The early indications, however, are that the regime sowed by political compromise with traditional political elites lacks channels of genuine democratic representation and is severely constrained by the power of those traditional politicians. If change is not impossible, many old practices have been written onto the system – some reinforced structurally, others not, and both types serve as major impediments to an extension of democracy at all levels of the political system.

THE FUTURE OF TRADITIONAL POLITICS IN BRAZIL

I have argued that though Brazil has experienced a transition to democracy, elite continuity threatens that democracy. But should it matter for democratization if traditional politicians are found in positions of power in the state and dominant parties if the rules of the game have changed? If "democratization," is understood as the road to a political system in which, in the Schumpeterian tradition, "its most powerful collective decision makers are selected through fair, honest, and periodic elections in which candidates freely compete for votes and in which virtually all the adult population is eligible to vote" (Huntington, 1991: 7), then perhaps it makes little or no difference. Arbitrary military abuses of human rights have been curbed, political rights restored to political "undesirables," censorship lifted, illiterates enfranchised, and direct elections resumed for state and national executive posts. The right to political expression is real. A Constituent Assembly elected after the retreat of the military constitutionally protected the right to strike and other interests of labor to a degree unprecedented in Brazilian history. The loosening of the electorate from the grip of old party bosses and the opportunity to cast votes of protest were made manifest in the groundswell of discontent that nearly elected the former union leader Luis Inácio da Silva to the presidency on the ticket of the Workers' Party in December 1989.

But if democracy is held to be something more than the institutions that limit state power and hold those who govern accountable to the governed, what Friedrich (1941) called "constitutionalism," and is understood instead in terms of the distribution of political power, the residual power of the traditional elite can be very consequential indeed. In Brazil today, political parties, local governments, the executive–legislative relationship, electoral codes, and modes of interest association and representation, even if not formally "authoritarian," are not like corresponding institutions and arrangements in a democratic polity that permit the fulfillment of Dahl's (1971: 1–2) requirements for a "polyarchy": that citizens have "unimpaired opportunities to formulate their preferences, to signify their preferences to their fellow citizens and the government by individual and collective action, and to have their preferences weighed equally in the conduct of government." They are well suited to restricting mass political participation and the arena of decision making. Party positions on issues are sacrificed systematically to the particularistic calculations of a closed elite, and weak parties suit a restricted democracy. While strong executives, weak parties, and pervasive clientelism do not in and of themselves undermine democracy – many democracies in the world today exhibit one or more of these characteristics – Brazilian democracy is flawed by each of these to an extreme paralleled by few countries. When these three are combined as they are in Brazil, moreover, their perverse effects on democracy are multiplied.

The traditional political elite does face constant challenges. In particular, the veil of authoritarianism has been dropped and the model of state-led capitalist development that dominated the Brazilian landscape for four decades and helped to preserve traditional politics during the dictatorship is exhausted. If state intervention in the economy structured representative politics, the relationship of industrial classes to the state, and political party identities, then the retreat of the state and a new pattern of economic development might be expected to trigger a realignment of political forces and recast state–society relations. Such an expectation has not been borne out, however, either in Brazil or in Mexico. Clientelism has actually proved to be a useful tool to state reformers in gaining the support of general electors in both countries and of key politicians as well in Brazil in scaling back the size of the state and the scope of its intervention in economic life (cf. Cornelius, Craig, and Fox, 1994). It may have strengthened the traditional political elite enough to resist the efforts of Fernando Henrique Cardoso, arguably the keenest analyst of Brazilian politics over the past quarter century and fully aware of the threat to representative democracy posed by the persistence of the traditional political elite and the clientelistic politics that it perpetuates, to reform the state and reduce the scope for the clientelism that has contaminated representative politics and government.

However doomed the old regime may appear, a century of traditional elite dominance should convince scholars and activists that the mere opportunity to loosen the stranglehold of this class on the Brazilian political system will not in itself bring about democracy. To democratize, Brazil must actively replace decaying channels of state–society mediation, not with corporatist ones headed by state autocrats or clientelistic ones headed by traditional political elites, but by more genuinely democratic ones. Developing democratic alternatives for political representation need not entail weakening the state, but merely that some political organization takes place outside its tentacles. Above all, political parties must be made more representative of and responsive to their constituents. Despite the obstacles, the opportunity to build a democracy in Brazil is perhaps greater than at any time in the nation's past. Although it may take some time for open political competition to create choice and encourage local opposition to form in the cities and the countryside, and eventually, for challengers to unseat incumbent cliques in the states and even in the federal government, formal democracy guarantees that what the political class in Brazil has long resisted may yet come to pass: the transformation and democratization of Brazilian politics.

Appendix: The Minas elite

The study of elites in Minas Gerais that forms a cornerstone of this study included all cabinet-rank positions except military portfolios. While the analysis attempts to consider the implications for traditional political elite persistence of the loss of the state security apparatus (the Department of Public Security) from 1970 to 1985, the social origins and career patterns of members of the military elite per se were not analyzed. Other executive positions in the state judged powerful were presidencies of state banks and the mayor of Belo Horizonte. In the federal arena, Mineiros who occupied national cabinet and bank positions were included in the study. Listed here are the posts included in the analysis.

State office

Governor
Lieutenant governor
Secretary of the interior and justice
Secretary of finance
Secretary of agriculture, industry, commerce, and labor (1956–63)
Secretary of agriculture (1963–82)
Secretary of education
Secretary of public works
Secretary of health
Secretary of public security (1956–70)
Secretary of administration (1963–82)
Secretary of government (1963–82)
Secretary of planning (1970–82)
Secretary of industry, commerce, and tourism (1972–82)
Secretary of economic development (1964–66)
Secretary of science and technology (1977–82)
Secretary of labor (1963–82)
Secretary of social action affairs (1964–66)
Secretary of rural credit and supply affairs (1964–66)
President, State Development Bank
President, Banco de Crédito Real
President, Caixa Ecônomica do Estado de Minas Gerais

President, Banco Mineiro da Produção (1956–67)
President, Banco Hipotecário e Agrícola do Estado de Minas Gerais (1956–67)
President, Banco do Estado de Minas Gerais (1967–82)
President, State Legislative Assembly
Mayor, Belo Horizonte

National office

President
Vice-president
Head, president's civil cabinet
Prime minister (1961–62)
Minister of justice
Minister of foreign relations
Minister of finance
Minister of transportation
Minister of agriculture
Minister of education and culture
Minister of labor and social security
Minister of health
Minister of mines and energy
Minister of industry and commerce
Minister of planning and general coordination
Minister of the interior
Minister of communications
President, Bank of Brazil
President, National Economic and Social Development Bank
President, Chamber of Deputies
President, Senate

No minimum was placed on the length of time an officeholder occupied a cabinet post; discrepancies in length of tenure were compensated for in the analysis by calculating the time (measured in months) that a post belonged to one or the other elite group. This procedure tends to overstate the displacement of political elites because, by Brazilian electoral law, public officials wishing to contest elective office must resign their posts several months before general elections to retain their eligibility. Hence, many politicians are replaced in the final months of a governor's term with administrators who do not intend to seek election.

Much of the data on which this study is based derives from the archives of the Centro de Estudos Mineiros, a research facility connected with the Federal University of Minas Gerais. Its archives, in turn, draw from the records of the Arquivo Público de Minas Gerais, questionnaires completed by relatives and prominent informants from the subjects' hometowns, obituaries, personal interviews, the work of such historians as David Fleischer, and studies of congressional representatives conducted in the 1970s. I supplemented these data for officeholders in the state banking system and all recent officeholders from the departments and banks that these elites headed, newspaper and magazine accounts, and the curriculum vitaes of officeholders obtained from the state governor's staff.

Data were obtained about the vital statistics, civil status, descendants, occupations of parents and in-laws, secondary, university, and postgraduate education, occupations and work experience, relatives in politics, and local, state, and federal careers in executive, legislative, and party service. Also generally available were the records of descent from traditional families, landholding, elite posts held in other states, ambassadorships, unsuccessful candidacies, judicial posts held, foreign travel, publications, honors, and specialized information such as famous classmates, courses attended at the Superior War College, and inclusion as signatory of the *Manifesto dos Mineiros*.

References

Abranches, Sérgio Henrique (1977). "Empresa estatal e capitalismo: Uma análise comparada." Pp. 5–53 in Carlos Estevam Martins (ed.), *Estado e Capitalismo no Brasil*. São Paulo: HUCITEC-CEBRAP.

Alexander, Robert (1973). *Latin American Political Parties*. New York: Praeger.

Alvarez, Sonia E. (1990). *Engendering Democracy in Brazil: Women's Movements in Transition Politics*. Princeton, NJ: Princeton University Press.

Alves, Maria Helena Moreira (1985). *State and Opposition in Military Brazil*. Austin: University of Texas Press.

Ames, Barry (1973). *Rhetoric and Reality in a Militarized Regime: Brazil since 1964*. Beverly Hills, CA: Sage Publications.

(1987). *Political Survival: Politicians and Public Policy in Latin America*. Berkeley: University of California Press.

(1991). "Electoral Strategy and Legislative Politics in Brazil, 1978–1990." A progress report. Department of Political Science, Washington University, St. Louis.

(1994). "The Reverse Coattails Effect: Local Party Organization in the 1989 Brazilian Presidential Election." *American Political Science Review* 88, 1 (March): 95–111.

Anderson, Charles W. (1967). *Politics and Economic Change in Latin America: The Governing of Restless Nations*. Princeton, NJ: D. Van Nostrand.

Andrade, Francisco de Assis (1975). "Relação dos Chefes do Governo Mineiro e Seus Secretários, 1894 a 31 de dezembro de 1974." *Revista do Arquivo Público Mineiro* 26 (May): 7–62.

Andrade, Luis Aureliano Gama de (1980). "Technocracy and Development: The Case of Minas Gerais." Ph.D. diss., University of Michigan.

Andrade, Thompson A. (1980). "Industrialização e Incentivo Fiscal: Minas Gerais no Período 1970/1977." Instituto de Planejamento Econômico e Social (IPEA), No. 30 (October).

Araújo, Aloízio G. de Andrade (1980). "As Eleições Legislativas de 1978, II – As Eleições em Minas Gerais." *Revista Brasileira de Estudos Políticos* 51 (July): 37–70.

Araújo, Braz José de (1977). "Intervenção Econômica do Estado e Democracia." Pp. 221–39 in Carlos Estevam Martins (ed.), *Estado e Capitalismo no Brasil*. São Paulo: HUCITEC-CEBRAP.

Arriagada Herrera, Genaro (n.d.). "Carta a los militantes: La reforma del Estatuto del Partido."

Bacha, Edmar (1977). "Issues and Evidence on Recent Brazilian Economic Growth." *World Development* 5, 1–2: 47–67.

Baer, Werner, Richard Newfarmer, and Thomas Trebat (1976). "On State Capitalism in Brazil: Some New Issues and Questions." *Inter-American Economic Affairs* 30 (Winter): 69–96.

Baer, Werner, and Claudio Paiva (1994). "Brazil's Drifting Economy: Stagflation and Inflation during 1987–93." Paper prepared for the Conference "What Kind of Market? What Kind of Democracy?" McGill University, Montreal, Canada (April 6–8).

Banco de Desenvolvimento de Minas Gerais (BDMG) (1968). *Diagnóstico da Economia Mineira*, 6 volumes. Belo Horizonte: BDMG.

Banco Interamericano de Desarrollo (BID) (1984). *Progreso Económico y Social en América Latina*. Washington, DC: BID.

Barbosa, Julio (1964). "Minas Gerais." Pp. 171–204 in Themistocles Cavalcanti and Reisky Dubnic (eds.), *Comportamento Eleitoral no Brasil*. Rio de Janeiro: Fundação Getúlio Vargas.

Barros de Castro, Antonio, and Francisco Eduardo Pires de Souza (1985). *A Economia Brasileira em Marcha Forçada*. Rio de Janeiro: Paz e Terra.

Bastos, Tocary A. (with the assistance of Nilza da S. Rocha) (1964). "Análise das Eleições em 1962 em Minas Gerais." *Revista Brasileira de Estudos Políticos* 16 (January): 307–91.

Bastos, Tocary A., and Thomas W. Walker (1971). "Partidos e Forças Políticas em Minas Gerais." *Revista Brasileira de Estudos Políticos* 31 (May): 117–57.

Benevides, Maria Victoria de Mesquita (1981). *A UDN e o Udenismo: Ambigüidades do Liberalismo Brasileiro (1945–1965)*. Rio de Janeiro: Paz e Terra.

Berger, Suzanne, and Michael Piore (1980). *Dualism and Discontinuity in Industrial Societies*. Cambridge: Cambridge University Press.

Berry, R. Albert, and Mauricio Solaún (1980). "Notes toward an Interpretation of the National Front." Pp. 435–60 in R. Albert Berry, Ronald G. Hellman, and Mauricio Solaún (eds.), *Politics of Compromise: Coalition Government in Colombia*. New Brunswick, NJ: Transaction Books.

Boschi, Renato R. (ed.) (1983). *Movimentos Coletivas no Brasil Urbano*. Rio de Janeiro: Zahar/Instituto Universitário de Pesquisas do Rio de Janeiro (IUPERJ).

  (1987). "Social Movements and the New Political Order in Brazil." Pp. 179–212 in John D. Wirth, Edson de Oliveira Nunes, and Thomas E. Bogenschild (eds.), *State and Society in Brazil: Continuity and Change*. Boulder, CO: Westview Press.

Brazil (1981). *A Nova Constituição do Brasil*. Rio de Janeiro: Gráfica Auriverde.

  (1988). *A Constituição do Brasil*. Rio de Janeiro: Forense Universitária.

Bresser Pereira, Luiz Carlos (1978). *O Colapso de uma Aliança de Classes*. São Paulo: Brasiliense.

  (1984). *Development and Crisis in Brazil, 1930–1983*. Trans. Marcia Van Dyke. Boulder, CO: Westview Press.

Bruneau, Thomas C. (1982). *The Church in Brazil: The Politics of Religion*. Austin: University of Texas Press.

Câmara dos Deputados (1991). *Deputados Brasileiros, 49ª Legislatura, 1991–1995. Repertório Biográfico*. Brasília.

Cammack, Paul (1982). "Clientelism and Military Government in Brazil." Pp. 53–75 in Christopher Clapham (ed.), *Private Patronage and Public Power*. New York: St. Martin's Press.

Campello de Souza, Maria do Carmo (1976). *Estado e Partidos Políticos no Brasil (1930–1964)*. São Paulo: Editora Alfa-Omega, Ltda.

(1989). "The New Republic: Under the 'Sword of Damocles.' " Pp. 351–94 in Alfred Stepan (ed.), *Democratizing Brazil: Problems of Transition and Consolidation.* New York: Oxford University Press.

Campolina Diniz, Clélio (1978). "Estado e Capital Estrangeiro na Industrialização Mineira." Master's thesis, Universidade de Campinas.

Campos Coelho, Edmundo (1976). *Em Busca de Identidade: O Exército e a Política na Sociedade Brasileira.* Rio de Janeiro: Forense-Universitária.

Cardoso, Fernando Henrique (1965). "The Structure and Evolution of Industry in São Paulo: 1930–1960." *Studies in Comparative International Development* 1, 5: 43–47.

(1972). "Dependency and Development in Latin America." *New Left Review* 74 (July–August): 83–95.

(1973). "Associated-Dependent Development: Theoretical and Practical Implications." Pp. 142–76 in Alfred Stepan (ed.) *Authoritarian Brazil: Origins, Policies, and Future.* New Haven, CT: Yale University Press.

(1975). *Autoritarismo e Democratização.* Rio de Janeiro: Paz e Terra.

(1978). "Partidos e Deputados em São Paulo: O Voto e a Representação Política." Pp. 45–75 in Fernando Henrique Cardoso and Bolivar Lamounier (eds.), *Os Partidos e as Eleições no Brasil.* 2nd edition. Rio de Janeiro: Paz e Terra.

(1979). "On the Characterization of Authoritarian Regimes." Pp. 33–57 in David Collier (ed.), *The New Authoritarianism in Latin America.* Princeton, NJ: Princeton University Press.

(1985). "Opinião: O PMDB." *Folha de São Paulo* (February 19).

(1989). "Associated-Dependent Development and Democratic Theory." Pp. 299–326 in Alfred Stepan (ed.), *Democratizing Brazil: Problems of Transition and Consolidation.* New York: Oxford University Press.

Cardoso, Fernando Henrique, and Enzo Faletto (1979). *Dependency and Development in Latin America.* Trans. Marjorie Mattingly Urquidi. Berkeley: University of California Press.

Cardoso, Fernando Henrique, and Bolivar Lamounier (eds.) (1978). *Os Partidos e as Eleições no Brasil.* 2nd edition. Rio de Janeiro: Paz e Terra.

Cardoso, Ruth C. L. (1984). "Movimentos Sociais Urbanos: Balanço Crítico." Pp. 215–39 in Bernardo Sorj and Maria Hermínia Tavares de Almeida (eds.), *Sociedade e Política no Brasil Pós-64.* 1st edition, 1983. São Paulo: Brasiliense.

Cardoso Silva, Vera Alice (1982). "O Significado da Participação dos Mineiros na Política Nacional, Durante a Primeira República." Pp. 145–63 in Centro de Estudos Mineiros, *V Seminário de Estudos Mineiros, A República Velha em Minas.* Proceedings of a seminar held in Belo Horizonte, August 22–24, 1977. Belo Horizonte: UFMG/PROED.

Carone, Edgard (1976). *O Estado Nôvo (1937–1945).* São Paulo: DIFEL.

(1978). *A República Velha I: Instituições e Classes Sociais.* 4th edition. São Paulo: DIFEL.

Carvalho, Carlos Alberto Penna Rodrigues de (1980). "As Eleições Legislativas de 1978, III – As Eleições no Município de Barbacena (MG)." *Revista Brasileira de Estudos Políticos* 51 (July): 71–99.

Carvalho, Orlando M. (1960). "Os Partidos Políticos de Minas Gerais e as Eleições de 1958." *Revista Brasileira de Estudos Políticos* 8 (April): 279–87.

Cavarozzi, Marcelo (1986). "Peronism and Radicalism: Argentina's Transitions in Perspective." Pp. 143–74 in Paul W. Drake and Eduardo Silva (eds.), *Elections and Democratization in Latin America, 1980–85.* San Diego, CA: Center for Iberian and Latin American Studies, University of California, San Diego.

(1989). "El Esquema Partidario Argentino: Partidos Viejos, Sistema Débil." Pp. 297–334 in Marcelo Cavarozzi and Manuel Antonio Garretón (eds.), *Muerte y Resurrección: Los Partidos Políticos en el Autoritarismo y las Transiciones del Cono Sur*. Santiago de Chile: FLACSO.

Cavarozzi, Marcelo, and Manuel Antonio Garretón (eds.) (1989). *Muerte y Resurrección: Los Partidos Políticos en el Autoritarismo y las Transiciones del Cono Sur*. Santiago de Chile: FLACSO.

Centro de Estudios de la Realidad Contemporanea (1992). "Informe de Prensa: Encuesta Gran Santiago." Santiago: CERC.

Chacon, Vamireh (1964). "Pernambuco." Pp. 207–26 in Themistocles Cavalcanti and Reisky Dubnic (eds.), *Comportamento Eleitoral no Brasil*. Rio de Janeiro: Fundação Getúlio Vargas.

Chaves de Mendonça, Aureliano (1978). *Mensagem à Assembléia Legislativa*. Belo Horizonte: Imprensa Oficial.

Chilcote, Ronald H. (1990). *Power and the Ruling Classes in Northeast Brazil: Juazeiro and Petrolina in Transition*. Cambridge: Cambridge University Press.

Chubb, Judith (1981). "The Social Bases of an Urban Political Machine: The Christian Democratic Party in Palermo." Pp. 57–90 in S. N. Eisenstadt and René Lemarchand (eds.), *Political Clientelism, Patronage and Development*. Contemporary Political Sociology, volume 3. Beverly Hills, CA: Sage Publications.

(1982). *Patronage, Power and Poverty in Southern Italy: A Tale of Two Cities*. Cambridge: Cambridge University Press.

Cintra, Antônio Octávio (1979). "Traditional Brazilian Politics: An Interpretation of Relations between Center and Periphery." Pp. 127–66 in Neuma Aguiar (ed.), *The Structure of Brazilian Development*. New Brunswick, NJ: Transaction Books.

Cipolla, Francisco Paulo (1977). "A Estatização Segundo Wilson Suzigan." Pp. 95–109 in Carlos Estevam Martins (ed.), *Estado e Capitalismo no Brasil*. São Paulo: HUCITEC-CEBRAP.

Coelho, Levindo (1957). "Depoimento de Um Velho Político Mineiro." *Revista Brasileira de Estudos Políticos* 2 (July): 116–31.

Cohen, Youssef (1982). " 'The Benevolent Leviathan': Political Consciousness among Urban Workers under State Corporatism." *American Political Science Review* 76 (March): 46–59.

Collier, Ruth Berins (1982). "Popular Sector Incorporation and Political Supremacy: Regime Evolution in Brazil and Mexico." Pp. 57–109 in Sylvia Ann Hewlett and Richard S. Weinert (eds.), *Brazil and Mexico: Patterns in Late Development*. Philadelphia: Institute for the Study of Human Issues.

Collier, Ruth Berins, and David Collier (1979). "Inducements versus Constraints: Disaggregating Corporatism" *American Political Science Review* 73 (December): 967–86.

(1991). *Shaping the Political Arena: Critical Junctures, The Labor Movement, and Regime Dynamics in Latin America*. Princeton, NJ: Princeton University Press.

Cornelius, Wayne A., Ann L. Craig, and Jonathan Fox (eds.) (1994). *Transforming State-Society Relations in Mexico: The National Solidarity Strategy*. La Jolla: Center for U.S.-Mexican Studies, University of California, San Diego.

Correia Brasiliense (Brasília) (1984–85).

Coutinho, Luciano G., and Henri-Philippe Reichstul (1977). "O Setor Produtivo Estatal e o Ciclo." Pp. 55–93 in Carlos Estevam Martins (ed.), *Estado e Capitalismo no Brasil*. São Paulo: HUCITEC-CEBRAP.

Dahl, Robert A. (1961). *Who Governs: Democracy and Power in an American City*. New Haven, CT: Yale University Press.

(1971). *Polyarchy: Participation and Opposition*. New Haven, CT: Yale University Press.

Dean, Warren (1969). *The Industrialization of São Paulo*, 1880–1945. Austin: Institute of Latin American Studies, University of Texas Press.

De Cew, Judson (1978). "A Decisão Eleitoral em Caxias do Sul." Pp. 184–211 in Fábio Wanderley Reis (ed.), *Os Partidos e o Regime: A Lógica do Processo Eleitoral Brasileiro*. São Paulo: Símbolo.

De Lima, Venicio A. (1993). "Brazilian Television in the 1989 Presidential Election: Constructing a President." Pp. 97–117 in Thomas E. Skidmore (ed.), *Television, Politics, and the Transition to Democracy in Latin America*. Baltimore: Johns Hopkins University Press and Washington, DC: Woodrow Wilson Center Press.

Della Cava, Ralph (1989). "The 'People's Church,' the Vatican, and *Abertura*." Pp. 143–67 in Alfred Stepan (ed.), *Democratizing Brazil: Problems of Transition and Consolidation*. New York: Oxford University Press.

Departamento Intersindical de Assessoria Parlamentar (DIAP) (1988). *Quem Foi Quem na Constituinte nas Questões de Interesse dos Trabalhadores*. São Paulo: OBORÉ/Cortez.

De Riz, Liliana (1989). "Política y Partidos. Ejercicio de Análisis Comparado: Argentina, Chile, Brasil y Uruguay." Pp. 35–78 in Marcelo Cavarozzi and Manuel Antonio Garretón (eds.), *Muerte y Resurrección: Los Partidos Políticos en el Autoritarismo y las Transiciones del Cono Sur*. Santiago de Chile: FLACSO.

De Riz, Liliana, Marcelo Cavarozzi, and Jorge Feldman (1987). *Concertación, estado, y sindicatos en la Argentina contemporánea*. Buenos Aires: CEDES.

Dias, Fernando Correia (1968–69). "Estado e Desenvolvimento em Minas Gerais." *Revista Brasileira de Estudos Políticos* 25–26 (July–January): 111–36.

D'Incao, Maria Conceição (1975). *O Boiá Fria: Acumulação e Miséria*. Petrópolis: Vozes.

Diniz, Eli (1980). "Máquinas Políticas e Oposição: O MDB no Rio de Janeiro." *Dados* 23, 3: 335–57.

(1982). *Voto e Máquina Política: Patronagem e Clientelismo no Rio de Janeiro*. Rio de Janeiro: Paz e Terra.

(1986). "The Political Transition in Brazil: A Reappraisal of the Dynamics of the Political Opening." *Studies in Comparative International Development* 21 (Summer): 63–73.

Domhoff, G. William (1967). *Who Rules America?* Englewood Cliffs, NJ: Prentice-Hall.

Dreifuss, René Armand (1981). *1964: A Conquista do Estado: Ação Política, Poder, e Golpe de Classe*. Petrópolis: Vozes.

Dresser, Denise (1994). "Bringing the Poor Back In: National Solidarity as a Strategy of Regime Legitimation." Pp. 143–65 in Wayne A. Cornelius, Ann L. Craig, and Jonathan Fox (eds.), *Transforming State–Society Relations in Mexico: The National Solidarity Strategy*. La Jolla: Center for U.S.-Mexican Studies, University of California, San Diego.

Economist (1991). "Drunk, Not Sick: A Survey of Brazil." (December 7): 1–24.

Eloy de Carvalho Guimarães, Carlos (1956). "A Vida Política de Dores do Indaiá." *Revista Brasileira de Estudos Políticos* 1 (December): 170–79.

Erickson, Kenneth Paul (1977). *The Brazilian Corporative State and Working Class Politics.* Berkeley: University of California Press.

(1985). "Brazil: Corporative Authoritarianism, Democratization, and Dependency." Pp. 160–211 in Howard J. Wiarda and Harvey F. Kline (eds.), *Latin American Politics and Development.* 2nd edition. Boulder, CO: Westview.

Estado de Minas (Belo Horizonte). (1980–86).

Evans, Peter B. (1979). *Dependent Development: The Alliance of Multinational, State, and Local Capital in Brazil.* Princeton, NJ: Princeton University Press.

Evans, Peter B., Dietrich Rueschemeyer, and Theda Skocpol (eds.) (1985). *Bringing the State Back In.* Cambridge: Cambridge University Press.

Faoro, Raymundo (1958). *Os Donos do Poder: Formação do Patronato Político Brasileiro.* Porto Alegre: Globo.

Faria, Vilmar E. (1978). "As Eleições de 1974 no Estado de São Paulo: Uma Análise das Variações Inter-regionais." Pp. 205–42 in Fernando Henrique Cardoso and Bolivar Lamounier (eds.), *Os Partidos e as Eleições no Brasil.* 2nd edition. Rio de Janeiro: Paz e Terra.

(1984). "Desenvolvimento, Urbanização, e Mudanças na Estrutura do Emprego: A Experiência Brasileira dos Últimos Trinta Anos." Pp. 118–63 in Bernardo Sorj and Maria Hermínia Tavares de Almeida (eds.), *Sociedade e Política no Brasil Pós-64.* 1st edition, 1983. São Paulo: Brasiliense.

(1986). "Mudanças na Composição do Emprego e na Estrutura das Ocupações." Pp. 75–109 in Edmar Lisboa Bacha and Herbert S. Klein (eds.), *A Transição Incompleta: Brasil Desde 1945,* volume 1, *População, Emprego, Agricultura e Urbanização.* Rio de Janeiro: Paz e Terra.

Faucher, Philippe (1980). "Industrial Policy in a Dependent State: The Case of Brazil." *Latin American Perspectives* 24 (Winter): 3–22.

(1981). "The Paradise That Never Was: The Breakdown of the Brazilian Authoritarian Order." Pp. 11–39 in Thomas C. Bruneau and Philippe Faucher (eds.), *Authoritarian Capitalism: Brazil's Contemporary Economic and Political Development.* Boulder, CO: Westview Press.

Fausto, Boris (1981). *A Revolução de 1930: Historiografia e Historia.* 7th edition. São Paulo: Brasiliense.

Federação de Indústrias de Minas Gerais (FIEMG) (1980). *Guia Econômico e Industrial do Estado de Minas Gerais.* Belo Horizonte: FIEMG.

Ferreira, Oliveiros S. (1964). "São Paulo." Pp. 229–62 in Themistocles Cavalcanti and Reisky Dubnic (eds.), *Comportamento Eleitoral no Brasil.* Rio de Janeiro: Fundação Getúlio Vargas.

Fishlow, Albert (1973). "Some Reflections on Post-1964 Brazilian Economic Policy." Pp. 69–118 in Alfred Stepan (ed.), *Authoritarian Brazil: Origins, Policies, and Future.* New Haven, CT: Yale University Press.

(1989). "A Tale of Two Presidents: The Political Economy of Crisis Management." Pp. 83–119 in Alfred Stepan (ed.), *Democratizing Brazil: Problems of Transition and Consolidation.* New York: Oxford University Press.

FitzGerald, E. V. K. (1979). *The Political Economy of Peru, 1956–78: Economic Development and the Restructuring of Capital.* Cambridge: Cambridge University Press.

Fleischer, David V. (n.d.). "O Poder Legislativo em Minas Gerais: Uma Análise da Composição Socio-Econômica, Recrutamento e Padrões de Carreira, 1947–1977." Brasília: Fundação Universidade de Brasília.

(1976). "Concentração e Dispersão Eleitoral: Um Estudo da Distribuição

Geográfica do Voto em Minas Gerais (1966/1974)." *Revista Brasileira de Estudos Políticos* 43 (July): 333–60.

(1977). "A Bancada Federal Mineira: Trinta Anos de Recrutamento Político, 1945/1975." *Revista Brasileira de Estudos Políticos* 45 (July): 7–58.

(1980a). "A Evolução do Bipartidarismo Brasileiro 1966–1979." *Revista Brasileira de Estudos Políticos* 51 (July): 155–85.

(1980b). "Renovação Política – Brasil 1978: Eleições Parlamentares Sob a Egide do 'Pacote de Abril.' " *Revista de Ciência Política* 23 (August): 57–82.

(1981a). "A Evolução do Sistema Bipartidário." Pp. 183–202 in David V. Fleischer (ed.), *Os Partidos Políticos no Brasil*, volume 1. Brasília: Editora Universidade de Brasília.

(1981b). "As Origens Sócio-Econômicas e Regionais das Lideranças Partidárias em Minas." Pp. 96–115 in David V. Fleischer (ed.), *Os Partidos Políticos no Brasil*, volume 2. Brasília: Editora Universidade de Brasília.

(1982). "A Cúpula Mineira na República Velha – Origens Socio-Econômicas e Recrutamento de Presidentes e Vice-Presidentes do Estado e de Deputados Federais." Pp. 11–61 in Centro de Estudos Mineiros, *V Seminário de Estudos Mineiros, A República Velha em Minas*. Proceedings of a seminar held in Belo Horizonte, August 22–24, 1977. Belo Horizonte: UFMG/PROED.

(1987). "O Congresso-Constituinte de 1987: Um Perfil Socio-Econômico e Político." Unpublished paper, University of Brasília.

Folha de São Paulo (São Paulo). (1984–85, 1992).

Forjaz, Maria Cecília Spina (1977). *Tenentismo e Política: Tenentismo e Camadas Médias Urbanas na Crise da Primeira República*. Rio de Janeiro: Paz e Terra.

Foxley, Alejandro (1983). *Latin American Experiments in New-conservative Economics*. Berkeley: University of California Press.

Freeman, John (1982). "State Entrepreneurship and Dependent Development." *American Journal of Political Science* 26 (February): 90–112.

Frey, Frederick W. (1965). *The Turkish Political Elite*. Cambridge, MA: MIT Press.

Friedrich, Carl J. (1941). *Constitutional Government and Politics*. Lexington, MA: Ginn Custom.

Fundação João Pinheiro (FJP) (n.d.). *Análise da Evolução da Despesa Pública do Estado de Minas Gerais – Administração Direta, Autarquias, e Fundações*, 4 volumes. Belo Horizonte: Fundação João Pinheiro.

Furtado, Celso (1968). "De l'oligarchie à l'état militaire." Pp. 1–23 in Celso Furtado (ed.), *Brasil: Tempos Modernos*. Rio de Janeiro: Paz e Terra.

Garcia, Hélio (1985). *Mensagem à Assembléia Legislativa*. Belo Horizonte: Imprensa Oficial.

Garretón, Manuel Antonio (1989). *The Chilean Political Process*. Trans. Sharon Kellum in collaboration with Gilbert W. Merkx. Boston: Unwin Hyman.

Gazeta da Varginha (1981).

Geddes, Barbara (1990). "Building 'State' Autonomy in Brazil, 1930–1964." *Comparative Politics* 22 (January): 217–35.

(1994). *Politician's Dilemma: Building State Capacity in Latin America*. Berkeley: University of California Press.

Gerschenkron, Alexander (1962). *Economic Backwardness in Historical Perspective*. Cambridge, MA: Harvard University Press.

Gillespie, Charles G. (1986). "Activists and Floating Voters: The Unheeded Lessons of Uruguay's 1982 Primaries." Pp. 215–244 in Paul W. Drake and Eduardo Silva (eds.), *Elections and Democratization in Latin America, 1980–85*. San Diego: Center for Iberian and Latin American Studies, University of California, San Diego.

(1991). *Negotiating Democracy: Politicians and Generals in Uruguay*. Cambridge: Cambridge University Press.

Gillespie, Charles Guy, and Luis Eduardo González (1989). "Uruguay: The Survival of Old and Autonomous Institutions." Pp. 207–46 in Larry Diamond, Juan J. Linz, and Seymour Martin Lipset (eds.), *Democracy in Developing Countries*, volume 4, *Latin America*. Boulder, CO: Lynne Rienner.

González, Luis E. (1985). "Political Parties and Redemocratization in Uruguay." Working Paper no. 163, Woodrow Wilson Center, Washington, DC.

Graciarena, Jorge (1972). *Poder e Clases Sociales en el Desarrollo de América Latina*. Buenos Aires: Editorial Paidós.

Graham, Lawrence S. (1968). *Civil Service Reform in Brazil: Principles versus Practice*. Austin: University of Texas Press.

Graham, Richard (1990). *Patronage and Politics in Nineteenth Century Brazil*. Stanford, CA: Stanford University Press.

Gramsci, Antonio (1971). *Selections from the Prison Notebooks*. Trans. and ed. Quintin Hoare and Geoffrey Nowell Smith. New York: International Publishers.

Greenfield, Sidney M. (1977). "Patronage, Politics, and the Articulation of Local Community and National Society in Pre-1968 Brazil." *Journal of Interamerican Studies and World Affairs* 19 (May): 139–72.

Grossi, Maria das Graças (1977). "Minas Gerais: Del Estancamiento al Boom: Una Réplica Local del Modelo Brasileño." *Revista Mexicana de Sociología* 39 (January–March): 251–67.

(1979). "Système Politique et Developpement Industriel: Le Cas de Minas Gerais (Brésil)." Thèse pour le Doctorat de Troisième Cycle, École des Hautes Études en Sciences Sociales, Paris.

Guimarães, Cesar (1977). "Empresariado, Tipos de Capitalismo e Ordem Política." Pp. 191–204 in Carlos Estevam Martins (ed.), *Estado e Capitalismo no Brasil*. São Paulo: HUCITEC-CEBRAP.

(1985). "Avanço à Esquerda, Inclinação à Direita." Pp. 37–42 in "As Eleições Municipais de 85 e a Conjuntura Política," *Cadernos de Conjuntura*, no 3. Rio de Janeiro: Instituto Universitário de Pesquisas do Rio de Janeiro (IUPERJ).

Haddad, Paulo (1980). *Participação, Justiça Social e Planejamento*. Rio de Janeiro: Zahar Editores.

Hagopian, Frances (1990). "Democracy by Undemocratic Means?: Elites, Political Pacts, and Regime Transition in Brazil." *Comparative Political Studies* 23 (July): 147–70.

(1992). "The Compromised Consolidation: The Political Class in the Brazilian Transition." Pp. 243–93 in Scott Mainwaring, Guillermo O'Donnell, and J. Samuel Valenzuela (eds.), *Issues in Democratic Consolidation: The New South American Democracies in Comparative Perspective*. Notre Dame, IN: University of Notre Dame Press.

(1993). "After Regime Change: Authoritarian Legacies, Political Representation, and the Democratic Future of South America." *World Politics* 45 (April): 464–500.

Hagopian, Frances, and Scott Mainwaring (1987). "Democracy in Brazil: Problems and Prospects." *World Policy Journal* 4 (Summer): 485–514.

Hall, Peter (1986). *Governing the Economy: The Politics of State Intervention in Britain and France*. New York: Oxford University Press.

Hamilton, Nora (1982). *The Limits of State Autonomy: Post-Revolutionary Mexico*. Princeton, NJ: Princeton University Press.

Hartyln, Jonathan (1988). *The Politics of Coalition Rule in Colombia.* Cambridge: Cambridge University Press.

Hippolito, Lucia (1985). *De Raposas e Reformistas – o PSD e a Experiência Democrática Brasileira (1945–64).* Rio de Janeiro: Paz e Terra.

Hirschman, Albert O. (1963). *Journeys toward Progress: Studies of Economic Policy-Making in Latin America.* New York: Twentieth Century Fund.

(1971). *A Bias for Hope: Essays on Development in Latin America.* New Haven, CT: Yale University Press.

(1987). "The Political Economy of Latin American Development: Seven Exercises in Retrospection." *Latin American Research Review* 22, 3: 7–36.

Humphrey, John (1982). *Capitalist Control and Workers' Struggle in the Brazilian Auto Industry.* Princeton, NJ: Princeton University Press.

Huntington, Samuel P. (1968). *Political Order in Changing Societies.* New Haven, CT: Yale University Press.

(1984). "Will More Countries Become Democratic?" *Political Science Quarterly* 99 (Summer): 193–218.

(1991). *The Third Wave: Democratization in the Late Twentieth Century.* Norman: University of Oklahoma Press.

Inglehart, Ronald (1977). *The Silent Revolution: Changing Values and Political Styles among Western Publics.* Princeton, NJ: Princeton University Press.

(1990). *Culture Shift in Advanced Industrial Society.* Princeton, NJ: Princeton University Press.

Instituto Brasileiro de Administração Municipal (IBAM) (1975). *Municípios do Brasil: Quinze Anos Depois.* Rio de Janeiro: IBAM.

(1976). *O FPM e a Política de Receitas Vinculadas.* Rio de Janeiro: IBAM.

Instituto Brasileiro de Geografia e Estatística (IBGE). (1950).

(1970). *Sinopse Preliminar do Censo Demográfico.* Rio de Janeiro: IBGE.

(1975). *Censo Agropecuário,* 2 volumes. Rio de Janeiro: IBGE.

(1977). *Geografia do Brasil, Região Sudeste,* volume 3. Rio de Janeiro: IBGE.

(1979a). *Annuário Estatístico do Brasil.* Rio de Janeiro: IBGE (published 1980).

(1979b). *Areas de atração e evasão populacional no Brasil no período 1960–1970.* Série Estudos e Pesquisas, 4. Rio de Janeiro: IBGE.

(1980a). *Censo Agropecuário, Minas Gerais,* 1a. parte. Rio de Janeiro: IBGE (published 1984).

(1980b). *Censo Demográfico, Minas Gerais.* Volume 3, *Dados Distritais.* Volume 5, *Mão de Obra.* Rio de Janeiro: IBGE (published 1983).

(1980c). *Estatísticas Económicas do Setor Público, Atividade Empresarial.* Rio de Janeiro: IBGE.

(1983). *Annuário Estatístico do Brasil.* Rio de Janeiro: IBGE.

(1984). *Sinopse Estatística do Brasil.* Rio de Janeiro: IBGE.

(1993). *Annuário Estatístico do Brasil.* Rio de Janeiro: IBGE.

Instituto de Desenvolvimento Industrial (INDI) (1978). *Economic Information on Minas Gerais, Brasil.* Belo Horizonte: INDI.

(1980). *Posição de Projetos em 30.06.80.* Belo Horizonte: INDI.

Istoé (1984–86).

Istoé/Senhor (1991). *Perfil Parlamentar Brasileiro.* São Paulo: Editora Três.

Jaguaribe, Hélio (1968). "Brasil: Estabilidade social pelo colonial-fascismo?" Pp. 25–47 in Celso Furtado (ed.), *Brasil: Tempos Modernos.* Rio de Janeiro: Paz e Terra.

Johnson, John (1958). *Political Change in Latin America: The Emergence of the Middle Sectors.* Stanford, CA: Stanford University Press.

Jornal da Casa (Belo Horizonte) (1981–82).

Jornal da Tarde (São Paulo) (1983–85).
Jornal do Brasil (Rio de Janeiro) (1984–85).
Karl, Terry Lynn (1990). "Dilemmas of Democratization in Latin America." *Comparative Politics* 23 (October): 1–21.
Kaufman, Robert R. (1973). *The Politics of Chilean Land Reform, 1950–1970.* Cambridge, MA: Harvard University Press.
   (1977). "Corporatism, Clientelism, and Partisan Conflict: A Study of Seven Latin American Countries." Pp. 109–48 in James M. Malloy (ed.), *Authoritarianism and Corporatism in Latin America.* Pittsburgh: University of Pittsburgh Press.
Keck, Margaret E. (1989). "The 'New Unionism' in the Brazilian Transition." Pp. 252–96 in Alfred Stepan (ed.), *Democratizing Brazil: Problems of Transition and Consolidation.* New York: Oxford University Press.
   (1992). *The Workers' Party and Democratization in Brazil.* New Haven, CT: Yale University Press.
Key, V. O., Jr. (with the assistance of Alexander Heard) (1984). *Southern Politics in State and Nation.* 1st edition, 1949. Knoxville: University of Tennessee Press.
Kinzo, Maria D'Alva Gil (1988). *Oposição e Autoritarismo: Gênese e trajectória do MDB, 1966/1979.* São Paulo: Vértice.
   (1993). "The 1989 Presidential Election: Electoral Behaviour in a Brazilian City." *Journal of Latin American Studies* 25 (May): 313–30.
Kohli, Atul, and Vivienne Shue (1994). "State Power and Social Forces: On Political Contention and Accommodation in the Third World." Pp. 293–326 in Joel S. Migdal, Atul Kohli, and Vivienne Shue (eds.), *State Power and Social Forces: Domination and Transformation in the Third World.* Cambridge: Cambridge University Press.
Kurth, James (1979). "Industrial Change and Political Change: A European Perspective." Pp. 319–62 in David Collier (ed.), *The New Authoritarianism in Latin America.* Princeton, NJ: Princeton University Press.
Laclau, Ernesto (1979). *Politics and Ideology in Marxist Theory: Capitalism – Fascism – Populism.* London: Verso.
Lage de Resende, Maria Efigênia (1982). *Formação da Estrutura de Dominação em Minas Gerais: O Novo PRM (1989–1906).* Belo Horizonte: UFMG/PROED.
Lamounier, Bolivar (1978). "Presidente Prudente: O Crescimento da Oposição num Reduto Arenista." Pp. 1–89 in Fábio Wanderley Reis (ed.), *Os Partidos e O Regime: A Lógica do Processo Eleitoral Brasileiro.* São Paulo: Símbolo.
   (1980). "O Voto em São Paulo, 1970–1978." Pp. 15–80 in Bolivar Lamounier (ed.), *Voto de Desconfiança: Eleições e Mudança Política no Brasil: 1970–1979.* São Paulo: Vozes/CEBRAP.
   (1984). "Opening through Elections: Will the Brazilian Case Become a Paradigm?" *Government and Opposition* 19 (Spring): 167–77.
   (1989a). "*Authoritarian Brazil* Revisited: The Impact of Elections on the *Abertura.*" Pp. 43–79 in Alfred Stepan (ed.), *Democratizing Brazil: Prospects of Transition and Consolidation.* New York: Oxford University Press.
   (1989b). "Brazil: Inequality against Democracy." Pp. 111–57 in Larry Diamond, Juan J. Linz, and Seymour Martin Lipset (eds.), *Democracy in Developing Countries,* volume 4, *Latin America.* Boulder, CO: Lynne Rienner.
   (1994a). "Brazil: Toward Parliamentarism." Pp. 179–219 in Juan J. Linz and Arturo Valenzuela (eds.), *The Failure of Presidential Democracy,* volume 2, *The Case of Latin America.* Baltimore: Johns Hopkins University Press.
   (1994b). "Brazilian Democracy from the 1980's to the 1990's: The Hyper-Active Paralysis Syndrome." Paper prepared for the Inter-American Dialogue Work-

shop, "Democratic Governance in the Americas," Washington, DC (September 12–13).

Lamounier, Bolivar, and Alkimar R. Moura (1986). "Economic Policy and Political Opening in Brazil." Pp. 165–96 in Jonathan Hartlyn and Samuel A. Morley (eds.), *Latin American Political Economy: Financial Crisis and Political Change*. Boulder, CO: Westview Press.

Lamounier, Teodoro Alves (n.d.). "Estrutura Empresarial de Minas Gerais." Belo Horizonte: Banco de Desenvolvimento de Minas Gerais.

Levine, Robert M. (1978). *Pernambuco in the Brazilian Federation, 1889–1937*. Stanford, CA: Stanford University Press.

Lewin, Linda (1987). *Politics and Parentela and Paraíba*. Princeton, NJ: Princeton University Press.

Lima Jr., Olavo Brasil de (1978). Articulação de Interesses, Posição Sócio-Econômica e Ideologia: As Eleições de 1976 em Niterói." Pp. 91–144 in Fábio Wanderley Reis (ed.), *Os Partidos e o Regime: A Lógica do Processo Eleitoral Brasileiro*. São Paulo: Símbolo.

(1981). "O Sistema Partidário Brasileiro, 1945–1962." Pp. 24–45 in David V. Fleischer (ed.), *Os Partidos Políticos no Brasil*, volume 1. Brasília: Editora Universidade de Brasília.

(1984). "ARENA" and "MDB." Pp. 66–68 of volume 1 and 2322–2324 of volume 2 in Israel Beloch and Alzira Alves de Abreu (eds.), *Dicionário Histórico Biográfico Brasileiro, 1930–1983*. Rio de Janeiro: Fundação Getúlio Vargas, Financiadora de Projetos (FINEP), and Forense Universitária.

Linz, Juan J. (1973). "The Future of an Authoritarian Situation or the Institutionalization of an Authoritarian Regime: The Case of Brazil." Pp. 233–54 in Alfred Stepan (ed.), *Authoritarian Brazil: Origins, Politics and Future*. New Haven, CT: Yale University Press.

(1975). "Totalitarian and Authoritarian Regimes." Pp. 191–357 in Fred I. Greenstein and Nelson W. Polsby (eds.), *Handbook of Political Science*, volume 3. Reading, MA: Addison-Wesley.

(1978). *The Breakdown of Democratic Regimes: Crisis, Breakdown, and Reequilibration*. Baltimore: Johns Hopkins University Press.

Lipset, Seymour Martin (1960). *Political Man: The Social Basis of Politics*. New York: Doubleday.

Lipset, Seymour Martin, and Stein Rokkan (1967). "Cleavage Structures, Party Systems, and Voter Alignments: An Introduction." Pp. 1–64 in Seymour Martin Lipset and Stein Rokkan (eds.), *Party Systems and Voter Alignments: Cross National Perspectives*. New York: Free Press.

Love, Joseph L. (1970). "Political Participation in Brazil, 1881–1969." *Luso-Brazilian Review* 7 (December): 3–24.

(1971). *Rio Grande do Sul and Brazilian Regionalism, 1882–1930*. Stanford, CA: Stanford University Press.

(1980). *São Paulo in the Brazilian Federation, 1889–1937*. Stanford, CA: Stanford University Press.

Mainwaring, Scott (1986a). *The Catholic Church and Politics in Brazil, 1916–1985*. Stanford, CA: Stanford University Press.

(1986b). "The Transition to Democracy in Brazil." *Journal of Inter-American Studies and World Affairs* 28 (Spring): 149–79.

(1987). "Urban Popular Movements, Identity, and Democratization in Brazil." *Comparative Political Studies* 20 (July): 131–59.

(1988). "Review Article: Political Parties and Democratization in Brazil and the Southern Cone." *Comparative Politics* 21 (October): 91–120.

(1989a). "Grass-roots Catholic Groups and Politics in Brazil." Pp. 151–92 in Scott Mainwaring and Alexander Wilde (eds.), *The Progressive Church in Latin America*. Notre Dame, IN: University of Notre Dame Press.

(1989b). "Grassroots Popular Movements and the Struggle for Democracy: Nova Iguaçu." Pp. 168–204 in Alfred Stepan (ed.), *Democratizing Brazil: Problems of Transition and Consolidation*. New York: Oxford University Press.

(1991a). "Clientelism, Patrimonialism, and Economic Crisis: Brazil since 1979." Paper prepared for the Latin American Studies Association Meetings, Washington DC, (April 4–7).

(1991b). "Politicians, Parties, and Electoral Systems: Brazil in Comparative Perspective." *Comparative Politics* 24 (October): 21–43.

(1992–93). "Brazilian Party Underdevelopment in Comparative Perspective." *Political Science Quarterly* 107 (Winter): 677–707.

(1994). "Explaining Choices of Political Institutions: Interests and Ideas in Brazil, 1985–1988." Paper prepared for the Annual Meeting of the American Political Science Association, New York (September 1–4).

(1995). "Brazil: Weak Parties, Feckless Democracy." Pp. 354–98 in Scott Mainwaring and Timothy R. Scully (eds.), *Building Democratic Institutions: Party Systems in Latin America*. Stanford, CA: Stanford University Press.

Mainwaring, Scott, and Donald Share (1986). "Transition through Transaction: Democratization in Brazil and Spain." Pp. 175–215 in Wayne A. Selcher (ed.), *Political Liberalization in Brazil: Dynamics, Dilemmas, and Future Prospects in Brazil*. Boulder, CO: Westview Press.

Malloy, James (1979). *The Politics of Social Security in Brazil*. Pittsburgh, PA: University of Pittsburgh Press.

Martinez-Alier, Verena, and Armando Boito Júnior (1978). "1974: Enxada e Voto." Pp. 243–62 in Fernando Henrique Cardoso and Bolivar Lamounier (eds.), *Os Partidos e as Eleições no Brasil*. 2nd edition. Rio de Janeiro: Paz e Terra.

Martins, José de Souza (1977). "El café y la génesis de la industrialización en São Paulo." *Revista Mexicana de Sociología* 39 (July–September): 781–97.

Martins, Luciano (1965). "Os Grupos Bilionários Nacionais (De 1 a 4 Bilhões)." *Revista do Instituto de Ciências Sociais* 2 (January–December): 79–115.

(1977). "A Expansão Recente do Estado: Seus Problemas, Seus Atores." Relatório de Pesquisa. Rio de Janeiro: Instituto Universitário de Pesquisas do Rio de Janeiro (IUPERJ) and Financiadora de Projetos (FINEP).

(1985). *Estado Capitalista e Burocracia no Brasil pós 64*. Rio de Janeiro: Paz e Terra.

(1986). "The 'Liberalization' of Authoritarian Rule in Brazil." Pp. 72–94 in Guillermo O'Donnell, Philippe C. Schmitter, and Laurence Whitehead (eds.), *Transitions from Authoritarian Rule*, volume 2, *Latin America*. Baltimore: Johns Hopkins University Press.

Martins Filho, Amilcar Vianna (1981). *A Economia Política do Café Com Leite (1900–1930)*. Belo Horizonte: UFMG/PROED.

(1983). "The Mineiro Political Elite during the Brazilian First Republic: A Collective Biography." Paper presented to the 11th International Conference of the Latin American Studies Association, Mexico City (September).

Martins Rodrigues, Leôncio (1990). *CUT: Os militantes e a ideologia*. São Paulo: Paz e Terra.

Marx, Karl, and Friedrich Engels (1972). "Manifesto of the Communist Party." Pp. 331–62 in Robert C. Tucker (ed.), *The Marx-Engels Reader*. New York: Norton.

Matthews, Donald R. (1954). *The Social Background of Political Decision-Makers.* New York: Random House.

Maybury-Lewis, David (1968). "Growth and Change in Brazil since 1930: An Anthropological View." Pp. 159–72 in Raymond S. Sayers (ed.), *Portugal and Brazil in Transition.* Minneapolis: University of Minnesota Press.

Mayer, Arno J. (1981). *The Persistence of the Old Regime: Europe to the Great War.* New York: Pantheon Books.

McClintock, Cynthia, and Abraham F. Lowenthal (eds.) (1983). *The Peruvian Experiment Reconsidered.* Princeton, NJ: Princeton University Press.

McDonough, Peter (1981a). "Mapping an Authoritarian Power Structure: Brazilian Elites during the Médici Regime." *Latin American Research Review* 16, 1: 79–106.

   (1981b). *Power and Ideology in Brazil.* Princeton, NJ: Princeton University Press.

Mendes, Cândido (1980). "The Post-1964 Brazilian Regime: Outward Redemocratization and Inner Institutionalization." *Government and Opposition* 15 (Winter): 48–74.

Mendonça de Barros, José, and Douglas H. Graham (1978). "The Brazilian Economic Miracle Revisited: Private and Public Sector Initiative in a Market Economy." *Latin American Research Review* 13, 2: 5–38.

Mericle, Kenneth S. (1977). "Corporatist Control of the Working Class: Authoritarian Brazil Since 1964." Pp. 303–38 in James M. Malloy (ed.), *Authoritarianism and Corporatism in Latin America.* Pittsburgh: University of Pittsburgh Press.

Meynaud, Jean (1968). *Technocracy.* Trans. Paul Barnes. London: Faber and Faber.

Miceli, Sérgio (1979). *Intelectuais e Classe Dirigente no Brasil (1920–1945).* São Paulo: DIFEL.

Migdal, Joel S. (1994). "The State in Society: An Approach to Struggles for Domination." Pp. 7–34 in Joel S. Migdal, Atul Kohli, and Vivienne Shue (eds.), *State Power and Social Forces: Domination and Transformation.* Cambridge: Cambridge University Press.

Mills, C. Wright (1956). *The Power Elite.* New York: Oxford University Press.

Minas Gerais (1983–87).

Ministério da Fazenda (1981). *Finanças do Brasil.* Volume 23, *Receita e Despesa, União, Estados e Municípios, 1965–1975.* Brasília.

   (1984). *Finanças do Brasil.* Volume 27, *Receita e Despesa da União, Estados e Municípios.* Brasília.

Miyamoto, Shiguenoli (1980). "Eleições de 1978 em São Paulo: A Campanha." Pp. 111–72 in Bolivar Lamounier (ed.), *Voto de Desconfiança: Eleições e Mudança Política no Brasil, 1970–1979.* São Paulo: Vozes/CEBRAP.

Moisés, José Alvaro (1979). "Current Issues in the Labor Movement in Brazil." *Latin American Perspectives* 6 (Fall): 51–70.

   (1982). "Qual é a Estrategia do Novo Sindicalismo?" Pp. 11–39 in José Alvaro Moisés (ed.), *Alternativas Populares da Democracia: Brazil, Anos 80.* Petrópolis: Vozes.

   (1993). "Elections, Political Parties and Political Culture in Brazil: Changes and Continuities." *Journal of Latin American Studies* 25 (October): 575–611.

Montes Claros em Foco (1981). 14 (October): 39.

Moore, Barrington, Jr. (1966). *Social Origins of Dictatorship and Democracy: Lord and Peasant in the Making of the Modern World.* Boston: Beacon Press.

Mora y Araújo, Manuel (1986). "The Nature of the Alfonsín Coalition." Pp. 175–

88 in Paul W. Drake and Eduardo Silva (eds.), *Elections and Democratization in Latin America, 1980–85.* San Diego: Center for Iberian and Latin American Studies, University of California, San Diego.

Motta, Paulo Roberto (1971). *Movimentos Partidários no Brasil: A Estrategia da Elite e dos Militares.* Rio de Janeiro: Fundação Getúlio Vargas.

Murilo de Carvalho, José (1966). "Barbacena, a Família, a Política, e uma Hipótese." *Revista Brasileira de Estudos Políticos* 20 (January): 153–93.

——— (1968–69). "Estudos de poder local no Brasil." *Revista Brasileira de Estudos Políticos* 25–26 (July–January): 231–48.

——— (1980). *A Construção da Ordem: A Elite Política Imperial.* Brasília: Editora Universidade de Brasília.

Nordlinger, Eric A. (1987). "Taking the State Seriously." Pp. 353–90 in Myron Weiner and Samuel P. Huntington (eds.), *Understanding Political Development.* Boston: Little Brown.

Nunes, Edson de Oliveira (1978). "Legislativo, Política e Recrutamento de Elites no Brasil." *Dados* 17: 53–78.

Nunes Leal, Victor (1977). *Coronelismo: The Municipality and Representative Government in Brazil.* Trans. June Henfrey. Cambridge: Cambridge University Press. [Originally published in Portuguese as *Coronelismo: Enxada e Voto. O Município e o Regime Representativo no Brasil.* Rio de Janeiro: Revista Forense, 1949].

O Estado de São Paulo (São Paulo) (1983–85).

O Globo (Rio de Janeiro) (1983–85).

O'Connor, James (1973). *The Fiscal Crisis of the State.* New York: St. Martin's Press.

O'Donnell, Guillermo (1973). *Modernization and Bureaucratic-Authoritarianism: Studies in South American Politics.* Berkeley: Institute of International Studies, University of California.

——— (1978). "Reflections on the Patterns of Change in the Bureaucratic-Authoritarian State." *Latin American Research Review* 13, 1: 3–38.

——— (1979). "Tensions in the Bureaucratic-Authoritarian State and the Question of Democracy." Pp. 285–318 in David Collier (ed.), *The New Authoritarianism in Latin America.* Princeton, NJ: Princeton University Press.

——— (1988). "State and Alliances in Argentina, 1956–1976." Pp. 176–205 in Robert H. Bates (ed.), *Toward a Political Economy of Development: A Rational Choice Perspective.* Berkeley: University of California Press.

O'Donnell, Guillermo, and Philippe C. Schmitter (1986). *Tentative Conclusions about Uncertain Democracies.* Volume 4, *Transitions from Authoritarian Rule.* Baltimore: Johns Hopkins University Press.

Oliveira, Lucia Meria Lippi (1981). "O Partido Social Democrático." Pp. 108–14 in David V. Fleischer (ed.), *Os Partidos Políticos no Brasil,* volume 1. Brasília: Editora Universidade de Brasília.

Oliveira Vianna, Francisco José de (1974). *Instituições Políticas Brasileiras,* 2 volumes. 3rd edition. 1st edition, 1949. Rio de Janeiro: Fundação Oliveira Vianna, Distribuidora Record.

Pacheco, Rondon (1975). *Mensagem à Assembléia Legislativa.* Belo Horizonte: Imprensa Oficial.

Palermo, Vicente (1986). *Democracia Interna en los Partidos: Las Elecciones Partidarias de 1983 en el Radicalismo y Justicialismo Porteños.* Buenos Aires: IDES.

Pang, Eul-Soo (1973). "Coronelismo in Northeast Brazil." Pp. 65–88 in Robert Kern (ed.) (with the assistance of Ronald Dolkert), *The Caciques: Oligarchi-*

cal Politics and the System of Caciquismo in the Luso-Hispanic World. Albuquerque: University of New Mexico Press.

Pereira, Anthony (1991). "Regime Change without Democratization: Sugar Workers' Unions in Pernambuco, Northeast Brazil, 1961–89." Ph.D. diss., Harvard University.

Pereira dos Santos, Francelino (1983). *Mensagem à Assembléia Legislativa.* Belo Horizonte: Imprensa Oficial.

Przeworski, Adam (1986). "Some Problems in the Study of the Transition to Democracy." Pp. 47–63 in Guillermo O'Donnell, Philippe C. Schmitter, and Laurence Whitehead (eds.), *Transitions from Authoritarian Rule,* part 3: *Comparative Perspectives.* Baltimore: Johns Hopkins University Press.

(1989). "Democracy as a Contingent Outcome of Conflicts." Pp. 59–80 in Jon Elster and Rune Slagsted (eds.), *Constitutionalism and Democracy.* Cambridge: Cambridge University Press.

(1991). *Democracy and the Market: Political and Economic Reforms in Eastern Europe and Latin America.* Cambridge: Cambridge University Press.

(1992). "The Games of Transition." Pp. 105–52 in Scott Mainwaring, Guillermo O'Donnell, and J. Samuel Valenzuela (eds.), *Issues in Democratic Consolidation: The New South American Democracies in Comparative Perspective.* Notre Dame, IN: University of Notre Dame Press.

Purcell, Susan Kaufman (1981). "Mexico: Clientelism, Corporatism and Political Stability." Pp. 191–216 in S. N. Eisenstadt and René Lemarchand (eds.), *Political Clientelism, Patronage and Development.* Contemporary Political Sociology, volume 3. Beverly Hills, CA: Sage Publications.

Putnam, Robert D. (1976). *The Comparative Study of Political Elites.* Englewood Cliffs, NJ: Prentice-Hall.

Queiroz, Mauricio Vinhas de (1965). "Os Grupos Multibilionários." *Revista do Instituto de Ciências Sociais* 2 (January–December): 47–78.

Rebelo Horta, Cid (1956). "Famílias Governamentais de Minas Gerais." Pp. 45–91 in Universidade de Minas Gerais, *Segundo Seminário de Estudos Mineiros,* Belo Horizonte (October 22–27).

Reis, Elisa P. (1980). "The Agrarian Roots of Authoritarian Modernization in Brazil, 1880–1930." Ph.D. diss., Massachusetts Institute of Technology.

(1985). "Change and Continuity in Brazilian Rural Politics." Paper prepared for presentation at the LASA Convention, Albuquerque, New Mexico (April).

(1989). "Brazil: One Hundred Years of the Agrarian Question." Unpublished paper, Instituto Universitário de Pesquisas do Rio de Janeiro (IUPERJ) and Fundação Getúlio Vargas.

Reis, Fábio Wanderley (with the assistance of Rubem Barboza Filho) (1978a). "Classe Social e Opção Partidária: As Eleições de 1976 em Juiz de Fora." Pp. 213–87 in Fábio Wanderley Reis (ed.), *Os Partidos e o Regime: A Lógica do Processo Eleitoral Brasileiro.* São Paulo: Símbolo.

(1978b). "As Eleições em Minas Gerais." Pp. 127–151 in Fernando Henrique Cardoso and Bolivar Lamounier (eds.), *Os Partidos e as Eleições no Brasil,* 2nd edition. Rio de Janeiro: Paz e Terra.

(1981). "O Bipartidarismo nas Eleições Municipais de 1976." Pp. 202–20 in David V. Fleischer (ed.), *Os Partidos Políticos no Brasil,* volume 1. Brasília: Editora Universidade de Brasília.

Remmer, Karen L. (1985). "Redemocratization and the Impact of Authoritarian Rule in Latin America." *Comparative Politics* 17 (April): 253–75.

(1989). *Military Rule in Latin America.* Boston: Unwin Hyman.

Rial, Juan (1986). "The Uruguayan Elections of 1984: A Triumph of the Center."

Pp. 245–71 in Paul W. Drake and Eduardo Silva (eds.), *Elections and Democratization in Latin America, 1980–85*. San Diego: Center for Iberian and Latin American Studies, University of California, San Diego.

(1989). "Continuidad y Cambio en las Organizaciones Partidárias en el Uruguay: 1973–1984." Pp. 243–96 in Marcelo Cavarozzi and Manuel Antonio Garretón (eds.), *Muerte y Resurrección: Los Partidos Políticos en el Autoritarismo del Cono Sur*. Santiago de Chile: FLACSO.

Ribeiro, Fávila (1964). "Ceará." Pp. 63–120 in Themistocles Cavalcanti and Reisky Dubnic (eds.), *Comportamento Eleitoral no Brasil*. Rio de Janeiro: Fundação Getúlio Vargas.

Rios, José Arthur (1964). "Guanabara." Pp. 123–68 in Themistocles Cavalcanti and Reisky Dubnic (eds.), *Comportamento Eleitoral no Brasil*. Rio de Janeiro: Fundação Getúlio Vargas.

Rodrigues, Carlos (ed.) (1984). *Brasília: Personalidades*. Brasília: C. R. Editora Ltda.

Roett, Riordan (1984). *Brazil: Politics in a Patrimonial Society*. 3rd edition. New York: Praeger.

Rouquié, Alain (1978). "Clientelist Control and Authoritarian Contexts." Pp. 19–35 (notes 215–19) in Guy Hermet, Richard Rose, and Alain Rouquié (eds.), *Elections without Choice*. New York: Halstead Press/John Wiley and Sons.

Sampaio, Nelson de Souza (1964). "Bahia." Pp. 5–60 in Themistocles Cavalcanti and Reisky Dubnic (eds.), *Comportamento Eleitoral no Brasil*. Rio de Janeiro: Fundação Getúlio Vargas.

Santos, Wanderley Guilherme dos (1971). "Governadores-Políticos, Governadores-Técnicos, Governadores-Militares." *Dados* 8: 123–28.

(1979). "The Calculus of Conflict: Impasse in Brazilian Politics and the Crisis of 1964." Ph.D. diss., Stanford University.

(1986). *Sessenta e Quatro: Anatomia da Crise*. São Paulo: Vértice.

Sarles, Margaret J. (1982). "Maintaining Political Control through Parties: The Brazilian Strategy." *Comparative Politics* 15 (October): 41–71.

(1985). "Government and Politics: Brazil." *Handbook of Latin American Studies* 47: 554–68.

Sarles Jenks, Margaret (1979). "Political Parties in Authoritarian Brazil." Ph.D. diss., Duke University.

Sartori, Giovanni (1966). "European Political Parties: The Case of Polarized Pluralism." Pp. 137–76 in Joseph LaPalombara and Myron Weiner (eds.), *Political Parties and Political Development*. Princeton, NJ: Princeton University Press.

Sartori, Giovanni (1976). *Parties and Party Systems: A Framework for Analysis*. Cambridge: Cambridge University Press.

Schamis, Hector E. (1991). "Reconceptualizing Latin American Authoritarianism in the 1970s: From Bureaucratic-Authoritarianism to Neoconservatism. *Comparative Politics* 23 (January): 201–20.

Schmitter, Philippe C. (1971). *Interest Conflict and Political Change in Brazil*. Stanford, CA: Stanford University Press.

(1973). "The 'Portugalization' of Brazil?" Pp. 179–232 in Alfred Stepan (ed.), *Authoritarian Brazil: Origins, Policies and Future*. New Haven, CT: Yale University Press.

Schneider, Ronald M. (1971). *The Political System of Brazil*. New York: Columbia University Press.

Schwartzman, Simon (1970). "Representação e Cooptação Política no Brasil." *Dados* 7: 9–41.

(1975). *São Paulo e o Estado Nacional*. São Paulo: DIFEL.

(1982). *Bases do Autoritarismo Brasileiro.* Rio de Janeiro: Campus.

Scott, James C. (1972). "Patron–Client Politics and Political Change in Southeast Asia." *American Political Science Review* 66 (March): 91–113.

Secretaria da Fazenda do Estado de Minas Gerais (1979). "Finanças Públicas: Uma Experiência nos Últimos Anos." Prepared by the Secretaries of Finance of Minas Gerais, Paraná, Rio Grande do Sul, Rio de Janeiro, Santa Catarina, and São Paulo. Belo Horizonte.

Secretaria da Fazenda do Estado de Minas Gerais. Typesheets.

Secretaria de Estado do Planejamento e Coordenação Geral (SEPLAN) (1978). *Comportamento de Economia Mineira Período 1960–1977.* No. 5, *Evolução da Estrutura Espacial.* No. 6, *Setor Público,* 2 volumes. No. 7, *Agropecuário,* 2 volumes. No. 8, *Indústria de Transformação.* Belo Horizonte.

(1981). "Palestra pronunciado pelo Governador do Estado de Minas Gerais, Francelino Pereira dos Santos, no dia 15 de agosto de 1981, aos estagiários da Escola Superior de Guerra – ESG." Belo Horizonte.

(1983). *O Prefeito Mineiro (1982–1988).* Jack Siqueira, coordinator. Belo Horizonte.

Senhor (1985–86).

Serra, José (1979). "Three Mistaken Theses Regarding the Connection between Industrialization and Authoritarian Regimes." Pp. 99–163 in David Collier (ed.), *The New Authoritarianism in Latin America.* Princeton, NJ: Princeton University Press.

Shefter, Martin (1977). "Party and Patronage: Germany, England, and Italy." *Politics and Society* 7, 4: 403–51.

Singer, André (1990). "Collor na periferia: A volta por cima do populismo." Pp. 135–52 in Bolivar Lamounier (ed.), *De Geisel A Collor: O Balanço da transição.* São Paulo: IDESP/Sumaré.

Siqueira, Moema Miranda de (1970). "Elites Políticas em Minas Gerais." *Revista Brasileira de Estudos Políticos* 29 (July): 173–79.

Skidmore, Thomas E. (1967). *Politics in Brazil, 1930–1964: An Experiment in Democracy.* New York: Oxford University Press.

(1973). "Politics and Economic Policy Making in Authoritarian Brazil, 1937–71." Pp. 3–46 in Alfred Stepan (ed.), *Authoritarian Brazil: Origins, Policies, and Future.* New Haven, CT: Yale University Press.

(1988). *The Politics of Military Rule in Brazil, 1964–85.* New York: Oxford University Press.

Skocpol, Theda (1979). *States and Social Revolution.* Cambridge: Cambridge University Press.

Smith, Peter H. (1979). *Labyrinths of Power: Political Recruitment in Twentieth-Century Mexico.* Princeton, NJ: Princeton University Press.

Smith, William C. (1989). *Authoritarianism and the Crisis of the Argentine Political Economy.* Stanford, CA: Stanford University Press.

Soares, Glaucio Ary Dillon (1967). "The Politics of Uneven Development: The Case of Brazil." Pp. 467–96 in Seymour Martin Lipset and Stein Rokkan (eds.), *Party Systems and Voter Alignments: Cross-National Perspectives.* New York: Free Press.

(1973). *Sociedade e Política no Brasil.* São Paulo: DIFEL.

(1981). "A Formação dos Partidos Nacionais." Pp. 7–24 in David V. Fleischer (ed.), *Os Partidos Políticos no Brasil,* volume 1. Brasília: Editora Universidade de Brasília.

(1984). *Colegio Eleitoral, Convenções Partidárias e Eleições Diretas.* Petrópolis: Vozes.

Sorj, Bernardo (1980). *Estado e Classes Sociais na Agricultura Brasileira*. Rio de Janeiro: Zahar Editores.

(1984). "Public Enterprises and the Question of the State Bourgeoisie, 1968–75." Pp. 72–93 in David Booth and Bernardo Sorj (eds.), *Military Reformism and Social Classes: The Peruvian Experience, 1968–80*. New York: St. Martin's Press.

Spindel, Chewya R. (1983). "O Trabalho Temporário na Agricultura Brasileira: O 'Boiá-Fria,' Uma Categoria em Estudo." Paper prepared for the International Labor Organization. São Paulo: PUC.

Stallings, Barbara (1977). *Class Conflict and Economic Development in Chile, 1958–1973*. Stanford, CA: Stanford University Press.

Starling, Heloisa Maria Murgel (1986). *Os Senhores das Gerais: Os Novos Inconfidentes e o Golpe Militar de 1964*. 5th edition. Petrópolis: Vozes.

Stepan, Alfred (1971). *The Military in Politics: Changing Patterns in Brazil*. Princeton, NJ: Princeton University Press.

(ed.) (1973a). *Authoritarian Brazil: Origins, Politics, and Future*. New Haven, CT: Yale University Press.

(1973b). "The New Professionalism of Internal Warfare and Military Role Expansion." Pp. 47–65 in Alfred Stepan (ed.), *Authoritarian Brazil: Origins, Policies, and Future*. New Haven, CT: Yale University Press.

(1977). *The State and Society: Peru in Comparative Perspective*. Princeton, NJ: Princeton University Press.

(1978). "Political Leadership and Regime Breakdown: Brazil." Pp. 110–37 in Juan J. Linz and Alfred Stepan (eds.), *The Breakdown of Democratic Regimes: Latin America*. Baltimore: Johns Hopkins University Press.

(1985). "State Power and the Strength of Civil Society in the Southern Cone of Latin America." Pp. 317–43 in Peter B. Evans, Dietrich Rueschemeyer, and Theda Skocpol (eds.), *Bringing the State Back In*. Cambridge: Cambridge University Press.

(1988). *Rethinking Military Politics: Brazil and the Southern Cone*. Princeton, NJ: Princeton University Press.

(1989). "Introduction." Pp. vii–xvii in Alfred Stepan (ed.), *Democratizing Brazil: Problems of Transition and Consolidation*. New York: Oxford University Press.

Straubhaar, Joseph, Organ Olsen, and Maria Cavaliari Nunes (1993). "The Brazilian Case: Influencing the Voter." Pp. 118–44 in Thomas E. Skidmore (ed.), *Television, Politics, and the Transition to Democracy in Latin America*. Baltimore: Johns Hopkins University Press and Washington, DC: Woodrow Wilson Center Press.

Suleiman, Ezra (1974). *Politics, Power, and Bureaucracy in France: The Administrative Elite*. Princeton, NJ: Princeton University Press.

(1977). "The Myth of Technical Expertise: Selection, Organization, and Leadership." *Comparative Politics* 20 (October): 137–58.

Suzzi, Patrizia (1980). "Estado, Empresa e Desenvolvimento Regional: O Caso do Instituto de Desenvolvimento Industrial de Minas Gerais – INDI." Relatório de Pesquisa. Rio de Janeiro: Financiadora de Projetos (FINEP).

Tarrow, Sidney (1978). "Introduction." Pp. 1–27 in Sidney Tarrow, Peter J. Katzenstein, and Luigi Graziano (eds,), *Territorial Politics in Industrial Nations*. New York: Praeger.

Tavares de Almeida, Maria Hermínia (1981). "Tendências Recentes da Negociação Coletiva no Brasil." *Dados* 24, 2: 161–89.

(1983). "O Sindicalismo Brasileiro Entre a Conservação e a Mudança." Pp. 191–

214 in Bernardo Sorj and Maria Hermínia Tavares de Almeida (eds.), *Sociedade e Política no Brasil Pós-64*. São Paulo: Brasiliense.

(1987). *"Novo Sindicalismo* and Politics in Brazil." Pp. 147–78 in John D. Wirth, Edson de Oliveira Nunes, and Thomas E. Bogenschild (eds.), *State and Society in Brazil: Continuity and Change*. Boulder, CO: Westview Press.

Trebat, Thomas J. (1981). "Public Enterprises in Brazil and Mexico: A Comparison of Origins and Performance." Pp. 41–58 in Thomas C. Bruneau and Philippe Faucher (eds.), *Authoritarian Capitalism: Brazil's Contemporary Economic and Political Development*. Boulder, CO: Westview Press.

(1983), *Brazil's State-Owned Enterprises: A Case Study of the State as Entrepreneur*. Cambridge: Cambridge University Press.

Tribunal Regional Eleitoral de Minas Gerais (TRE-MG) (1962).

(1966). "Eleições de 15 de novembro de 1966, Senado, Deputado Federal, Deputado Estadual." Relatório da Comissão Apuradora.

(1970). "Eleições de 15 de novembro de 1970, Senado, Deputado Federal, Deputado Estadual." Relatório da Comissão Apuradora.

(1974). "Eleições de 15 de novembro de 1974, Senado, Deputado Federal, Deputado Estadual." Relatório da Comissão Apuradora.

(1978). "Eleições de 15 de novembro de 1978, Senado, Deputado Federal, Deputado Estadual." Relatório da Comissão Apuradora.

(1982). "Eleições de 15 de novembro de 1982, Governo do Estado, Senado Federal, Câmara dos Deputados, Assembéia Legislativa." Relatório da Comissão Apuradora.

(1989). "Prefeitos e Vice-Prefeitos Eleitos em 15/11/88."

Division of Statistics, File Data.

Division of Party Registration, File Data.

Tribunal Superior Eleitoral (1973). *Dados Estatísticos.*Volume 7, *Eleições Federais e Estaduais*. Brasília: Departamento de Imprensa Nacional.

Trindade, Helgio (1978). "Padrões e Tendências do Comportamento Eleitoral no Rio Grande do Sul." Pp. 153–204 in Fernando Henrique Cardoso and Bolivar Lamounier (eds.), *Os Partidos e as Eleições no Brasil*, 2nd edition. Rio de Janeiro: Paz e Terra.

Truman, David B. (1951). *The Governmental Process*. New York: Knopf.

Uricoechea, Fernando (1980). *The Patrimonial Foundations of the Brazilian Bureaucratic State*. Berkeley: University of California Press.

Valenzuela, Arturo (1977). *Political Brokers in Chile: Local Government in a Centralized Policy*. Durham, NC: Duke University Press.

(1978). *The Breakdown of Democratic Regimes: Chile*. Baltimore: Johns Hopkins University Press.

(1987). "Party Politics and the Failure of Presidentialism in Chile: A Proposal for a Parliamentary System of Government." Paper presented at the annual meeting of the American Political Science Association, Chicago (September 3–6).

(1989). "Chile: Origins, Consolidation, and Breakdown of a Democratic Regime." Pp. 159–206 in Larry Diamond, Juan J. Linz, and Seymour Martin Lipset (eds.), *Democracy in Developing Countries*, volume 4, *Latin America*. Boulder, CO: Lynne Rienner.

Valenzuela, Arturo, and J. Samuel Valenzuela (1986). "Party Oppositions under the Chilean Authoritarian Regime." Pp. 184–229 in J. Samuel Valenzuela and Arturo Valenzuela (eds.), *Military Rule in Chile: Dictatorship and Oppositions*. Baltimore: Johns Hopkins University Press.

Valenzeula, J. Samuel, and Arturo Valenzuela (eds.) (1986). *Military Rule in Chile: Dictatorship and Oppositions*. Baltimore: Johns Hopkins University Press.

Veja (1981–94).

Velasco e Cruz, Sebastião C., and Carlos Estevam Martins (1984). "De Castello a Figueiredo: Uma Incursão na pré-História da 'Abertura.' " Pp. 13–61 in Bernardo Sorj and Maria Hermínia Tavares de Almeida (eds.), *Sociedade e Política no Brasil Pós-64*, 2nd edition. São Paulo: Brasiliense.

Veliz, Claudio (1980). *The Centralist Tradition in Latin America.* Princeton, NJ: Princeton University Press.

Ventura de Morais, Jorge (1989). "A Esperança dos Homens: Sindicato e Assistência Social." Paper prepared for delivery at the Congress of the Latin American Studies Association, Miami (December).

Verba, Sidney (1965). "Germany: The Remaking of Political Culture." Pp. 130–70 in Lucian W. Pye and Sidney Verba (eds.), *Political Culture and Political Development.* Princeton, NJ: Princeton University Press.

Viola, Eduardo, and Scott Mainwaring (1984). "Transitions to Democracy: Brazil and Argentina in the 1980s." Working Paper no. 21, Kellogg Institute, University of Notre Dame.

Visão (1981). "Quem é Quem na Economia Brasileira." 30, 34A (August 29).

 (1983). "Quem é Quem na Economia Brasileira." 32, 35A (August 31).

 (1984). "Quem é Quem na Economia Brasileira." 33, 35A (August 31).

Waisman, Carlos (1987). *Reversal of Development in Argentina: Postwar Counterrevolutionary Policies and their Structural Consequences.* Princeton, NJ: Princeton University Press.

Wallerstein, Michael (1980). "The Collapse of Democracy in Brazil: Its Economic Determinants." *Latin American Research Review* 15, 3: 3–30.

Weffort, Francisco C. (1970). "State and Mass in Brazil." Pp. 385–406 in Irving Louis Horowitz (ed.), *Masses in Latin America.* New York: Oxford University Press.

 (1978). *O Populismo na Política Brasileira.* Rio de Janeiro: Paz e Terra.

 (1989). "Why Democracy?" Pp. 327–50 in Alfred Stepan (ed.), *Democratizing Brazil: Problems of Transition and Consolidation.* New York: Oxford University Press.

Werneck Viana, Luiz (1985). "A Ofensiva do Antigo Regime e a Conjuntura Pós-Eleitoral." Pp. 31–36 in "As Eleições Municipais de 85 e a Conjuntura Política," *Cadernos de Conjuntura,* no. 3. Rio de Janeiro: Instituto Universitário de Pesquisas do Rio de Janeiro (IUPERJ).

Wesson, Robert, and David V. Fleischer (1983). Brazil in Transition. New York: Praeger and Stanford, CA: Hoover Institution Press, Stanford University.

Whitehead, Laurence (1989). "Political Change and Economic Stabilization: The 'Economic Solidarity Pact.' " Pp. 181–213 in Wayne A. Cornelius, Judith Gentleman, and Peter H. Smith (eds.), *Mexico's Alternative Political Futures.* La Jolla: Center for U.S.-Mexican Studies, University of California, San Diego.

Wilde, Alexander (1978). "Conversations among Gentlemen: Oligarchical Democracy in Colombia." Pp. 28–81 in Juan J. Linz and Alfred Stepan (eds.), *The Breakdown of Democratic Regimes: Latin America.* Baltimore: Johns Hopkins University Press.

Wirth, John D. (1977). *Minas Gerais in the Brazilian Federation, 1889–1937.* Stanford, CA: Stanford University Press.

Zapata, Francisco (1994). "Sindicalismo y Regimen Corporativo en Mexico." Paper presented to the Conference "What Kind of Market? What Kind of Democracy?" McGill University, Montreal, Canada (April 6–8).

Zeitlin, Maurice, and Richard Earl Ratcliff (1975). "Research Methods for the Analysis of the Internal Structure of Dominant Classes: The Case of Landlords and Capitalists in Chile." *Latin American Research Review* 10 (Fall): 5–61.

Index

Abi-Ackel, Ibrahim, 136
Acordo de Minas ("Minas Agreement"),
224–25, 227
agrarian elites, 19–20; and agricultural policy of the military, 151, 217; and Neves,
218–19, 219; and the 1964 coup, 69;
and the Old Republic, 38–39, 40–41,
43–44; and populism, 262; and the
PSD, 63; and the Revolution of 1930,
51; see also landownership
agrarian reform, 69, 152; in the Constituent
Assembly, 236, 237, 238, 251
agriculture: modernization of, 88–93; state
programs for, 156, 157, 164–65
Alagoas, 184, 243
Alberto, João, 52
Aleixo, Pedro, 62–63
Alfonsín, Raul, 273–74, 275
Alkmim, José Maria, 70
Almeida, Sebastião Paēs de, 261
Alves, Aluísio, 229
Alves Filho, João, 246
Alves, Oscar, 223–24
Amapá, 246
Amazonas, 242
Ames, Barry, 157, 160, 161, 166, 245
Anderson, Charles W., 8, 255
Andrada family, 58, 133, 214; Antônio Car-
los de, 54; Bonifácio José Tamm de,
201, 204, 221; José Bonifácio Lafayette
de, 204; José Bonfácio Tamm de, 204
Andreazza, Mário, 160
Antunes Corporation, 85
"April package," 150, 247
ARENA (Aliança Renovadora Nacional),
108, 152–54
control of resources and recruitment by,
118, 141, 160–61, 179, 187, 190–92
divisions within, 188–89, 193–94
elections: pre-1974, 148; of 1974, 149,
156, 158, 173; of 1978, 158, 172, 174,
199–200; of 1966–76, 195, 196

and the PDS, 175
post-1979 fate of members: in cabinets,
219–20, 226, 250; in the Constituent Assembly, 233, 237; in elections, 215, 240–
41; in parties, 231, 232
reelection rates for, 202, 205–7
traditional elite control of, 184–87
see also PDS (Partido Democrático
Social)
Argentina, 5, 7; corporatism in, 273–74,
278; economic policy under military in,
259; party change in, 275–76, 278; populist coalitions in Brazil and, 265–66;
postwar politics in Brazil and, 257; repression in, 261; transition from authoritarianism in, 279
authoritarianism in Brazil: elite turnover under, 190–92, 202–8; and party system
change, 5, 21, 178–79, 210; and the personal vote, 192–98, 199–202; political
competition under, 184–90, 198; see
also bureaucratic authoritarianism; military in Brazil
Avellar Azeredo family, 248
Avellar Marques Ferreira, Afrânio de, 169
Azeredo, Eduardo, 248
Azeredo, Renato, 216, 219

Bahia, 246; and governors' politics, 40; in-
dustry in, 86, 88; and the PTB, 182,
184–86
Bank of Brazil, 109, 152, 158–60
Barbacena: elections in, 214, 240; family
politics in, 58, 63, 133, 191, 201
Barros, Adhemar de, 57, 63, 68
BDMG (Banco de Desenvolvimento de Mi-
nas Gerais), 87, 115, 126–27
Belo Horizonte, 43, 75, 83, 99; elections in,
148, 214; mayoralty of, 120, 124, 135, 225
Bernardes, Artur da Silva, 54, 63, 65,
117–18
Bernardes Filho, Artur, 117